MS-DOS®
batch file
utilities

Ronny Richardson

WINDCREST®

FIRST EDITION
FIRST PRINTING

Library of Congress Cataloging-in-Publication Data

Richardson, Ronny.
   MS-DOS batch file utilities / by Ronny Richardson.
     p.   cm.
   Includes index.
   ISBN 0-8306-2482-1   ISBN 0-8306-2481-3 (pbk.)
   1. Utilities (Computer programs) 2. Electronic data processing-
-Batch processing. 3. MS-DOS. I. Title.
QA76.76.U84R53   1991
005.4'46—dc20   91-16045
                                        CIP

TAB Books offers software for sale. For information and a catalog, please contact TAB Software Department, Blue Ridge Summit, PA 17294-0850.

Acquisitions Editor: Ron Powers
Book Editor: David M. McCandless
Production: Katherine G. Brown
Book Design: Jaclyn J. Boone
Cover: Sandra Blair Designs, Harrisburg, PA.   WR1

Contents

2   Communicating with the user   **49**

Acknowledgments

I want to say a special thanks to William (Bill) R. Moller and Ted de Castro. I don't have a CompuServe account, so Bill spent a lot of time on CompuServe looking for the latest and greatest versions of many of these utilities for me. Ted is the librarian for a large users group and spent a great deal of time pulling programs out of the library for me. Between Bill and Ted, I was able to grab the latest versions of programs actively being upgraded as well as copies of older programs not well known and not upgraded. Without their work, this book wouldn't have been possible.

Personally, I want to thank my wife Cicinda, my son Tevin, and my daughter Dawna for their support and patience. Because I have only a limited pool of time available, some of the time I spent writing this book had to come from the time I would have spent with my family. They were all very understanding and supportive.

About the author

Ronny Richardson was born in Oak Ridge, Tennessee and raised in Atlanta, Georgia. He has undergraduate degrees in Electronics and Mathematics, as well as graduate degrees in Decision Sciences and Business Administration.

He began using computers in 1983 and won an IBM clone at the Atlanta Comdex the following year, which spurred his interest in learning about computers. Later that year, he began teaching computer classes at a local computer store; and, in 1986, he began writing articles for Computer Shopper. Since then, he has published over 200 articles as well as five books. He currently writes for *Computer Monthly*, *Atlanta Computer Currents*, and *PC/Computing*.

Introduction

The idea for this book came out of the research I did writing my *MS-DOS Batch File Programming* book. While only a few batch file utilities are commercial, I found a great number of shareware and public domain batch file utilities. At first, I was going to include every one in the *MS-DOS Batch File Programming* book, but there were just too many utilities. Instead, I mentioned the best in that book and then collected every utility I could find for this one.

What do you need to know first?

In writing this book, I am assuming that you know the basics of writing and using batch files. If you don't, you should read the first three chapters of *MS-DOS Batch File Programming* (TAB book #3916) before reading this book. While you need to understand the basics of batch files, however, you don't need to be a batch file expert. In fact, many of these utilities remove the need for complex batch file tricks.

A note about/to public domain utility authors

One of the things you will read a lot about in this book are tiny utilities that only do one or two things. Many times these utilities have been released into the public domain, meaning their authors didn't copyright them and thus anyone can copy and use them. We owe these authors a real debt of gratitude. Originally, they most likely wrote the utility to fulfill a need they had. Then, instead of leaving the utility on their system or just trying to make a quick buck or two, they released it into the public domain in case anyone else was having a similar problem.

Now, having said some nice things about public domain program authors, I have two very important notes for them. First, while writing this book, I had trouble trying to verify the status of many programs. Often, programs get separated from their documentation in their progress through the very loose network supporting public domain and shareware software. If you are releasing software into the public domain, you should definitely place a note to that effect *in the code itself* so that it can't become separated from the software.

Second, I want to hear from the authors of batch software, no matter what type. If your program is in this book and I erred in describing it or didn't have the latest version, let me know and then send me the latest version. If you have a batch utility I didn't cover, again drop me a line. Hopefully, this book will gain enough popularity to warrant an update. If you keep me abreast of your activities and software, I can include that information in the next version. Write to me at this address:

Ronny Richardson
c/o TAB Books
Blue Ridge Summit, PA 17294-0214

An outline of the book

The chapters in the book are as follows:

Chapter 1: Getting input from the user. The only native way a batch file can get information from the user is through replaceable parameters. However, these are less than optimum because you must enter all of them on the command line prior to starting the batch file. The utilities in this chapter overcome this limitation in several interesting ways.

Chapter 2: Communicating with the user. The only native way a batch file can present information to the reader is through the ECHO and TYPE commands. Both of these print information one line at a time and scroll from the bottom to the top like a Teletype machine. Batch file utilities give batch files the ability to communicate with the user in fantastic ways.

Chapter 3: Menu programs. You can use literally hundreds of menu programs on your computer, and I don't plan to cover them all. However, a couple of them rely almost exclusively on batch files. Those are the menu systems I cover in this chapter.

Chapter 4: Dealing with files and disks. Batch files have only the standard DOS commands for dealing with files. For example, they can't find out how much free space a disk has or discover the date of a file. A number of batch file utilities overcome these limitations.

Chapter 5: Windows batch files. You don't need anything special to write batch files for Windows because almost all of your existing batch files will run under Windows without any problems. However, if you want to take full advantage of Windows, then you need a special type of program. This chapter covers those programs.

Chapter 6: Major utility sets. Batch file utilities tend to be small, single-purpose programs. As such, they are difficult to market. To get around this, some programs have combined a number of disjoint programs into sets that they sell.

Chapter 7: Other. A number of batch file utilities didn't fit into one of the above categories. Those that were left out are covered here.

Chapter 8: Alternative batch languages. This chapter covers languages that completely replace the DOS batch file language and compilers that will turn batch files into programs. In the process, the alternative languages and compilers add a number of improvements to the language.

Chapter 9: Using the environment. The AUTOEXEC.BAT and CONFIG.SYS file play a major role in determining the state of the DOS environment. Many utilities have been written to aid these files.

Chapter 10: Multiple configurations. It is becoming more and more difficult to develop one single configuration that works with all your programs. If you have a network, it eats up so much memory that some memory-hogging programs won't run. If you want to run Windows 3.0, you may find that the configuration it wants is less than optimal for your non-Windows software. Also, as in the past, some programs want extended memory and some programs want you to use a memory manager to turn your extended memory into expanded memory. What is a poor user to do? This chapter tells you!

Getting the software

A few of these utilities are commercial products that you can buy at your local software store or order from a mail order vendor. However, most of them are not. Those programs that aren't commercial programs fall somewhere along a continuum from shareware to public domain.

The best way to understand shareware is to see how the experts define it. According to the Association of Shareware Professionals,

> . . . Shareware distribution gives users a chance to try software before buying it. If you try a shareware program and continue using it, you are expected to register. Individual programs differ on details—some request registration while others require it, some specify a maximum trial period. With registration, you get anything from the simple right to continue using the software to an updated program with printed manual.
>
> Copyright laws apply to both shareware and commercial software, and the copyright holder retains all rights, with a few specific exceptions as stated below. Shareware authors are accomplished programmers, just like commercial authors, and the programs are of comparable quality. (In both cases, there are good programs and bad ones!) The main difference is in the method of distribution. The author specifically grants the right to copy and distribute the software, either to all and sundry or to a specific group. For example, some authors require written permission before a commercial disk vendor may copy their shareware.
>
> So, shareware is a distribution method, not a type of software. You should find software that suits your needs and pocketbook, whether it's commercial or shareware. The shareware system makes fitting your needs easier, because you can try before you buy. And because the overhead is low, prices are low also. Shareware has the ultimate money-back guarantee, if you don't use the product, you don't pay for it.

At the other end of the continuum are public domain programs. These are programs the author wrote and released to the public without making any claim on the program and without copyrighting the program.

Not all of these programs fall into either of these two neat categories. For example, one of the utilities bills itself as shareware but charges no fee. It does, however, restrict its use to nonmilitary applications.

Where I could, I obtained permission from the author and included the utility on the disk that comes with this book. However, the space on the disk was limited; thus, I couldn't contact all the authors, and some authors I reached didn't want their programs included with a commercial product. As a result, not all the utilities are on this sampler disk.

You can obtain shareware from many bulletin boards, including CompuServe and PC-Link. Other sources are the many vendors who specialize in selling shareware by the disk through the mail. Using this method, you don't need a modem. Personally, I use Public Brand Software, but many other good companies exist. Finally, your local users group should have many of these programs; they are often the best and cheapest source.

About the book

You may be interested in knowing about the hardware and software I used to write this book.

I wrote the book on a Osicom 386/25 and printed out my information on an HP Laserjet III. For a word processor, I used Microsoft Word 5.0 for everything except the ASCII files and tables. I edited batch files and other ASCII files with the extremely nice editor built into DOS 5.5. Finally, I created all the tables using Word for Windows; while too slow for general writing, it has the best table editing engine I have ever seen.

Disclaimer

All the batch file utilities were tested on wide variety of DOS versions. TAB Books and I have done everything possible to ensure that the programs and batch files included with this book and on the disk either run under all versions of DOS or are clearly labeled as to which version(s) they require. We have also done our best to make sure that every program and batch file does exactly what we claim it will do. Neither TAB Books nor I make any warranty of any type, expressed or implied, regarding the programs, batch files, and documentation included in this book and on the included diskette. In addition, we aren't liable for incidental or consequential damages in connection with, or arising from, the performance of these programs and batch files.

1
Getting input from the user

Communication with a batch file is always one direction; the batch file "talks" to the user using ECHO statements. You can only communicate with the batch file by using replaceable parameters when starting the batch file. Once the batch file is running, you have no control over it.

The IF command gives batch files the ability to branch and take different courses of action depending on conditions. You can write more effective batch files by basing this branching on user input. DOS itself offers only one way to do this: through replaceable parameters. *Replaceable parameters* are information the user enters on the command line following the batch file's name.

Unfortunately, DOS lacks a method for asking the user a question and then responding according to the answer. Luckily, many utilities have been written for just this purpose.

All of the utilities in this chapter allow a batch file to ask the user a question. Most accept a single keystroke and place a value to represent that keystroke in the ERRORLEVEL for testing. For that reason, I call these programs ERRORLEVEL-askers.

A few utilities manage to go beyond simple ERRORLEVEL-askers. Generally, they accept a multiple-character response and store it under an environmental variable. While an ERRORLEVEL-asker is adequate for most applications, these advanced programs allow you to develop more complex applications.

Answer

Name:	Answer
Version:	1.0
Price:	Free
Category:	Public Domain

Summary: Queries the user and places the multi-character response in the environment.
Author: Frank Schweiger
Availability: Included on the disk bound in this book.

Unluckily, DOS is very inhospitable to query programs. A program gets a copy of the environment to work with; but when the program terminates, its copy of the environment is erased. As a result, query programs can't easily use the environment to transfer information back to the calling batch file.

To combat this, a query program could search through memory for the original copy of the environment and modify it. Answer uses this approach.

To use Answer, you enter a command like

ANSWER Prompt

Answer displays the prompt and then has the user enter information directly after it. For better appearance, you should include a couple of trailing spaces in the prompt.

Answer stores the user's response in the master environment under the environmental variable ANSWER. Even though Answer was written in early 1986, it still works perfectly under DOS 5.0! If you want to ask the user more than one question, you should ensure that the contents of the answer environmental variable are transferred to another variable after each question.

If you must obtain multi-character responses from the user, Answer is about the best program you'll find.

Ask (T. A. Davis)

Name: Ask
Version: 1.0
Price: Free
Category: Public Domain
Summary: Ask will prompt the user for a response and only accept a Y or N. It sets ERRORLEVEL accordingly.
Author: T. A. Davis
Availability: The file is available on many bulletin board systems.

This version of Ask is a simple ERRORLEVEL-asker that only accepts a y or n key. If the user presses any other key, it responds with an "(Y/N)?" prompt and continues to do so until the user presses the y or n key. If you enter a prompt after the Ask command, it displays that prompt on the first line, although not with its own "(Y/N)" message added. The user enters his/her response directly next to the prompt, so you will want to include a few trailing spaces in the prompt.

Ask 1.0 works well and is especially useful when you want to force the user to answer yes or no to a question.

Ask (Sid Gudes)

Name:	Ask
Version:	1.0
Price:	Free
Category:	Public Domain
Summary:	An ERRORLEVEL-asker that converts lowercase responses to uppercase and limits responses to those specified on the command line.
Author:	Sid Gudes
Availability:	Included on the disk bound in this book.

Ask is an ERRORLEVEL-asker with three improvements:

- Ask displays a user-specified prompt. Ask has the user enter their response directly after the prompt, so you should include trailing spaces in the prompt.
- Ask is case-insensitive.
- Ask limits responses to those specified on the command line.

To use Ask, you include the command

```
ASK "Prompt" Characters
```

in the batch line. Characters represent those characters that Ask will accept from the user in response to the question; Ask assigns an ERRORLEVEL value of 1 to the first character, 2 to the second, and so on. The three mentioned improvements make Ask an excellent ERRORLEVEL-asker.

Ask (Norton)

Name:	Norton Utilities
Version:	5.0
Price:	$150.00
Category:	Commercial
Summary:	A small portion of the Norton Utilities that allows you to ask the user a question. It stores the answer in the ERRORLEVEL.
Author:	Peter Norton Computing, Incorporated
	2210 Wilshire Boulevard
	Santa Monica, California 90403
Availability:	Available at any software store.

Norton includes the Batch Enhancer in his utilities. (Norton Utilities 4.0 had both a standard and advanced version, with only the advanced version containing the Batch Enhancer. With NU 5.0, that dual distinction of the utilities has been dropped.) Batch

Enhancer began as a couple of small utilities like BEEP.COM. After a couple of versions, these small utilities were compiled into a single program called BE.EXE. BE [short for Batch Enhancer] contains several different routines that you call up with a keyword after the BE. One of the more useful options, ASK, gets information from the user. You run it with the command:

BE ASK "prompt" list [default =] [timeout =] [adjust =] [color]

The components of this command are as follows:

BE invokes the Norton Utilities Batch Enhancer.

ASK invokes the Ask option of the Batch Enhancer and is used to obtain input from the user.

Prompt is the text that tells the user what to do. An example would be "Press Y to delete the file or N to leave it alone."

List is the list of all the keystrokes Ask will accept. It assigns an ERRORLEVEL of 1 to the first character, 2 to the second, and so on. Ask normally ignores capitalization, so a list of "ABC" would assign 1 to A, 2 to B, and 3 to C no matter whether an upper- or lowercase letter was entered. If you don't include a list, Ask accepts any character and assigns its ASCII value to ERRORLEVEL. In this case, it assigns different values to upper- and lowercase.

Default = is the value that Ask assigns either if the user presses enter or if the timeout option is used and the user doesn't press a keystroke in time. If a list is defined and default isn't used, Ask won't accept enter. With a default assigned, Ask accepts enter and assigns the default value to it.

Timeout = is the number of seconds Ask must wait before assigning the default value and allowing the batch file to continue. If you don't have a default assigned, Ask assigns an ERRORLEVEL of 255 when it times out.

Adjust = is a number that Ask assigns to the ERRORLEVEL after the user responds. For example, assume that the acceptable responses are "ABC," that the adjustment is 10, and that the user presses B. This would result in an ERRORLEVEL of 2; but Ask would add 10 to it, giving a result of 12. Thus, you can pass multiple responses back to the batch file as a single ERRORLEVEL value. However, this requires very careful coding because DOS resets the ERRORLEVEL each time you run any program, including the Batch Enhancer. Table 1-1 illustrates this concept.

Table 1-1   NORTON1.BAT shows how, with very careful coding, you can use the adjust option in the Norton Utilities Batch Enhancer to pass multiple responses back to the batch file as a single ERRORLEVEL value.

Batch File Line	Explanation
@ECHO OFF	Turns command-echoing off.
REM NORTON1.BAT	Remark giving the name of the batch file.
REM Illustrate ability of Ask to	Documentation remark.
REM adjust the ERRORLEVEL value to	Documentation remark.
REM return more than one response.	Documentation remark.

Batch File Line	Explanation
`CLS`	Clears the screen.
`BE ASK "Do you want option A, B or C ", abc`	Ask the user to select from three options and sets ERRORLEVEL according to A=1, B=2, and C=3.
`CLS`	Clears the screen.
`IF ERRORLEVEL 3 GOTO THREE`	If ERRORLEVEL is greater than or equal to three, go to THREE. Because Ask only had three alternatives, three will be the maximum value.
`IF ERRORLEVEL 2 GOTO TWO`	If ERRORLEVEL equals two, jumps to TWO. Normally, this would test for greater than or equal to two, but the line above removed all the values of three or larger.
`IF ERRORLEVEL 1 GOTO ONE`	If ERRORLEVEL equals one, jumps to ONE. Because Ask will require a value, one is the minimum ERRORLEVEL value, so the batch file will only make it past this point using a GOTO command.
`:THREE`	Label used by a GOTO command.
`BE ASK "Do you want option 1 or 2 ",12,ADJUST=10`	Ask the user a question and add ten to his/her response.
`CLS`	Clears the screen.
`GOTO NEXT`	Continues processing below.
`:TWO`	Label used by a GOTO command.
`BE ASK "Do you want option 1 or 2 ",12,ADJUST=20`	Ask the user a question and add twenty to his/her response.
`CLS`	Clears the screen.
`GOTO NEXT`	Continues processing below.
`:ONE`	Label used by a GOTO command.
`BE ASK "Do you want option 1 or 2 ",12,ADJUST=30`	Asks the user a question and add thirty to his/her response.
`CLS`	Clears the screen.
`GOTO NEXT`	Continues processing below.
`:NEXT`	Label used by GOTO.

`IF ERRORLEVEL 32 GOTO A2`
`IF ERRORLEVEL 31 GOTO A1`
`IF ERRORLEVEL 22 GOTO B2`
`IF ERRORLEVEL 21 GOTO B1`
`IF ERRORLEVEL 12 GOTO C2`
`IF ERRORLEVEL 11 GOTO C1`
	A series of ERRORLEVEL tests used to determine which set of responses the user selected above. Notice the logic allows the batch file to store two responses in the single slot provided by ERRORLEVEL.

`:A2`
`ECHO A2 SELECTED`
`GOTO END`
`:A1`
`ECHO A1 SELECTED`
`GOTO END`
`:B2`
`ECHO B2 SELECTED`
`GOTO END`
`:B1`
`ECHO B1 SELECTED`
`GOTO END`
	Tells users what they selected and exits the batch file.

Table 1-1 Continued.

Batch File Line	Explanation
:C2 ECHO C2 SELECTED GOTO END :C1 ECHO C1 SELECTED GOTO END	
:END	Label marketing the end of the batch file.

Color allows you to specify the prompt color. Simply enter the color, not a color-=red-type statement.

Table 1-2 summarizes all the Ask options.

Of all the ERRORLEVEL-askers, Ask is without a doubt the most powerful. Interestingly, it's also one of the simpler ones to use. It handles capitalization easily; and, because it automatically assigns ERRORLEVEL values beginning with 1, it makes testing easy as well.

Table 1-2   Optional ASK keywords in the Norton Utilities Batch Enhancer.

Options	Function
Adjust	Lets you add a specified value to the ERRORLEVEL returned by Ask. By careful coding and decoding, you can use this feature to ask the user multiple questions and pass the answers back to a batch file as one ERRORLEVEL value.
Color	Lets you change the color of the prompt.
Default	The value Ask assigns if the user presses return or Ask times out.
Keys	This is what really sets Ask apart from other ERRORLEVEL tests. The keys you enter here are the only ones Ask will accept. If the user presses any other key, Ask just beeps and waits for an acceptable keystroke. And no more fooling with ASCII tables to get the ERRORLEVEL values either. Ask sets ERRORLEVEL to one for the first key in the list, to two for the second key, and so on. Ask is case-insensitive so you do not have to test for "Y" and "y". That effectively cuts your number of tests in half for character responses.
Prompt	The message that Ask displays. Typically, you would want to put a space at the end of the prompt so you do not enter the answer directly next to the prompt.
Timeout	The number of seconds Ask will wait for the user to press any key. If he/she does not press a key in that period to time, Ask defaults to the value you specify and returns control to the batch file. Note that Timeout uses the clock and is independent of processor speed. You can use the Timeout feature without a prompt to cause a batch file to pause for a given period of time.

Askkey

Name:	Askkey
Version:	1.0
Price:	Free
Category:	Copyrighted
Summary:	A standard ERRORLEVEL-asker that converts lowercase responses to uppercase.
Availability:	Complete directions for creating Askkey were published in the June 1987 issue of *PC Tech Journal*.

Askkey is a standard ERRORLEVEL-asker with two extensions:

- Askkey can display a prompt. You enter the prompt after the Askkey command. Because Askkey has the user enter the response directly after the prompt, you should include trailing spaces in the prompt.

- Askkey converts all lowercase responses to uppercase, which reduces the required amount of ERRORLEVEL-testing in half without sacrificing the quality of the information.

For more information on Askkey, see the June 1987 issue of *PC Tech Journal*.

B(DISK

Name:	B(DISK
Version:	Unknown
Price:	Unknown[1]
Category:	Copyrighted
Summary:	A collection of batch file utilities for working with files and performing other tasks.
Author:	G. Estes
Availability:	Available on many bulletin board systems.

The B(DISK of Batch Programmer Tools contains 34 separate utilities. The utilities are an odd mixture of programs that work best from within a batch file and other programs that would generally be used from the command line. Those dealing with the user input are covered next.

---

[1]The author includes documentation with the programs but fails to mention the status of the files, so I was unable to determine if they are public domain, shareware, or commercial. The author includes no name, address, or copyright notice in the documentation, although the programs are marked internally as copyright G. Estes. As a result, I don't know the status of the B(DISK programs.

B(CADOFF is a small (.7K) memory-resident program that disables the Ctrl-Alt-Del system reset. The system reset capabilities can't be restored without turning the computer off and back on or by pressing the hardware reset button.

B(CBOFF is a small (.7K) memory-resident program that disables Ctrl-Break. Like B(CADOFF, Ctrl-Break can only be restored by resetting the computer. If you are concerned about users stopping batch files with Ctrl-Break, you should enter this command in your AUTOEXEC.BAT configuration file.

B(QINKEY waits for the user to press any key and sets ERRORLEVEL to the ASCII value of that keystroke. The program is case-sensitive.

B(QY1N0 waits for the user to press a y or n key and sets ERRORLEVEL accordingly. It can display an optional prompt entered on the command line, or it will use its own prompt if none is specified.

The documentation for B(DISK fails to distinguish whether the programs are public domain, shareware, or commercial programs. In fact, the documentation fails to include a copyright notice (although, internally, the programs contain one). For that reason, you might want to avoid B(DISK to ensure you don't violate any copyrights. For more information on the B(DISK utilities, see Chapter 6.

Batpopup

Name:	Batpopup
Version:	1.0
Price:	$5.00
Category:	Shareware
Summary:	A batch file pop-up menu program.
Author:	J. R. McConnell
	Interfaces, People, and Magic
	Post Office Box 4496
	Middletown, Rhode Island 02841
Availability:	Available on many bulletin board systems.

Despite its name, Batpopup isn't a memory resident program. When you start Batpopup, it displays a very nice menu on the screen. The user uses a moving lightbar menu to select one of the items on the menu. Alternatively, the user can select an item using a number of a function key. Once the user makes a selection, Batpopup terminates and passes an ERRORLEVEL back to the batch file.

To display a menu using Batpopup, you issue the command

    BATPOPUP r c f b Title Item-1 Item-2 Item-3...Item-9

where r is the row and c is the column to use for the top left corner of the menu. Batpopup sizes the remainder of the menu automatically. F sets the foreground color and b sets the background color. These settings only affect the menu; the remainder of the screen is unaffected. The menu has a title and from two to nine menu items. Batpopup uses the spaces on the command line to separate the items, so the title and menu items can't include spaces. You can, however, simulate a space using Alt-255. Of course, the 127-character limit on the length of the command line prohibits long descriptive menu options.

Batpopup sets ERRORLEVEL to 1 for the first item, 2 for the second, and so on. After five minutes, the menu will "time-out" and exit automatically. If that happens, it sets ERRORLEVEL to 0. If the user presses Escape, the documentation claims to set ERRORLEVEL to -1. It also claims to set ERRORLEVEL to -2 if an internal error occurs. However, ERRORLEVEL only has room for a single byte of information, limiting it to numbers between 0 and 255. Actually, when the user presses Escape, ERRORLEVEL is set to 255.

Batpopup is easy to configure and produces very attractive menus. By making the menu options simple—like yes or no—you can easily obtain answers to simple questions using Batpopup. Table 1-3 illustrates both uses of Batpopup. Its ease-of-use combined with its low price makes Batpopup very attractive.

Table 1-3   SHOWP-UP.BAT shows how Batpopup can be used for menus or to ask simple questions.

Batch File Line	Explanation
`@ECHO OFF`	Turns command-echoing off.

`REM NAME:    SHOWP-UP.BAT`
`REM PURPOSE: Demonstrate Batpopup`
`REM VERSION: 1.00`
`REM DATE:    April 2, 1991`
	Documentation remarks.

`:TOP`	Label marking the top of the loop used to display the menu.
`CLS`	Clears the screen before displaying the menu.

`BATPOPUP 12 30 1 15 Ronny's_Menu`
`   Word_Processor Data_Base`
`   Spreadsheet Graphics`
`   Communications Games Exit_Menu`
	The command to display the menu. In the actual batch file, the underscores (_) have been replaced with Alt-255, which appear like spaces from DOS but are not treated like a divider by DOS.

`IF ERRORLEVEL 7    GOTO END`
`IF ERRORLEVEL 6    GOTO PLAY`
`IF ERRORLEVEL 5    GOTO TALK`
`IF ERRORLEVEL 4    GOTO GRAPHICS`
`IF ERRORLEVEL 3    GOTO 123`
`IF ERRORLEVEL 2    GOTO DATABASE`
`IF ERRORLEVEL 1    GOTO WP`
`GOTO END`
	Goes to the appropriate section to handle the user's menu selection.

`:WP`
`   CLS`
`   ECHO Run Word Processor Here`
`   PAUSE`
`   GOTO TOP`
	If this were an actual menu, this section would handle running the word processor and then redisplaying the menu. (In the actual batch file, this section is formatted with a box around it.)

Table 1-3 Continued.

Batch File Line	Explanation

`:DATABASE`
`  CLS`
`  ECHO Run Data Base Here`
`  PAUSE`
`  GOTO TOP`
	If this were an actual menu, this section would handle running the data base and then redisplaying the menu. (In the actual batch file, this section is formatted with a box around it.)

`:123`
`  CLS`
`  ECHO Run Spreadsheet Here`
`  PAUSE`
`  GOTO TOP`
	If this were an actual menu, this section would handle running the spreadsheet and then redisplaying the menu. (In the actual batch file, this section is formatted with a box around it.)

`:GRAPHICS`
`  CLS`
`  ECHO Run Graphics Program Here`
`  PAUSE`
`  GOTO TOP`
	If this were an actual menu, this section would handle running the graphics processor and then redisplaying the menu. (In the actual batch file, this section is formatted with a box around it.)

`:TALK`
`  CLS`
`  ECHO Run Communication Program Here`
`  PAUSE`
`  GOTO TOP`
	If this were an actual menu, this section would handle running the communications program and then redisplaying the menu. (In the actual batch file, this section is formatted with a box around it.)

`:PLAY`
`  CLS`
`  ECHO Run Games Menu Here`
`  PAUSE`
`  GOTO TOP`
	If this were an actual menu, this section would handle displaying the games menu and then redisplaying the main menu. (In the actual batch file, this section is formatted with a box around it.)

`:END`	Label marking the exit point in the menu.
`CLS`	Clears the screen.
`BATPOPUP 12 35 1 15 Do_You_Really_` `  Want_To_Exit? Yes No`	This command displays a menu that gives the user a yes/no choice. In the actual batch file, the underscores (_) are replaced with Alt-255 spaces.
`IF ERRORLEVEL 2 GOTO TOP`	If the user selects no, redisplays the original menu.
`CLS`	If the user selects yes, erases the menu before exiting.

Batquery

Name:	Batquery
Version:	1.0
Price:	Free
Category:	Public Domain
Summary:	An ERRORLEVEL-asker that allows you to assign ERRORLEVEL values to various keystrokes.
Author:	T. G. Browning
	MorganSoft
	2170 Raynor Street SE
	Salem, Oregon 97302
Availability:	Available on many bulletin board systems.

To use Batquery, you issue a command like

```
BATQUERY AaBb1,CcDd2,Ee3,FfGgHh4 Select A-H
```

Everything before the first comma is assigned an ERRORLEVEL of 1, everything between the first and second commas is assigned an ERRORLEVEL of 2, and so on. Everything after the first space is displayed as a prompt.

Batquery contains a significant bug that prevents it from functioning properly. It assigns ERRORLEVELs correctly for the first two groups of values but only recognizes the first character in the third group; everything beyond the third group is ignored completely. This flaw makes Batquery unacceptable for most applications.

BATUTIL

Name:	BATUTIL
Version:	1.0
Price:	$39.00 (Includes STACKEY)
Category:	Shareware
Summary:	A powerful batch file utility that allows you to do almost anything required in a batch file.
Author:	The Support Group
	Lake Technology Park
	Post Office Box 130
	McHenry, Maryland 21541
	(800) 872-4768
Availability:	Available on many bulletin board systems.

BATUTIL is far more than just a batch utility—it's really a batch language disguised as a batch utility. To use BATUTIL, you enter a command like

BATUTIL [HOUR]

on the command line. When you enclose the command in square [ ] brackets, BATUTIL returns results in ERRORLEVEL. If you enclose the command in curly {} brackets, BATUTIL also returns the results as an environmental variable. BATUTIL only needs the first two characters of the command and ignores capitalization, so [HOUR], [Ho], [HoUr] and [ho] all mean the same thing.

Covered here are BATUTIL's many nice features for getting information from the user.

EDITENV allows you to interactively edit environmental variables. When you issue the command, it calls a screen letting you edit any and all of the environmental variables much like a word processor lets you edit text. While this is nice for systems development, you most likely don't want batch file users to be able to modify the PATH or CONSPEC variables.

If you issue the EDITENV command followed by a variable name, then the user can only enter contents for that name. So the BATUTIL command

BATUTIL [ECHO Enter Your Name][EDITENV UserName]

would let the user enter his/her name in a box without being able to disturb the contents of the other environmental variables.

GETKEY gets a single keystroke from the user. You can control almost every aspect of the way GETKEY operates, and it's flexible enough to emulate almost any of the ERRORLEVEL-askers discussed in this chapter.

ASCIIREAD gets the ASCII value of a keystroke from the user.

PMATCH compares information provided by the user (perhaps on the command line) against a list of acceptable values and sets ERRORLEVEL to indicate which position (if any) in the list the match occurred.

QLOCK checks the status of the CapsLock, NumLock, or ScrollLock and sets ERRORLEVEL accordingly. If you have a batch file that runs a long time and must ask a yes/no question in the middle, QLOCK provides a nice way for you to answer the question ahead of time.

SCANREAD gets the scan code of a keystroke from the user.

USERNAME gets the user's name and branches accordingly. You can limit the number of attempts by the user to enter a matching user name, so USERNAME can function as a crude password program. Of course, because you can look at the batch file from DOS and see the codes, it would only be effective against very inexperienced users.

BATUTIL is an extremely powerful tool for controlling the operation of batch files. As part of its toolkit, BATUTIL has more powerful tools for getting information from the user than any other program.

For more information on BATUTIL, see Chapter 6.

BEN

Name:	BEN
Version:	March 1991
Price:	$15.00
Category:	Shareware
Summary:	A batch file utility that gives the user a great deal of control over the screen.
Author:	Hutchins Software
	5232 West Townley Avenue
	Glendale, Arizona 85302
Availability:	Included on the disk bound in this book.

BEN (short for Batch File Enhancement Program) is a single program (BEN.EXE) that gives you a great deal of flexibility in designing screens for batch files.

BEN requires ANSI.SYS to be attached in the CONFIG.SYS in order to work. Also, BEN works with keywords. For each command, you enter BEN followed by a keyword and perhaps by additional instructions. Two of those keywords allow you to obtain user input:

AREPLY is another ERRORLEVEL-asker allowing the user to enter any letter. It sets ERRORLEVEL to 1 for A, 2 for B, and so on. For any other response, it sets the ERRORLEVEL to 0. If you insist upon the user entering a letter response, you can loop back through the question until you get an ERRORLEVEL other than 0.

NREPLY is an ERRORLEVEL-asker that allows the user to enter 1-9. It sets the ERRORLEVEL accordingly—to 1 for 1, 2 for 2, and so on. For any other response, it sets the ERRORLEVEL to 0. If you insist upon the user entering a 1-9 response, you can loop back through the question until you get an ERRORLEVEL other than 0.

All of the BEN commands are covered in detail in Chapter 2.

BQ

Name:	BQ
Version:	2.5
Price:	$10.00 (Included in the registration of the author's other package, SCR.
Category:	Shareware
Summary:	An advanced ERRORLEVEL-asker with mouse support.
Author:	T. G. Browning
	MorganSoft
	2170 Raynor Street SE
	Salem, Oregon 97302
Availability:	Included on the disk bound in this book.

Most ERRORLEVEL-askers don't support mice. However, because more and more programs are adding mouse support, users naturally expect to find it in every program. In addition, because ERRORLEVEL-askers only accept a single character response, it can be difficult to clearly explain the possible answers.

BQ overcomes both of these problems. To use BQ, first draw a menu on the screen using either SCR or simple ECHO commands. Next, run BQ and pass it the characters to accept, the location of the menu on the screen, and a prompt. SHOW-BQ.BAT in Table 1-4 illustrates this.

**Table 1-4   SHOW_BQ.BAT sets up a menu
and then, through BQ, lets the user make a selection.**

Batch File Line	Explanation
`@ECHO OFF`	Turns command-echoing off.
`REM SHOW-BQ.BAT`	Remark giving the name of the batch file.
`CLS`	Clears the screen. This is necessary because BQ needs to know the exact location of the menu. If you display the text using DOS, the only way you can be sure of its location is to clear the screen so it will be at the top left of the screen.

`ECHO 1)  dBASE`
`ECHO 2)  Lotus 1-2-3`
`ECHO 3)  Microsoft Word`
`ECHO 4)  Games Menu`
	Displays the menu. Notice only standard DOS commands are used, using nothing special.

`BQ 1Dd,2Ll,3MmWw,4Gg 1 1 4 25` `    31 Select Program`	This is the command that runs BQ. The "1Dd,2Ll,3MmWw,4Gg" tells BQ which keystrokes to accept and what ERROR-LEVEL to assign. The 1 1 4 25 tells BQ the menu starts at the top left of the screen, contains 4-rows and is 25-characters wide. The 31 sets the cursor to blue, and the "Select Program" is a prompt to the user.

The BQ line in SHOW-BQ.BAT is fairly complex, so we'll take a closer look at it:

BQ 1Dd,2Ll,3MmWw,4Gg 1 1 4 25 31 Select Program

The line's components are as follows:

BQ runs the program.

1Dd,2Ll,3MmWw,4Gg tells BQ which characters to accept and what ERRORLEVEL values to assign. Everything before the first comma is assigned a 1, everything between the first and second comma is assigned a 2, and so on. Notice each cell has both the upper- and lowercase letters to deal with capitalization. Finally, notice that the user can select the program using the number in the menu or the first letter of the program name. In the case of Microsoft Word, they can select it with the first letter of Microsoft or Word.

1 1 4 25 tells BQ that the menu begins in column 1, row 1, contains four lines, and is 25 characters wide.

31 sets the cursor color to blue.

Select Program is a user prompt.

The syntax for BQ is a little complex but unavoidable, given its ability to return the same ERRORLEVEL value for multiple keystrokes.

BUBA

Name:	BUBA
Version:	1.0
Price:	Free
Category:	Public Domain
Summary:	Five utilities to measure file size, select a file and input information.
Author:	Bill Reamy
Availability:	Available on many bulletin board systems.

BUBA (short for Bill's Unique Batch Arsenal) is a collection of five utilities. Four of them work with files (and thus are covered in Chapter 4); but the fifth—Input—obtains general information from the user and is covered here.

Input allows the user to enter any text string and have it placed in the environmental variable name supplied after the Input command. Input requires that you define the variable first; and it only uses the characters supplied by the user up to the predefined size of the variable. Thus, if you define the variable with SET USED = 1234 and then issue the command INPUT used, Input will only use the first four characters supplied by the user because USED is predefined to be four characters long.

Although slightly more difficult to use than necessary because of the demands of pre-defining variables, Input is otherwise an excellent utility.

BUBA itself is covered in more detail in Chapter 4.

Check

Name:	Check
Version:	11-18-87
Price:	Free
Category:	Copyrighted
Summary:	A program that can determine a great deal of information about the computer hardware and pass that information back to the batch file. It can also prompt the user for a single character response to a question. All information is passed using the ERRORLEVEL.
Author:	Jeff Prosese from *PC Magazine*
Availability:	All *PC Magazine* files are available from their area on CompuServe. See any issue of *PC Magazine* for details.

Check is one of the many useful batch file utilities published by *PC Magazine* over the years, with Check's most helpful function being to ask the user a question and wait for a response using the KEYPRESS keyword. It's a fairly standard ERRORLEVEL-asker that returns the ASCII value of the entered keystroke. (It returns a 0 for all extended codes.)

As helpful as this is, Check does much more: it uses 16 keywords to communicate with the user. The keywords follow the Check command and are covered in detail in Chapter 7.

CLUTIL

Name:	CLUTIL
Version:	1.3
Price:	$18.00
Category:	Shareware
Summary:	A collection of general file-handling utilities.
Author:	William S. Mezian
	105 1/2 20th Avenue, Apartment 2
	Saint Petersburg Beach, Florida 33706
Availability:	Many bulletin board systems carry CLUTIL.

CLUTIL [short for Command Line UTILities] is a collection of utilities designed primarily for use on the command line. However, some of the utilities are useful in batch files. CLUTIL is covered in detail in Chapter 7; but, because CALLKEY is used to obtain information from the user, it's covered here.

CALLKEY is an excellent ERRORLEVEL-asker program. Rather than storing its results in the ERRORLEVEL like other programs, it converts the user's response to uppercase and then stores its ASCII value in an environmental variable called CALLKEY. This simplifies equality testing, using a line like IF %CALLKEY%==68 rather than dealing with the greater-than-or-equal tests of ERRORLEVEL.

If you must get a multi-character response from the user, then run CALLKEY with the S option. CALLKEY converts the input to uppercase and stores the entire response in the CALLKEY environmental variable.

CALLKEY works under DOS 4.x and earlier. However, it doesn't work under DOS 5.0, failing in both the single- and multi-character response mode.

All of the CLUTIL programs require the computer to have ANSI.SYS loaded, without which many of them won't run. Even if the programs manage to run without ANSI .SYS, they tend to clutter the screen with escape sequences intended for ANSI.SYS. Therefore, you shouldn't consider CLUTIL unless you routinely load ANSI.SYS.

Except for CALLKEY and COLOR, the programs in CLUTIL aren't all that useful. They either operate dangerously—like MOVE—or are inferior to other available shareware programs, like LIST.COM as a replacement for VIEW. ANSI.SYS users, however, will find CALLKEY and COLOR very useful.

DDDBATCH

Name:	DDDBATCH
Version:	1.0
Price:	$10 Single User
	$30 Site License
Category:	Shareware
Summary:	A collection of 12 utilities to improve batch files.
Author:	J. Barrett
Availability:	Included on the disk bound in this book.

DDDBATCH offers up to twelve useful utility programs, all of them separate. Because two of DDDBATCH's programs are ERRORLEVEL-askers, those two are discussed here.

0-9 is an ERRORLEVEL-asking program that only accepts the numbers 0-9 as a response, setting the ERRORLEVEL equal to the number the user enters. This makes it useful as a menu selection program where you want to force the user to pick between a limited number of options. However, it won't beep if the user enters an invalid response, and it can't display a prompt. Both of these limitations can be overcome using clear messages in the batch file before running the program.

YES_NO is a simple ERRORLEVEL-asker that only accepts the y or n key. It sets ERRORLEVEL to 1 for the y key and to 2 for the n key, which simplifies the asking of questions like "Do you really want to delete all the files?" in a batch file.

All of the DDDBATCH programs are discussed in detail in Chapter 7.

F1toF10

Name:	F1toF10
Version:	1.0
Price:	Free
Category:	Public Domain
Summary:	An ERRORLEVEL-asker that only accepts function keys.
Author:	Glen Hammond
Availability:	One of several files included on the enclosed disk in a file called HAMMOND.ZIP.

F1toF10 is a modified ERRORLEVEL-asker. It only accepts the F1 through F10 function keys, ignoring any other keystrokes—including the F11 and F12 function keys found on many keyboards and the F13-F15 function keys found on Northgate keyboards. When the user presses a function key, it sets ERRORLEVEL to 59 for F1, 60 for F2, and so on. F1toF10 can't display a message and doesn't signal the user if an invalid key is pressed.

GET

Name:	GET
Version:	1.0
Price:	Free
Category:	Public Domain
Summary:	Passes information about the system to the batch file through the environment.
Author:	Bob Stephan
Availability:	Available on many bulletin board systems.

Get has a number of options for obtaining information. It then passes this information back to the batch file by either the environmental variable GET or by ERRORLEVEL. The GET options that get information from the user are as follows:

C   Accepts a single character response from the user, converts it to uppercase, and stores it in the environment. It also stores the ASCII value of the uppercase character in ERRORLEVEL. Storing the response in the environment makes batch files much more readable (for example, compare the easily read IF %GET% = = A GOTO Lotus to IF ERRORLEVEL 65 IF NOT ERRORLEVEL 66 GOTO Lotus).

N   Accepts either the y or n single character response from the user, converting it to uppercase and storing it both in the environmental variable GET and as an ERRORLEVEL.

S   Accepts a full string from the user and stores it in the environmental variable GET string (*not* converting it to uppercase). The ERRORLEVEL stores the length of this new variable.

T   Accepts a single keystroke from the user just like the C option but displays a different prompt; C displays an optional prompt entered on the command line, while T reads a file containing up to 4096 bytes and displays that as a scrolling message at the screen bottom.

GET is a very powerful program for getting information from the user and about the system—especially for a public domain program. For more information on GET, please see Chapter 6.

Getecho

Name:	Getecho
Version:	2.0
Category:	Public Domain

Summary: Displays a prompt, waits for the user to press a key, converts that keystroke to uppercase, and sets the ERRORLEVEL equal to its ASCII value.
Author: Richard N. Wisan
Availability: Included on the disk bound in this book.

Getecho is an ERRORLEVEL-asking program with two nice enhancements; it converts all keystrokes to uppercase, and it can display a message. The format for the command is as follows:

GETECHO message

Getecho displays the message and waits for the user to press any key. If the key pressed is a letter, it's converted to uppercase. Then Getecho sets ERRORLEVEL equal to the ASCII value of the keystroke.

GetKey (Glen Hammond)

Name: Getkey
Version: 1.0
Price: Free
Category: Public Domain
Summary: A standard ERRORLEVEL-asker.
Author: Glen Hammond
Availability: One of several files included on the enclosed disk in a file called HAMMOND.ZIP.

Getkey is a standard ERRORLEVEL-asker with no enhancements. It waits for the user to press a key and then sets the ERRORLEVEL to the ASCII value of that keystroke. It can't display a prompt, selectively assign ERRORLEVEL values, or do anything else fancy. Surprisingly, Getkey is only an incredible 8 bytes long, which makes it one of the shortest programs that performs a useful function.

Getkey (Ken Hipple)

Name: Getkey
Version: 1.0
Price: Free
Category: Public Domain
Summary: An ERRORLEVEL-asker that lets you control the valid responses and displays a message.
Author: Ken Hipple
Availability: Available on many bulletin board systems.

While the syntax is difficult, Getkey is one of the most flexible ERRORLEVEL-askers available. To use Getkey, you enter the command

GETKEY [?][*][W = #]{keystrokes}[!][@][&] [message]

While you can skip various components of this command, the ones you use must be in this exact order. Those components are as follows:

?	Displays a help screen. Generally, you wouldn't use the other components with this one.
*	Turns off echoing. Without this switch, Getkey echoes the pressed character to the screen.
W = #	Defines how long Getkey will wait for a valid response, the time being entered in 10-second increments. If the user doesn't enter a valid response in this period of time, the program terminates with the default ERRORLEVEL of 0.
{}	Acceptable keystrokes are entered inside these brackets. Getkey is case-insensitive, so you only must enter each letter once. Getkey can also accept a function key as an input.
!	Causes Getkey to display an error message if the user presses an invalid keystroke. Getkey always beeps for an invalid response.
@	Suppresses the return after the user's response.
&	Causes Getkey to accept Return as a valid keystroke.
Message	Takes up the remainder of the line. It must be preceded by a space and should include several spaces at the end.

Once the user presses a valid keystroke, Getkey converts it to uppercase if it's a lower-case letter and then returns the ASCII value as an ERRORLEVEL.

Because Getkey returns the ASCII value through ERRORLEVEL rather than by returning a 1 for the first character, 2 for the second, and so on, it's somewhat more difficult to set up all the necessary ERRORLEVEL tests. Otherwise, its ability to limit responses, timeout, display an error message, and beep for an invalid response makes Getkey one of the more useful ERRORLEVEL-askers available.

Getyes

Name:	Getyes
Version:	1.1
Category:	Public Domain
Summary:	Accepts a y or n from the user and sets ERRORLEVEL accordingly.
Author:	Richard N. Wisan
Availability:	Included on the disk bound in this book.

The command to run Getyes is

    GETYES message

where the message is optional. If you enter a message, Getyes adds a " (Y/N) " to the end of the prompt. If the user presses anything other than a y or n, the program just beeps and waits for a valid keystroke. Once the user presses either y or n, it sets ERRORLEVEL to 0 for y and to 1 for n.

Getyorn

Name:	Getyorn
Version:	1.0
Price:	Free
Category:	Public Domain
Summary:	An ERRORLEVEL-asker that accepts only a capital Y or N keystroke.
Author:	Glen Hammond
Availability:	One of several files included on the enclosed disk in a file called HAMMOND.ZIP.

Getyorn is an ERRORLEVEL-asker that accepts only a capital Y or N. Getyorn will accept nothing else, not even a lowercase y or n. If the user presses any other keystroke, the program ignores it and gives no signal that the user pressed an invalid keystroke. When a capital Y or N is pressed, it sets ERRORLEVEL to 89 for Y and 78 for N, their regular ASCII values.

IFF

Name:	IFF
Version:	5.0
Price:	$20.00
Category:	Shareware
Summary:	A utility set designed to ask different types of questions.
Author:	John Knauer, Junior
	Post Office Box 747
	Brookfield, Connecticut 06804
Availability:	Available on many bulletin board systems.

IFF is a batch toolkit designed around queries. All of IFF's options run by issuing the IFF question followed by an option letter and generally return information via ERRORLEVEL. In addition, many of the questions can display information on the screen—although this can be disabled for batch files.

The I option prompts the user to enter a string, which is converted to uppercase and stored in the environment under the name IFF. Unlike similar routines, this option allows you to restrict the length of the information the user enters. In addition, the Q option prompts the user for a y or n response and won't accept anything else.

IFF works well and is fairly easy to use. For more information, see Chapter 6.

InKey

Name:	InKey
Version:	1.0
Price:	Free
Category:	Copyrighted
Summary:	Ask the user a question and wait for a response. That response is placed in ERRORLEVEL. InKey converts all lowercase responses to uppercase to reduce the amount of required testing.
Author:	Stephen Moore
Availability:	Three versions of InKey (for different keyboards) and their source code are included on the sampler disk.

InKey was written by Stephen Moore, the network manager for TAB Books.

The command to use InKey in your batch file is

INKEY [prompt]

InKey displays the prompt and waits for the user to press any key, setting the ERRORLEVEL value based on the key pressed.

The prompt can be up to 80 characters long and can contain anything except the four DOS redirection operators >, |, <, or >> and the dollar sign $. The INKEY prompt routine can include almost any character string, including ANSI.SYS cursor positioning and video attribute commands; these provide the opportunity to generate some highly creative menu screens.

For the standard ASCII characters Ctrl-A through lowercase z, InKey returns the normal ASCII value of the key. You must test the alphabetic characters for their uppercase forms only, ASCII 65-90, because InKey converts all lowercase keystrokes to uppercase; this makes testing for menu selections much easier. For the nonASCII keys (such as the function keys), obtain the key's ERRORLEVEL value from the appropriate keyboard table in Appendix D. If a key you need isn't listed, you can run InKey and then use CHECKERR .BAT (from Chapter 2) to test the ERRORLEVEL value.

An interesting side effect for the standard keys is that Ctrl-C (ASCII 3) is reported just like any other character without stopping your batch file. Because InKey doesn't flush the keyboard buffer, however, Ctrl-Break brings up the "Terminate batch job (Y/N)?" message. This quirk allows you to give your users the familiar Ctrl-C "escape pod" without bombing the whole routine.

InKey is very flexible and can be highly modified, although most users will never need to do that. The diskette included with your book has a version for the regular, enhanced, and older Tandy keyboards. If you have a special application for which you must modify InKey, you will find complete instructions in Appendix A. These instructions are somewhat technical in nature, however; most users should be able to ignore Appendix A and just use one of the versions of InKey on the disk.

INPUT

Name:	INPUT
Version:	1.0
Price:	Free
Category:	Copyrighted
Summary:	Queries the user and places the multi-character response in the environment.
Author:	William C. Parke; written for
	Capitol Health Users' Group
	Post Office Box 16406
	Arlington, Virginia 22215
Availability:	Available from many bulletin board systems.

INPUT takes a character string from the user and places it in the environment using the environmental variable ANS. INPUT expands on the power of Answer by adding two switches. The /b switch causes the environmental variable's values to retain the capitalization used by the user. Otherwise, everything is uppercase. The /# switch cause INPUT to truncate the user's response to the indicated number of characters. If the user presses return without entering a response or the response won't fit in the environment, INPUT sets ERRORLEVEL to 1.

If you must obtain multi-character responses from the user, INPUT is the best program you'll find.

Insist
Insist2

Name:	Insist
	Insist2
Version:	1.0
Category:	Public Domain
Summary:	Insist beeps constantly until a key is pressed. Once pressed, the key is converted to uppercase and the ASCII value is stored in ERRORLEVEL. Insist2 is identical but beeps only 600 times.
Author:	Richard N. Wisan
Availability:	Included on the disk bound in this book.

Sometimes batch files can take a very long time to run. This usually happens when the batch file executes a program that runs for a long time (for example, a batch file for an accounting program that first performs a daily closing, then a weekly closing, and then a monthly closing).

If a long-running batch file needs user input between steps, it might have trouble drawing attention to itself. Insist and Insist2 correct this problem. Both are ERRORLEVEL-askers; they take the user's input, convert it to uppercase, and then set the ERRORLEVEL equal to the ASCII value of the response.

While the uppercase conversion is nice, both Insists have an additional feature useful for long batch files. Insist will beep constantly until the user presses a key, which makes it very hard to forget about or ignore. In fact, this makes Insist useful for standard batch files as well as long batch files. Insist2 works identically except that it only beeps 600 times. I've put both on the included diskette.

Keypress (Glen Hammond)

Name:	Keypress
Version:	1.0
Price:	Free
Category:	Public Domain
Summary:	An ERRORLEVEL-asker that is case-insensitive and lets the user assign ERRORLEVEL values.
Author:	Glen Hammond
Availability:	One of several files included on the enclosed disk in a file called HAMMOND.ZIP.

Keypress is an ERRORLEVEL-asker that allows the user to assign the keystrokes equated with ERRORLEVEL codes. In the process, it allows the user to perform case-insensitive input testing. To use Keypress, you enter the command followed by the allowable characters. You don't have to specify upper- and lowercase separately, and the program can't display a prompt.

When the user presses a keystroke, the program checks to see if it was one of the keystrokes specified on the command line. If it was, it sets ERRORLEVEL to 1 if it was the first character on the command line, 2 if it was the second, and so on. This portion isn't case-sensitive. If the keystroke wasn't specified on the command line, it sets ERRORLEVEL to 0. If you must ensure that the user enters an acceptable keystroke, you can have the batch file loop back through until the program sets ERRORLEVEL to something other than 0.

KeyPress (Louis J. Cutrona Jr.)

Name: KeyPress
Version: 1.0
Price: Free
Category: Copyrighted
Summary: Ask the user a question and wait for a response, which is placed in
                 ERRORLEVEL. You can assign specific ERRORLEVEL values to
                 keystrokes, although KeyPress will accept any keystroke from the user.
Author: Louis J. Cutrona Jr.
Availability: All *PC Magazine* files are available from their area on CompuServe. See
                 any issue of *PC Magazine* for details.

With KeyPress, you specify the desired keystrokes on the command line. For example, you might use

```
KEYPRESS ABCDE
```

as a command. KeyPress assigns an ERRORLEVEL value of 1 to the first desired keystroke, a 2 to the second, and so on. KeyPress is case-insensitive, so upper and lowercase work identically.

   While you can specify the desired keystrokes on the command line, KeyPress will accept any keystrokes; those not on the desired keystroke list result in an ERRORLEVEL value of 0. Thus, KeyPress is less useful than ERRORLEVEL-askers that allow you to limit the responses to valid responses. However, you can overcome this limitation by looping back through the batch file until the user enters an acceptable keystroke. PRESSKEY .BAT in Table 1-5 illustrates this.

Table 1-5   PRESSKEY.BAT negates KeyPress's weakness of accepting any keystroke by looping back until a valid response is entered.

Batch File Line	Explanation
`@ECHO OFF`	Turns command-echoing off.
`REM PRESSKEY.BAT`	Remark giving the name of the batch file.
`:TOP`	Label marking the top of the loop.
`ECHO Enter A B or C`	Tells the user what to do.
`KEYPRESS ABC`	Run KeyPress and asks for A, B or, C.
`IF NOT ERRORLEVEL 1 ECHO Invalid Response`	If the user enters any other keystroke, the ERRORLEVEL value will be zero and this test will fail, so tell the user there is a mistake.
`IF NOT ERRORLEVEL 1 GOTO TOP`	If the user entered an invalid keystroke, jumps to the top of the loop.
`REM Rest of batch file here`	Documentation remark.

MicroMacroBat

Name:	MicroMacroBat
Version:	3.0
Price:	$35.00
Category:	Shareware
Summary:	A very powerful tool for developing advanced screens for batch files.
Author:	Sitting Duck Software
	Post Office Box 130
	Veneta, Oregon 97487
Availability:	Included on the disk bound in this book.

MicroMacroBat is primarily a tool to control displaying information on the screen from within a batch file; for that reason, it's covered in Chapter 2. However, MicroMacroBat has a keyword (GETKEY) in the registered version that allows you to obtain information from the user. You specify a list of acceptable keystrokes after the GETKEY keyword, and it accepts only those keystrokes while ignoring all others. GETKEY accepts any of the keystrokes in the list without regard to capitalization and sets ERRORLEVEL to 1 for the first, 2 for the second, and so on. While GETKEY can't display text on the screen, Micro-MacroBat has many other keywords to do that.

For more information, see Chapter 2.

MYMENU

Name:	MYMENU
Version:	1.0
Price:	Free
Category:	Copyrighted
Summary:	A very nice program that lets you select options off a moving lightbar menu.
Author:	Brian E. Smith
	59 Main Street
	Piedmont, South Carolina 29673
Availability:	Included on the disk bound in this book.

One reason for using an ERRORLEVEL-asker is to let the user select one item from a list. For that purpose, MYMENU is one of the nicest ERRORLEVEL-askers available.

To use MYMENU, you first create a disk file containing the menu. You can have as many menus as you like. As a minimum, the menu contains a title and list of options. The program draws a box around the menu and displays everything in a nice format, giving you a moving lightbar to make your selection. You move the cursor to the menu item you want and press return. MYMENU sets the ERRORLEVEL to 0 for the first item, 1 for the second, and so on.

Unfortunately, MYMENU doesn't support alternative methods of selecting menu items. You can't quickly jump to an item by pressing the first letter of the item, nor does MYMENU support a mouse for moving the cursor.

What really makes MYMENU special are the customizing commands you can include in the menu file. You can position the menu anywhere on the screen with the POSITION command. You must clear the screen first, however, because MYMENU doesn't.

The menu is made up of five areas: the title, selected item, items in the menu, the border, and the shadow. You can change the foreground and background colors for each using the keywords TITLE, SELECT, ITEM, BORDER, and SHADOW. For example, to change the color of the title you would add the following to the menu file:

```
TITLE TEXT WHITE
TITLE BACKGROUND BLUE
```

MYMENU is a tiny, easy-to-use program that makes getting information from the user painless.

Option

Name:	Option
Version:	1.0
Price:	Free
Category:	Copyrighted
Summary:	Ask the user a question and wait for a response, which is placed in ERRORLEVEL. You can assign specific ERRORLEVEL values to keystrokes; however, the process can be difficult.
Author:	Edward Morris
Availability:	Available from the PC Magazine forum on CompuServe.

Option has two sets of inputs. The first input is a list of allowable keystrokes and the associated ERRORLEVEL values. Thus, the list A1a1B2b2C3c3 would set the ERROR-LEVEL to 1 if either a capital or lowercase A is pressed, to 2 for a B, or to 3 for a C. The second input is the prompt that Option displays for the user. In addition to displaying a prompt, Option sounds a beep. If you don't like the beep, the documentation includes Debug instructions to path Option to turn the beep off.

Coming up with the list of allowable keystrokes and associated ERRORLEVEL values can become more complex than it sounds at first. You use the plus sign to represent return (which, coincidentally, makes the plus sign unavailable.) You can also allow a space by including a space in the input string. If you enter an odd number of keypress arguments, Option uses the last number as the working value of ERRORLEVEL if any other key is pressed. If you don't include this, Option doesn't allow keystrokes other than the ones you specify.

The real complexity comes in if you must assign ERRORLEVEL values greater than 9. To do that, you use the ASCII codes directly following the 9. The next few values are a colon for 10, a semi-colon for 11, a less than sign for 12, and an equal sign for 13. Thus, a keypress argument to assign ERRORLEVEL values of 0 − 13 would look like this:

```
A0B1C2D3E4F5G6H8I9J:K;L<M=
```

Clearly, it would be less confusing if you just entered the acceptable keystrokes and Option assigned 1 to the first, 2 to the second, and so on. However, this method does let you treat upper and lowercase differently. Still, a simpler program simply returning the ASCII value in ERRORLEVEL does this as well.

When the user enters an invalid keystroke, Option just beeps. When the user enters a valid keystroke, Option clears the screen and moves the cursor to the upper left corner of the screen. The documentation includes a Debug patch modifying Option so that the cursor just moves down one line for a valid keystroke.

Option is one of the most difficult ERRORLEVEL-askers to configure. In addition, it offers no features not available in other programs. For those reasons, you should avoid Option for one of the other programs.

QUERY.COM

Name:	QUERY.COM
Version:	1.0
Price:	Free
Category:	Copyrighted
Summary:	A user query program that creates a batch file to place information into the environment.
Author:	Brett Glass
Availability:	Complete directions for creating QUERY.COM were printed in the March 1991 issue of *PC/Computing*.

DOS is very inhospitable to query programs. A program works with a copy of the environment; but when the program terminates, its copy of the environment is erased. As a result, query programs can't easily use the environment to transfer information back to the calling batch file.

To combat this, a program could search through memory for the original copy of the environment and modify it; however, this is difficult, and most programs choose not to do this. Query programs also could store information in the ERRORLEVEL. Unlike the environment, only one copy of ERRORLEVEL exists, so it remains intact when control returns to the batch file. However, the ERRORLEVEL has room for only 1 byte, and running any other DOS program resets the ERRORLEVEL to 0.

QUERY.COM doesn't use either of these methods, instead taking advantage of a quirk in the way DOS manages the environment. Programs, both .COM and .EXE, get a copy of the environment when they run; but batch files run with the master copy of the environment. When you run QUERY.COM, it asks the user for information but doesn't place the user's response in the environment. Rather, it creates a batch file containing the user's response. After QUERY.COM terminates, the batch file can call the batch file created by QUERY.COM to place the user's response into the environment. Because only batch files are running at this point, the response is placed in the master copy of the environment.

The prompt to run QUERY.COM consists of three parts: the query command, the prompt, and the batch file in which to place the response. A typical line might look like this:

```
QUERY Enter Your First Name > FIRST.BAT
```

After the user enters his/her name, QUERY.COM creates FIRST.BAT with the single line SET ASK = Response, where Response is whatever the user entered.

QUERY.COM always stores the response under the environmental variable ASK. If you need more than one piece of information from the user, you must handle transferring the contents of ASK to another environmental variable each time you run QUERY.COM. In addition, QUERY.COM has no mechanism to clean up the short batch files it leaves on the disk, so you must handle all this manually. Table 1-6 illustrates using QUERY.COM and tackling these problems.

Table 1-6   NAME.BAT uses QUERY.COM
to place the user's full name in the environment.

Batch File Line	Explanation
`@ECHO OFF`	Turns command-echoing off.
`REM NAME.BAT`	Remark giving the name of the batch file.
`QUERY Enter Your First Name >FIRST.BAT`	Ask the user his/her first name. QUERY.COM places their response in a single-line batch file with the line "SET ASK= Response". That allows you to CALL that batch file to configure the environment.
`CALL FIRST`	Runs the batch file created by QUERY.COM to set ASK equal to the user's first name.
`SET FIRST=%ASK%`	Stores the user's first name under another environmental variable name so QUERY.COM can be used again.
`QUERY Enter Your Last Name > LAST.BAT`	Asks for the user's last name.
`CALL LAST`	Places that last name in the environment.
`SET LAST=%ASK%`	Stores that last name under another name.
`ECHO Hello %FIRST% %LAST%`	Displays the user's name.

Table 1-6 Continued.

Batch File Line	Explanation
DEL FIRST.BAT	Deletes the first batch file created by QUERY.COM
DEL LAST.BAT	Deletes the second batch file.
SET ASK=	Resets the ASK environmental variable because it is no longer needed.

Because of the DOS limitation of 127 characters on a command line, the SET ASK = Response line QUERY.COM creates is also limited to 127 characters. If you equal or surpass this limit, QUERY.COM locks up and forces you to reboot the computer. You can use QUERY.COM to gather most of the information.

Complete directions for creating QUERY.COM were printed in the March 1991 issue of *PC/Computing*.

Query2

Name:	Query2
Version:	1.0
Price:	Free
Category:	Public Domain
Summary:	An ERRORLEVEL-asker that can display a prompt and restrict choices to those specified on the command line.
Author:	Torsten Hoff
Availability:	Available on many bulletin board systems.

To ask a question using Query2, use the following command:

```
QUERY2 "responses" "message"
```

Query2 displays the message and waits for the user to press a keystroke. If that keystroke isn't one of those listed in response, it ignores it. Once the user presses a valid keystroke, Query2 sets ERRORLEVEL equal to the ASCII value of that keystroke.

Query2 is case-sensitive, so you must specify both the upper- and lowercase forms of all the valid letter responses—a time-consuming task. In addition, Query2 doesn't alert the user when an invalid response is entered; it simply ignores that response, possibly confusing the user.

Ronset

Name:	Ronset
Version:	2.1
Price:	$20.00
Category:	Shareware
Summary:	A very powerful tool for manipulating environmental variables. Unfortunately, it doesn't work with newer versions of DOS.
Author:	Ron Bemis
	9601 Forest Lane
	Apartment #222
	Dallas, Texas 75243
Availability:	Available on many bulletin board systems.

Under DOS, you can do very little with environmental variables. Basically, you can either create and erase them using the SET command, print them, or test them in batch files by surrounding their names with percent signs. Beyond that, however, there is little DOS can use them for.

All that changes, though, under Ronset. Using Ronset, there suddenly is little you can't do with environmental variables. The basic command to use Ronset is as follows:

```
RONSET A = XYZ(n,m)
```

In this command, A represents the environmental variable that the results will be stored in when the command finishes. The XYZ represents one of almost 100 functions you can perform (for example, the ADD function sums two numbers). The n and m represent the parameters being passed to the function. Most of the functions in Ronset perform tasks other than data input, so it's covered in detail in Chapter 9; but two functions deal with user input:

CHAR gets a single character from the user. The format is

```
RONSET A = CHAR(prompt,allowed,seconds)
```

The prompt is displayed on the command line. Allowed is a list of characters the program is allowed to accept from the user. Finally, seconds is how long the program waits for the user to enter a character before aborting.

STRING is a very useful function that allows the user to enter an entire line of information. The format is

```
RONSET A = STRING(prompt,length)
```

The prompt is displayed on the command line. The length defines how much information the user is allowed to enter, with a default length of 80 characters.

Once the information has been received from the user, Ronset offers a number of string manipulation functions to adjust that information. See Table 9-2 later in the book for a list of those functions.

Were it not for one flaw, Ronset would be one of the most powerful and useful batch utilities available. Unfortunately, Ronset can't run under any current version of DOS. I tested it under IBM DOS 3.3 and 4.0, as well as under Microsoft DOS 5.0; regretfully, it wouldn't work under any of them. However, I finally located a copy of DOS 2.1, under which it worked perfectly. Thus, once Ronset is upgraded to work with more modern versions of DOS, I can highly recommend it.

Scanion Enterprises Batch File Utilities

Name: Scanion Enterprises Batch File Utilities
Version: 2.2.0
Price: $9.95
Category: Shareware
Summary: A collection of over 100 batch file utilities.
Author: Paul Scanion
Availability: Included on the disk bound in this book.

The Scanion Enterprises Batch File Utilities [SEBFU for short] is a collection of over 100 batch file utilities discussed in detail in Chapter 7. However, the programs that accept user input are discussed here.

Each of the commands in SEBFU is a separate *.COM file. As a result, your disk can end up cluttered with quite a number of small program files. You might consider erasing those program files you aren't likely to use.

CR pauses the batch file until the enter key is pressed; it ignores other keystrokes, although it beeps for invalid ones. Pressing escape will exit the program. In essence, CR functions as a specialized PAUSE command.

CURKEY returns either an ERRORLEVEL value for each cursor movement key or a 0 for any other key. CURKEY is primarily used to allow the user to move the cursor around a batch file menu, rather than accepting input.

FUNKEY waits for the user to press F1-F10 and sets the ERRORLEVEL accordingly. It ignores other keystrokes, although it beeps for invalid ones. Pressing escape will exit the program. FUNKEY doesn't recognize the F11-F15 keys found on newer keyboards. Today, with more programs using function keys, this program is an especially nice way to get input from the user.

GALF waits for the user to press a letter key; it then converts that keystroke to uppercase and sets ERRORLEVEL accordingly. A is set to 1, B to 2, and so on, rather than using the ASCII values (making it easier to get an alphabetic response from the user).

GETNUM waits for the user to press a number and sets the ERRORLEVEL accordingly. It ignores other keystrokes, although it beeps for invalid ones. Pressing escape will exit the program. Accepting only numbers makes GETNUM an excellent way for the user to select a menu option.

INKEY accepts a single keystroke from the user and sets the ERRORLEVEL to its ASCII value. This resembles the typical ERRORLEVEL-asking program.

PASSWORD gives the user three chances to enter the correct password. If the user succeeds, the batch file continues. Otherwise, it locks up the computer and requires a cold reboot to continue. This version didn't work properly under DOS 4.0 or later. If the user entered a wrong password twice, it accepted the second password and prompted the user to enter a new password.

RESPONSE accepts a multi-character response from the user and stores it under the environmental variable specified on the command line. This surpasses other programs because you can specify the environmental variable name to use. Generally, you would only use RESPONSE when a single character response isn't enough, such as when you want to know the name of either the user, a program to run, or a data file.

YN waits for the user to press either the y or n key and then sets the ERRORLEVEL accordingly. It ignores other keystrokes, although it beeps for invalid ones. Pressing escape will exit the program. YN is perfect for questions like "Do you want to delete these files?" or "This takes three hours. Do you want to continue?"

For more detail on SEBFU, see Chapter 7.

Select

Name:	Select
Version:	Unknown
Price:	Unknown
Category:	Unknown
Summary:	An ERRORLEVEL-asker that converts the response to uppercase.
Author:	Steve Olensky
Availability:	Available on many bulletin board systems.

Select is a fairly standard ERRORLEVEL-asker. It optionally will display a prompt if one is entered after the SELECT command, and it automatically adds trailing spaces. Also, it nicely converts all letter responses to uppercase before assigning their ASCII value to ERRORLEVEL.

Select has no documentation, and I was unable to contact the author; thus, I am unsure if the program is actually shareware or public domain and therefore appropriate to be posted on bulletin board systems. For that reason, you might want to ignore Select to avoid violating any copyrights.

tBU

Name:	tBU
Version:	3.0
Price:	Free
Category:	Copyrighted
Summary:	A collection of very powerful functions for manipulating environmental variables.
Author:	Todd R. Hill
	Claude N. Warren Jr.
Availability:	Available on many bulletin board systems.

Most of the batch utilities in this book are programs that perform some specific task. However, tBU (short for the Batch Utility) doesn't work this way, functioning instead for the most part as an intermediary. You run tBU to perform some manipulation of an environmental variable you want to use to perform some other task.

To run tBU, you provide it with a symbol instructing it what to do, an environmental variable to manipulate, and optional parameters as required. tBU sometimes sets ERRORLEVEL, but the really useful information is stored in the environmental variable. Accordingly, you really should expand your environment while using tBU (for help doing so, see Appendix B).

The general format of the tBU command is

TBU -S VAR options

where S is the symbol telling tBU what to do. Please note that the symbol is case-sensitive. The VAR is the environmental variable tBU uses to store the results, while options are the remaining symbol-specific parameters required by tBU.

The symbols supported by tBU and their general function are covered in detail in Chapter 6, but those dealing with user inputs are covered here:

c Allows the user to enter a single keystroke from the keyboard.

s Has the user enter a string for the keyboard and stores it in the environmental variable.

Unfortunately, tBU uses a complex syntax difficult to learn, and the extremely terse documentation makes learning tBU even more difficult. Fortunately, tBU is so powerful that you will soon wonder how you got along without it. In fact, after this book was finished, tBU is one of only a handful of utilities that found a permanent home on my crowded hard disk. I highly recommend tBU.

Ultimate Screen Manager

Name:	Ultimate Screen Manager
Version:	1.20
Price:	$39.00
Category:	Shareware
Summary:	Creates, modifies and displays advanced screens.
Author:	MDFlynn Associates
	Post Office Box 5034
	Redwood City, California 94063
Availability:	Included on the disk bound in this book.

Normally, the information you want to get from the user is either a menu selection or some short input like a filename. The programs in this chapter handle these sort of tasks well.

Occasionally, you might want to get other information from the user. The Ultimate Screen Manager helps you construct a database front end using a batch file. This front end then asks the user questions and stores the responses in environmental variables for further use by the batch file.

For more information on the Ultimate Screen Manager, please see Chapter 7.

Well

Name:	Well
Version:	1.0
Price:	Free
Category:	Public Domain
Summary:	An ERRORLEVEL-asker that allows you to control the ERRORLEVEL value assigned to different keystrokes.
Author:	Laurence Shusta
	523 Green Hill Road
	Madison, Connecticut 06443
Availability:	Available on many bulletin board systems.[2]

To ask a question using Well, you issue a command like this:

```
WELL 14 18 "Do You Want To Continue? (y/n)" Y N
```

The 14 and 18 respectively define the column and row where the prompt will be displayed. The prompt must be enclosed in quotes and doesn't need extra spaces at the end. Following the prompt, you list the acceptable responses.

---

[2]Generally distributed as a set containing both Rite and Well and named BATIN-IT.ZIP after the name of the demonstration batch file.

If the user presses an invalid keystroke, the program ignores it. Once the user presses the proper keystroke, it sets ERRORLEVEL to 1 if it's the first keystroke in the list, 2 if it's the second, and so on. Well is both flexible and easy to use.

WHAT

Name:	WHAT
Version:	1.47
Price:	Free
Category:	Public Domain
Summary:	WHAT can determine a great deal of information about the computer and pass that information back to the batch file. It can also prompt the user for a single character response to a question. Information is passed using the ERRORLEVEL and an environmental variable.
Author:	Tom Peters
Availability:	Available on many bulletin board systems.

Sometimes you can write a more effective batch file if you know information about the environment under which the batch file is running. WHAT is an excellent program for obtaining that information.

The general format for the WHAT command is

WHAT X [E] Parameter-1 Parameter-2

where X is the option to run and E is the optional enhanced mode.

Some of the WHAT options require additional parameters. Most of the WHAT options return a value in the environmental variable what and in ERRORLEVEL. However, a few of the options allow the user to input information. These options are as follows:

C prompts the user for a single keystroke. You can limit the keystrokes the program will accept from the user. The program is case-insensitive and treats all letters as uppercase. The actual uppercase version of the letter is stored in the environment, and the ERRORLEVEL is set to the ASCII value of the uppercase letter. Adding the E option prevents the keystroke from echoing to the user.

S lets the user enter a string, such as a password or their name (the E option will prevent echoing of the string.) S stores the string in the environment and sets ERRORLEVEL equal to the length of the string.

WHAT is extremely powerful and also easy to use. It belongs in everyone's batch file toolkit.

For more information on WHAT, see Chapter 7.

X-BATCH

Name:	X-BATCH
Version:	1.0
Price:	$20.00
Category:	Shareware
Summary:	A collection of 13 useful utilities.
Author:	Gary R. Pannone
	9 Brady Road Ext.
	Westboro, Massachusetts 01581
Availability:	Available on many bulletin board systems.

X-BATCH is a collection of thirteen useful batch file utilities. Concerning queries, it has a command called GETCHAR that gets information from the user in the form of a single keystroke. You either can accept any character or limit the user to a specific list of keystrokes. Letters are converted to uppercase, and the ASCII value of the keystroke is returned.

The X-BATCH commands are useful and easy to learn, possessing a sensible format that reads almost like English.

For more information on X-BATCH, see Chapter 6.

Zerobat

Name:	Zerobat
Price:	Free
Category:	Copyrighted
Summary:	A batch file to create 0 length files, a program to accept a y or n input, and a replacement for the PAUSE command.
Author:	John C. Van Lund
Availability:	Zerobat is available on many bulletin board systems.

Zerobat actually consists of three different programs: CALLYN, CONTINUE, and ZERO.BAT. Because CALLYN allows a batch file to communicate with the user, it's discussed here. CONTINUE is discussed below in pausing programs, and all three are discussed in Chapter 6.

CALLYN sets ERRORLEVEL to 255 for a y key, 254 for an n key, 1 for a function key, and 0 for anything else. Unfortunately, it requires ANSI.SYS to operate properly and doesn't work under DOS 5.0, where it sets ERRORLEVEL to 34 no matter which key is pressed. These weaknesses make CALLYN less useful than similar programs.

Pausing programs

These programs don't get information from the user in the typical sense (i.e., when they finish, no information is transferred back to the user). Rather, they resemble the DOS PAUSE command, stopping the batch file until the user presses a key and then restarting the batch file. However, each of these programs offers some improvement over the PAUSE command.

AT

Name:	AT
Version:	1.0
Price:	Free
Category:	Copyrighted
Summary:	Runs a program at a specified time and date.
Author:	Kevyn Ford
	CSI Research & Development
Availability:	Available on many bulletin board systems.

Most pausing programs simply wait until the clock reaches a specific time and then return control over to a batch file. AT differs from this in two ways.

First, AT not only waits for a specific time, it also waits for a specific date. While at first glance that might sound like an advantage, it really greatly reduces the usefulness of AT. To run your backup program next Monday, you might enter a command like

```
AT 01:00 06/17 C: \ BAT \ BACKALL.BAT
```

and on June 17 at 1 AM, AT would run your backup batch file. This approach works fine from the command line but makes AT very difficult to use within a batch file. Essentially, you must edit the batch file each time you run it in order to update the date. To make a backup *every* night after 1 AM, I could enter the commands manually using AT, but that defeats the purpose of using a batch file. Basically, because I must include the date with AT, the batch file I run one night won't work the next.

Second, AT wants to run the program for you rather than allowing a batch file to resume execution—necessary for use as a command line utility but not in a batch file. To circumvent this, you can enter an invalid command for AT to run, allowing the batch file to resume at the proper time once AT fails to find its program.

AT probably will fail to find its program anyway; it won't search the PATH for a program or batch file, so you must enter the entire path as well as the extension on the command line. Finally, internal commands (like DEL *.BAK) won't work with AT at all. Because users rarely enter the full path and extension for a program, most are likely to improperly specify the program that AT should run. AT doesn't check the program prior to running it, so you will likely ask AT to run something at night only to discover the next morning that it didn't run at all!

AT isn't compatible with DOS 5.0. Depending on my memory configuration, AT would either lock up the computer or violate Microsoft's memory manager in such a way to force a cold reboot.

AT has too many problems to justify using it, especially considering that a large number of good pausing programs are available.

B(DISK

Name:	B(DISK
Version:	Unknown
Price:	Unknown[3]
Category:	Copyrighted
Summary:	A collection of batch file utilities for working with files and performing other tasks.
Author:	G. Estes
Availability:	Available on many bulletin board systems.

The B(DISK of Batch Programmer Tools contains 34 separate utilities. The utilities are an odd mixture of programs that work best from within a batch file and of other programs that would generally be used from the command line. The B(DISK utilities dealing with pausing are as follows:

B(DELAY pauses the batch file for a specified period of time and can't be aborted by any key combination except for Ctrl-Break.

B(PAUSE pauses the batch file for a specified period of time and can be aborted by pressing any key.

B(UNTIL pauses the batch file until a specified time has passed and can't be aborted by any key combination except for Ctrl-Break.

B(WAIT pauses the batch file until a specified time is reached and can be aborted by pressing any key.

The documentation for B(DISK fails to mention whether the programs are public domain, shareware, or commercial programs. In fact, the documentation fails to include a copyright notice although the programs contain one internally. For that reason, you might want to ignore B(DISK to avoid violating any copyrights.

For more information on the B(DISK utilities, see Chapter 6.

---

[3]The author includes documentation with the programs but fails to mention the status of the files, so I was unable to determine if they are public domain, shareware, or commercial. The author includes no name, address, or copyright notice in the documentation, although the programs are marked internally as copyright G. Estes. As a result, I don't know the status of the B(DISK programs.

EC

Name:	EC
Version:	1.00
Price:	Free
Category:	Public Domain
Summary:	Pauses the batch file until the specified time is reached and then runs EXEC-CLK.BAT.
Author:	Lonnie J. Rolland
Availability:	Available on many bulletin board systems

When run, EC displays a clock in the top right corner of the screen and pauses until the specified time is reached. If you didn't specify a time, EC pauses until midnight. Once either the specified time or midnight is reached, EC runs a batch file called EXEC-CLK.BAT.

The arrangement of running a specific batch file means you can easily use EC as either a command line or batch file utility. You might choose to run EC as a command line utility if you always plan to run the same task—say a tape backup. In this case, you would build EXEC-CLK.BAT to perform the backup and then run EC with a time (or without, if midnight was acceptable) from the command line.

If you must perform several different tasks using EC—say a tape backup on Mondays and Thursdays, a full disk check on Wednesdays and an account closing on Friday—EC will be difficult to run from the command line because you constantly will need to change the contents of EXEC-CLK.BAT.

A better approach in this case would be to build separate batch files for the tape backup, disk checking, and account closing, each of which can run EC to pause. If EXEC-CLK.BAT doesn't exist or simply contains a trivial command like ECHO RUNNING, then EC will return control to the calling batch file once EXEC-CLK.BAT executes. Thus, each batch file can use EC to simply pause until a specified time is reached.

While EC is pausing, it displays both a message telling the user what time it will execute EXEC-CLK.BAT and a clock in the top right side of the screen; but, otherwise, it doesn't clear the screen. This gives the batch file author a great deal of flexibility in designing informational screens to display while EC is running.

To regain control of the computer while EC is pausing, simply press a key to abort EC without running EXEC-CLK.BAT. Of course, if an underlying batch file is using EC as a pausing program, then that batch file will resume execution.

GPAUSE.COM

Name:	GPAUSE.COM
Version:	Unknown
Price:	Unknown

Category:	Unknown
Summary:	A replacement for the DOS PAUSE command.
Author:	Unknown
Availability:	Available on many bulletin board systems.

GPAUSE.COM displays a "Type in GO to continue or Press <Ctrl-Break> to quit" message. If you enter anything other than GO or Control-Break, it redisplays the message. GO continues the batch file, while Control-Break aborts it.

Of course, the advantage over the PAUSE command is that the user must read the instructions and perform them specifically to continue, rather than simply pressing a key. Thus, the warning is much harder to ignore.

IFF

Name:	IFF
Version:	5.0
Price:	$20.00
Category:	Shareware
Summary:	A utility set designed to ask different types of questions.
Author:	John Knauer, Junior
	Post Office Box 747
	Brookfield, Connecticut 06804
Availability:	Available on many bulletin board systems.

IFF is a batch toolkit designed around queries. All of IFF's options run by issuing the IFF question followed by an option letter and generally return information via ERRORLEVEL. In addition, many of the questions can display information on the screen—although this can be disabled for batch files.

IFF's W option pauses the batch file for the specified number of minutes or seconds.

IFF works well and is fairly easy to use. For more information, see Chapter 6.

MicroMacroBat

Name:	MicroMacroBat
Version:	3.0
Price:	$35.00
Category:	Shareware
Summary:	A very powerful tool for developing advanced screens for batch files.
Author:	Sitting Duck Software
	Post Office Box 130
	Veneta, Oregon 97487
Availability:	Included on the disk bound in this book.

MicroMacroBat is primarily a tool to control displaying information on the screen from within a batch file. However, MicroMacroBat has several keywords (SLEEP, WAIT, and WAIT-ROTATE) that pause the batch file. SLEEP pauses the batch file for a specified number of seconds. WAIT displays text and pauses the batch file until the user presses a key. WAIT-ROTATE displays text in a moving marquee fashion and pauses the batch file until the user presses a key (this keyword is available only in the registered version).

For more information, see Chapter 2.

PAUSE3

Name:	PAUSE3
Version:	1.0
Price:	Free
Category:	Public Domain
Summary:	Replaces the DOS PAUSE command and also displays a message.
Author:	Scott Pakin
	6007 North Sheridan Road
	Chicago, Illinois 60660
Availability:	Available on many bulletin board systems.

When you issue the DOS PAUSE command, it always displays the same boring "Strike any key to continue . . ." message. PAUSE3 simulates the PAUSE command, but any text entered after the PAUSE3 command is displayed as a message.

Of course, you can do the same thing with DOS by using echo to display the message first and then piping the "Strike any key to continue . . ." message off the screen using the command PAUSE > NUL. This makes PAUSE3 useless or at least redundant.

Rebeep

Name:	Rebeep
Version:	1.0
Price:	Free
Category:	Copyrighted
Summary:	Beeps at user in selected intervals until a key is pressed.
Author:	Community Educational Services Foundation
	Post Office Box 636
	Arlington, Virginia 22216
Availability:	Available on many bulletin board systems.

You call Rebeep with the command REBEEP n, where n is the number of seconds between beeps. Rebeep pauses the batch file and beeps every n seconds until the user presses any keystroke.

Scroll

Name:	Scroll
Version:	3a
Price:	Free
Category:	Copyrighted
Summary:	Pauses the batch file while displaying a large, moving message on the screen.
Author:	Bill Stewart
Availability:	Available on many bulletin board systems.

Scroll is the cream of the pausing programs. It displays your message in very large letters (formed from ASCII characters) that scroll across the screen from right to left. After the message finishes, it pauses briefly and then redisplays the message. Messages can be as long as the DOS 127-character command limit allows. When you press any key, Scroll terminates.

In addition to displaying message, Scroll gives you the ability to control the foreground and background colors as well as the ASCII characters used to construct the large characters.

In addition to letters, Scroll has a number of symbols built in (such as a car, flag, and house). These are formed from ASCII characters just like the letters, so they do appear crude on the screen. Still, they scroll by fast enough that they tend to draw attention to the screen.

The moving display of Scroll is attractive and works well enough that you could set up a PC screen in a store and use it as an advertising gimmick.

SIGNALX.COM

Name:	SIGNALX.COM
Version:	Unknown
Price:	Unknown
Category:	Unknown
Summary:	A replacement for the DOS PAUSE command.
Author:	Unknown
Availability:	Available on many bulletin board systems.

SIGNALX.COM is much like the PAUSE command. It displays a "Press any key to continue" message and terminates when you press a key. Unlike PAUSE, however, it beeps constantly until you press a key. Thus, SIGNALX.COM is a good program to signal that a long batch file is finished or otherwise needs attention.

Sleep

Name:	Sleep
Version:	1.1
Price:	Unknown
Category:	Unknown
Summary:	Pauses the batch file until a specified period has passed or until a specific time is reached.
Author:	John Parnell & Associates
Availability:	Sleep is available on many bulletin board systems, although it's undocumented and possibly unappropriate for posting.

The command SLEEP FOR hh:mm:ss instructs Sleep to pause the batch file the requested number of hours (hh), minutes (mm), and seconds (ss). The command SLEEP UNTIL hh:mm:ss instructs Sleep to pause the batch file until the specified time is reached. Sleep uses ANSI.SYS to display either a countdown when sleeping for a specified length of time or the current time when sleeping until a specified time. It can run without ANSI, although the screen will be cluttered with ANSI escape sequences.

Sleep is useful when a task must be performed within a certain time period. For example, on the network at my office, we can backup our local hard disks across the network after midnight. Adding a SLEEP UNTIL 00:00:01 to my backup batch file takes care of the after-midnight requirement.

Unfortunately, Sleep has no documentation, and I was unable to contact the author; thus, I am unsure if the program is actually shareware or public domain and therefore appropriate to be posted on bulletin board systems. For that reason, you might want to ignore Sleep to avoid violating any copyrights.

T_Minus

Name:	T_Minus
Version:	1.2
Price:	Free
Category:	Copyrighted
Summary:	Pauses the batch file for the specified number of seconds.
Author:	Harry M. Carver
Availability:	Available on many bulletin board systems.

The command T_Minus n pauses the batch file for n seconds. While pausing, T_Minus displays the message "T Minus m seconds . . . and counting" and updates the counter every second. You can press Ctrl-Break to abort the program.

T_Minus was able to handle very large numbers of seconds and worked very well.

Time__In

Name:	Time__In
Version:	1.0
Price:	Free
Category:	Copyrighted
Summary:	Allows the user to run a program based on a configured time limit.
Author:	John W. Wulff
	260 Terranova Drive
	Warrenton, Virginia 22186
Availability:	Available on many bulletin board systems.

Technically, Time__In isn't a pausing program. However, I have included it here because it's actually more qualified than many pausing programs. To use Time__In, you issue a command like this:

```
TIME__IN 10:00-12:00 18:00-24:00 02:00-04:30
```

Time__In then checks to see if the time falls within any of those blocks. If it does, it sets ERRORLEVEL to 1; otherwise, it sets it to 0. You can use up to ten blocks.

Time__In is actually superior to most pausing programs because it allows you to work with multiple blocks. By looping until ERRORLEVEL is 1, Time__In effectively functions as a pausing program using multiple time blocks. The following batch file segment illustrates that:

```
:TOP
TIME__IN 10:00-12:00 18:00-24:00 02:00-04:30
IF ERRORLEVEL 0 IF NOT ERRORLEVEL 1 GOTO TOP
```

TIMEJOB

Name:	TIMEJOB
Version:	Unknown
Price:	Unknown
Category:	Unknown
Summary:	Pauses a batch file until a specified time is reached.
Author:	Unknown
Availability:	Available on many bulletin board systems.[4]

---

[4] I was unable to determine the status of the program, so you may want to ignore it to avoid violating any copyrights.

TIMEJOB is a typical pausing program in that it pauses the batch file until a specified time is reached. It is atypical, however, for two reasons. First, you enter a description of the batch file executing on the command line, and it displays the first 30 characters of that description while pausing. Second, it produces a very nice screen (white letters in a red box on a blue background) without relying on ANSI.SYS.

After running for a few minutes, TIMEJOB clears the screen to protect against monitor burn-in and displays a brief moving message to press any key for screen restoration. If the user presses Escape, TIMEJOB aborts and sets ERRORLEVEL to 1, allowing you to ensure that TIMEJOB was able to wait until the specified time before the batch file ran a program.

Until

Name:	Until
Version:	1.0
Price:	Free
Category:	Copyrighted
Summary:	Pauses the batch file until a specified time is reached.
Author:	Jerry A. Shank
	2596 Old Philadelphia Pike
	Bird-in-Hand, Pennsylvania 17505
Availability:	Available on many bulletin board systems.

The command UNTIL time causes the batch file to pause until the specified time is reached. Until clears the screen and displays the author's name and address, as well as the time Until started and the time it's waiting until. Pressing Ctrl-Z aborts the program without setting ERRORLEVEL and allows the batch file to resume.

Wait (Glen Hammond)

Name:	Wait
Version:	1.0
Price:	Free
Category:	Public Domain
Summary:	Pauses the batch file for up to 59 seconds in 1-second increments.
Author:	Glen Hammond
Availability:	One of several files included on the enclosed disk in a file called HAMMOND.ZIP.

The command WAIT n pauses the batch file for n seconds where n is an integer value between 1 and 59. If you enter a number higher than 59, the program repeatedly subtracts

59 from it until the remaining value is 59 or less. If the user presses a key during the wait, the program exits without setting ERRORLEVEL, giving the user a chance to read the screen and abort the batch file if necessary without unduly delaying it if it's running unattended.

Wait (Software Research)

Name:	Wait
Price:	Unknown
Category:	Unknown
Summary:	Pauses a batch file until a specified time is reached.
Author:	Software Research
Availability:	The file is available on some bulletin board systems, although it's not clear if it was intended to be distributed that way. The code contains a 1983 copyright notice.

Wait doesn't pause a batch file until a key is pressed but rather until a specific time is reached. You enter the command WAIT HH:MM:SS in the batch file, where HH is the hour in 24-hour format, MM is the minute, and SS is the second. When the batch file encounters this line, Wait displays a small digital clock on the screen and pauses the batch file until that time is reached. Once the specified time is reached, the batch file continues without user intervention.

Wait's a very useful program, but its pedigree is unknown. The file is available on some bulletin board systems but has no documentation. The code contains a 1983 copyright notice by Software Research, so I'm uncertain that the program can be distributed by bulletin board system. Until more is known about this program's source, you might want to ignore Wait to avoid violating Software Research's copyright.

Waitil

Name:	Waitil
Version:	1.00
Price:	Free
Category:	Copyrighted
Summary:	Pauses the batch file until the specified time is reached.
Author:	George A. Stanislav
Availability:	The author has restricted distribution to non-profit organizations, so the program may be hard to find.

The command WAITIL hh:mm causes the batch file to pause until the specified time is reached. Pressing any key while waiting causes Waitil to abort and the batch file to continue.

X-BATCH

Name:	X-BATCH
Version:	1.0
Price:	$20.00
Category:	Shareware
Summary:	A collection of 13 useful utilities.
Author:	Gary R. Pannone
	9 Brady Road Ext.
	Westboro, Massachusetts 01581
Availability:	Available on many bulletin board systems.

X-BATCH is a collection of thirteen useful batch file utilities, of which the WAIT command can pause batch files for a specific period of time or until a specific time is reached.

The X-BATCH commands are useful and easy to learn, with a sensible format reading almost like English.

For more information, see Chapter 6.

Zerobat

Name:	Zerobat
Price:	Free
Category:	Copyrighted
Summary:	A batch file to create 0 length files, a program to accept a y or n input, and a replacement for the PAUSE command.
Author:	John C. Van Lund
Availability:	Zerobat is available on many bulletin board systems.

Zerobat actually consists of three different programs: CALLYN, CONTINUE and ZERO .BAT. CALLYN was discussed earlier in the section on getting input from the user; CONTINUE is discussed next because it's a pausing program. All three programs are discussed in Chapter 6.

CONTINUE displays a flashing red "Continue with any key" message at the top right of the screen and waits for the user to press any key before continuing. CONTINUE doesn't need ANSI.SYS to run and is the most useful of the three programs in ZERO .BAT.

2

Communicating with the user

DOS offers only the very bland TYPE and ECHO commands for batch files to use to communicate with the user. These are, as my 14-year old daughter would say, "boooooooring." If you use ANSI.SYS (and very few of you do), then you can change the color of the text and background but only through complex escape sequences difficult to understand and use. You can't even use ANSI.SYS when writing batch files for others because you never know if they use it.

The utilities in this chapter all improve on batch file communications. They range from a very simple program that skips a line to programs that let you control almost every aspect of the screen. Among them, you will find just the thing to protect you from boring screens.

Ansihere

Name:	Ansihere
Version:	1.0
Price:	Free
Category:	Copyrighted
Summary:	Tests to see if ANSI.SYS is loaded and sets ERRORLEVEL accordingly.
Availability:	All *PC Magazine* files are available from their area on CompuServe. See any issue of *PC Magazine* for details.

If ANSI.SYS is loaded, you can design nice colorful screens by echoing the proper escape sequences. However, if you echo those same escape sequences without ANSI.SYS loaded, the screen becomes a real mess. Your batch file needs a way to determine if ANSI .SYS is loaded so it can use a colorful screen if it is and a plain one if it's not.

While DOS offers no method to test for ANSI.SYS, Ansihere does just that. Running Ansihere without any parameters will display a message on the screen indicating if ANSI

.SYS is loaded. Even better for your batch file, Anishere will set ERRORLEVEL to 0 if ANSI.SYS is missing and to 1 if present. That way, your batch file can jump to different screen handling sections depending on the status of ANSI.SYS.

BATUTIL

Name:	BATUTIL
Version:	1.0
Price:	$39.00 (Includes STACKEY)
Category:	Shareware
Summary:	A powerful batch file utility that allows you to do almost anything required in a batch file.
Author:	The Support Group
	Lake Technology Park
	Post Office Box 130
	McHenry, Maryland 21541
	(800) 872-4768
Availability:	Available on many bulletin board systems.

BATUTIL is far more than just a batch utility—it's really a batch language disguised as a batch utility. To use BATUTIL, you enter a command like

    BATUTIL [HOUR]

on the command line. When you enclose the command in square [ ] brackets, BATUTIL returns results in ERRORLEVEL. If you enclose the command in curly {} brackets, BATUTIL also returns the results as an environmental variable. BATUTIL only needs the first two characters of the command and ignores capitalization, so [HOUR], [Ho], [HoUr] and [ho] all mean the same thing.

BATUTIL has some very nice features for displaying information on the screen, which are covered here.

BATUTIL supports all the prompt metastrings (like $p and $g) along with some of its own. These include

$E   The date in English (e.g. April 20, 1991).
$M   The month as a two-digit number.
$T   The time in HHMM format.
$W   The day of the week in English

and several more. These metastrings can be used in conjunction with the other BATUTIL display features discussed below.

BATUTIL is designed to use yellow text on a blue background for all its display actions, although commands exist to change this. Some of the commands BATUTIL uses to control the display are as follows:

BECHO displays text on the screen in large letters.

CLS clears the screen using the BATUTIL colors.

ECHO displays text, much like the DOS ECHO command, but using the BATUTIL colors, extra metastring characters and additional BATUTIL control.

MENU and **FMENU** fantastic built-in functions for menu development. MENU works from the command line, while FMENU reads from the file. These two functions alone are worth the registration fee for BATUTIL.

PRETTY resembles the ECHO command but simplifies the displaying of text in multiple colors.

ROW and **COL** position the cursor.

BATUTIL is an extremely powerful tool for controlling the operation of batch files. As part of its toolkit, BATUTIL has some very nice tools for displaying information on the screen.

For more detailed information on BATUTIL, see Chapter 6.

BEN

Name:	BEN
Version:	March 1991
Price:	$15.00
Category:	Shareware
Summary:	A batch file utility giving the user a great deal of screen control.
Author:	Hutchins Software
	5232 West Townley Avenue
	Glendale, Arizona 85302
Availability:	Included on the disk bound in this book.

BEN (short for Batch File Enhancement Program) is a single program (BEN.EXE) that gives you great flexibility in designing screens for batch files. To work, BEN requires ANSI.SYS to be attached in the CONFIG.SYS. BEN works with keywords; for each command, you enter BEN followed by a keyword and perhaps by additional instructions. The keywords available in BEN are as follows:

AREPLY is another ERRORLEVEL-asker that allows the user to enter any letter. It sets ERRORLEVEL to 1 for A, 2 for B, and so on.For any other response, it sets the ERRORLEVEL to 0. If you want to insist the user enter a letter response, you can loop back through the question until you get an ERRORLEVEL other than 0.

ATTRIB controls several attributes of the color. You can reset the color to normal or set it to high intensity, underline (monochrome only), blinking, reverse, or invisible.

BEEP sounds the speaker the specified number of times. You can't control the frequency or duration using BEN.

BOX draws a single-line box on the screen at the specified coordinates.

COLOR allows you to control the display color. You supply the color command with both the foreground and background colors.

CURSOR positions the cursor at the specified location on the screen.

DATE displays the date from within the batch file.

DBOX draws a double-line box on the screen at the specified coordinates.

DIRECT displays the current subdirectory. It doesn't set ERRORLEVEL, so the batch file can't make use of it.

DIREXIST tests to see if the specified subdirectory exists and sets the ERRORLEVEL accordingly.

DISKFREE displays the amount of free disk space. It doesn't set ERRORLEVEL, so the batch file can't make use of it.

DRIVE displays the current drive. It doesn't set ERRORLEVEL, so the batch file can't make use of it.

ECHOB echoes the specified number of blank lines, especially useful because of the difficulty in echoing blank lines using DOS.

FINDTEXT tests to see if the specified file contains specified text. The text can't contain any spaces, and the text searching isn't case-sensitive.

MEMFREE displays the amount of free conventional memory. It doesn't set ERRORLEVEL, so the batch file can't make use of it.

NREPLY is an ERRORLEVEL-asker that allows the user to enter 1-9. It sets the ERRORLEVEL accordingly, to 1 for 1, 2 for 2, and so on. For any other response, it sets the ERRORLEVEL to 0. If you want to insist the user enter a 1-9 response, you can loop back through the question until you get an ERRORLEVEL other than 0.

TIME displays the time from within the batch file.

WAIT pauses the batch file for the specified number of seconds.

Table 2-1 shows a summary of the BEN keywords and their syntax. Table 2-2 shows SHOW-BEN.BAT, a batch file illustrating many of the BEN keywords. BEN also comes with two stand-alone programs; one turns the cursor off, and the other turns the cursor back on.

**Table 2-1 BEN has numerous keywords that
you can use to control the display from within the batch file.**

Keyword	Syntax Function
	When the command BEN is used without a keyword, it displays a help screen.
AREPLY	AREPLY Waits for the user to enter a letter and sets ERRORLEVEL accordingly.

Keyword	Syntax Function
ATTRIB	`ATTRIB #` Selects the color attribute to use.
BEEP	`BEEP n` Beeps the speaker n-times.
BOX	`BOX r1 c1 r2 c2` Draws a single-line box beginning at row r1, column c1 going to row r2, column c2.
COLOR	`COLOR n m` Selects the foreground (n) and background (m) colors to use.
CURSOR	`CURSOR r c` Positions the cursor at row r and column c.
DATE	`DATE` Displays the current date.
DBOX	`DBOX r1 c1 r2 c2` Draws a double-line box beginning at row r1, column c1 going to row r2, column c2.
DIRECT	`DIRECT` Displays the current subdirectory.
DIREXIST	`DIREXIST subdirectory` Checks to see if the specified subdirectory exists and sets ERROR-LEVEL accordingly.
DISKFREE	`DISKFREE` Displays the amount of free disk space.
DRIVE	`DRIVE` Displays the current drive.
ECHOB	`ECHOB n` Echoes n-blank lines.
FINDTEXT	`FINDTEXT filename text` Checks the file named filename to see if it contains the specified text and sets ERRORLEVEL accordingly. The text can not contain any spaces and the testing is case-insensitive.
MEMFREE	`MEMFREE` Displays the amount of free conventional memory.
NREPLY	`NREPLY` Waits for the user to enter a number 1-9 and sets ERRORLEVEL accordingly.
TIME	`TIME` Displays the current time.
WAIT	`WAIT n` Pauses the batch file for n-seconds.

**Table 2-2   SHOW-BEN.BAT illustrates
many of the keywords available in BEN.**

Batch File Line	Explanation
`@ECHO OFF`	Turns command-echoing off.

`REM Name:     SHOW-BEN.BAT`
`REM Version: 1.00`
`REM Date:     March 23, 1991`
`REM Purpose: Demonstrate Ben`
	Documentation remarks.

Table 2-2   Continued.

Batch File Line	Explanation
CLS	Clears the screen.
BEN ATTRIB 0	Resets display type to normal.
ECHO This Line Is Normal Intensity	Echoes text.
BEN ATTRIB 1 ECHO This Line Is High Intensity	Echoes high intensity text.
BEN ATTRIB 0	Resets the display before changing to another display mode.
BEN ATTRIB 5 ECHO This Line Will Be Blinking	Displays blinking text.
BEN ATTRIB 0 BEN ATTRIB 7 ECHO This Line Is Reverse Video	Displays text in inverse video.
BEN ATTRIB 0 BEN ATTRIB 4 ECHO This Line Is Underlined (Monochrome Only)	Displays underlined text.

The batch file displays several combinations of attributes in a similar fashion.

Batch File Line	Explanation
BEN ATTRIB 1	Sets the attributes to high intensity.
BEN COLOR 37 40	Sets the colors.
ECHO This Is White On Black	Displays text.
BEN COLOR 37 41 ECHO This Is White On Red	Displays text in another color.
BEN COLOR 37 42 ECHO This Is White On Green	Displays text in another color.

The batch file displays several more combinations of different colors in a similar fashion.

Batch File Line	Explanation
BEN ATTRIB 0	Resets the display attributes.
ECHO Batch File Is Now Pausing For 3 Seconds	Tells the user what will happen next.
BEN WAIT 3	Pauses the batch file for three seconds.
CLS	Clears the screen.
BEN ECHOB 1	Skips one blank line.
ECHO 5 Beeps	Tells the user what will happen next.
BEN BEEP 5	Beeps the speaker five times.
BEN ECHOB 1	Displays a blank line.
BEN DATE	Displays the date.
BEN ECHOB 1	Displays a blank line.
BEN TIME	Displays the time.
BEN ECHOB 1	Displays a blank line.
ECHO Press Any Key To Continue	Tells the user how to continue.
PAUSE >NUL	Pauses the batch file and pipe the "Press any key to continue" message from DOS to NUL.
:GETAGN	Label marking the top of a section.

Batch File Line	Explanation
CLS	Clears the screen.
BEN ECHOB 5	Skips five blank lines.
ECHO Enter Selection Number (1 - 4)	Tells the user what to do.
BEN NREPLY	Gets any number 1-9.
IF ERRORLEVEL 5 GOTO BADSEL	If ERRORLEVEL is five or above, the user entered an invalid number, so jumps to an error-handling section.
IF ERRORLEVEL 4 GOTO SEL4 IF ERRORLEVEL 3 GOTO SEL3 IF ERRORLEVEL 2 GOTO SEL2 IF ERRORLEVEL 1 GOTO SEL1	The user made a valid selection, so jumps to a section to handle that selection.
GOTO BADSEL	If the batch file reaches this point, ERRORLEVEL was zero meaning the user did not enter a number so the batch file jumps to an error-handling routine.
:SEL1 ECHO Selected 1 GOTO DONESEL	Tells the user what selection she/he made and jump to the next section. In a more realistic batch file, this section would most likely run a program and then redisplay a menu.
:SEL2 ECHO Selected 2 GOTO DONESEL	Section to handle the user entering a two.
:SEL3 ECHO Selected 3 GOTO DONESEL	Section to handle the user entering a three.
:SEL4 ECHO Selected 4 GOTO DONESEL	Section to handle the user entering a four.
:BADSEL	Label marking the beginning of the error-handling routine.
BEN ECHOB 1	Skips a line.
BEN BEEP 1	Beeps the speaker.
ECHO Bad Selection ECHO Try Again	Tells the user the problem.
GOTO GETAGN	Goes through the loop again.
:DONESEL	Label marking the exit point for valid selections.
BEN ECHOB 1	Skips a blank line.
ECHO System Information	Tells the user what will happen next.
BEN ECHOB 1	Skips another line.
BEN MEMFREE	Displays the free memory.
BEN DISKFREE	Displays the free disk space.
BEN DRIVE	Displays the drive.
BEN DIRECT	Displays the subdirectory.
BEN ECHOB 1	Skips another line.
ECHO Press Any Key To Continue	Tells the user how to continue.
PAUSE >NUL	Pauses the batch file.

Table 2-2 Continued.

Batch File Line	Explanation
CLS	Clears the screen.
BEN FINDTEXT C:\CONFIG.SYS FILES	Checks to see if the file C:\CONFIG.SYS contains the text FILES. This test is case-insensitive.
IF ERRORLEVEL 2 GOTO NOFIND IF ERRORLEVEL 1 GOTO NOFILE IF ERRORLEVEL 0 GOTO FOUND	Jumps to the appropriate section to handle the results of the test.
:NOFIND ECHOB 1 ECHO Your System CONFIG.SYS Does Not ECHO Contain A "FILES" Statement GOTO DEXIST	Tells the user the results and goes ahead to the next section.
:NOFILE ECHOB 1 ECHO The File CONFIG.SYS Does Not ECHO Exist On Your System GOTO DEXIST	Tells the user the results and goes ahead to the next section.
:FOUND ECHOB 1 ECHO A "FILES" Statement In Your CONFIG.SYS	Tells the user the results. This section does not need a GOTO statement because the next section directly follows it.
:DEXIST	Label marking the exit point for the about routines.
BEN ECHOB 1	Skips a line.
BEN DIREXIST \BEN	Checks to see if the subdirectory \BEN exists on the default drive.
IF ERRORLEVEL 2 GOTO NODIR IF ERRORLEVEL 1 GOTO EMPTY	Jumps to a section to handle the results.
ECHOB 1 ECHO The Directory \BEN Exists ECHO And Has Files In It GOTO LAST	The batch file reaches this point if ERRORLEVEL is zero, meaning the subdirectory exists. Tell the user and jumps to the next section.
:EMPTY ECHOB 1 ECHO The Directory \BEN Exists ECHO But Does Not Have Any Files GOTO LAST	Tells the user the results and jumps to the next section.
:NODIR ECHOB 1 ECHO The Directory \BEN Does Not Exist	Tell the user the results and then continue with the batch file.
:LAST	Label marking the exit point for the above batch files.
BEN ECHOB 1	Skips a line.
ECHO Press Any Key To Continue	Tells the user how to continue.
PAUSE >NUL	Pauses the batch file.
CLS	Clears the screen.
BEN CURSOR 4 8	Positions the cursor.
ECHO This Line Starts At Row 4, Column 8	Displays text at the new position.

Batch File Line	Explanation
BEN CURSOR 10 20	Positions the cursor again.
ECHO This Line Starts At Row 10, Column 20	Displays more text.
BEN BOX 1 1 23 79	Draws a box from 1,1 to 23,79.
BEN DBOX 3 3 21 77	Draws a box from 3,3 to 21,77.
BEN CURSOR 15 15	Positions the cursor.
ECHO Press Any Key To Exit	Tells the user how to exit.
BEN CURSOR 15 34	Repositions the cursor.
PAUSE >NUL	Pauses the batch file.
CLS	Clears the screen.

BEN performs the work for some of its keywords (ATTRIB, COLOR, BEEP, CURSOR, BOX, and DBOX) by feeding ANSI escape sequences to DOS. You can pipe these escape sequences to a file using DOS redirecting. Later, you can use those escape sequences without BEN by typing the file. For example, if you wanted to draw a box from row 5, column 5 to row 10, column 60, you could issue the command BEN BOX 5 5 10 60 > BOX and later draw the box without BEN by issuing the command TYPE BOX. This gives you a method of creating batch files that will run on any system using ANSI.SYS even if BEN isn't present.

If you use ANSI.SYS, BEN gives you a nice way to control the screen. Its ability to pipe instructions into a file you can later use without BEN is a good addition.

Bigecho

Name:	Bigecho
Version:	1.0
Price:	Free
Category:	Postware (Send the authors a post card.)
Summary:	Displays text in large letters.
Author:	Barry Simon
	Richard Wilson
Availability:	Available on many bulletin board systems.

Bigecho can display ten characters per line and show three lines per screen. You typically use Bigecho in batch files, and you must have ECHO OFF for the screen to look right. Ctrl-A sends a happy face to the screen, while Ctrl-B sends a reverse happy face to the screen.

The distribution package also includes a program called Goodday. This program reads the system clock and displays the appropriate greeting in large Bigecho-like letters on the screen.

You may have some difficulty finding Bigecho. The authors allow you to copy the software and give away the disks but don't allow you to sell them. In addition, the authors are no longer supporting Bigecho and have incorporated its features into a shareware package called Batutil. If you would like a copy of Bigecho, check with your local users group and bulletin board to see if they have a copy.

DDDBATCH

Name:	DDDBATCH
Version:	1.0
Price:	$10 Single User
	$30 Site License
Category:	Shareware
Summary:	A collection of 12 utilities to improve batch files.
Author:	J. Barrett
Availability:	Included on the disk bound in this book.

DDDBATCH offers twelve useful utilities, each a separate program. The following programs communicate with the user:

CLW clears a small user-specified portion of the screen, which makes it useful for managing windows within a batch file.

DR_BOX draws a box on the screen at the user-specified coordinates. Combined with the CLW program for clearing away screen portions and the PRTAT program for locating the cursor and printing, this makes it possible to place complex-looking windows on the screen within batch files.

FCLS1 is a fancy way of clearing the entire screen by splitting the display across the middle. The top half of the screen scrolls up, while the bottom half scrolls down.

FCLS2 is another fancy way of clearing the entire screen. The screen again splits in half, with the top and bottom halves converging in the middle.

PRTAT locates the cursor at any position on the screen and then optionally prints text. This is how the batch file would print text once a window is drawn with DR_BOX or a section of the screen has been cleared with CLW.

All of the DDDBATCH programs are discussed in detail in Chapter 7.

ECHO-N

Name:	ECHO-N
Price:	Free
Category:	Copyrighted

Summary: Displays text on the screen like the ECHO command, except it doesn't move the cursor to the next line and doesn't strip off leading spaces.
Author: Paul Johnson
Availability: Available on many bulletin board systems.

ECHO-N overcomes two minor limitations of the DOS ECHO command. Using the echo command, it's difficult to center text on the screen because echo strips off all the leading spaces. To overcome that problem, you must begin the leading spaces with a nonprinting character like Alt-255. Echo also complicates constructing long and complex prompts because it automatically issues a line feed after every line.

ECHO-N overcomes both of these limitations. To use ECHO-N, you simply issue the command ECHO-N message from the batch file. ECHO-N only strips out the first space of the message (i.e., the separator between program and message). It also leaves the cursor positioned at the end of the line after displaying the message.

Cursor positioning becomes trickier using ECHO-N. Your last message in a series must be displayed using ECHO, or the cursor remains at the end of the last message. As a result, DOS messages are displayed in unusual positions and possibly split over two lines—making them difficult to read.

ECHOF

Name:	ECHOF
Version:	1.02
Price:	$15.00
Category:	Shareware
Summary:	A version of ECHO that lets you send formatting characters to the display.
Author:	Steven M. Georgiades
Availability:	Available on many bulletin board systems.

If you don't use ANSI.SYS, the DOS ECHO command gives you very little formatting capability over the text you are displaying in a batch file. ECHOF overcomes that. Using ECHOF, you embed formatting codes inside the message itself. Those codes are as follows:

\b Backspaces the cursor.

\e Sends an escape, generally followed by an ANSI escape code.

\g Rings the bell.

\l Issues a line feed but not a carriage return.

\n Issues a line feed and carriage return, making it perfect for printing blank lines within a batch file.

\r Issues a carriage return but not a line feed.

These codes give more flexibility in displaying messages. Typical messages might look like these:

```
ECHO The Following Line is Blank \n\n
ECHO Do You Really Want To Delete These Files? \g
```

If you use Christopher J. Dunford's CED Command Editor, ECHOF includes a version you can make resident for faster echoing.

Ecoh

Name:	Ecoh
Version:	1.0
Price:	Free
Category:	Public Domain
Summary:	Imitates the DOS ECHO command, except it displays text in reverse video.
Author:	Glen Hammond
Availability:	One of several files included on the enclosed disk in a file called HAMMOND.ZIP.

The command ECOH text works just like the ECHO text command except that Ecoh displays its text in reverse video. Issuing the ECOH command by itself doesn't display a blank line.

Locate

Name:	Locate
Version:	1.0
Price:	Free
Category:	Public Domain
Summary:	Positions the cursor on the screen.
Author:	Glen Hammond
Availability:	One of several files included on the enclosed disk in a file called HAMMOND.ZIP.

The command LOCATE n m positions the cursor at the n row and the m column. The next time DOS writes to the screen, it writes to that position. Generally, you would follow a Locate command with an ECHO to place text at a specific location on the screen.

MicroMacroBat

Name:	MicroMacroBat
Version:	3.0
Price:	$35.00
Category:	Shareware
Summary:	An extremely powerful program for displaying information on the screen from inside a batch file.
Author:	Sitting Duck Software
	Post Office Box 130
	Veneta, Oregon 97487
Availability:	Included on the disk bound in this book.

MicroMacroBat is a program designed to give a batch file designer complete control over the appearance of the screen. The key to MicroMacroBat is the small 7K program MB.EXE. Despite its small size, MicroMacroBat is very powerful.

You control MicroMacroBat by issuing the MB command followed by a keyword. Often, that keyword is followed by additional instructions. The keywords are as follows:

BIG prints large characters on the screen at a specified location. Because the large characters are formed using ASCII characters, this command (like all MicroMacroBat commands) will work on a monochrome screen. You would typically use this command as a banner at the start of a batch file.

BOX draws a box on the screen. You control its size, shape, and color. Typically, you would use a box to set off or highlight important information.

CBUF clears the keyboard buffer. You would typically use this just prior to asking the user a question where you want to make sure the user has read the question before responding. For example, "Do you really want to delete all these files? (y/n)"

CHIME sounds the speaker using one of ten distinctive sounds.

CURSOROFF or CURSORON let you control the cursor. Typically, you would turn the cursor off before beginning to construct a complex screen to keep the flashing cursor from distracting the user.

FILLSCRN fills a selected area of the screen with a single character. If you are managing several boxes on the screen, filling them with spaces is one easy way to erase them.

GETKEY waits for the user to press a keystroke and assigns an ERRORLEVEL to indicate the value of that keystroke. You specify the allowable keystrokes on the command line. GETKEY only accepts those keystrokes and sets ERRORLEVEL to 1 for the first, 2 for the second, and so on. This keyword currently only works with the registered version.

LIST prints on the screen a list of words stacked vertically on top of each other. This is an unusual way to put information on the screen; and such, used sparingly, it increases the chance the user will take the time to read the information. If you overuse this method, however, it will lose its emphasis and become difficult to read.

LOCATE positions the cursor on the screen. You don't need this command for Micro-MacroBat keywords that write to the screen, as all of them are able to position the cursor themselves. You would use this keyword to position the cursor prior to issuing a DOS command that will write to the screen.

OCPRINT prints text to the screen one character at a time. If not overdone, the single character printing adds effect to the batch files.

PRINT is MicroMacroBat's version of the DOS ECHO command. It lets you print information to the screen while controlling its location and color.

RECOLOR changes the colors in a selected area of the screen without changing or erasing the text displayed in that area.

USCROLL, DSCROLL, LSCROLL, and RSCROLL all let you scroll a selected area of the screen in any direction without altering the other areas of the screen.

SLEEP pauses a batch file for a specified period of time.

VPRINT prints text in a vertical column, another good way to draw attention to an important message if used sparingly.

WAIT causes the batch file to wait for the user to press a keystroke, like the DOS PAUSE command. It also lets you display a message and control the color of that message.

WAIT-ROTATE is like WAIT, except that the text is displayed scrolling right-to-left in a small window. This keyword currently only works with the registered version.

For all of the commands that allow you to control the color, MicroMacroBat controls the color in an unusual way. Rather than specifying the foreground and background colors individually, the documentation has a color matrix. This matrix has foreground colors vertically and background colors horizontally at the border. Inside are the numbers 0-127, where each digit represents a unique combination of foreground and background colors. You then use that number in the batch files to control the colors. This is more cumbersome than specifying the colors individually, but it still works.

Table 2-3 summarizes the MicroMacroBat keywords, while Table 2-4 shows a batch file using some of the MicroMacroBat keywords.

Table 2-3   Summary of the MicroMacroBat keywords, not all of which work with the shareware version.

Keyword	Syntax Function
BIG	`BIG/TEXT/CHR/ROW/COLUMN/COLOR` Prints text in large characters on the screen. It uses the ASCII character specified as CHR to construct the large characters.
BOX	`BOX/BR/BC/ER/EC/CHARACTER/COLOR/C/S` Draws a box on the screen beginning at row BR and column BC and ending at row ER and column EC. The box is drawn using either a single or double line depending on the number used for CHARACTER. COLOR defines the color. /C clears the background color inside the box and /S adds a shadow around the box.
CBUF	`CBUF` Clears the keyboard buffer.

Keyword	Syntax Function
CHIME	`CHIME/N` Plays one of ten chimes depending on the number indicated in N.
CURSOROFF	`CURSOROFF` Turns the cursor off.
CURSORON	`CURSORON` Turns the cursor on.
DSCROLL	`DSCROLL/BR/BC/ER/EC/TIMES` Scroll the selected area of the screen dows the indicated number of times without affecting the other areas of the screen.
FILLSCRN	`FILLSCRN/BR/BC/ER/EC/COLOR/ASCII` Fills an area of the screen defined by BR/BC/ER/EC using the character defined in ASCII using the combination of foreground and background colors defined by COLOR.
GETKEY	`GETKEY/TEXT` Pauses for the user to press a key. Only those keystrokes listed in TEXT are accepted. The first one is assigned an ERRORLEVEL on one, the second two, and so on. **(Only the registered version has this feature.)**
LIST	`LIST/ROW/COLUMN/COLOR/X/WORD1/WORD2...` Prints a vertical list of words on the screen. The first word is printed at the row and column given in ROW/COLUMN. The second word is printed at row and column ROW+1/COLUMN, and so on.
LOCATE	`LOCATE/ROW/COLUMN` Positions the cursor on the screen at the indicated position.
LSCROLL	`LSCROLL/BR/BC/ER/EC/TIMES` Scroll the selected area of the screen left the indicated number of times without affecting the other areas of the screen.
OCPRINT	`OCPRINT/ROW/COLUMN/TEXT/COLOR` Prints the text one character at a time at the specified location and in the selected color.
PRINT	`PRINT/ROW/COLUMN/TEXT/COLOR` Prints the text at the specified location and in the selected color.
RECOLOR	`RECOLOR/OLD/NEW` Change all the old color combinations to a new color combination without changing the text.
RSCROLL	`RSCROLL/BR/BC/ER/EC/TIMES` Scroll the selected area of the screen right the indicated number of times without affecting the other areas of the screen.
SLEEP	`SLEEP/SECONDS` Pauses the batch file.
USCROLL	`USCROLL/BR/BC/ER/EC/TIMES` Scroll the selected area of the screen up the indicated number of times without effecting the other areas of the screen.
VPRINT	`VPRINT/ROW/COLUMN/TEXT/COLOR/C` Prints text vertically and waits for the user to press a keystroke. Adding /C sounds a chime.
WAIT	`WAIT/ROW/COLUMN/COLOR/TEXT/C` Prints text normally and waits for the user to press a keystroke.

Table 2-3   Continued.

Keyword	Syntax Function
	Adding /C sounds a chime. **(Only the registered version has this feature.)**
WAIT-ROTATE	`WAIT-ROTATE/ROW/COLUMN/TEXT/COLOR` Prints text in a marquee fashion and waits for the user to press a keystroke. Adding /C sounds a chime. **(Only the registered version has this feature.)**

Table 2-4   SHOW-MB.BAT illustrates
some of the MicroMacroBat keywords.

Batch File Line	Explanation
`@ECHO OFF`	Turns command-echoing off.

`REM Name:     SHOW-MB.BAT`
`REM Purpose: Demonstrate MicroMacroBat`
`REM Version: 1.00`
`REM Revised: March 23, 1991`
	Documentation remarks.

`MB FILLSCRN/1/1/25/80/0/32`	Fills the screen with colored spaces. This is one way of clearing the screen.
`MB BIG/WELCOME/75/1/1/79`	Prints welcome in large colored letters.
`MB BIG/ONE-ALL/85/12/1/124`	Prints one-all in large colored letters.
`MB SLEEP/6`	Pauses for six seconds.
`MB FILLSCRN/1/1/24/80/79/32`	Clears the screen using colored spaces.
`MB LIST/10/35/31/Press/Any/Key/` `   To/Continue/Demonstration`	Puts a message on the screen using the LIST keyword. This will print one word per line in a vertical column.
`MB CBUF`	Clears the keyboard buffer.
`MB WAIT/20/34/15/Press any key` `   to continue/c`	Pauses until the user presses a keystroke.
`MB FILLSCRN/1/1/24/80/112/32`	Fills the screen with colored spaces.
`ECHO`	Uses DOS to echo a blank line by echoing ALT-255, a non-printing space. MB does not always position the cursor correctly. By echoing a blank line, you can be sure the cursor is in the left column because DOS resets it there after an echo command.
`ECHO Press A, B or C`	Tells the user to press a specific key.

Batch File Line	Explanation
MB GETKEY/ABC	Has the batch file wait until the user presses the specified keystroke. (**This is not currently available in the shareware version. You must register to receive this feature.**)

IF ERRORLEVEL 1 IF NOT ERRORLEVEL 2
    ECHO A-Pressed
IF ERRORLEVEL 2 IF NOT ERRORLEVEL 3
    ECHO B-Pressed
IF ERRORLEVEL 3 IF NOT ERRORLEVEL 4
    ECHO C-Pressed
	Tells the user which key was pressed.

CLS	Uses DOS to clear the screen.
MB BOX/1/1/12/40/1/79/c MB BOX/8/15/15/45/3/48/C/S MB BOX/20/1/22/80/1/59/c MB BOX/2/50/11/76/2/47/c	Draws four different boxes on the screen.
MB PRINT/3/52/Notice This/47 MB PRINT/5/55/Your Batch File/47 MB PRINT/6/55/Can Write Anywhere/47 MB PRINT/9/60/On the Screen/47	Writes a message in one of the boxes.
MB PRINT/2/2/You Can Even Write/79 MB PRINT/4/2/In Multiple Boxes!/79 MB PRINT/6/6/Imagine The Possibilities!/79	Writes a message in another of the boxes.
MB SLEEP/6	Waits six seconds.
CLS	Clears the screen using DOS.

The major drawback to MicroMacroBat is its lack of error checking. While the author warns about this in the documentation, it's still difficult to write error-free batch files on your first go-around. Thus, you can end up with mistakes that inadvertently lock up the computer.

If you like MicroMacroBat, you are definitely going to want to register it. When you register, you receive

- A newer version of MB.EXE that supports any commands added since the last shareware version of MB.EXE, as well as those few commands not supported in the shareware version.

- Three smaller programs that split the MicroMacroBat functions into three separate programs. These would be useful on a system where space was at a real premium and you only needed a few of the keywords.

- A typeset manual. While the manual doesn't contain any information not in the ASCII file, it's nicely formatted and very easy to follow.

Overall, MicroMacroBat is one of the most powerful screen control programs available for batch files. It is an even better program because it's fairly easy to use.

Unlike most software vendors, the author of MicroMacroBat actively requests your suggestions on improving his product. Not only that, he listens to your suggestions and responds rapidly. I sent him a list of eight suggestions and heard back from him a mere few weeks later. Already, he had incorporated five of my suggestions into his programs, written a new program for one of my suggestions, and decided not to follow the last two. Now that's responsive service!

MSG

Name:	MSG
Version:	1.0
Price:	Free
Category:	Copyrighted
Summary:	Improves the ability to display messages from within a batch file.
Author:	Ralph Dratman
Availability:	Available on many bulletin board system.

MSG controls the displaying of messages by embedding the C-style escape sequences shown here:

\# A backslash followed by a number sends the character with the corresponding ASCII value. For example, \033 sends an escape.

\\ Prints a single backslash.

\b Backspaces the cursor without erasing the text being backspaced over.

\f Sends a formfeed. Of course, you must pipe this to the printer with a command like MSG \f >LPT1.

\n Moves the cursor to a new line.

\r Sends a character return.

\s Prints a space; this is required if you want multiple spaces between items because MSG strips off all but one space between items.

\t Tabs the cursor.

\v Sends a vertical tab. I couldn't make this work on my system.

While MSG improves the ECHO command, other programs in this chapter are far more powerful.

ProBat

Name:	ProBat
Version:	1.0
Price:	$35 American
	$45 Canadian
Category:	Shareware
Summary:	A batch file development environment.

Author: Mark Tigges
2925 Altamont Circle
West Vancouver B.C. Canada V7V 3B9
Availability: Available on many bulletin board systems.

ProBat is both a combination word processor for writing batch files and a screen processor for designing display screens within a batch file. See Chapter 7 for more details.

Rite

Name:	Rite
Version:	1.0
Price:	Free
Category:	Public Domain
Summary:	A display program that allows you to control the location and color of text.
Author:	Laurence Shusta
	523 Green Hill Road
	Madison, Connecticut 06443
Availability:	Available on many bulletin board systems.[1]

To display a message with Rite, you enter a command like this:

```
RITE 28 16 " \ #10 WARNING: This Process Takes Five Hours! \ #10" 0 1
```

The 28 and 16 define the column and row respectively where the text will be displayed. The text inside the quote marks is what's displayed on the screen. All spaces beyond a single space between items is ignored. The \ #10 switch tells the program to add ten spaces to both sides of the message. The 0 and 1 define the colors used to display the message.

Rite is fairly picky about how commands are entered. There must be a space between all parameters, and messages must be surrounded by quotation marks. The documentation doesn't list the colors corresponding to various colors, so you will have to experiment. Beyond those minor problems, Rite works well and gives you a great deal more control than does the ECHO command.

Scanion Enterprises Batch File Utilities

Name:	Scanion Enterprises Batch File Utilities
Version:	2.2.0
Price:	$9.95
Category:	Shareware

---

[1]Generally distributed as a set containing both Rite and Well and named BATIN-IT.ZIP after the name of the demonstration batch file.

Summary: A collection of over 100 batch file utilities.
Author: Paul Scanion
Availability: Included on the disk bound in this book.

The Scanion Enterprises Batch File Utilities [SEBFU for short] is a collection of over 100 batch file utilities. Those programs displaying information for the user are discussed here.

Each of the commands in SEBFU is a separate *.COM file. As a result, your disk can end up cluttered with quite a number of small program files. You might consider erasing the program files you aren't likely to use.

BIGLTR displays a large 10-character message on the screen. The program wouldn't work with a VGA system.

CGABORDR changes the color of the border on a CGA display.

CHGC changes the color of the screen in a specific range, useful for printing a window on the screen in a different color than the rest of the screen.

CLR clears a specified portion of the screen, useful for erasing the text in a window on the screen.

COLOR changes the screen colors.

DBLBOX draws a box on the screen using a double line, useful for outlining a window on the screen.

DLINE draws a double line on the screen using the user-supplied coordinates.

FCHR fills a selected area on the screen with a specified character.

GCURS finds the coordinates of the cursor and returns either one as an ERRORLEVEL value or both as environmental variables. This is useful for finding the position of the cursor after the user has entered some information.

GETCC finds the column of the cursor and returns it as either an ERRORLEVEL or an environmental variable.

GETCOLR returns an ERRORLEVEL to indicate the current screen color, useful for restoring the screen to the appropriate color after a batch file is finished.

GETCR detects the cursor position and returns the row number as an ERRORLEVEL or environmental variable.

INVERT swaps the foreground and background colors, useful for developing warning screens that stand out.

LINE draws a line on the screen using the user-supplied coordinates.

LOCATE positions the cursor at a specific location on the screen.

MOVCUR moves the cursor by a specified amount.

SCROLL moves a specified portion of the screen, useful for creating and maintaining windows within a batch file.

SCROLMSG displays a moving message at the bottom of the screen.

SNGLBOX draws a box on the screen using a single line.

SROWS sets the ERRORLEVEL to indicate what row the cursor is currently on.

SWIDTH sets ERRORLEVEL to indicate the width of the display.

WRITE displays a message on the screen.

WRITEF writes a small file to the screen, useful for displaying a menu or help text quickly.

All of the programs in SEBFU are described in Chapter 7.

Send

Name:	Send
Version:	1.6
Price:	Free
Category:	Public Domain
Summary:	A screen display program designed to control ANSI.SYS.
Author:	Howard Rumsey
Availability:	Available on many bulletin board systems.

If you load ANSI.SYS in your CONFIG.SYS configuration file, it gives you greatly extended control over the screen from within your batch files. However, controlling ANSI from within a batch file can be difficult. The Send program overcomes that difficulty handily.

Send works like ECHO, except that it treats a couple of characters differently. In a Send message, any character preceded by a *caret* (a ^, typed by pressing Shift-6) is replaced by a control character. For example, ^[is replaced by Escape, and ^\ is replaced by Hex 1C. This saves you from having to write long prompt statements to control ANSI. In addition, Send doesn't terminate lines with a carriage return and line feed as does echo, allowing you the flexibility of using more than one line to display long messages.

Send supports the $-meta characters of the prompt command. Thus, a dollar sign preceding a character has a special meaning to Send. For example, $d will display the date, $t the time, and $_ a line feed and carriage return combination.

There are two significant differences between the prompt command and Send. First, $h in the prompt is a destructive backspace (it erases the characters it backs over), while $h in Send is a nondestructive backspace. Second, Send supports a few extensions to the prompt $-meta characters using uppercase characters, shown here:

$T   Displays the time in HHSS format (for example, 2:05 PM is displayed as 1405).

$M   Displays the month as a two-digit number, with January as 01 and December as 12.

$D   Displays the date as a two-digit number.

$Y   Displays the last two digits of the year.

Nicely enough, Send allows you to redirect its output using standard piping symbols. For example, the command SEND @SET DAY = $D > SETDAY.BAT will make a one-line batch file creating an environmental variable containing today's date. By issuing this command in the AUTOEXEC.BAT file and then issuing a CALL SETDAY command, the day of the month will always be available from the environment. You could then, for example, perform a backup automatically on the 10th and 20th of each month. By redirecting Send's output to your printer, you have an easy way to send escape characters to your printer using batch files rather than loading Basic.

If you load ANSI.SYS in your CONFIG.SYS configuration file, Send is a very powerful way to format the screen and control your printer from within batch files.

Show

Name:	Show
Price:	Free
Category:	Copyrighted
Summary:	Displays text from within a batch file using various screen attributes.
Author:	HBP Systems
Availability:	Available on many bulletin board systems.

When you use the DOS ECHO command in a batch file, you are fairly limited in what you can do to highlight a statement if you aren't using ANSI.SYS. About all you can do is surround the message with ASCII characters, which results in echoes like "***WARN-ING***" or "===Hello===".

Show overcomes the limitations of DOS by allowing you to highlight messages without using ANSI. You display messages using the command SHOW /switches message. The switches supported by Show are as follows:

/h Prints the message in bright text.
/u Prints the message in underlined text on a monochrome display. On my VGA color screen, it produces a blue message.
/i Prints the message in inverse video.
/b Prints the message in blinking text.

If you don't use any switches, Show prints normal text. Several of the switches can be combined to produce, for example, a blinking underlined message.

SkipLine

Name:	SkipLine
Version:	1.0
Price:	Free
Category:	Copyrighted. (You may use SkipLine on all of the machines you own, no matter how many, but you may not give copies of the program to anyone else.)
Summary:	Inserts a blank line on the screen.

Author: Ronny Richardson
Availability: Included on the disk bound in this book.

DOS doesn't offer a nice neat way to skip a line when echoing output to the screen. Consider a batch file segment like this one:

```
ECHO You are about to erase
ECHO important files
ECHO
ECHO Is this what you want?
```

On the third line, you want DOS to skip a line, so you enter ECHO with nothing after it. However, DOS thinks you are asking about the status of command echoing and replies with an "ECHO is on" message (or "off," depending on its status).

There are a couple of ways you can force DOS to skip a line:

- Depending on the version of DOS you have, a command like ECHO. might skip a line. Table 2-5 lists the ECHO quirks that can give you a blank line. It is, however, a good idea to avoid these because they don't work with all versions of DOS and can make exchanging batch files or upgrading DOS versions very difficult.

- ECHO a non-printing character like a Ctrl-H backspace or Alt-255 space. This works under all versions of DOS but not with all editors.

- ECHO a small printing character like a period, which makes the screen less attractive but works with all editors and versions of DOS.

Because of all the problems skipping a line on the screen, I wrote a small program called SkipLine. When you want a blank line, just place the SkipLine command on a line by itself. Of course, SKIPLINE.COM must be in the current subdirectory or in your path.

Table 2-5   ECHO quirks.

Dots	2.x versions of DOS let you replace the ECHO command with a dot. So the two batch file lines below are equivalent. . Your message here ECHO Your message here
Special Characters	< Do not include in an ECHO statement > Do not include in an ECHO statement | Do not include in an ECHO statement % Include a % % in your ECHO statement to ECHO a single % ^H Start your lines with and ECHO ^H to center messages, ECHO a blank line, or begin a message with ON or OFF ^G ECHO ^G sounds the PC bell
@	Beginning with DOS 3.3, you can suppress command echoing, even when ECHO is ON by preceding the batch command with a @.
SKIPLINE	With any version of DOS, you can use this command in conjunction with SKIPLINE.COM on the diskette to produce a blank line on the screen.

Using SkipLine, the above batch file segment would look like this:

```
ECHO You are about to erase
ECHO important files
SKIPLINE
ECHO Is this what you want?
```

Timedget

Name:	Timedget
Version:	1.0
Price:	Free
Category:	Copyrighted
Summary:	Pauses briefly for the user to press a keystroke and sets ERRORLEVEL accordingly.
Author:	C. David Moran
Availability:	Available on many bulletin board systems.

Timedget isn't very useful as a ERRORLEVEL-asker. You enter TIMEDGET on the command line, and it pauses briefly for the user to enter a keystroke. It then sets the ERRORLEVEL to 255 if that keystroke was the spacebar and to 0 for any other keystroke or if time ran out before the user pressed a key.

As if the choice of the spacebar or anything else wasn't limited enough, the pause itself is too brief. The documentation claims it pauses for 12 seconds, and it probably does on a 4.77 MHz PC; but on my 386/20, the pause is less than 1.5 seconds. Additionally, Timedget can't even display a prompt.

Because of its limited selection of ERRORLEVEL values and inability to pause for a reasonable period of time, Timedget is a program you should avoid.

Title

Name:	Title
Version:	1.0
Price:	Free
Category:	Public Domain
Summary:	Displays a 32-character message on the screen in large letters.
Author:	D. W. Martin
Availability:	Available on many bulletin board systems.

To run Title, you enter the command TITLE font message. Title first clears the screen and then displays the message in large characters in the screen's middle. The message can be up to 32 characters long in any of the three available fonts (Gothic, Sans-Serif, and Triplex). After about four seconds, Title clears the screen and allows the batch file to continue.

Typo

Name:	Typo
Version:	1.0
Price:	$5.00
Category:	Shareware
Summary:	A replacement for the DOS ECHO command that can center text and easily display blank lines.
Author:	Sapphire Software
	4141 Ball Road, Suite 166
	Cypress, California 90630
Availability:	Available from many bulletin board systems.

Typo is a small program designed to make two minor improvements in the DOS ECHO command. When you enter the Typo command followed by a number, Typo displays that many blank lines. When you enter the Typo command followed by text, Typo displays that text and automatically centers it on the screen. If you enter the text in quotes, Typo displays it without centering it.

Typo also uses an interesting method of displaying text on the screen. The asterisk moves across the screen like a large cursor and blinks for each character it displays. In addition, the speaker makes a very low, dull sound for each character. The sound is quiet and at a very low frequency to avoid being annoying.

Because Typo uses a leading number telling it how many blank lines to display, Typo can't display any message beginning with a number. When the message begins with a number, Typo displays that many blank lines and then ignores the rest of the message, even if you assign the message to an environmental variable and then try to display that environmental variable as such. For example,

```
SET ADDRESS = 1234 MAIN STREET
TYPO %ADDRESS%
```

Typo doesn't display more than nine blank lines; thus, in the above example, all the numbers after the 1 are also ignored.

Typo doesn't always position the cursor on the left side of the screen after displaying a message. As a result, messages from other sources can end up split with a few characters displayed on the right side and the remaining characters displayed on the next line on the left side. This can affect DOS messages like "Abort, Ignore, or Fail" or the prompt when Typo terminates.

Ultimate Screen Manager

Name:	Ultimate Screen Manager
Version:	1.20
Price:	$39.00
Category:	Shareware
Summary:	Creates, modifies, and displays advanced screens.
Author:	MDFlynn Associates
	Post Office Box 5034
	Redwood City, California 94063
Availability:	Included on the disk bound in this book.

The Ultimate Screen Manager allows you to construct very complex screens to communicate with the user. It also allows you to design menus and obtain information from the user to be stored in environmental variables.

The Ultimate Screen Manager is covered in Chapter 7.

Write

Name:	Write
Version:	1.1
Price:	Free
Category:	Public Domain
Summary:	Replaces the DOS echo command with a more powerful screen-control program.
Author:	Markus Fischer
	University of Geneva
	Department of Anthropology
	12, rue Gustave Revilliod
	1227 Carouge (Geneve)
	Switzerland
Availability:	Available on many bulletin board systems.

Write is a replacement for the DOS ECHO command. In addition to simply displaying text on the screen, it has a number of switches you can include in the text to control its appearance. Those switches are as follows:

\ $	Displays a dollar sign.
\ _	Displays a carriage return and line feed character.
\ b	Displays the vertical bar (|) sign and avoids having DOS pipe the command.
\ d	Displays the date.
\ e	Sends an escape character.
\ f	Sends a form feed. Generally, you would pipe this to a printer.

\g	Displays the greater than ($>$) sign and avoids having DOS pipe the command.
\h	Backspaces the cursor.
\l	Displays the less than ($<$) sign and avoids having DOS pipe the command.
\n	Displays the default drive letter.
\p	Displays the current logical subdirectory.
\q	Displays the equal ($+$) sign.
\r	Displays the current physical directory.
\t	Displays the time.
\v	Displays the volume label.

Write works very well and has a number of nice applications, especially when combined with the piping symbols. For example, when using Write, you can easily pipe a time/date stamp to the end of an ASCII file or send a form feed to the printer.

X-BATCH

Name:	X-BATCH
Version:	1.0
Price:	$20.00
Category:	Shareware
Summary:	A collection of 13 useful utilities.
Author:	Gary R. Pannone
	9 Brady Road Ext.
	Westboro, Massachusetts 01581
Availability:	Available on many bulletin board systems.

X-BATCH is a collection of thirteen useful batch file utilities. Commands that deal with communicating with the user are as follows:

BOX draws a box on the screen. You can control the size, location, and color of the box, as well as display it without erasing text already on the screen.

CURSOR positions the cursor at a specific location on the screen, useful for controlling where DOS programs display their messages.

DISPFILE reads a file and displays it in a box on the screen. If the file is too large to fit, only the portion that fits will be displayed. DISPFILE doesn't allow you to scroll around in the file.

DISPLAY displays text on the screen, allowing you to position the cursor first and control the color of the text.

SHOW displays the date, day, and time in a better format than that of DOS.

SOUND sounds the speaker, allowing you to control the frequency and duration.

The X-BATCH commands are useful and easy to learn, with a sensible format reading almost like English.

For detailed information on X-BATCH, see Chapter 6.

3

Menu programs

A menu is nothing more than a list of options on the screen. While a number of utilities are currently available to handle menus, I have long been an advocate of using simple menus mostly through batch files. In fact, my *MS-DOS Batch File Programming . . . Including DOS 5.0* book (TAB Book #3916) devotes a full chapter to batch file menu development.

If you develop your menu system using DOS, you'll face two problems. First, you'll need a way to display the actual menu; second, you'll need a way to select the various options. You can put text on the screen through DOS in many ways. For example, you can store the menu in a file and TYPE it to the screen, or you can display the menu using a series of ECHO commands. Of course, you could also use many of the screen enhancement tools in Chapter 2 to construct nicer looking screens.

The menu will give numbers for each option on the menu. To run any of the programs on the menu, the user types in the number for the program to run and presses Enter. Thus, if the first menu option is "Press 1 for Wordstar" the user would press 1 and Enter to activate the word processor.

Entering a 1 at the DOS prompt to run a word processor does nothing by itself. You must create a batch file called 1.BAT to perform the action under option 1 in the menu. Thus, entering a 1 runs 1.BAT. In addition to running the word processor, 1.BAT would typically contain a final command to redisplay the menu. The exact format of that command would depend on the type of menu being used.

Menu options can do more than just automatically run a program; they can also control how dangerous programs are used. For example, formatting a disk without the drive (for example, C> FORMAT) can erase the entire hard disk with some versions of DOS but can be avoided by formatting diskettes from the menu. The menu option to format a disk runs a batch file, thus preventing the user from entering the format command incorrectly.

Managing all the batch files necessary to work with even a moderate number of programs can be a daunting task for an inexperienced user. That's where these batch file-based menu programs come in.

Batch'in

Name:	Batch'in
Price:	$40.00
Category:	Commercial
Summary:	A screen design and batch file authoring system for menu development.
Author:	Leber Enterprises
	Post Office Box 9281
	Peoria, Illinois 61612
	(309) 693-0634
Availability:	Batch'in is a commercial program that should be available at many software stores.

While Batmenu (discussed later in this chapter) is strong on batch file creation and weak on screen design, Batch'in is a batch file menu system strong on menu design and batch file creation. Unlike Batmenu, Batch'in allows you to create *nested menus* (menus on which choosing an option simply brings up another menu).

When you install Batch'in, it checks out your system and makes suggestions for modifications to your AUTOEXEC.BAT and CONFIG.SYS files if they aren't up to Batch'in's standards. If you like, Batch'in will make the changes for you. Batch'in wants you to have ANSI.SYS loaded because it depends on ANSI.SYS to control colors in the menus. Otherwise, it constructs straight ASCII menus.

You begin by constructing a menu. Batch'in lets you add a company name to the top line and a menu title to the next line. Below that, you enter a single line for each menu option. Figure 3-1 shows a typical Batch'in menu.

```
            ┌──────────────────────┐
            │    Ronny Richardson    │
            ├──────────────────────┤
            │       Main Menu        │
            └──────────────────────┘




        1:   Lotus 1-2-3

        2:   Lotus 1-2-3 Release 3.1

        3:   Microsoft Word

        4:   Microsoft Windows


        0:   Exit To DOS
```

3-1 A typical Batch'in menu.

When Batch'in creates this menu, it creates an ASCII file. If you are using ANSI .SYS, it appends the necessary ANSI escape-sequences to the file to control the colors. To display the menu, the batch files type this file to the screen. Because of this, you can't have fancy formatting such as selecting the option by use of a moving lightbar menu or by pressing the first letter of the menu option. The only way to select a menu option is by entering its number and pressing return, which in turn runs an associated batch file.

Batch'in works with nested menus in a very clever fashion. Because each menu has an option number 1, Batch'in must create a 1.BAT for each menu. It does that by keeping the batch files for each menu in a separate subdirectory.

The batch files for the main menu are in the Batch'in subdirectory. If you create a submenu off main called GAMES, for example, Batch creates a subdirectory called \BATCHIN\GAMES. It stores the batch files for the games submenu in this subdirectory. When you select the games submenu from the main menu, the batch file changes to the GAMES subdirectory and types the new menu. Because DOS will run 1.BAT from the current subdirectory before searching the PATH, it runs the correct batch file when you start a batch file from a submenu. Select option 0 from the submenu (which is always Return to the Prior Menu), and the batch file moves down the directory tree one level and redisplays the menu it finds there.

As long as you have Batch'in write all your batch files, this structure works flawlessly no matter how complex your menu structure. However, if you decide to go in and modify or create some of the menus yourself, you can get lost in all the subdirectories and end up with a batch file that redisplays the wrong menu.

While Batch'in does a very good job of creating screens and managing multiple menus, it falls a little short when it goes to create the actual batch files. To create a batch file, you supply the following information to Batch'in:

- *Command to start.* Batch'in will actually check to see if a .EXE or .COM program exists to match this command or if it runs a .BAT file. If not, it will warn you.

- *Default directory.* This is the drive and directory needed to run the program.

- *Path.* This is any special path needed by the program. If you specify a special path, Batch'in saves the old path and restores it when the program terminates.

- *Parameters.* This is anything you would enter on the command line when starting the program. For example, you might start the card game in Windows with the command WIN SOL. In this case, WIN is the command to start and SOL is a parameter.

- *Environmental variables.* Some programs, most notably compilers, require environmental variables to point define how the program is to operate or how it was installed. Batch'in defines these before running the application and deletes them after the application terminates.

- *Floppy disk.* If you have an old, nasty program that requires you to insert a floppy disk before running, Batch'in can handle it.

- *Prompts.* This is any information you want to supply to the user before the program runs. For example, "This program takes three hours to run" or "Be sure to turn the printer on first."

- *Return menu.* This is the menu you want Batch'in to return to once the program terminates. Generally, this will be the menu that started the application.
- *Pause after running.* This causes Batch'in to insert a PAUSE command before redisplaying the menu.

Batch'in creates a solid menu structure and set of batch files to run it.

The menu system Batch'in creates is based on three things: the batch files themselves, the subdirectory structure it creates to manage nested menus, and the typing of the files to the screen to display the menu. Because none of the day-to-day operation of the menu system uses any Batch'in files, you can legally copy the resulting batch file menu system (although not the Batch'in program) to more than one computer. This is especially nice if you have more than one computer in an office with the same structure. You can create a menu system on one machine and then carefully copy it to the other machines in order to maintain the subdirectory structure. Avoid copying any Batch'in files, and all the computers will have the same menu structure.

Batch'in isn't without a few problems. When the command to start a program is a nonBatch'in batch file, it gives you the option of incorporating the batch file's code into the Batch'in batch file or calling the batch file using COMMAND/C. This is an old trick used prior to DOS 3.3 to allow control to return to a batch file when that batch file ran another batch file. Since DOS 3.3, however, the CALL command has been available to do this without the extra memory requirements of COMMAND/C. While Batch'in is able to figure out the version of DOS it's running under, it never takes advantage of the CALL command.

When you are on the batch file definition screen and you make a mistake, too bad. Once you pass a prompt, you can't go back without first completing that batch file and then returning to recreate the batch file (which is much more cumbersome than necessary.)

If you want to use Batch'in menu for a task requiring more than one command to run, you must do some work outside of Batch'in because it only allows a single DOS command to start an application. You have two options. First, before running Batch'in, you can create a batch file to perform the tasks and then have Batch'in reference that batch file. Alternatively, you can edit the batch file once Batch'in creates it.

The manual that comes with Batch'in is clearly written with the beginner in mind. It is likely that anyone with only a few months experience with a computer could read the manual and construct their very own menu system without a lot of difficulty.

Batch Menu

Name:	Batch Menu
Version:	5.4
Price:	Free
Category:	Copyrighted
Summary:	Allows the user to select from an on-screen menu and sets ERRORLEVEL accordingly.

Author: HFK Software
68 Wells Road
Lincoln, Massachusetts 01773

Availability: Available on many bulletin board systems.

Using Batch Menu, you can display a fairly nice menu using a single command. To display a menu, you enter

CHOOSE Title \ Option 1 \ Option 2 \ ... \ Option 9

The program displays three boxes on the screen. The top box has a centered title. The second box has the menu options listed on top of each other. While you can have only a maximum of nine menu options, you don't have to specify all nine. The bottom box displays the message "BATCH MENU compliments of HFK Software."

You select the option you want by moving the cursor to that item and pressing return. If the first letters of the items are unique, you can also make your selection by pressing the first letter. Choose sets ERRORLEVEL to 9 for the first item (even if less than nine are specified), 8 for the second, down to 1 for the ninth. You can get out of the menu by pressing Escape; Choose then sets ERRORLEVEL to 0.

Table 3-1 shows a batch file using Batch Menu to make a menu selection.

Table 3-1   B-MENU.BAT uses Batch Menu to display a menu.

Batch File Line	Explanation
`@ECHO OFF`	Turns command-echoing off.

`REM NAME:     B-MENU.BAT`
`REM PURPOSE: Demonstrate Batch`
`             Menu`
`REM VERSION: 1.00`
`REM DATE:    March 25, 1991`
	Documentation remarks.

`:TOP`	Label marking the top of the loop that keeps the menu going.
`CLS`	Clears the screen.

`CHOOSE Ronny's Menu\Word`
`    Processing\Spreadsheet`
`    \Database\Microsoft Windows`
	The command to draw the menu on the screen. The first parameter becomes the menu and the remaining parameters become the menu items.

`IF ERRORLEVEL 10 GOTO ERROR`
`IF ERRORLEVEL  9   GOTO WORD`
`IF ERRORLEVEL  8   GOTO 123`
`IF ERRORLEVEL  7   GOTO DATABASE`
`IF ERRORLEVEL  6   GOTO WIN`
`IF ERRORLEVEL  0   GOTO ESCAPE`
	Choose sets the ERRORLEVEL to nine for the first menu option, eight for the second on down to one for the last. It sets ERRORLEVEL to zero for escape. These tests direct the batch file to the appropriate section based on the user's selection.

`:ERROR`
`CLS`
`ECHO Error In Batch File`
`ECHO Press Any Key to Exit`
`PAUSE>NUL`
`GOTO END`
	The batch file will only reach this point if there is an error in the program to inform the user and exit.

Table 3-1 Continued.

Batch File Line	Explanation
| ```
:WIN
CLS
ECHO Would Run Windows Here
ECHO Press Any Key to Continue
PAUSE>NUL
GOTO TOP
``` | This section would handle running Windows and redisplaying the menu in an actual menu system. Here it just puts a prompt on the screen and then loops back through the menu. |
| ```
:DATABASE
CLS
ECHO Would Run Database Here
ECHO Press Any Key to Continue
PAUSE>NUL
GOTO TOP
``` | This section would handle starting the database. |
| ```
:123
CLS
ECHO Would Run Spreadsheet Here
ECHO Press Any Key to Continue
PAUSE>NUL
GOTO TOP
``` | This section would handle starting the spreadsheet. |
| ```
:WORD
CLS
ECHO Would Run Word Processor
     Here
ECHO Press Any Key to Continue
PAUSE>NUL
GOTO TOP
``` | This section would handle running the word processor. |
| ```
:ESCAPE
CLS
ECHO You Pressed Escape
ECHO Press Any Key to Exit
GOTO END
``` | This section handles exiting the menu. |
| ```
:END
``` | Label marking the end of the batch file. |

The default display mode for Batch Menu is black and white; but, by using built-in keywords, you can change the foreground and background colors as well as several other display options. Those changes are written back to the Batch Menu, so they remain in effect until you change them again.

As said before, Batch Menu is limited to nine items. Also, because the DOS command line is limited to 127 characters, you are further limited to the length of the individual menu items. If you can write your menu within those two limits, Batch Menu is a very good menuing program.

Batmenu

Name:	Batmenu
Version:	2.5[1]
Price:	$19.95

---

[1]The version I discuss here is 2.0. V 2.5 arrived too late for me to include in the discussion. However, I was able to include v2.5 on the disk rather than v2.0.

Category: Shareware
Summary: A batch file database for creating and managing the batch files to run a menu system.
Author: Masterware
               2442 Tilghman Street #1
               Allentown, Pennsylvania 18104
Availability: Available on many bulletin board systems.

Batmenu is an extremely clever marriage of batch files and a database program. After installing Batmenu, you enter BM followed by a number to create a batch file. Batmenu brings up a data entry screen where you enter the information Batmenu needs to create the batch file. You tell it the name of the program, the drive to use, the subdirectory to use, and the commands necessary to run the program. You get seven lines to enter the program-specific commands; however, Batmenu handles changing to the proper location before running the program, changing back to the root directory and redisplaying the menu afterwards, so all seven commands can be used to start the program.

Batmenu uses this information to construct a DOS batch file and modify the ASCII file it uses to display the menu. The menu can display up to sixty items in three columns of twenty. You don't have to use the numbers sequentially, so you can group different types of programs together.

For each item on the menu, Batmenu constructs a matching batch file with the name of the batch file matching the number on the menu. For example, item 39 in the menu results in a batch file called 39.BAT.

Batmenu's behavior after this sets it apart from the other menu packages. Each menu item in Batmenu results in a database entry storing all of the information you entered in the original screen. That way, you can easily modify the menu by going into the database and editing the individual lines of the batch file. When you finish, Batmenu automatically recreates all the batch files.

While Batmenu does an excellent job of creating and managing the batch files, the program is a little quirky. It insists on being in the \BM subdirectory on the C drive and won't run from any other location. Every time you exit the program, Batmenu automatically returns you to the root directory.

Batpopup

Name: Batpopup
Version: 1.0
Price: $5.00
Category: Shareware
Summary: A batch file pop-up menu program.
Author: J. R. McConnell
               Interfaces, People, and Magic
               Post Office Box 4496
               Middletown, Rhode Island 02841

Availability: Available on many bulletin board systems.

Despite its name, Batpopup isn't a memory-resident program. When you start Batpopup, it displays a very nice menu on the screen. The user uses a moving lightbar menu to select one of the items on the menu. Alternatively, the user can select an item using a number of function keys. Once the user makes a selection, Batpopup terminates and passes an ERRORLEVEL back to the batch file.

To display a menu using Batpopup, you issue the command

BATPOPUP r c f b Title Item-1 Item-2 Item-3...Item-9

where r is the row and c is the column to use for the top left corner of the menu. Batpopup sizes the remainder of the menu automatically. F sets the foreground color, and b sets the background color. These settings only affect the menu; the remainder of the screen is unaffected. The menu has a title and from two to nine menu items. Batpopup uses the spaces on the command line to separate the times, so the title and menu items can't include spaces. However, they can simulate a space using Alt-255. Of course, the 127-character limit on the length of the command line prohibits long descriptive menu options.

Batpopup sets ERRORLEVEL to 1 for the first item, 2 for the second, and so on. After five minutes, the menu will "time-out" and exit automatically. If that happens, it sets ERRORLEVEL to 0. If the user presses Escape, the documentation claims to set ERRORLEVEL to -1. It also claims to set ERRORLEVEL to -2 if an internal error occurs. However, ERRORLEVEL only has room for a single byte of information, limiting it to numbers between 0 and 255. What actually happens when the user presses Escape is that ERRORLEVEL is set to 255.

Batpopup is easy to configure and produces very attractive menus. By making the menu options simple—like yes or no—it's just as easy to obtain answers to simple questions using Batpopup. Its ease of use combined with its low price makes Batpopup very attractive.

Table 3-2 illustrates both uses of Batpopup.

Table 3-2   SHOWP-UP.BAT uses
Batpopup for menus or to ask simple questions.

Batch File Line	Explanation
`@ECHO OFF`	Turns command-echoing off.

`REM NAME:     SHOWP-UP.BAT`
`REM PURPOSE: Demonstrate Batpopup`
`REM VERSION: 1.00`
`REM DATE:     April 2, 1991`
	Documentation remarks.

`:TOP`	Label marking the top of the loop used to display the menu.
`CLS`	Clears the screen before displaying the menu.

`BATPOPUP 12 30 1 15 Ronny's_Menu`
`  Word_Processor Data_Base`
`  Spreadsheet Graphics`
`  Communications Games Exit_Menu`
	The command to display the menu. In the actual batch file, the underscores (_) have been replaced with Alt-255, which appear like spaces from DOS but are not treated like a divider by DOS.

Batch File Line	Explanation
| ```
IF ERRORLEVEL 7   GOTO END
IF ERRORLEVEL 6   GOTO PLAY
IF ERRORLEVEL 5   GOTO TALK
IF ERRORLEVEL 4   GOTO GRAPHICS
IF ERRORLEVEL 3   GOTO 123
IF ERRORLEVEL 2   GOTO DATABASE
IF ERRORLEVEL 1   GOTO WP
GOTO END
``` | Goes to the appropriate section to handle the user's menu selection. |
| ```
:WP
  CLS
  ECHO Run Word Processor Here
  PAUSE
  GOTO TOP
``` | If this were an actual menu, this section would handle running the word processor and then redisplaying the menu. (In the actual batch file, this section is formatted with a box around it.) |
| ```
:DATABASE
  CLS
  ECHO Run Data Base Here
  PAUSE
  GOTO TOP
``` | If this were an actual menu, this section would handle running the data base and then redisplaying the menu. (In the actual batch file, this section is formatted with a box around it.) |
| ```
:123
  CLS
  ECHO Run Spreadsheet Here
  PAUSE
  GOTO TOP
``` | If this were an actual menu, this section would handle running the spreadsheet and then redisplaying the menu. (In the actual batch file, this section is formatted with a box around it.) |
| ```
:GRAPHICS
  CLS
  ECHO Run Graphics Program Here
  PAUSE
  GOTO TOP
``` | If this were an actual menu, this section would handle running the graphics processor and then redisplaying the menu. (In the actual batch file, this section is formatted with a box around it.) |
| ```
:TALK
  CLS
  ECHO Run Communication Program Here
  PAUSE
  GOTO TOP
``` | If this were an actual menu, this section would handle running the communications program and then redisplaying the menu. (In the actual batch file, this section is formatted with a box around it.) |
| ```
:PLAY
  CLS
  ECHO Run Games Menu Here
  PAUSE
  GOTO TOP
``` | If this were an actual menu, this section would handle displaying the games menu and then redisplaying the main menu. (In the actual batch file, this section is formatted with a box around it.) |
| ```
:END
``` | Label marking the exit point in the menu. |
| ```
  CLS
``` | Clears the screen. |
```

Table 3-2 Continued.

Batch File Line	Explanation
BATPOPUP 12 35 1 15 Do_You_Really_ Want_To_Exit? Yes No	This command displays a menu that gives the user a yes/no choice. In the actual batch file, the underscores (_) are replaced with Alt-255 spaces.
IF ERRORLEVEL 2 GOTO TOP	If the user selects no, redisplays the original menu.
CLS	If the user selects yes, erases the menu before exiting.

BATUTIL

Name: BATUTIL
Version: 1.0
Price: $39.00 (Includes STACKEY)
Category: Shareware
Summary: A powerful batch file utility that allows you to do almost anything required in a batch file.
Author: The Support Group
            Lake Technology Park
            Post Office Box 130
            McHenry, Maryland 21541
            (800) 872-4768
Availability: Available on many bulletin board systems.

BATUTIL is far more than just a batch utility—it's really a batch language disguised as a batch utility. To use BATUTIL, you enter a command like

    BATUTIL [HOUR]

on the command line. When you enclose the command in square [ ] brackets, BATUTIL returns results in ERRORLEVEL. If you enclose the command is curly {} brackets, BATUTIL also returns the results as an environmental variable. BATUTIL only needs the first two characters of the command and ignores capitalization, so [HOUR], [Ho], [HoUr] and [ho] all mean the same thing.

While BATUTIL has several features enhancing its menus, the primary menu commands are MENU and FMENU. MENU works from the command line, while FMENU reads from the file. These two functions alone are worth the registration fee for BATUTIL.

What makes them particularly nice is how little work you must do to use them. You can construct a simple but working menu with the command:

    BATUTIL {MENU Lotus Word dBASE Graphics Games Quit}

That simple command will clear the screen and display a colored menu in the screen's center, with the six options listed after the MENU command. The user can select one either by pressing the first uppercase letter on each line, by moving the lightbar cursor to an option and pressing return, or by double-clicking with the mouse. The first menu option gets an ERRORLEVEL value of 1, the second a value of 2, and so on.

BATUTIL figures out the options by dividing them by spaces. If you really need a space in a menu option, you can replace it with a $S metastring character in the command to make BATUTIL display the space properly. Thus, the above menu line could easily become

```
BATUTIL {MENU Lotus$S1-2-3 Microsoft$SWord dBASE$SIII+ Graphics Games
        Quit}
```

and the $S metastring characters would be replaced by spaces.

If you want to add a title to the menu, you can do so with the HEADER command. The command for the mentioned menu with a title would look like this:

```
BATUTIL {HEADER Sample Menu}{MENU Lotus$S1-2-3 Microsoft$SWord
dBASE$SIII+ Graphics Games Quit}
```

BATUTIL adds several more keywords to control the display of the menu:

NMOUSE   Causes BATUTIL not to use the mouse if it finds one.

POP   Causes the menu to pop up onto the screen as it's being displayed and pop off the screen after a selection is made. You can also add sound effects to go along with this popping.

SHADOW   Places a shadow behind the menu.

FKEY   Lets the user select the menu items by function keys, where F1 selects the first option, F2 selects the second option, and so on. Of course, the normal selection methods continue to work.

What really makes the BATUTIL menus powerful is their ease of use. For example, the command

```
BATUTIL {POP S}{SHADOW}{FKEY}{HEADER Sample Menu}{MENU
        Lotus$S1-2-3 Microsoft$SWord dBASE$SIII+ Graphics Games Quit}
```

is all that is required to display a menu that pops onto the screen with sound effects and a shadow behind it; allows you to select from six options using the first uppercase letter, a mouse, the cursor keys or a function key; and then pops off the screen with sound effects!

While fitting all the BATUTIL commands for the menu onto one line is not difficult, DOS's 127-character limit could give you problems. You can avoid this completely by creating a file called MENU.TXT (or some other arbitrary name) containing the following text:

```
Lotus 1-2-3
Microsoft Word
dBASE III+
micrografx Designer
Games
Quit
```

You could then recreate the fancy menu above with the command:

```
BATUTIL  {POP S}{SHADOW}{FKEY}{HEADER Sample Menu}{FMENU
          MENU.TXT}
```

The FMENU command causes BATUTIL to read the menu text from a file. With the file, each line is treated as a single menu option, so you don't have to use the $S metastring character as a space.

Obtaining the menu text from a file is nice, allowing you to completely avoid the 127-character DOS command line limit. It also allows for a few nice additions. First, you can include multiple menus in the same file by adding a batch file label (a colon followed by a name) at the top of each set of text. When you do this, you follow the file name with the label name, so {FMENU MENU.TXT} becomes {FMENU MENU.TXT MAINMENU} if the menu label is MAINMENU.

You can also add help text to the file. After you finish entering the menu text in the file, add a @ character to the line below the text. Then enter one line of explanation text per menu line. All this might make MENU.TXT look like

```
:MAINMENU
Lotus 1-2-3
Microsoft Word
dBASE III +
micrografx Designer
Games
Quit
@
Run the Lotus spreadsheet program
Run the word processing program
Run the database program
Run the graphics program—This option will automatically load
Windows 3.0
Load the games menu (Watch out for the boss)
Quit using the menu
:GAMEMENU
Chess
Checkers
```

and so on. When the user highlights the "dBASE III +" option, the menu program will show the help text "Run the database program" at the bottom of the screen—much like when Lotus displays a line of help text below the menu depending on which option is highlighted.

As you can see, BATUTIL is an extremely powerful menu program. Also, once the user makes a selection from the menu, you have all the power of BATUTIL to process that selection.

For detailed information on BATUTIL, see Chapter 6.

Bmenu

Name:	Bmenu
Version:	5.4
Price:	$10
Category:	Shareware
Summary:	Automates displaying a menu and selecting a menu option.
Author:	Mark Strong
	6029 Eastridge Lane
	Cincinnati, Ohio 45247
Availability:	Available on many bulletin board systems.

Bmenu offers two easy means of creating moving lightbar menus. Using the first method, you can issue all the commands on a single line in a batch file, like this:

```
BMENU n m – a b c "Title" "Option 1" "Option 2" "Option 3"
```

This menu is then displayed with its top left corner at row n and column m. The optional – a b c switches define the colors of the menu. The title is printed at the top center of the menu as part of a box drawn around the menu. The menu options are listed one per row.

The author realized that the 127-character limit on the DOS command line placed a rather severe limit on the number and complexity of menu items supported by Bmenu. To overcome this, he developed the second menu definition methodology: you can create an ASCII file that contains one or more menus with each of the above items on a line by itself.

To have more than one menu in a file, you must start each menu with a dollar sign followed by a menu name on a line by itself. You must also end each menu with $END on a line by itself. Other than storing the parameters in a file, this menu behaves exactly like the one defined on the command line.

To select a menu option, the user moves the cursor around the menu and, after highlighting the desired option, presses return. Bmenu sets ERRORLEVEL to 1 for the first menu option, 2 for the second, and so on.

The one drawback to Bmenu is that the author doesn't adequately describe how to use various numbers to define the menu colors. Thus, you must experiment to get a menu that looks right. Other than this, Bmenu works very well.

Table 3-3 shows a batch file that displays two Bmenu menus, and Fig. 3-2 shows the menu definition file called by SHOWBMEN.BAT.

Table 3-3   SHOWBMEN.BAT reads information from the file TABMENUS to display its menus.

Batch File Line	Explanation
`@ECHO OFF`	Turns command-echoing off.

`REM NAME:     SHOWBMENU.BAT`
`REM PURPOSE: ILLUSTRATE BMENU54`
`REM VERSION: 1.00`
`REM DATE:    APRIL 4, 1991`
	Documentation remarks.

`:TOP`	Label marking the top of the section that displays the first menu.
`CLS`	Clears the screen.
`BMENU @TABMENUS FIRST`	Reads the menus from a file called TABMENUS and looks for the menu in that file labeled first.

`FOR %%J IN (1 2 3 4 5 6) DO IF`
`   ERRORLEVEL %%J SET ERROR=1%%J`
`GOTO %ERROR%`
	Stores the ERRORLEVEL set by BMENU in an environmental variable with a one added to the front of it. Then, uses that environmental variable as the label for a GOTO command.

`:11`
`CLS`
`ECHO Word Processor Runs Here`
`PAUSE`
`GOTO TOP`
	Section that handles the first menu selection and then redisplays the menu.

`:12`
`CLS`
`ECHO Database Runs Here`
`PAUSE`
`GOTO TOP`
	Section that handles the second menu selection and then redisplays the menu.

`:13`
`CLS`
`ECHO Spreadsheet Runs Here`
`PAUSE`
`GOTO TOP`
	Section that handles the third menu selection and then redisplays the menu.

`:14`
`CLS`
`ECHO Games Menu Runs Here`
`PAUSE`
`GOTO TOP`
	Section that handles the forth menu selection and then redisplays the menu.

`:15` `GOTO NEXT`	Section that handles jumping to the DOS command menu.
`:16` `GOTO END`	Section that handles exiting the menu.
`:NEXT`	Label marking the beginning of the next menu area.
`CLS`	Clears the screen.
`BMENU @TABMENUS SECOND`	Displays the next menu.

`FOR %%J IN (1 2 3 4 5 6) DO IF`
`   ERRORLEVEL %%J SET ERROR=2%%J`
`GOTO %ERROR%`
	Jumps to the appropriate section of the batch file.

Batch File Line	Explanation

`:21`
`CLS`
`DIR`
`PAUSE`
`GOTO NEXT`
	Section that handles the first menu selection and then redisplays the menu.

`:22`
`CLS`
`CHKDSK`
`PAUSE`
`GOTO NEXT`
	Section that handles the second menu selection and then redisplays the menu.

`:23`
`CLS`
`ECHO Would Format A-Drive Here`
`PAUSE`
`GOTO NEXT`
	Section that handles the third menu selection and then redisplays the menu.

`:24`
`CLS`
`ECHO Would Format B-Drive Here`
`PAUSE`
`GOTO NEXT`
	Section that handles the forth menu selection and then redisplays the menu.

`:25`
`CLS`
`MEM`
`PAUSE`
`GOTO NEXT`
	Section that handles the fifth menu selection and then redisplays the menu. Note that MEM is a DOS 4.0 command.

`:26` `GOTO END`	Section that handles exiting the menu.
`:END`	Label marking the end of the batch file.

3-2 TABMENUS defines the two menus displayed by SHOWBMEN.BAT.

```
$FIRST
12
35
-5
9
15
First Menu
Word Processor
Database
Spreadsheet
Games
DOS Commands
Exit Menus
$END
$DR
$SECOND
12
30
-6
12
4
----DOS Commands---
Perform a Directory
Run Chkdsk
Format Disk In A-Drive
Format Disk In B-Drive
Find Out How Much Memory
Exit Menu
$END
```

IFF

Name:	IFF
Version:	5.0
Price:	$20.00
Category:	Shareware
Summary:	A utility set designed to ask different types of questions.
Author:	John Knauer, Junior
	Post Office Box 747
	Brookfield, Connecticut 06804
Availability:	Available on many bulletin board systems.

IFF is a batch toolkit designed around queries. All of IFF's options run by issuing the IFF question followed by an option letter and generally return information via ERRORLEVEL. In addition, many of the questions can display information on the screen—although this can be disabled for batch files.

IFF has two menu options:

M   Reads a file from the disk, displays it, and then prompts the user to make a choice. You can restrict the choice but the method is not very flexible. The choices go from 0-9 and then A-Z, of which you can select the ending point but not the starting point. As a result, if your menu had eleven items, you would have to use 0-9 and then A as your choices.

P   Works just like the M question except it doesn't read a file from the disk first. Thus, the batch file would have to handle displaying the menu.

Overall, IFF works well and is fairly easy to use. However, its menu options aren't all that powerful when compared to other programs in the chapter.

For detailed information on IFF, see Chapter 6.

Ultimate Screen Manager

Name:	Ultimate Screen Manager
Version:	1.20
Price:	$39.00
Category:	Shareware
Summary:	Creates, modifies and displays advanced screens.
Author:	MDFlynn Associates
	Post Office Box 5034
	Redwood City, California 94063
Availability:	Included on the disk bound in this book.

The Ultimate Screen Manager allows you to easily construct menus that permit the user to select options using a moving lightbar menu. The program also allows you to obtain from the user information to be stored in environmental variables.

The Ultimate Screen Manager is covered in Chapter 7.

4

Dealing with files, disks, and subdirectories

Batch files have only the standard DOS commands for dealing with files. For example, they can't find out how much free space a disk has or the date of a file. A number of batch file utilities overcome these limitations.

B(DISK

Name:	B(DISK
Version:	Unknown
Price:	Unknown[1]
Category:	Copyrighted
Summary:	A collection of batch file utilities for working with files and performing other tasks.
Author:	G. Estes
Availability:	Available on many bulletin board systems.

The B(DISK of Batch Programmer Tools contains 34 separate utilities. The utilities are an odd mixture of programs that work best from within a batch file and of other programs that would generally be used from the command line. The B(DISK utilities that deal with files are as follows:

B(CFDATE compares the date on two files and sets ERRORLEVEL to indicate which is newer.

---

[1]The author includes documentation with the programs but fails to mention the status of the files, so I was unable to determine if they are public domain, shareware, or commercial. The author includes no name, address, or copyright notice in the documentation, although the programs are marked internally as copyright G. Estes. As a result, I don't know the status of the B(DISK programs.

B(CFTIME compares the date and time on two files and sets ERRORLEVEL to indicate which is newer. This is very useful in a batch file to prevent writing over a newer file with an older one.

B(QFDATE compares the date on a file against the date entered on the command line and sets ERRORLEVEL accordingly.

Attributes

Generally, you would run the B(DISK file attribute utilities from the command line rather than from the keyboard. Most utilities all run from one program (like the DOS ATTRIB program), using switches to control specific attributes. However, B(DISK uses a cumbersome arrangement where you use one utility to set an attribute, another to remove it, and a third utility to test for an attribute.

To test for, add, and remove the *archive* attribute, you use B(AFARCH, B(ARCH, and B(UNARCH respectively. For the *system* attribute, you use B(QFSYS, B(FSYS, and B(UNSYS respectively. For the *hidden* attribute, you use B(QFHID, B(HIDE, and B(UNHIDE respectively. For the *read-only* attribute, you use B(QFRO, B(RO, and B(UNRO respectively. B(QFNORM tests to see if any attributes other than archive are present and sets ERRORLEVEL accordingly. B(QFSUB sets ERRORLEVEL to indicate if a file is a subdirectory.

The documentation for B(DISK fails to mention if the programs are public domain, shareware, or commercial programs. In fact, the documentation fails to include a copyright notice although the programs contain one internally. For that reason, you might want to ignore B(DISK to avoid violating any copyrights.

The B(DISK utilities are covered in detail in Chapter 6.

Batcd

Name:	Batcd
Version:	Unknown
Price:	Unknown
Category:	Unknown
Summary:	Changes subdirectories using DOS piping.
Author:	Unknown
Availability:	Available on many bulletin board systems.

The DOS CD command can pipe its output to a file (CD > file) but can't accept input from a file (CD < file). Batcd overcomes that problem. It accepts input from a file, so the command BATCD < file in a batch file would work. You can use this to return to the starting directory by first issuing the command CD > \ file to pipe the current subdirectory to a file in the root directory. When the batch file is ready to return, it issues the command BATCD < \ file.

Batcd has documentation, but it fails to mention the status of Batcd. I am unsure if the program is actually shareware or public domain and therefore appropriate to be posted on a bulletin board system. For that reason, you might want to ignore Batcd to avoid violating any copyrights.

BATUTIL

Name:	BATUTIL
Version:	1.0
Price:	$39.00 (Includes STACKEY)
Category:	Shareware
Summary:	A powerful batch file utility that allows you to do almost anything required in a batch file.
Author:	The Support Group
	Lake Technology Park
	Post Office Box 130
	McHenry, Maryland 21541
	(800) 872-4768
Availability:	Available on many bulletin board systems.

BATUTIL is far more than just a batch utility—it's really a batch language disguised as a batch utility. To use BATUTIL, you enter a command like

    BATUTIL [HOUR]

on the command line. When you enclose the command in square [ ] brackets, BATUTIL returns results in ERRORLEVEL. If you enclose the command in curly {} brackets, BATUTIL also returns the results as an environmental variable. BATUTIL only needs the first two characters of the command and ignores capitalization, so [HOUR], [Ho], [HoUr] and [ho] all mean the same thing.

BATUTIL has some very nice features for working with files. It can find out whether a file exists in the current subdirectory or along the path, whether a file has today's date, whether a path exists, the number of files matching one or more file specifications, and which of two files is older. It also can discover the current drive (A=0, B=1, and so on), the total disk space (in 8K blocks for floppy disk or 256K blocks for hard disks) and the free disk space (in 8K blocks), and the number of floppy disk drives you have.

BATUTIL's file-working tools, along with all the others, are discussed in detail in Chapter 6.

BG

Name:	BG
Version:	Unknown
Price:	Unknown

Category:	Unknown
Summary:	Generates a custom batch file based on the text and filenames you supply.
Author:	Unknown
Availability:	Available on many bulletin board systems.[2]

You run BG with a filename (*.* for example) and it then prompts you for a "skeleton" to go with the names. For example, you might run BG with the filename *.BAK and then supply the skeleton DEL. BG will generate a batch file with one line for each file matching the filename. For example, the resulting batch file might look like:

```
DEL ONE.BAK
DEL TWO.BAK
DEL LAST.BAK
```

The created batch file is named NAMES.BAT (which you must, of course, run for these commands to work).

If BG did nothing else, it would basically only offer as much as wildcards; however, BG has several additional abilities:

@   Allows you to use only the name part. Thus, you could supply the skeleton REN @ @.OLD to the above example, renaming all the *.BAK files to *.OLD. This ability is duplicated by wildcards, but other applications are possible that wildcards can't mimic. For example, you might have a number of documents where you want to copy the *.DOC files to a floppy if a .BAK file exists—indicating a recent modification; you can't do this with wildcards. However, starting BG with a *.BAK filename and entering the COPY @.DOC A: skeleton will accomplish this.

.@   Allows you to use only the file extension part. Thus, starting BG with the *.BAK filename and entering the skeleton DIR *.@ would list all the .BAK files.

#.   Creates the same list as @ except the period between the name and extension is dropped.

Several switches also are available for use with BG:

?   Displays a help screen in case you forget how to use BG.

F   Allows you to change the name of the batch file BG creates. Without this switch, the default is NAMES.BAT.

H   Allows you to enter a header line in the batch file BG creates.

L   Converts all filenames to lowercase in the batch file.

P   Prompts you for every file matching the filename and only includes those you select in the final batch file.

T   Allows you to enter a trailing line in the batch file.

---

[2]I was unable to determine the status of the program so you may want to avoid using it to make sure you don't violate any copyrights.

While BG is useful for handling situations too complex for wildcards, I was unable to determine the status of the program. As a result, you may not want to use it, thus avoiding the violation of any copyrights.

BUBA

Name:	BUBA
Version:	1.0
Price:	Free
Category:	Public Domain
Summary:	Five utilities to measure file size, select a file, and input information.
Author:	Bill Reamy
Availability:	Available on many bulletin board systems.

BUBA (short for Bill's Unique Batch Arsenal) is a collection of five utilities. Those utilities are as follows:

DiskSize reports the type of drive in the ERRORLEVEL. There are unique ERRORLEVEL values for the four common floppy diskette sizes (360K, 720K, 1.2 Mb, and 1.44 Mb) and five ERRORLEVEL values for various ranges of hard disk sizes. DiskSize can test floppies without triggering the DOS "Abort, Ignore, or Fail" error message if the drive isn't ready and will report that fact through ERRORLEVEL.

FileFits only needs you to supply the name of a file and a size. The program sets ERRORLEVEL to indicate if the file will fit into the given amount of RAM. You would use this to test a file before trying to edit it with an editor requiring the entire file to fit into memory.

FileSize reports the size of a file in kilobytes in ERRORLEVEL. FileSize reports the largest number of kilobytes smaller than the actual file. For example, a file that contains 13,311 bytes will be reported in ERRORLEVEL as 12 because it doesn't quite contain 13K. (1K is 1,024 bytes, so 13K is 13*1024 or 13,312 bytes.)

Input allows the user to enter any text string and have it placed in the environment in the environmental variable name supplied after the Input command. Input requires that you define the variable first, and it only uses the characters supplied by the user up to the predefined size of the variable. Thus, if you define the variable with SET USED = 1234 and then issue the command INPUT used, Input will only use the first four characters supplied by the user because USED is predefined to be four characters long.

Selector lets you select a single file from a list of all files matching a predefined criteria by scrolling through the list and pressing return on the file you want. To begin with, you must predefine an environmental variable just as you did with Input. Because it will store a filename, you would want to use a definition like SET FILE = 12345678.123 so any file will fit. Next, you start Selector with a command like

```
SELECTOR file *.TXT *.DOC READ.ME "Select Documentation File"
```

where file is the name of the environmental variable to use. Selector can handle multiple file specifications. It clears the screen and lists all the files in the current subdirectory matching any of these specifications. If you enter an optional message in quotes, it displays that message at the bottom of the screen. You move a cursor around the screen until it highlights the file to select, and then you press return. That file name is stored in the environment using the given variable name.

Selector and Input are a tiny bit more difficult to use than they should be, because you first must predefine the variables, but otherwise are two excellent utilities. While less useful, DiskSize, FileFits, and FileSize work well and can be useful in certain situations.

CHKVOLID

Name:	CHKVOLID
Version:	1.0
Price:	Free
Category:	Public Domain
Summary:	Will check the volume label on a disk, return status, or display the volume label. It will also return the disk type or status.
Author:	Wayne Mingee
Availability:	Available on many bulletin board systems.

CHKVOLID is a utility designed to work primarily with the volume label. If you enter the command by itself, it will display the volume label, just like the VOL command. If you enter a volume label after the CHKVOLID command, it will compare that with the volume label and set ERRORLEVEL to let you know if they match. The comparison is case-insensitive, so D-DRIVE will match D-Drive.

Running CHKVOLID without a volume label to compare does more than just display the current volume label. CHKVOLID also checks the disk drive to see if it can read and write to it. If an error exists, CHKVOLID sets ERRORLEVEL to 2 plus the bios error code. If the drive is working, CHKVOLID sets ERRORLEVEL to indicate the type of drive found.

Normally, you would use CHKVOLID to ensure that the user had inserted a floppy disk with the proper volume label before continuing with some process requiring a specific floppy disk. However, while CHKVOLID worked properly with the hard disk drive, it failed to display the volume label or set ERRORLEVEL properly when working on floppy disks under DOS 4.0 or later; thus, its usefulness is severely limited.

CLUTIL

Name:	CLUTIL
Version:	1.3

Price:	$18.00
Category:	Shareware
Summary:	A collection of general file-handling utilities.
Author:	William S. Mezian
	105^1/$_2$ 20th Avenue, Apartment 2
	Saint Petersburg Beach, Florida 33706
Availability:	Many bulletin board systems carry CLUTIL.

CLUTIL [short for Command Line UTILities] is a collection of utilities designed primarily for use on the command line. However, some of the utilities are useful in batch files. The programs working with files are covered here:

CLSHELL is a small DOS shell. Unlike more advanced shells, it doesn't show the disk visually, and you don't operate on files by tagging them. Rather, CLSHELL simply prompts you one piece at a time for the information the command needs. For example, to delete files, it asks you for the drive, subdirectory, and file specification. More likely, anyone knowing this information would find it easier to enter the information on the command line.

CDIR is a replacement for the DOS DIR command. It shows files in a multi-column format and displays different types of files in different colors.

CDIR displays the number of files, the size of the files, and the amount of free space—just like DOS 5.0. However, CDIR doesn't display any subdirectories, making it difficult to use for navigating the hard disk. If you display a file specification (like CDIR *.NOT) that doesn't exist, CDIR states that one file containing 0 bytes exists. In addition, CDIR displays a few characters of ANSI.SYS escape-sequences on the screen.

FREE reports the amount of available disk space and memory. It doesn't set the ERRORLEVEL.

MBAK is a quasi-backup program, copying the specified files to the specified drive. Unlike most backup programs, it leaves the files intact on the target disk and can't split large files across multiple disks. Like MOVE, it doesn't copy files to the disk unless they are newer than the backups already on the disk. Because MBAK expects to check the disk before backing up, MBAK is really useful only for small backups that will fit on a single disk.

MDEL is a safer replacement for the DOS DEL/ERASE commands. You enter MDEL file specification at the command line, and it lists the files one at a time. You press the DEL-key to delete the file, the Enter-key to skip it, or the Escape-key to exit the program.

MERGE combines two or more files into one large file. The format of the command is MERGE first second output, but either the first or second set of files can be specified using wildcards. MERGE is cumbersome to use only because you must specify two sets of files to merge, even if you specify the first set using wildcards. You can't fool it by giving an invalid specification for the second set because it checks before running. If your output file exists, the program asks if you want to overwrite it. You don't have the option of appending to the file.

You can accomplish the same thing using the DOS COPY command. For example, COPY first + second output performs identically to the MERGE command.

MOVE performs the same function as NCOPY except it deletes the source file after copying. MOVE actually copies and then deletes the files. Much better moving programs are available that only change the subdirectory information associated with the file without copying the file. Using that approach, you don't need twice the disk space as you do with MOVE.

MOVE has a flaw dangerous enough that you should never use this program to move files. When MOVE first tries to copy the files to the new location, it behaves exactly like NCOPY. If the target file is newer than the source file, it doesn't copy the file. However, it does delete the source file. As a result, the older file is lost. Normally, that wouldn't be a problem; but it would be if the newer files had mistakes and you wanted to replace it with the older file. Before deleting a file not saved somewhere else, MOVE should always ask the user.

NCOPY is a replacement for the DOS COPY command and has the advantage of not overwriting files unless the file being copied is newer than the file being overwritten.

While not overwriting newer files with older files is an excellent safety feature, NCOPY's implementation is poor. The program doesn't tell you it's not overwriting the file. In fact, it only indicates when it has started copying and when it has finished. Although it doesn't overwrite the files unless the source file is newer, these copying messages fool you into believing that the file has been overwritten. Especially troublesome would be the times when you actually wanted to overwrite the files and wouldn't be sure if it had been done.

VIEW displays an ASCII file one screen at a time but is far less useful than other programs of this type. For one, you can't scroll backwards. Once you start viewing a file, you must scroll to the end of the file one screen at a time in order to stop. Also, VIEW doesn't accept wildcards. If you must view files, LIST.COM from Vernon D. Buerg (also shareware) is a much better program.

All of the CLUTIL programs require the computer to have ANSI.SYS loaded, without which many of them won't run. Even when the programs do run without ANSI.SYS, they tend to clutter the screen with escape-sequences intended for ANSI.SYS. Therefore, you shouldn't consider CLUTIL unless you routinely load ANSI.SYS.

Except for CALLKEY and COLOR, the programs in CLUTIL aren't all that useful. They either operate dangerously, like MOVE, or other far superior shareware programs are available (like LIST.COM as a replacement for VIEW). ANSI.SYS users, however, will find CALLKEY and COLOR to be very useful.

For detailed information on all CLUTIL programs, see Chapter 7.

Drvdir

Name: Drvdir
Version: 1.0

Category:	Public Domain
Summary:	Stores the current drive and subdirectory in an environmental variable.
Author:	Richard N. Wisan
Availability:	Included on the disk bound in this book.
Also See:	PPPD in Chapter 4.

A number of tricks can obtain either the current subdirectory or the current drive. Authors need this information to write batch files that return to their starting location.

Drvdir is a simple program that makes all these tricks unnecessary. When you issue the command DRVDIR, it stores the current drive (with colon) in the environmental variable named DRV and puts the full path to the current subdirectory in the environmental variable named CUR. Once set, a batch file can return either to the drive stored in the environment with the command %DRV% or to the subdirectory stored in the environment with the command CD\ %CUR%. By having the batch file transfer this information to other variables, you can write a batch file to nest these subdirectories.

In case you run out of environmental space, Drvdir also stores the current drive as an ERRORLEVEL value, where 0=A, 1=B, and so on. There are two switches you can use with Drvdir. The /F switch changes what is stored in ERRORLEVEL to the number of files in the current subdirectory. The /R switch changes how Drvdir stores the subdirectory in the environment when it's the root directory. Normally, Drvdir would store a blank variable for the root directory, so the command CD\ %CUR% would work properly. However, some versions of DOS won't work with this line when CUR is empty. For them, the /R switch causes Drvdir to store "ROOT" in CUR when in the root directory. In that case, the batch file would have to check the contents of the CUR variable before using it in the CD\ %CUR% command.

Dskchk

Name:	Dskchk
Version:	1.0
Category:	Public Domain
Summary:	Checks to see if the specified drive can be read and written to and sets ERRORLEVEL accordingly.
Author:	Richard N. Wisan
Availability:	Included on the disk bound in this book.

One problem with a batch file needing to write to a floppy drive is that you never can be sure the drive is ready. If the batch file tries to change over to an unready floppy drive, DOS issues the familiar "Abort, Retry, or Ignore" error message and the batch file can't recover without user intervention.

Dskchk overcomes this problem. It checks to see if it can read the specified drive using a method that doesn't trigger the "Abort, Retry, or Ignore" error message; if it fails, it stores the results in the ERRORLEVEL. If you include an optional /W switch, it will test to see if it can write to the drive as well, again without triggering the "Abort, Retry, or Ignore" error message.

Dskchk returns a 0 in ERRORLEVEL if the drive is ready, a 1 if it's not, a 2 if the user specified the /W switch and the drive is read-only, and a 255 for other errors. The batch file can test on the values and prompt the user to correct any problems before it tries to continue.

FD

Name:	FD
Version:	Unknown
Price:	Unknown
Category:	Unknown
Summary:	Checks to see if a file or subdirectory exists.
Author:	Martin Telfer
Availability:	Available on many bulletin board systems.

With FD, you enter the following command on the command line:

    FD \ subdirectory \ file

(with \ file being optional). It sets ERRORLEVEL to 3 if the specified file or subdirectory doesn't exist. If you don't specify a file, it sets ERRORLEVEL to 2 if the subdirectory exists. If you specify a file, it sets ERRORLEVEL to 1 if the file exists. FD doesn't support wildcards, so you must check for each file individually.

The file checking ability of FD offers no real advantage over the IF EXIST file except that it sets ERRORLEVEL. However, your batch file can branch on the results of the IF EXIST file easier than IF ERRORLEVEL, so in most circumstances setting ERRORLEVEL offers no real advantage. However, a batch file can't easily check to see if a subdirectory exists using DOS commands, so FD's ability to perform that task is useful.

FT

Name:	FT (Floppy Test)
Version:	1.0
Price:	Free
Category:	Copyrighted
Summary:	Reports on the status of a floppy drive.
Author:	Jeffrey S. Morley
Availability:	Available on many bulletin board systems.

The command FT drive issues a quick and complete report on any floppy drive (see Fig. 4-1 for a copy of the report). Normally, you would use this feature from the command line and not in a batch file.

```
FT.COM - Floppy Type/Status
Copyright 1989 Jeffrey S. Morley

Drive       :  B:
Drive Type  :  1.4M floppy (3.5")
Disk Type   :  1.4M High density
Total Space :  1,457,664
Used Space  :  265,728

Free Space  :  1,191,936
Status      :  Ready for use
```

4-1 Floppy Tests (FT) reports on the status of floppy drives.

FT also sets ERRORLEVEL as follows:

0   Floppy ready.
1   Disk not formatted.
2   The drive specified isn't a floppy drive.
3   The drive specified is a network drive.
4   Drive or BIOS not supported.
5   Invalid drive.
6   Drive door open.
7   Drive not specified.

These ERRORLEVEL values allow your batch files to react to any unusual conditions when dealing with a floppy drive. FT is a great program.

GET

Name:	GET
Version:	1.0
Price:	Free
Category:	Public Domain
Summary:	Passes information about the system to the batch file through the environment.
Author:	Bob Stephan
Availability:	Available on many bulletin board systems.

Get has a number of options for obtaining information. It then passes this information back to the batch file by either the environmental variable GET or sometimes

ERRORLEVEL. The GET options dealing with files are as follows:

F   Gets the size of a specified file in kilobytes and stores it in the environmental variable GET and ERRORLEVEL.

K   Gets the free space on the specified drive in kilobytes and stores it in the environmental variable GET and ERRORLEVEL.

Y   Stores the current subdirectory in the environmental variable GET and the drive number in ERRORLEVEL.

GET is a very powerful program for getting information from the user and about the system—especially for a public domain program.

For detailed information on GET, please see Chapter 6.

IFF

Name:	IFF
Version:	5.0
Price:	$20.00
Category:	Shareware
Summary:	A utility set designed to ask different types of questions.
Author:	John Knauer, Junior
	Post Office Box 747
	Brookfield, Connecticut 06804
Availability:	Available on many bulletin board systems.

IFF is a batch toolkit designed around queries. All of IFF's options run by issuing the IFF question followed by an option letter and generally return information via ERRORLEVEL. In addition, many of the questions can display information on the screen—although this can be disabled for batch files.

Several IFF options let you work with files:

C   Searches the entire drive to see if the specified file exists. It reports the results in ERRORLEVEL and changes to the subdirectory containing the file.

E   Tests to see if a specified file exists but doesn't search all subdirectories and doesn't change to the subdirectory. Unlike the DOS IF EXIST command, this test doesn't trigger the DOS "Abort, Ignore, or Retry" error message if a drive has a problem.

F   Searches the drive for a file (like the C option) but doesn't change to the subdirectory when it finds it.

L   Compares the disk label against a label entered on the command line.

R   First, you create a file listing up to ten filenames. The R option then searches the drive for each of those ten filenames and sets ERRORLEVEL to indicate the first file it found.

S   Compares the available disk space against a number you enter on the command line and sets ERRORLEVEL to indicate if that much free space exists.

T   Tests to see which drives are available and working on your system. For example, this option won't report an A drive without a disk in it because, although the drive's available, it's not currently working.

IFF works well and is fairly easy to use. For more detailed information, see Chapter 6.

IsDir

Name:	IsDir
Version:	1.0
Category:	Public Domain
Summary:	Checks to see if a subdirectory exists and sets the ERRORLEVEL accordingly.
Author:	Richard N. Wisan
Availability:	Included on the disk bound in this book.

When writing a batch file to copy files to someone else's machine, you often never know whether the subdirectory you want to copy to exists. My solution has always been to issue the make directory command to attempt the creation of the subdirectory I want. If it already exists, the MD command results in an error message but no damage; however, if the subdirectory doesn't exist, then this method simply creates it.

IsDir provides an alternative solution to the problem. To check for the existence of a subdirectory, you issue this command:

```
SDIR SUBDIRECTORY
```

Isdir sets the ERRORLEVEL to 0 if the subdirectory exists, 1 if it doesn't exist, and 255 if the syntax is incorrect. IsDir is fairly forgiving if you omit the first or last backslash, so incorrect syntax will be a rare problem. Once the ERRORLEVEL is set, your batch file can branch to a special section if the subdirectory doesn't exist.

Lastdir

Name:	Lastdir
Version:	2.0
Price:	Free
Category:	Public Domain
Summary:	Stores the current drive and subdirectory in an environmental variable.

Author:	Ken Hipple
Availability:	Available on many bulletin board systems.

The command LASTDIR causes the program to store the current drive and subdirectory in an environmental variable called LASTDIR. You can then return to that subdirectory by issuing a CD %LASTDIR% command in a batch file. Due to a limitation of DOS, this command won't work from the command line. This is useful for a batch file where you must change to a specific subdirectory to run a program but want the batch file to return to the subdirectory where it started. If Lastdir encounters an error, it sets the ERRORLEVEL to flag the error.

Because Lastdir uses an environmental variable, you can't nest multiple Lastdir commands in a batch file. In addition, Lastdir refused to work under DOS 4.x or DOS 5.x.

Lookfor

Name:	Lookfor
Version:	1.0
Price:	Free
Category:	Public Domain
Summary:	Checks to see if a file exists and sets ERRORLEVEL accordingly.
Author:	Wayne King
Availability:	Available on many bulletin board systems.

Lookfor checks to see if the file or files specified on the command line exists. It does this without triggering the DOS "Abort, Ignore, or Fail" error message if a drive isn't ready and sets the ERRORLEVEL to indicate its results. The documentation says it sets ERRORLEVEL to 152 if a drive isn't ready but doesn't offer any other values. The program sets ERRORLEVEL to 18 if it doesn't find the file and to 15 if the drive specified on the command line is invalid. Also, the examples in the documentation and sample batch file perform ERRORLEVEL testing improperly. This misuse of ERRORLEVEL causes me to wonder about the quality of the code going into Lookfor, although it worked properly in my testing.

Menuware Batch File Utilities

Name:	Menuware Batch File Utilities
Version:	1.0
Price:	$10.00[3]

---

[3]The author adds a strange extension to shareware called menuware. Under this, the author allows you to register only those programs you want to use. The individual registration fee is one dollar. However, many of the utilities (especially the system variable ones) work together, so it seems to me that you would be better off just registering all of them.

Category:	Shareware
Summary:	A collection of utilities primarily for counting.
Author:	Interfaces, People, and Magic
	Post Office Box 4496
	Middletown, Rhode Island 02840
Availability:	Available on many bulletin board systems.

Menuware Batch File Utilities [MWBAT2 for short] is a collection of utilities primarily designed to allow counting in batch files and to measure time. Several of the MWBAT2 utilities work with the disk, so they are covered here. They are as follows:

AMIAT checks to see if the batch file is currently in the subdirectory specified on the command line and sets ERRORLEVEL accordingly.

CMPDS compares the amount of free disk space on the default drive with the amount specified on the command line and sets ERRORLEVEL accordingly.

GDRIVE sets ERRORLEVEL to indicate the current drive.

For a complete discussion of MWBAT2, see Chapter 7.

PPD/PPPD

Name:	PPD
	PPPD
Version:	1.0
Category:	Public Domain
Summary:	PPD stores and recalls the current drive and subdirectory using a file. PPPD performs all the functions of PPD while also storing the current path.
Author:	Richard N. Wisan
Availability:	Included on the disk bound in this book.

A number of tricks can obtain either the current subdirectory or the current drive. Authors need this information to write batch files that return to their starting location.

PPD completely automates this process. The command PPD PUSH stores the current drive and subdirectory in a file stored in the root directory of the C drive. Issue the command again, and the second set of values for the current drive and subdirectory are added to the file. Issue the command PPD POP, and PPD changes to the current drive and subdirectory last entered in the PPD file and removes that entry from the file. Issue the command again, and it repeats the process. This allows nesting of multiple sets of current drive and subdirectories.

PPPD operates just like PPD. It stores and recalls the current drive and subdirectory from a file, also storing and recalling the path using this file.

Ronset

Name:	Ronset
Version:	2.1
Price:	$20.00
Category:	Shareware
Summary:	A very powerful tool for manipulating environmental variables. Unfortunately, it doesn't work with newer versions of DOS.
Author:	Ron Bemis
	9601 Forest Lane
	Apartment #222
	Dallas, Texas 75243
Availability:	Available on many bulletin board systems.

Under DOS, you can do very little with environmental variables. You can either create and erase them using the SET command or print and test them in batch files by surrounding their names with percent signs. Beyond that, DOS has little use for them.

All that changes under Ronset. Using Ronset, there is little you can't do with environmental variables. The basic command to use Ronset is as follows:

```
RONSET A = XYZ(n,m)
```

In this command, A represents the environmental variable the results will be stored in when the command finishes. The XYZ represents one of almost 100 functions you can perform. (For example, the ADD function sums two numbers.) The n and m represent the parameters being passed to the function.

Ronset adds a number of new environmental variable manipulation functions and offers a number of file-manipulation functions, which are covered here. (For a detailed list of Ronset file functions, look far ahead at Table 9-2.)

BYTE   Stores the ASCII value of a character from a specific file position.
LONG   Stores the 32-bit value from a specific location in a file.
WORD   Stores the 16-bit value from a specific location in a file.

Clearly, Ronset has a very powerful set of tools for manipulating files and filenames. Because you then can use the environmental variable in a batch command by surrounding its name with percent signs, Ronset is a powerful tool for file manipulation in batch files.

As you can see, Ronset gives you the ability to do almost anything you can imagine with environmental variables. Were it not for one flaw, Ronset would be one of the most powerful and useful batch utilities available. Unfortunately, it doesn't run under any current version of DOS. I tested it under IBM DOS 3.3 and 4.0, as well as under Microsoft DOS 5.0; it wouldn't work under any of them. I finally located a copy of DOS 2.1, under which it worked perfectly. Once Ronset is upgraded to work with more modern versions of DOS, I will highly recommend it.

Scanion Enterprises Batch File Utilities

Name: Scanion Enterprises Batch File Utilities
Version: 2.2.0
Price: $9.95
Category: Shareware
Summary: A collection of over 100 batch file utilities.
Author: Paul Scanion
Availability: Included on the disk bound in this book.

The Scanion Enterprises Batch File Utilities [SEBFU for short] is a collection of over 100 batch file utilities. Some of the programs will work with disks and files and are discussed here.

Each of the commands in SEBFU is a separate *.COM file. As a result, your disk can end up cluttered with quite a number of small program files. You might consider erasing the program files you aren't likely to use.

CDD moves down toward the root directory a specified number of levels.

CHKSUM computes a checksum for a specified file and can also test the results against a specified value. This is an excellent way for a batch file to perform a quick-and-dirty test to see if a critical file had been specified by a virus.

DFREE measures the amount of free space on the specified drive and either sets ERRORLEVEL or an environmental variable to report its results. A batch file could run DFREE prior to running a program requiring a lot of disk space.

DLST displays a list of all the files in the current subdirectory.

DRVCK checks to see if a drive exists and sets ERRORLEVEL accordingly. It can perform this task without triggering the DOS "Abort, Ignore, or Fail" error message.

DSKRDY checks to see if a drive is ready to receive data and sets ERRORLEVEL accordingly. It can perform this task without triggering the DOS "Abort, Ignore, or Fail" error message.

FILES checks to see how many files exist in the current subdirectory and sets ERRORLEVEL accordingly.

FSIZE checks to see how large a file is and sets ERRORLEVEL accordingly. By combining this with DFREE, a batch file could test to see if a file would fit on a floppy disk before trying to copy it.

GDIR sets the environmental variable DIR equal to the current path, useful for writing batch files that return to their starting directory when finished running.

GDRIVE sets ERRORLEVEL to indicate the current drive, useful for writing batch files that return to their starting directory when finished running.

LOGON can write a name, date, and time to a file, useful for logging who runs a program or usage for taxes.

LST displays an ASCII file on the screen one page at a time.

PATHCK checks to see if the specified subdirectory exists in the path, useful for a batch file to check if a program's subdirectory is in the path before trying to run that program.

PRINTF prints any ASCII file up to 64K.

WRITEF displays a small (under 4K) file on the screen, useful for quickly displaying a menu or help text.

All SEBFU programs are described in Chapter 7.

tBU

Name:	tBU
Version:	3.0
Price:	Free
Category:	Copyrighted
Summary:	A collection of very powerful functions for manipulating environmental variables.
Author:	Todd R. Hill
	Claude N. Warren Jr.
Availability:	Available on many bulletin board systems.

Most of the batch utilities in this book are programs run to perform some specific task. tBU (short for the Batch Utility) doesn't work that way; for the most part, it functions as an intermediary. You run tBU to perform some manipulation of an environmental variable that you then use for some other task.

To run tBU, you provide it with a symbol telling it what to do, an environmental variable to manipulate, and optional parameters as required. tBU sometimes sets ERRORLEVEL, but the really useful information is stored in the environmental variable. As a result, you really should expand your environment while using tBU (see Appendix B).

The general format of the tBU command is

TBU – S VAR options

where S is the symbol telling tBU what to do. Please note that the symbol is case-sensitive. VAR is the environmental variable tBU uses to store the results, and options are the remaining symbol-specific parameters required by tBU.

The symbols supported by tBU and their general function are covered in detail in Chapter 6. Those dealing with files are listed below:

- d   Stores the date and/or time a file was created to the environmental variable.
- E   Stores the size of the environment to the environmental variable.
- K   Stores the free disk space to the environmental variable.
- k   Indicates if a specified amount of space is available on a disk.
- L   Stores the current drive to the environmental variable.

n   Stores just the filename portion of a file specification in the environmental variable.
T   Checks to see if a file or subdirectory exists.
x   Stores a files extension to the environmental variable.
Y   Stores the current subdirectory to the environmental variable.
y   Stores the subdirectory portion of a file specification in the environmental variable.
z   Stores the size of a file in the environmental variable.

Unfortunately, tBU uses a complex syntax difficult to learn and terse documentation that makes learning tBU even more difficult. Luckily, tBU is so powerful that you will soon wonder how you got along without it. In fact, after this book was finished, tBU is one of only a handful of utilities that found a permanent home on my crowded hard disk. I highly recommend tBU.

WHAT

Name:	WHAT
Version:	1.47
Price:	Free
Category:	Public Domain
Summary:	Can determine a great deal of information about the computer and pass that information back to the batch file. It can also prompt the user for a single character response to a question. Information is passed using the ERRORLEVEL and an environmental variable.
Author:	Tom Peters
Availability:	Available on many bulletin board systems.

Sometimes you can write a more effective batch file if you have some information about the environment under which the batch file is running. WHAT is an excellent program for obtaining that information.

The general format for the WHAT command is as follows:

WHAT X [E] Parameter-1 Parameter-2

X is the option to run, and E is the optional enhanced mode. Some of the WHAT options require additional parameters. Most of the WHAT options return a value in the environmental variable what and in ERRORLEVEL. The options that work with files are as follows:

F   Returns the size of a single file and stores it in the environment and in ERRORLEVEL. Wildcards aren't supported. Adding the E option divides the results by ten. When combined with the K option, this allows you to make sure enough free space exists before trying to copy a file. You can also test to make sure a file is small enough for an editor with limited capacity before trying to edit the file.

K   Returns the free space on a drive and stores it in the environment and in ERRORLEVEL. Adding the E option divides the results by ten. This allows you to make sure adequate free space exists before you install software or copy a file.

Y   Stores the current subdirectory in the environment. You can then write a batch file that returns to this subdirectory with a CD \ %WHAT% command. The E option stores the drive rather than the subdirectory.

WHAT is extremely powerful and also easy to use; it belongs in everyone's batch file toolkit. Turn to Chapter 7 for complete information on WHAT and its full options.

X-BATCH

Name:	X-BATCH
Version:	1.0
Price:	$20.00
Category:	Shareware
Summary:	A collection of 13 useful utilities.
Author:	Gary R. Pannone
	9 Brady Road Ext.
	Westboro, Massachusetts 01581
Availability:	Available on many bulletin board systems.

X-BATCH is a collection of thirteen useful batch file utilities, two of which work with files. The command COMPFILE compares the dates/sizes of two files to see which is earlier/larger. In addition, the CREATE command creates a 0-length file if a file doesn't already exist with the given name. Of course, this isn't very useful because you can do the same thing using straight DOS. The command TYPE nofile > 0-LENGTH.TXT will create a 0-length file called 0-LENGTH.TXT if the file nofile *doesn't* exist.

The X-BATCH commands are useful and easy to learn, with a sensible format reading almost like English.

For detailed information on X-BATCH, see Chapter 6.

5

A first look at Windows batch file programs

DOS, Microsoft's "old" operating system offers batch files as a powerful tool for automating routine procedures. As you have seen in this book and my *MS-DOS Batch File Programming* book, batch files are a very powerful tool.

However, when Microsoft developed their "new" operating system—Windows[1]—they left out batch files. Windows has no native language for automating procedures!

Of course, the very nature of Windows means you have less of a need for batch files. Batch files are commonly used to write menus and start applications, while Windows handles the menuing automatically using icons. The main icons you see when you start Windows represent your various menus. Click on an icon and it pops up another group of icons, generally representing the program—the elements of most menus.

If the program you want to run is a Windows application, then its installation program handles configuring Windows so that clicking on the icon starts the application automatically. Even for most non-Windows applications, you can configure Windows to run the application without a batch file. Even when you must resort to a batch file, you can generally get by with having Windows run a DOS batch file.

Batch files are also commonly used to navigate around your hard disk. With Window's file manager, you don't need batch files for this; you just click on the subdirectory you want to go to.

While Windows has less of a need for batch files than does DOS, the need still exists and Windows offers nothing to support it. Fortunately, your DOS batch files will generally work fine under Windows. Because Windows was designed to coexist with and run DOS applications, it will run batch files. As a result, you can still automate your DOS applications under Windows. However, that still leaves you with no way to automate Windows applications under Windows.

---

[1]When I refer to Windows in this chapter, I am referring to Windows 3.0. I made no effort to test any of these programs under earlier versions of Windows.

Luckily, two other developers have stepped in to make up for Microsoft's shortcomings. PubTech BatchWorks from Publishing Technologies and Bridge Tool Kit from Softbridge Incorporated offers many of the advantages of DOS batch files under and for Windows.[2]

With a DOS batch file, once your application starts, the batch file is suspended until the application terminates. With either of these languages under Windows, the batch file can interact with the application in ways not possible under DOS. In fact, both of these programs are far more than just "ports" of the batch language under Windows. Both of them qualify as programming languages in their own right.

PubTech BatchWorks

Name:	PubTech BatchWorks
Version:	1.0
Price:	$99.95
Category:	Commercial
Summary:	A Windows 3.0 batch language.
Author:	Publishing Technologies, Incorporated
	7719 Wood Hollow Drive
	Suite 260
	Austin, Texas 78731
	(800) 782-8324
Availability:	Order directly from the vendor.

PubTech BatchWorks is a combination macro/batch package. Think of it as a combination of Borland's SuperKey and the DOS language. The batch portion works and feels very much like the DOS batch language. Two primary uses of batch files are to interface with DOS better than Windows can do alone and to do more in the way of starting Windows applications than Windows can itself.

Window's interaction with DOS programs is very primitive. It can only either run a batch file or issue a command when you click on an icon. I wanted to be able to run my tape drive from within Windows in one of six different ways. My only solution under straight Windows was to have a separate icon for each configuration. With PubTech BatchWorks, I wrote a batch file that first asked me if I wanted a full or incremental backup and then asked if I wanted the C drive, D drive, or both backed up. The file then ran a common DOS batch file and passed it the necessary parameters.

While working on my dissertation, I need to switch between Word for Windows and Excel and thus need them both loaded. With Windows, I must go to two separate icons and load them individually. With PubTech BatchWorks, I wrote a very short batch file that

---

[2]Both of these applications have just been released as I am writing this. Because of the newness of the Windows environment, it's likely that these programs will evolve quickly over the next year or so. For that reason, I haven't provided as much detail on these programs as I have the programs running under the much more stable DOS environment.

launches both applications and loads the appropriate files when I click on Dissertation.

If that was all PubTech BatchWorks did, it would be worth its very reasonable price. However, it does much more. In addition to being a batch language, it's also a macro program.

While writing this book, I created a lot of tables in Word for Windows. While the process isn't difficult, it's fairly repetitive—a perfect application for a macro program. I wrote a fairly simple macro in PubTech BatchWorks that asks a couple of questions and then creates the table, adding the heading and applying the appropriate formatting all automatically. Not only was PubTech BatchWorks able to do this, I was able to add the command to the Word For Windows menu.

Bridge Tool Kit

Name:	Bridge Tool Kit
Version:	1.0
Price:	$695
Category:	Commercial
Summary:	A Windows batch language.
Author:	Softbridge, Incorporated
	125 Cambridge Park Drive
	Cambridge, Massachusetts 02140
	(800) 955-9190
Availability:	Order directly from the vendor.

Like PubTech BatchWorks, Bridge Tool Kit allows you to construct powerful batch files to interact both with Windows and DOS applications. One area where Bridge Tool Kit greatly exceeds PubTech BatchWorks is in dialog boxes. Under PubTech BatchWorks, you have very limited control over their placement and use. With Bridge Tool Kit, however, you have precise control over their placement, and you can evaluate their content before removing the dialog box from the screen. If the user enters an invalid response, you can leave the original dialog box on the screen and pop up another box explaining the proper responses.

Bridge Tool Kit also offers extensive control over Windows applications, far more than PubTech BatchWorks. Bridge Tool Kit supports DDE (Dynamic Data Exchange), something PubTech BatchWorks doesn't do. It can answer DDE requests for data or send requests to other applications.

Thus, Bridge Tool Kit can do some very powerful things. I was able to program it to grab data out of Excel, squirt it into Word for Windows, and then create a Word for Windows table for the data.

Bridge Tool Kit offers advanced abilities to communicate with DOS applications *if* Windows is running in 386 Enhanced Mode. Using a small memory resident program, Bridge Tool Kit can send keystrokes to the DOS application and even take information from the DOS application and bring it back into Windows. It does all this interactively. Without the 386 Enhanced Mode, its communications with DOS applications is crippled;

but it can still send keystrokes to an application, even one like Lotus that doesn't support supplying information on the command line.

Conclusion

You may be wondering which of these to buy, if either. Unless you are heavily into Windows, writing Windows batch files might not be high on your priorities. Right now, that's OK. Because these programs are available now, you know they'll be around when you need them.

If you're ready for Windows batch files, then I suggest you begin with PubTech Batch-Works. It's less powerful than Bridge Tool Kit but, at one seventh the cost, a real bargain anyway. If you have any doubts of its power, then check out the February 1991 issue of *PC/Computing*: they used its macro abilities to add a number of useful features to the Windows notepad.

6
Batch utilities sets

Several authors haven't been content to produce a couple of batch utilities, instead producing entire sets of utilities. This chapter covers those sets.

Basically, you can produce a set of batch utilities in one of two ways. For one, you could simply collect a bunch of utilities onto a disk—like B(DISK or Scanion Enterprises Batch File Utilities—and then call it a set. Unfortunately, using this method, you end up with a lot of small utilities cluttering up your hard disk. Alternatively, following the example of Batchman and Check, you could build one massive program that does everything and then use keywords to tell the program which task to perform.

I strongly prefer this second approach for the basic reason that, under most conditions, using one program saves disk space—often lots of it.

B(DISK

Name: B(DISK
Version: Unknown
Price: Unknown[1]
Category: Copyrighted
Summary: A collection of batch file utilities for working with files and performing other tasks.
Author: G. Estes
Availability: Available on many bulletin board systems.

The B(DISK of Batch Programmer Tools contains 34 separate utilities. The utilities are an odd mixture of programs that work best from within a batch file and of other programs

---

[1] The author includes documentation with the programs but fails to mention the status of the files, so I am unable to determine if they are public domain, shareware, or commercial. The author includes no name, address, or copyright notice in the documentation, although the programs are marked internally as copyright G. Estes. As a result, I don't know the status of the B(DISK programs.

that would generally be used from the command line. The B(DISK utilities are as follows:

Time and date utilities

B(DATE displays the date and sets the ERRORLEVEL to the day of the week. It is useful for piping the date because you don't need to worry about piping a return to this command as with the DOS DATE command.

B(DELAY pauses the batch file for a specified period of time. It can't be aborted by any key combination but Ctrl-Break.

B(PAUSE pauses the batch file for a specified period of time and allows the user to abort pausing and continue by pressing any key.

B(QDATE compares the date entered on the command line against the system date and then sets ERRORLEVEL accordingly.

B(QTIME compares the time entered on the command line against the system time and then sets ERRORLEVEL accordingly.

B(TIME displays the time and sets the ERRORLEVEL to the hour of the day. It is useful for piping the time, as you don't need to worry about piping a return to this command as with the DOS TIME command.

B(UNTIL pauses the batch file until a specified time is reached. It can't be aborted by any key combination but Ctrl-Break.

B(WAIT pauses the batch file until a specified time is reached and allows the user to abort the wait by pressing any key.

Keyboard utilities

B(CADOFF is a small (.7K) memory-resident program that disables the Ctrl-Alt-Del system reset. The system reset capabilities can't be restored without turning the computer off and back on or by pressing the hardware reset button.

B(CBOFF is a small (.7K) memory-resident program that disables Ctrl-Break. Like B(CADOFF, Ctrl-Break can only be restored by resetting the computer. If you are concerned about users stopping batch files with Ctrl-Break, you should enter this command in your AUTOEXEC.BAT configuration file.

B(CBOOT performs a cold reboot.

B(QINKEY waits for the user to press any key and sets ERRORLEVEL to the ASCII value of that keystroke. The program is case-sensitive.

B(QY1N0 waits for the user to press a y or n key and then sets ERRORLEVEL accordingly. It can display an optional prompt entered on the command line, or it will use its own prompt if none is specified.

B(WBOOT performs a warm reboot.

Printer utilities

B(LPTSWP swaps the two logical printer ports.

B(PRTSC, when run, operates the same as Shift-PrintScreen and is good for documenting the operation of small sections of a batch file designed for unattended operation.

B(QLPT checks the status of the printer port and sets ERRORLEVEL accordingly.

File date/time utilities

B(CFDATE compares the date on two files and then sets ERRORLEVEL to indicate which file has the latest date.

B(CFTIME compares the date and time on two files and then sets ERRORLEVEL to indicate file has the latest date, very useful in a batch file to prevent writing over a newer file with an older one.

B(QFDATE compares the date on a file against the date entered on the command line and then sets ERRORLEVEL accordingly.

File attribute utilities

Generally, you would run these utilities from the command line rather than from the keyboard. More utilities nowadays run from one program (like the DOS ATTRIB program), using switches to control specific attributes. However, B(DISK tediously uses one utility to set an attribute, another to remove it, and a third utility to test for an attribute.

To test for, add, and remove the *archive* attribute, you use B(AFARCH, B(ARCH, and B(UNARCH, respectively. For the *system* attribute, you use B(QFSYS, B(FSYS, and B(UNSYS respectively. For the *hidden* attribute, you use B(QFHID, B(HIDE, and B(UNHIDE respectively. For the *read-only* attribute, you use B(QFRO, B(RO, and B(UNRO respectively. B(QFNORM tests to see if any attributes other than archive are present and then sets ERRORLEVEL accordingly. B(QFSUB sets ERRORLEVEL to indicate if a file is a subdirectory.

Conclusion

Table 6-1 summarizes the many B(DISK programs. About half of these are utilities you might use often in a batch file, while the remaining programs are really keyboard utilities. However, the cumbersome program arrangement of the file attribute utilities might force you to write batch files handling this task normally performed from the command line.

Table 6-1   A summary of the B(DISK utility programs.

Program	Function
B(CADOFF.COM	Loads a small (.7K) memory-resident program that disables keyboard rebooting.
B(CBOFF.COM	Loads a small (.7K) memory-resident program that disables Ctrl-Break.
B(CBOOT.COM	Performs a cold reboot.
B(CFDATE.COM	Compares the date of two files and sets ERRORLEVEL accordingly.
B(CFTIME.COM	Compares the date and time of two files and sets ERRORLEVEL accordingly.
B(DATE.COM	Echoes the current date without requiring a return after it like the DATE command and sets ERRORLEVEL to the day of the week where Sunday=0, Monday=1, and so on.
B(DELAY.COM	Pauses the batch file for a specified time.
B(LPTSWP.COM	Swaps LPT1 and LPT2.

Table 6-1   Continued.

Program	Function
B(PAUSE.COM	Pauses the batch file for a specified time, but allows the user to press any key to resume earlier.
B(PRTSC.COM	Issues a Shift-PrtSc command from within a batch file.
B(QDATE.COM	Compares the current date with a specified date and sets ERROR-LEVEL accordingly.
B(QFARCH.COM	Checks to see if a file has an archive attribute and sets ERRORLEVEL accordingly.
B(QFDATE.COM	Compares the date of a file to one specified on the command-line and sets ERRORLEVEL accordingly.
B(QFNORM.COM	Checks to see if a file has normal attributes and sets ERRORLEVEL accordingly.
B(QFRO.COM	Checks to see if a file is read-only and sets ERRORLEVEL accordingly.
B(QFSUB.COM	Checks to see if a file is a subdirectory and sets ERRORLEVEL accordingly.
B(QFSYS.COM	Checks to see if a file has a system attribute and sets ERRORLEVEL accordingly.
B(QINKEY.COM	Prompts the user for any character and sets ERRORLEVEL to the ASCII value of the character.
B(QLPT.COM	Checks to see if the printer is ready and sets ERRORLEVEL accordingly.
B(QTIME.COM	Compares the current time with a specified time and sets ERROR-LEVEL accordingly.
B(QY1N0.COM	Prompts the user to press y or n and sets ERRORLEVEL to one for y and zero for n.
B(TIME.COM	Echoes the current time without requiring a return after it like the TIME command and sets ERRORLEVEL to the hour.
B(UNTIL.COM	Pauses the batch file until a specified time is reached.
B(WAIT.COM	Pauses the batch file until a specified time is reached, but allows the user to press any key to resume earlier.
B(WBOOT.COM	Performs a warm reboot.

The documentation for B(DISK fails to mention if the programs are public domain, shareware, or commercial programs. In fact, the documentation fails to include a copyright notice, although internally the programs contain one. For that reason, you might want to ignore B(DISK to avoid violating any copyrights.

Batchman

Name:	Batchman
Version:	1.0
Price:	Free
Category:	Copyrighted

Summary: Batchman is an incredibly powerful collection of 48 batch utilities in one tiny program.

Author: Michael Mefford

Availability: All *PC Magazine* files are available from their area on CompuServe. See any issue of *PC Magazine* for details.

Batchman is a collection of a number of useful batch commands in one program. Having all commands in one program keeps Batchman small because each command otherwise would need one cluster of disk space. To run a command, you enter

    BATCHMAN command [options]

Commands

The commands available in Batchman are as follows:

ANSI tests to see if ANSI.SYS is loaded, storing a 0 in ERRORLEVEL if it is and a 1 in ERRORLEVEL if it's not.

BEEP sounds the bell, of which you can control the frequency and duration. You enter the frequency in hertz and the duration in $1/18$ of a second.

BREAK tests the status of break, returning a 0 in ERRORLEVEL if break is off and a 1 if break is on.

CANCOPY determines if the drive you specify has enough room for the file specification you enter and then returns the results in an ERRORLEVEL. Thus, if not enough room exists, the batch file can tell the user to swap disks before continuing.

CAPSLOCK toggles the setting of the CapsLocks key if no option is specified and sets Capslock to the designated value if a setting is specified.

CECHO displays text like the ECHO command in DOS, except you can avoid a carriage return at the end of a line as well as change the color of the text string. The carriage return is avoided by your specifying the optional C, while the color can be changed by your specifying a new color using the same scheme used with CLS. Combining these two options means you can print part of a string in one color and the remaining part in another.

CLS clears the screen. When used without the optional colors, Batchman clears the screen using the color scheme it finds at the current cursor position. Unlike CLS, it properly clears the screen even if it's for an EGA screen in 43-line mode or a VGA screen in 43- or 50-line mode.

You can also specify the colors on the command line to have Batchman change the default colors. You enter a color, select the number of the foreground and background color, and then compute a single number with (foreground + (background * 16)). Unfortunately, Batchman doesn't accept simple names like "red" or "blue."

Some of the available colors are

    1 = blue   5 = purple
    2 = green   6 = orange
    3 = light blue 7 = white
    4 = red   8 = gray

On my superVGA display, Batchman would set the background color correctly but wouldn't change the foreground color.

COLDBOOT performs a cold reboot of the computer.

COLS returns the number of columns DOS is currently configured for as an ERRORLEVEL value.

COMPARE performs a case-insensitive comparison between the two strings you specify and returns the results as an ERRORLEVEL value.

CPU returns the CPU type as an ERRORLEVEL where

1=8086/8088
2=80186
3=80286
4=80386.

CURSORTYPE m n changes the shape of the cursor, where **m** is the beginning scan line and **n** is the ending scan line. Entering CURSORTYPE by itself resets the cursor shape. It returns an ERRORLEVEL of 0 if it's successful and a 1 if it's unsuccessful.

DAY returns the day of the month as an ERRORLEVEL value.

DIREXIST checks to see if the specified subdirectory exists and then sets ERRORLEVEL accordingly.

DISPLAY returns the type of display as an ERRORLEVEL value.

DOSVER returns the DOS version in ERRORLEVEL. However, the format used by DOSVER isn't very useful. It returns an ERRORLEVEL value of 32 times the major version plus the minor version. Thus, DOS 3.1 returns 32*3+1 or 97.

DRIVEEXIST tests to see if the specified drive exists and then sets ERRORLEVEL accordingly. It only checks to see if the drive exists, disregarding whether or not the drive is ready to receive data.

E43V50 sets an EGA display to 43-line mode and a VGA display to 50-line mode. Batchman doesn't have a command to reset either to 24-line mode.

EXPMEN n r reports of expanded memory. If you specify an amount of expanded memory (the **n**), MAINMEN returns an ERRORLEVEL of 0 if you have that much expanded memory, a 1 otherwise. If you specify the **r**, it reports on the amount of expanded memory. Under DOS 5.0, this option always reports 0 memory.

EXTMEN n r reports on extended memory. If you specify an amount of extended memory (the **n**), MAINMEM returns an ERRORLEVEL of 0 if you have that much extended memory, a 1 otherwise. If you specify the **r**, it reports on the amount of extended memory. Under DOS 5.0, this option always reports 0 memory.

GETKEY prompts the user for information. If you don't specify a string, GETKEY returns the ASCII value of the keystroke as an ERRORLEVEL. If you specify a string, it returns the first keystroke in the string as a 1, the second as a 2, and so on. When a string is specified, the testing is case-insensitive. According to the documentation, you can specify function keys after the string as F1, F2, and so on. However, this didn't work, and GETKEY wouldn't recognize the function keys as valid keystrokes.

HOUR returns the hour as an ERRORLEVEL value.

ISVOL tests to see if the volume label of a disk matches the one specified on the command line and then sets the ERRORLEVEL accordingly. The test is case-insensitive, but ISVOL can't test for volume labels with spaces in them (which can't be created by DOS anyway, although programs like VOLABEL in the Norton Utilities can make them).

MAINMEM n r reports on main memory. If you specify an amount of memory (the **n**), MAINMEM returns an ERRORLEVEL of 0 if you have that much memory, a 1 otherwise. If you specify the **r**, it reports on the amount of memory.

MINUTE returns the minute as an ERRORLEVEL value.

MONTH returns the month as an ERRORLEVEL value where January=1, February=2, and so on.

NUMLOCK toggles the setting of the NumLock key. If a specific setting is specified, NumLock is set to that value.

PRTSC issues a print screen.

PUSHPATH stores the current drive and subdirectory in a 408-byte memory area. The POPPATH command returns to that drive and subdirectory. Multiple PUSHPATH commands can be nested as long as you don't exceed the 408-byte memory space. It returns an ERRORLEVEL of 0 if successful, a 1 otherwise.

QFORMAT redoes the formatting on a floppy disk. In the process, it erases all files and removes any subdirectories. The procedure rewrites to the file allocation table [FAT] and doesn't overwrite the actual files, so an unerasing program (such as UnErase in the Norton Utilities) can still recover the data. QFORMAT returns an ERRORLEVEL of 0 if successful, a 1 otherwise.

RENDIR changes the name of the old subdirectory to the new name.

ROWS returns the number of rows DOS is currently configured for as an ERRORLEVEL value.

SCROLLOCK toggles the setting of the ScrollLock key. If a specific setting is specified, ScrollLock is set to that value.

SECOND returns the second as an ERRORLEVEL value.

SETCURSOR moves the cursor to the location specified after the keyword. You even can locate the cursor off the screen, effectively hiding it. Still, you must be careful with this because a mistake can make text on the screen invisible. When I tried locating the cursor in column 0 by mistake, my computer locked up.

SETLOOP n reserves a small amount of memory and stores the number **n** in that space. Each time you issue the DECLOOP command, that counter is decreased by 1. In addition, DECLOOP sets the ERRORLEVEL value to the counter value so you can test on ERRORLEVEL to see if it's time to exit the batch file. Both the area for the counter and ERRORLEVEL are 1 byte large, so the counter is limited to 255 or smaller.

SHIFT returns a 1 in ERRORLEVEL if the specified toggle key is pressed, a 0 otherwise.

TYPEMATIC changes the keyboard typematic built into most AT and better keyboards. You can change the repeat rate and the delay before the keyboard begins repeating, or you can reset everything to normal.

VIDEOMODE returns the video mode as an ERRORLEVEL value.

WAITFOR pauses the batch file for the specified number of seconds. If you press any key, it aborts waiting and continues with the batch file. It returns an ERRORLEVEL of 0 if successful, a 1 otherwise.

WAITTIL pauses the batch file until the specified time. If you press any key, it aborts waiting and continues with the batch file. It returns an ERRORLEVEL of 0 if successful, a 1 otherwise.

WARMBOOT performs a warm reboot of the computer.

WEEKDAY returns the weekday as an ERRORLEVEL value where Sunday=0, Monday=1, and so on.

WINDOW draws a window on the screen using ASCII characters. While drawing the window, it erases all the text inside the window using the ASCII space character but ignores the text outside the window. You could then use the Batchman cursor positioning command to write text inside the window. Also, you optionally can set the color or change the type of border used.

YEAR returns the year as an ERRORLEVEL value. Because ERRORLEVEL values can't exceed 255, it returns 1980=1, 1981=2, and so on.

Conclusion

Table 6-2 summarizes the Batchman keywords, while Table 6-3 presents SHOWBMAN .BAT, a batch file illustrating many of the Batchman commands.

Batchman is clearly one of the most powerful and useful batch file utilities currently available. Although suffering from a few bugs, it's overall an excellent package.

Table 6-2   A summary of Batchman keywords.

Keyword	Syntax Usage
ANSI	ANSI Sets ERRORLEVEL to zero if ANSI.SYS is not loaded and to one if it is loaded.
BEEP	BEEP [frequency, duration] Sounds the speaker while letting the user control the frequency and duration.
BREAK	BREAK Sets the ERRORLEVEL to indicate if break is on or off.
CANCOPY	CANCOPY files drive Measures the space required by the files and the space available on the drive to determine if there is enough space to perform the copy. Returns the results as an ERRORLEVEL value.

Keyword	Syntax Usage
CAPSLOCK	CAPSLOCK [on | off] Either toggles the status of Capslock or turns it on or off.
CECHO	CECHO [C] [color] String Displays text on the screen much like ECHO. Optionally changes the color of the text and optionally writes the string to the display without a carriage return at the end.
CLS	CLS [color] Clears the screen and optionally resets the foreground and background colors to those specified by the user.
COLDBOOT	COLDBOOT Performs a cold reboot of the computer.
COLS	COLS Returns the number of columns DOS can display in the current video mode as an ERRORLEVEL value.
COMPARE	COMPARE string1 string2 Performs a case-insensitive string comparison and places the results in the ERRORLEVEL.
CPU	CPU Returns the type of CPU as an ERRORLEVEL value.
CURSORTYPE	CURSORTYPE [m,n] Changes the size of the cursor.
DAY	DAY Returns the day of the month as an ERRORLEVEL value.
DIREXIST	DIREXIST [drive:] subdirectory Tests to see if the specified subdirectory exists and sets ERROR-LEVEL accordingly.
DISPLAY	DISPLAY Returns the type of display as an ERRORLEVEL value.
DOSVER	DOSVER Returns the DOS version as an ERRORLEVEL value, although in a format that is difficult to use. The ERRORLEVEL value is the major DOS version (1.x, 2,x, and so on) times 32 plus the minor version number.
DRIVEEXIST	DRIVEEXIST drive Tests to see if the drive exists and sets ERRORLEVEL accordingly.
E43V50	E43V50 Sets an EGA display to 43-line mode and a VGA display to 50-line mode.
EXPMEM	EXPMEM n | r If an amount of expanded memory is entered, it returns an ERRORLEVEL of one if there is that amount of expanded memory in the system, a zero otherwise. If an r is specified, it reports on the expanded amount of memory.
EXTMEN	EXTMEN n | r If an amount of extended memory is entered, it returns an ERRORLEVEL of one if there is that amount of extended memory in

Table 6-2 Continued.

Keyword	Syntax Usage
	the system, a zero otherwise. If an r is specified, it reports on the amount of extended memory.
GETKEY	GETKEY ["string"] Returns the value of the key pressed in ERRORLEVEL. If a string is specified, it returns the first keystroke as an ERRORLEVEL of one, the second as two, and so on. If no string is specified, it returns the ASCII value.
HOUR	HOUR Returns the hour as an ERRORLEVEL.
ISVOL	ISVOL [drive:] volume Tests to see if the specified volume matches the one on the disk and sets ERRORLEVEL accordingly.
MAINMEM	MAINMEM n | r If an amount of memory is entered, it returns an ERRORLEVEL of one if there is that amount of memory in the system, a zero otherwise. If an r is specified, it reports on the amount of memory.
MINUTE	MINUTE Returns the minute as an ERRORLEVEL value.
MONTH	MONTH Returns the month as an ERRORLEVEL value where January=1, February=2, and so on.
NUMLOCK	NUMLOCK [on | off] Either toggles the numlock status or sets it directly to on or off.
PRTSC	PRTSC Issues a Print-Screen command.
PUSHPATH POPPATH	PUSHPATH POPPATH PUSHPATH stores the current drive and subdirectory into a memory-resident storage area. POPPATH returns to that drive and subdirectory. The total storage area is 408-bytes and sets of these commands can be imbedded.
QFORMAT	QFORMAT drive Completely erases the files and subdirectories from a floppy disk very quickly. Will not work on a hard disk.
RENDIR	RENDIR old new Changes the name of a subdirectory.
ROMDATE	ROMDATE Displays the ROM date.
ROWS	ROWS Returns the number of rows DOS can display in the current video mode as an ERRORLEVEL value.
SCROLLOCK	SCROLLOCK [on | off] Either toggles the status of Scrollock, or turns it on or off.
SETCURSOR	SETCURSOR row, column Locates the cursor at a specific position on the screen.

Keyword	Syntax Usage
SETLOOP DECLOOP	SETLOOP [n] DECLOOP SETLOOP establishes a counter in memory. DECLOOP reduces the value of that counter by one and transfers the counter into ERRORLEVEL so the batch file can test on it.
SHIFT	SHIFT ALT | CTRL Returns a one in ERRORLEVEL if the Alt or Ctrl key is pressed, a zero otherwise.
TYPEMATIC	TYPEMATIC [repeat rate, initial delay | default] Changes the keyboard typematic rate or reset it to normal.
VIDEOMODE	VIDEOMODE Returns the video mode as an ERRORLEVEL value.
WAITFOR	WAITFOR [mm:]ss Pauses the batch file for a specified amount of time.
WAITTIL	WAITTIL hh:mm[.ss] Halts execution of the batch file until the specified time.
WARMBOOT	WARMBOOT Performs a warm reboot of the computer.
WEEKDAY	WEEKDAY Returns the day of the week as an ERRORLEVEL where Sunday=0, Monday=1, and so on.
WINDOW	WINDOW row, column, width, height [color, border] Draws a box on the screen using the coordinates specified after the command. Can also set the color using the same method as the COLOR command and can specify either a single or double border.
YEAR	YEAR Returns the year as an ERRORLEVEL. Because ERRORLEVEL values are limited to one number, it returns 1980=1, 1981=2, and so on.

Table 6-3   SHOWBMAN.BAT illustrates many of the Batchman commands.

Batch File Line	Explanation
`@ECHO OFF`	Turns command-echoing off.
`REM SHOWBMAN.BAT`	Remark giving the name of the batch file.
`REM Illustrate Batchman Program`	Documentation remark.
`BATCHMAN CLS 33`	Clears the screen and reset the color.
`BATCHMAN CECHO C 19 This Batch File` `BATCHMAN CECHO C 35 Illustrates The` `BATCHMAN CECHO C 51 PC Magazine Program` `BATCHMAN CECHO    67 Called Batchman`	Writes a single line to the screen in four different colors.
`BATCHMAN CECHO The Next Message Will` `BATCHMAN CECHO Show Five Times` `BATCHMAN CECHO Press Any Key To Start` `PAUSE > NUL`	Tells the user what will happen next.

Table 6-3 Continued.

Batch File Line	Explanation
BATCHMAN SETLOOP 5 :LoopTop BATCHMAN CECHO Repeated Message BATCHMAN DECLOOP IF ERRORLEVEL 1 GOTO LOOPTOP	Loops through and displays the same message five times.
CLS BATCHMAN CECHO C The Current Subdirectory Is: CD BATCHMAN PUSHPATH CD\ BATCHMAN CECHO C Now The Subdirectory Is: CD BATCHMAN POPPATH BATCHMAN CECHO C Location Reset To: CD PAUSE	Stores the current subdirectory, displays that subdirectory, changes to another subdirectory, displays that subdirectory, and then changes back to the original subdirectory.
CLS BATCHMAN ANSI IF ERRORLEVEL 1 ECHO ANSI NOT LOADED IF ERRORLEVEL 1 GOTO SKIPANSI ECHO ANSI LOADED!	Determines if ANSI.SYS is loaded and tells the user.
BATCHMAN BEEP 392,3;523,3;659,3;784,3; 10,3;659,3;784,12 PAUSE	Plays a tune on the speaker.
CLS ECHO Batch File Will Now Pause For 10-Seconds BATCHMAN WAITFOR 10	Pauses the batch file for 10-seconds.
ECHO Cursor Will Now Change BATCHMAN CURSORTYPE 0,15 ECHO Notice New Cursor PAUSE ECHO Resetting Cursor BATCHMAN CURSORTYPE	Displays two different cursor types.
BATCHMAN BREAK IF ERRORLEVEL 1 ECHO Break Is On IF ERRORLEVEL 0 IF NOT ERRORLEVEL 1 ECHO Break Off PAUSE	Displays the status of break.
CLS BATCHMAN DRIVEEXIST A: IF ERRORLEVEL 1 ECHO A-Drive Exists continues B-I BATCHMAN DRIVEEXIST J: IF ERRORLEVEL 1 ECHO J-Drive Exists	Displays which drives exist.
ECHO BATCHMAN DIREXIST C:\SYSLIB IF ERRORLEVEL 1 ECHO C:\SYSLIB Exists BATCHMAN DIREXIST C:\BAT IF ERRORLEVEL 1 ECHO C:\BAT Exists PAUSE	Checks to see if two subdirectories exist and informs the user. Note that the ECHO command is followed by an Alt-255 to display a blank line.
CLS	
BATCHMAN YEAR IF ERRORLEVEL 10 IF NOT ERRORLEVEL 11 ECHO It's 1990 IF ERRORLEVEL 11 IF NOT ERRORLEVEL 12 ECHO It's 1991 IF ERRORLEVEL 12 IF NOT ERRORLEVEL 13 ECHO It's 1992 IF ERRORLEVEL 13 IF NOT ERRORLEVEL 14 ECHO It's 1993 IF ERRORLEVEL 14 IF NOT ERRORLEVEL 15 ECHO It's 1994 IF ERRORLEVEL 15 IF NOT ERRORLEVEL 16 ECHO It's 1995 IF ERRORLEVEL 16 IF NOT ERRORLEVEL 17 ECHO It's 1996 IF ERRORLEVEL 17 IF NOT ERRORLEVEL 18 ECHO It's 1997 IF ERRORLEVEL 18 IF NOT ERRORLEVEL 19 ECHO It's 1998	Displays the year.

Batch File Line	Explanation

`BATCHMAN MONTH`
`IF ERRORLEVEL  1 IF NOT ERRORLEVEL  2 ECHO It's Jan.`
`IF ERRORLEVEL  2 IF NOT ERRORLEVEL  3 ECHO It's Feb.`
`IF ERRORLEVEL  3 IF NOT ERRORLEVEL  4 ECHO It's Mar.`
`IF ERRORLEVEL  4 IF NOT ERRORLEVEL  5 ECHO It's Apr.`
`IF ERRORLEVEL  5 IF NOT ERRORLEVEL  6 ECHO It Is May`
`IF ERRORLEVEL  6 IF NOT ERRORLEVEL  7 ECHO It's June`
`IF ERRORLEVEL  7 IF NOT ERRORLEVEL  8 ECHO It's July`
`IF ERRORLEVEL  8 IF NOT ERRORLEVEL  9 ECHO It's Aug.`
`IF ERRORLEVEL  9 IF NOT ERRORLEVEL 10 ECHO It's Sep.`
`IF ERRORLEVEL 10 IF NOT ERRORLEVEL 11 ECHO It's Oct.`
`IF ERRORLEVEL 11 IF NOT ERRORLEVEL 12 ECHO It's Nov.`
`IF ERRORLEVEL 12 IF NOT ERRORLEVEL 13 ECHO It's Dec.`
	Displays the month.

`BATCHMAN DAY`
`FOR %%J IN (1 2 3 4 5 6 7 8 9 10)`
`     DO IF ERRORLEVEL %%J SET DAY=%%J`
`FOR %%J IN (11 12 13 14 15 16 17)`
`     DO IF ERRORLEVEL %%J SET DAY=%%J`
`FOR %%J IN (18 19 20 21 22 23 24)`
`     DO IF ERRORLEVEL %%J SET DAY=%%J`
`FOR %%J IN (25 26 27 28 29 30 31)`
`     DO IF ERRORLEVEL %%J SET DAY=%%J`
`ECHO Today Is The %DAY%th`
	Displays the day.

`BATCHMAN HOUR`
`FOR %%J IN (1 2 3 4 5 6 7 8 9 10)`
`     DO IF ERRORLEVEL %%J SET HOUR=%%J`
`FOR %%J IN (11 12 13 14 15 16 17)`
`     DO IF ERRORLEVEL %%J SET HOUR=%%J`
`FOR %%J IN (18 19 20 21 22 23 24)`
`     DO IF ERRORLEVEL %%J SET HOUR=%%J`
`ECHO The Hour Is %HOUR%`
	Displays the hour.

`BATCHMAN MINUTE`
`FOR %%J IN (1 2 3 4 5 6 7 8 9 10)`
`     DO IF ERRORLEVEL %%J SET MINUTE=%%J`
`FOR %%J IN (11 12 13 14 15 16 17)`
`     DO IF ERRORLEVEL %%J SET MINUTE=%%J`
`FOR %%J IN (18 19 20 21 22 23 24)`
`     DO IF ERRORLEVEL %%J SET MINUTE=%%J`
`FOR %%J IN (25 26 27 28 29 30 31)`
`     DO IF ERRORLEVEL %%J SET MINUTE=%%J`
`FOR %%J IN (32 33 34 35 36 37 38)`
`     DO IF ERRORLEVEL %%J SET MINUTE=%%J`
`FOR %%J IN (39 40 41 42 43 44 45)`
`     DO IF ERRORLEVEL %%J SET MINUTE=%%J`
`FOR %%J IN (46 47 48 49 50 51 52)`
`     DO IF ERRORLEVEL %%J SET MINUTE=%%J`
`FOR %%J IN (53 54 55 56 57 58 59 60)`
`     DO IF ERRORLEVEL %%J SET MINUTE=%%J`
`ECHO The Minute Is %MINUTE%`
	Displays the minutes.

`BATCHMAN SECOND`
`FOR %%J IN (1 2 3 4 5 6 7 8 9 10)`
`     DO IF ERRORLEVEL %%J SET SECOND=%%J`
`FOR %%J IN (11 12 13 14 15 16 17)`
`     DO IF ERRORLEVEL %%J SET SECOND=%%J`
`FOR %%J IN (18 19 20 21 22 23 24)`
`     DO IF ERRORLEVEL %%J SET SECOND=%%J`
`FOR %%J IN (25 26 27 28 29 30 31)`
`     DO IF ERRORLEVEL %%J SET SECOND=%%J`
`FOR %%J IN (32 33 34 35 36 37 38)`
`     DO IF ERRORLEVEL %%J SET SECOND=%%J`
`FOR %%J IN (39 40 41 42 43 44 45)`
`     DO IF ERRORLEVEL %%J SET SECOND=%%J`
`FOR %%J IN (46 47 48 49 50 51 52)`
`     DO IF ERRORLEVEL %%J SET SECOND=%%J`
`FOR %%J IN (53 54 55 56 57 58 59 60)`
`     DO IF ERRORLEVEL %%J SET SECOND=%%J`
`ECHO The Second Is %SECOND%`
	Displays the seconds.

Table 6-3   Continued.

Batch File Line	Explanation

`PAUSE`
`SET DAY=`
`SET HOUR=`
`SET MINUTE=`
`SET SECOND=`
	Resets environmental variables.

`BATCHMAN ROWS`
`FOR %%J IN (1 2 3 4 5 6 7 8 9 10)`
`    DO IF ERRORLEVEL %%J SET ROWS=%%J`
 	
`These ERRORLEVEL tests continue for 11-45`
 	
`FOR %%J IN (46 47 48 49 50 51 52)`
`    DO IF ERRORLEVEL %%J SET ROWS=%%J`
`ECHO Your Display Can Show %ROWS% Rows`
	Displays the number of rows the computer can display given its current configuration.

`BATCHMAN COLS`
`FOR %%J IN (1 2 3 4 5 6 7 8 9 10)`
`    DO IF ERRORLEVEL %%J SET COLS=%%J`
 	
`These ERRORLEVEL tests continue 11-134`
 	
`FOR %%J IN (35 36 37 38 39 40 41)`
`    DO IF ERRORLEVEL 1%%J SET COLS=1%%J`
`ECHO You Display Can Show %COLS% Columns`
	Displays the number of columns. Notice that the loop values for the ERRORLEVEL tests above 100 are only used at two digits and the 1 is added as part of %%J.

`PAUSE`
`BATCHMAN CLS`
`ECHO Placing Display in Tiny Mode`
`BATCHMAN E43V50`
`BATCHMAN SETCURSOR 1,1`
`ECHO Here`
`BATCHMAN SETCURSOR 5,30`
`ECHO No Here!`
`BATCHMAN SETCURSOR 15,55`
`ECHO Now Over Here`
`BATCHMAN SETCURSOR 25,1`
`ECHO Back Over Here`
`BATCHMAN SETCURSOR 36,55`
`ECHO Now I'm Over Here`
`BATCHMAN SETCURSOR 43,25`
`ECHO I'm Finished Playing`
`BATCHMAN SETCURSOR 44,25`
`ECHO Press Any Key To Continue`
`BATCHMAN SETCURSOR 51,1`
`PAUSE>NUL`
`MODE 80`
`BATCHMAN CLS`
	Displays messages at various positions on the screen.

`SET STRING1=ABCDEF`
`SET STRING2=abcdef`
`ECHO String1 is %STRING1%`
`ECHO String2 is %STRING2%`
`BATCHMAN COMPARE %STRING1% %STRING2%`
`IF ERRORLEVEL 1 ECHO No Match`
`IF ERRORLEVEL 0 IF NOT ERRORLEVEL 1 ECHO Match`
	Performs a case-insensitive string comparison.

`BATCHMAN CANCOPY SHOWBMAN.BAT C:\`
`IF ERRORLEVEL 1 ECHO No Room For SHOWBMAN.BAT On C:\`
`IF ERRORLEVEL 0 IF NOT ERRORLEVEL 1`
`    ECHO SHOWBMAN.BAT Will Fit On C:\`
	Tests to see if there is room for SHOW-BMAN.BAT in the root directory of the C-drive.

`ECHO Turning Toggle Switches On`
`BATCHMAN NUMLOCK    ON`
`BATCHMAN CAPSLOCK   ON`
`BATCHMAN SCROLLOCK ON`
`PAUSE`
`ECHO Turning Them Back Off`
`BATCHMAN NUMLOCK    OFF`
`BATCHMAN CAPSLOCK   OFF`
`BATCHMAN SCROLLOCK OFF`
`ECHO`
	Toggles the Numlock, Capslock, and Scrollock keys. Note the ECHO command is followed by an Alt-255 to produce a blank line.

Batch File Line	Explanation

`ECHO Your Romdate Is:`
`BATCHMAN ROMDATE`
`PAUSE`
`CLS`
	Displays the ROM date.

`ECHO Press Any Letter Key`
`ECHO Z Exits This`
`:ZTOP`
`BATCHMAN GETKEY "ABCDEFGHIJKLMNOPQRSTUVWXYZ"`
`IF ERRORLEVEL  1 IF NOT ERRORLEVEL  2 ECHO A Pressed`
`IF ERRORLEVEL  2 IF NOT ERRORLEVEL  3 ECHO B Pressed`
`IF ERRORLEVEL  3 IF NOT ERRORLEVEL  4 ECHO C Pressed`
`IF ERRORLEVEL  4 IF NOT ERRORLEVEL  5 ECHO D Pressed`
`IF ERRORLEVEL  5 IF NOT ERRORLEVEL  6 ECHO E Pressed`
`IF ERRORLEVEL  6 IF NOT ERRORLEVEL  7 ECHO F Pressed`
`IF ERRORLEVEL  7 IF NOT ERRORLEVEL  8 ECHO G Pressed`
`IF ERRORLEVEL  8 IF NOT ERRORLEVEL  9 ECHO H Pressed`
`IF ERRORLEVEL  9 IF NOT ERRORLEVEL 10 ECHO I Pressed`
`IF ERRORLEVEL 10 IF NOT ERRORLEVEL 11 ECHO J Pressed`
`IF ERRORLEVEL 11 IF NOT ERRORLEVEL 12 ECHO K Pressed`
`IF ERRORLEVEL 12 IF NOT ERRORLEVEL 13 ECHO L Pressed`
`IF ERRORLEVEL 13 IF NOT ERRORLEVEL 14 ECHO M Pressed`
`IF ERRORLEVEL 14 IF NOT ERRORLEVEL 15 ECHO N Pressed`
`IF ERRORLEVEL 15 IF NOT ERRORLEVEL 16 ECHO O Pressed`
`IF ERRORLEVEL 16 IF NOT ERRORLEVEL 17 ECHO P Pressed`
`IF ERRORLEVEL 17 IF NOT ERRORLEVEL 18 ECHO Q Pressed`
`IF ERRORLEVEL 18 IF NOT ERRORLEVEL 19 ECHO R Pressed`
`IF ERRORLEVEL 19 IF NOT ERRORLEVEL 20 ECHO S Pressed`
`IF ERRORLEVEL 20 IF NOT ERRORLEVEL 21 ECHO T Pressed`
`IF ERRORLEVEL 21 IF NOT ERRORLEVEL 22 ECHO U Pressed`
`IF ERRORLEVEL 22 IF NOT ERRORLEVEL 23 ECHO V Pressed`
`IF ERRORLEVEL 23 IF NOT ERRORLEVEL 24 ECHO W Pressed`
`IF ERRORLEVEL 24 IF NOT ERRORLEVEL 25 ECHO X Pressed`
`IF ERRORLEVEL 25 IF NOT ERRORLEVEL 26 ECHO Y Pressed`
`IF ERRORLEVEL 26 IF NOT ERRORLEVEL 27 ECHO Z Pressed`
`IF NOT ERRORLEVEL 26 GOTO ZTOP`
`PAUSE`
`CLS`
	Continues displaying the letter the user enters until the user enters a Z.

`ECHO Memory Reports Will Now Appear`
`ECHO Press Any Key To Begin`
`PAUSE`
`BATCHMAN MAINMEM R`
`PAUSE`
`BATCHMAN EXPMEM R`
`PAUSE`
`BATCHMAN EXTMEM R`
`PAUSE`
`CLS`
	Displays memory reports.

`BATCHMAN DISPLAY`
`FOR %%J IN (1 2 3 4 5 6 7 8 9 10 11)`
`    DO IF ERRORLEVEL %%J SET DISPLAY=%%J`
`IF ERRORLEVEL 1 IF NOT ERRORLEVEL 2 ECHO MDA`
`IF ERRORLEVEL 2 IF NOT ERRORLEVEL 3 ECHO CGA`
`IF ERRORLEVEL 4 IF NOT ERRORLEVEL 5 ECHO EGA COLOR`
`IF ERRORLEVEL 5 IF NOT ERRORLEVEL 6 ECHO EGA MONO`
`IF ERRORLEVEL 6 IF NOT ERRORLEVEL 7 ECHO PGS`
`IF ERRORLEVEL 7 IF NOT ERRORLEVEL 8 ECHO VGA MONO`
`IF ERRORLEVEL 8 IF NOT ERRORLEVEL 9 ECHO VGA COLOR`
`IF ERRORLEVEL 11 IF NOT ERRORLEVEL 12 ECHO MCGA MONO`
`IF ERRORLEVEL 12 IF NOT ERRORLEVEL 23 ECHO MCGA COL.`
	Shows display mode.

`BATCHMAN CPU`
`IF ERRORLEVEL 1 IF NOT ERRORLEVEL 2 ECHO 8086/8088`
`IF ERRORLEVEL 2 IF NOT ERRORLEVEL 3 ECHO 80186`
`IF ERRORLEVEL 3 IF NOT ERRORLEVEL 4 ECHO 80286`
`IF ERRORLEVEL 4 IF NOT ERRORLEVEL 5 ECHO 80386/486`
	Displays CPU type.

`BATCHMAN E43V50`
`BATCHMAN WINDOW 1,1,75,10,23,+`
`BATCHMAN WINDOW 2,2,75,30,44,=`
`BATCHMAN WINDOW 25,25,10,10,2,+`
	Draws several windows on the screen.

Table 6-3   Continued.

Batch File Line	Explanation
BATCHMAN WINDOW 26,26,8,8,66,- BATCHMAN WAITFOR 20 BATCHMAN CLS MODE 80	

BATUTIL

Name:	BATUTIL
Version:	1.0
Price:	$39.00 (Includes STACKEY)
Category:	Shareware
Summary:	A powerful batch file utility that allows you to do almost anything required in a batch file.
Author:	The Support Group
	Lake Technology Park
	Post Office Box 130
	McHenry, Maryland 21541
	(800) 872-4768
Availability:	Available on many bulletin board systems.

BATUTIL is far more than just a batch utility—it's really a batch language disguised as a batch utility. To use BATUTIL, you enter a command like

    BATUTIL [HOUR]

on the command line. When you enclose the command in square [ ] brackets, BATUTIL returns results in ERRORLEVEL. If you enclose the command in curly {} brackets, BATUTIL also returns the results as an environmental variable. BATUTIL only needs the first two characters of the command and ignores capitalization, so [HOUR], [Ho], [HoUr] and [ho] all mean the same thing.

BATUTIL can accept multiple commands on a single line—subject to the DOS 127-character command line limit. Because DOS must load BATUTIL from disk for each line, this can significantly speed the execution of batch files with a number of BATUTIL commands. However, you must use care when combining commands. When you need the information a command is returning in ERRORLEVEL, that command must come last because DOS has room for only a single ERRORLEVEL value.

BATUTIL can discover as much information about the environment as any other package in the book and more than most, including information about files, the console, memory, the computer itself, time, and date information.

Files

BATUTIL can discover if a file exists in the current subdirectory or along the path, if a file has today's date, if a path exists, the number of files matching one or more file specifications and which of two files is older.

Console

BATUTIL can discover if a mouse is attached, if ANSI.SYS is loaded, the number of monitors, the type of keyboard, the type of monitor (monochrome or color), and the video mode.

Memory

BATUTIL can find the total and free amount of conventional memory (in 4K blocks), environmental space (in 16-byte blocks for total space or 1-byte blocks for free space), expanded (LIM) memory (in 64K blocks), and extended memory (in 16K blocks). Because BATUTIL can check on the amount of free environmental space, you can use that as error checking before using BATUTIL to store information in the environment.

System information

BATUTIL can find out the alternative operating systems (for example, Carousel, DesqView, and Omniview—although not Windows), the current drive (A=0, B=1, and so on), the total disk space (in 8K blocks for floppy disk or 256K blocks for hard disks) and the free disk space (in 8K blocks), the DOS version (times 10, so DOS 5.0 is reported as 50), the type of processor (80486 not supported), the type of math coprocessor, and the LIM driver status (0 if not installed or the version times 10 if found). It also can find the status of the printer, the number of serial ports, the number of game ports, and the number of floppy disk drives.

Time

BATUTIL has numerous commands that obtain time and date information:

```
date      (1-31)
hour      (0-23)
minute    (0-59)
month     (1-12)
weekday   (0=Sunday up to 6=Saturday)
year      (years since 1980, so 1991=11, etc.).
```

Working with the environment

BATUTIL also gives you very powerful tools for working with the environment:

ADDPATH lets you add a subdirectory to your PATH.

DELPATH lets you delete a subdirectory—even if it's in the middle.

EDITENV lets you edit other environmental variables interactively.

EDITPATH lets you edit your PATH.

ENVREP displays all the environmental variables (like the DOS SET command) plus their length.

KILLENV deletes everything in the environment except the COMSPEC variable that DOS needs to find COMMAND.COM.

LOADENV will restore a version of the environment from a file or merge it into the current environment.

SAVENV will save a copy of the environment to a file.

SET installs environmental variables just like the DOS SET command, though it can install more than one variable per line and does metastring translation. Also, it performs %variable% translations differently than DOS, so you can create variables (including PATH) longer than the 127-character limit of DOS.

One nice thing the SET command can do is display a list of available files. The user moves a cursor over the desired file and presses return to set the environmental file to that filename.

Screen display

If finding information about the system and environment was all BATUTIL did, it would still be a very powerful package. However, BATUTIL can do much more, especially excelling at screen handling.

BATUTIL supports all the prompt metastrings (like $p and $g) along with some of its own,

$E The date in English, e.g. April 20, 1991.
$M The month as a two-digit number.
$T The time in HHMM format.
$W The day of the week in English.

plus others.

BATUTIL is designed to use yellow text on a blue background for all its display actions, although commands can change this. Some commands used to control the display are as follows:

BECHO displays text on the screen in large letters.

CLS clears the screen using the BATUTIL colors.

ECHO displays text, much like the DOS ECHO command, but using the BATUTIL colors, extra metastring characters, and additional BATUTIL control.

MENU and **FMENU** are fantastic built-in functions for menu development. MENU works from the command line, while FMENU reads from the file; and both alone are worth the registration fee for BATUTIL.

PRETTY resembles the ECHO command but simplifies displaying text in multiple colors.

ROW and **COLumn** position the cursor.

Getting information

In addition to the MENU and FMENU commands discussed above, BATUTIL has other ways to get information from the user:

GETKEY gets a single keystroke from the user. You can control almost every aspect of the way GETKEY operates. It is flexible enough that it can be made to emulate almost any of the ERRORLEVEL-askers discussed in Chapter 1.

ASCIIREAD gets the ASCII value of a keystroke from the user.

PMATCH compares information provided by the user (perhaps on the command line) against a list of acceptable values and sets ERRORLEVEL to indicate which position (if any) in the list the match occurred.

QLOCK checks the status of the CapsLock, NumLock, or ScrollLock and sets ERRORLEVEL accordingly. If you have a batch file that runs a long time and must ask a yes/no question in the middle, you can use QLOCK to answer the question ahead of time.

SCANREAD gets the scan code of a keystroke from the user.

USERNAME gets the users name and branches accordingly. You can limit the number of attempts the user can make to enter a matching user name, enabling USERNAME to function as a crude password program. Of course, because you can look at the batch file from DOS and see the codes, this will be effective only against very inexperienced users.

As you can see, BATUTIL offers a massive number of features. Table 6-4 summarizes them, while SHOW-BU.BAT (Table 6-5) shows many of these commands in action.

**Table 6-4   BATUTIL can perform almost
any task you could demand from a batch file utility.**

Option	Function	Returns
#ALTMON	The monitor type of the second monitor if one is attached.	A number corresponding to the type of monitor.
#COMM	The number of serial ports.	The number of serial ports.
#DISK	The total amount of free space.	Total disk space in 8K blocks for floppy disks up to a maximum of 1,592K and 256K blocks for hard disks up to a maximum of 49.75 Meg.
#ENV	The total amount of environmental space.	Total environmental space in 4-byte blocks to a maximum of 3,184-bytes.
#FLOPPY	The number of floppy disk drives.	The number of floppy disk drives.
#GAME	The number of game ports.	The number of game ports.
#INTEL	The processor installed in the computer.	A zero for an 8088/8086 through a three for an 80386, or a twenty for a NEC V20/V30. The 80486 is returned as an 80386.
#KEYBOARD	If the bios supported an enhanced (101-key) keyboard.	A one if it is supported, a zero otherwise.
#LIM	The total amount of expanded or LIM memory.	Total expanded memory in 64K blocks to a maximum of 12,736K.
#MEM	The total amount of convention memory.	Total conventional memory in 4K blocks.
#PRN	The number of printers attached to the system.	The number of printers.
#RODENT	If a Microsoft-compatible mouse is attached.	A one if a mouse if found, a zero otherwise.

Table 6-4 Continued.

Option	Function	Returns
#Terminal	The number of terminals.	The number of terminals, up to two.
#VMODE	The video mode.	The video mode as reported by interrupt 10H.
#WHICHMON	The monitor type.	A number corresponding to the type of monitor.
#XTENDED	The total amount of extended memory.	Total extended memory in 4K blocks to a maximum of 3,184K.
@ANSI	If ANSI.SYS is attached.	A one if ANSI.SYS is attached, a zero otherwise.
@DISK	The amount of free disk space.	In 8K blocks for all disk drives, up to a maximum of 1,592K.
@ENV	The amount of free environmental space.	Free environmental space in 4-byte blocks to a maximum of 3,184-bytes.
@FLOPPY	If the floppy disk drive is the A- or B-drive.	A number that allows you to determine a floppy drive is the A- or B-drive.
@INTEL	The type of math coprocessor installed.	A zero for not math coprocessor, a one for an 8087 through a three for an 80387. It returns the other brands of math DesqView as though they were Intel brand.
@LIM	The amount of free expanded or LIM memory.	Free expanded memory in 64K blocks to a maximum of 12,736K.
@MEM	The amount of free conventional memory.	Free conventional memory in 4K blocks.
@PRN	The status of the printer.	A number representing the status of the printer.
@TERMINAL	The type of terminal.	A zero for a monochrome monitor or a one for a color monitor.
@XTENDED	The amount of free extended memory.	Free extended memory in 4K blocks to a maximum of 3,184K.
ADDPATH	Adds a directory to the PATH.	A new path.
ASCIIREAD	Get information from the user.	The ASCII value of the keystroke.
ATTRIBUTE	Change the default color attributes BATUTIL uses for display.	Nothing.
BECHO	Displays text on the screen in very big letters.	Nothing.
BIGCHAR	Allows you to change the character used to build the large letters used by BECHO.	Nothing.
BPRETTY	Similar to the BECHO command but it makes it easier to change colors in the middle of a string.	Nothing.

Option	Function	Returns
CAROUSEL	Checks to see if Software Carousel is installed.	A zero if Software Carousel is not installed or the partition number if it is installed.
CHECK	Checks to see if a specified path exists.	A zero if the path exists and a nine if it does not.
CLS	Clears the screen.	Nothing.
COL	Position the cursor.	Nothing.
CSENT	Causes BATUTIL to treat character inputs for GETKEY as case-sensitive.	Nothing.
CURSOR	Turn the cursor on and off.	Nothing.
DATE	The current date.	The day of the month (1-31).
DELPATH	Removes a directory from the PATH.	A new path.
DOS	The DOS version.	Takes the version (say 4.01), multiplies it times ten (4.01*10=40.1) and then rounds it down to a whole number (40).
DRIVE	The current drive.	A=0, B=1, and so on.
DVIEW	Checks to see if DesqView is installed.	A zero if DesqView is installed or the partition number if it is installed.
ECHO	Displays text on the screen.	Nothing.
EDITENV	Lets you edit your environmental variables interactively.	A new environment.
ENVREP	Displays the contents of the environment.	Nothing.
EOLINE	Clears the current line from the cursor position to the end of the line.	Nothing.
ERRORLEVEL	Sets the ERRORLEVEL value.	The assigned ERRORLEVEL value.
EXIST	If a file exists.	A number to indicate if the file exists in the current subdirectory or along the path and which subdirectory contains it.
FDIR	Searches for a file.	Stores the subdirectory containing the file in the environment.
FECHO	Displays text read from a file.	Nothing.
FKEY	Display a menu where function keys are a valid choice.	The ERRORLEVEL associated with the menu choice.
FMENU	Reads the menu from a file rather than the batch file. This gets around the 127-character limit on a command-line.	The ERRORLEVEL associated with the menu choice.

Table 6-4 Continued.

Option	Function	Returns
FRETTY	Displays text from a file with easy color formatting.	Nothing.
GETKEY	Gets a single keystroke from the user.	The ERRORLEVEL of the keystroke.
HALTIF	Halts the batch file immediately if a given condition exits.	Nothing.
HOUR	The current hour.	The hour of the day in military format (0-23).
KILLENV	Deletes the entire environment except the COMSPEC variable, which DOS needs to operate.	Nothing.
LENGTH	Computes the length of a string.	The length of the string.
LIM	The version of the LIM manager.	Zero if no LIM manager is installed or the current version of the manager times ten.
LOADENV	Restores a copy of the environment from a file or merges an environmental file into the current environment.	A new environment.
MAKEFILE	Compares the date on two files.	A value indicating which file is older.
MENU	Display a menu on the screen.	The ERRORLEVEL associated with the menu choice.
MHEADER	Displays a header for a menu.	Nothing.
MINUTE	The minute.	The minute (0-59).
MNATTRIBUTE	Change the default color attributes BATUTIL uses for display.	Nothing.
MONTH	The current month.	One for January, Two for February through twelve for December.
NBEEP	Suppresses beeping.	Nothing.
NFLUSH	Causes BATUTIL not to flush the buffer before running GETKEY.	Nothing.
NMOUSE	Do not use the mouse for menu selections.	Nothing.
NSOUND	Suppresses the SOUND command.	Nothing.
NUMBERFILES	Counts the number of files matching one or more file specifications.	The number of files.
OVIEW	Checks to see if Omniview is installed.	A zero if Omniview is installed or the partition number if it is installed.
PATHEDIT	Edit the path.	A new path.

Option	Function	Returns
PMATCH	Check information from the user.	Compares information from the user against a list of allowable options and sets ERRORLEVEL to indicate the matching position or the lack of a match.
POP	Causes a menu to "pop" onto the screen.	Nothing.
PRETTY	Similar to the ECHO command but it makes it easier to change colors in the middle of a string.	Nothing.
QLOCK	Checks the status of the Caps-Num- or Scroll-Locks key.	Sets ERRORLEVEL accordingly.
REM	A non-executing remark.	Nothing.
ROW	Position the cursor.	Nothing.
RUN	Runs a non-BATUTIL program.	The ERRORLEVEL value the program returns.
SAVENV	Stores a copy of the environment to a file.	Nothing.
SCANREAD	Get information from the user.	The scan code of the keystroke.
SET	Create and install environmental variables. It is far more flexible than the DOS SET command.	Nothing.
SHADOW	Causes a menu to be displayed with a shadow.	Nothing.
SOUND	Plays a note or song.	A note or one of ten built-in song fragments.
STDOUT	Normally, ECHO writes directly to the screen. This causes it to use DOS.	Nothing.
TODAYFILE	If a file has today's date.	A value to indicate if a given file has today's date and if it exists.
USERNAME	Get information from the user.	Returns the ERRORLEVEL corresponding with the position in a list for the parameter matching the user's input.
VISUAL	Changes the visual feedback GETKEY provides.	Nothing.
WEEKDAY	The current weekday.	Zero for Sunday, One for Monday through six for Saturday.
YEAR	The current year.	The current year less 1980 so 1991 return (1991-1980=11) an eleven.

Table 6-5   SHOW-BU.BAT illustrates many of the features of BATUTIL.

Batch File Line	Explanation
`@ECHO OFF`	Turn off command-echoing.

`REM NAME:     SHOW-BU.BAT`
`REM PURPOSE: Illustrate Some of`
`REM          the Feature of BatUtil`
`REM VERSION: 1.0`
`REM DATE:     April 18, 1991`
	Documentation remarks.

`GOTO START`	Skip over the following text.

`:MENUTEXT`
`Lotus 1-2-3 Release 2.3`
`1-2-3 Release 3.2`
`dBASE III+`
`Microsoft Word`
`mIcrosoft Windows`
`micrografx Designer`
`Crosstalk`
`Games`
`Exit`
	FMENU reads in this file and searches for the MENUTEXT label. It uses the text below that down to the "@" sign as menu options. The first upper-case letter is used as an optional way to select a menu option.

`@`
`Run the latest 2.x version of Lotus (spreadsheet)`
`Run the latest 3.x version of Lotus (spreadsheet)`
`Run the database program`
`Run the word processor`
`Run Windows 3.0`
`Run the graphic package`
`Run the communications package`
`Play games (watch out for the boss)`
`Exit the menu`
	FMENU uses the text below the "@" sign as help text. When the first menu option is highlighted, it displays the first line of the help text, the second line for the second menu text, and so on.

`:START`	This label marks the actual start of the batch file.
`CLS`	Clears the screen.
`BATUTIL [@ENV]`	Check and make sure there is enough free environmental space to run the commands.
`IF NOT ERRORLEVEL 30 GOTO ERROR`	If there are 30-bytes or less of free environmental space, exit the batch file.
`BATUTIL {HOUR}`	Find the hour and store it in the RC environmental variable.
`SET HOUR=%RC%`	Store the hour under another variable name. Since BAT-UTIL uses the RC name for everything, you have to store its contents under another name before rerunning BAT-UTIL.
`BATUTIL {MINUTE}` `SET MINUTE=%RC%`	Find the minute and store it under another name.
`ECHO Time: %HOUR%:%MINUTE%`	Display the time.
`SET HOUR=` `SET MINUTE=`	Reset the variables used earlier.
`BATUTIL {DATE}` `SET DATE=%RC%`	Find the day of the month and store it under another name.

Batch File Line	Explanation
`BATUTIL {MONTH}` `SET MONTH=%RC%`	Find the month and store it under another name.
`BATUTIL [YEAR]`	Find the year and set the ERRORLEVEL accordingly.

`IF ERRORLEVEL 11 SET YEAR=1991`
`IF ERRORLEVEL 12 SET YEAR=1992`
`IF ERRORLEVEL 13 SET YEAR=1993`
`IF ERRORLEVEL 14 SET YEAR=1995`
`IF ERRORLEVEL 15 SET YEAR=1996`
`IF ERRORLEVEL 16 SET YEAR=1997`
`IF ERRORLEVEL 17 SET YEAR=1998`
`IF ERRORLEVEL 18 SET YEAR=1999`
`IF ERRORLEVEL 19 SET YEAR=2000 or Beyond`
	Since the year is greater than 255, it can not be stored directly in the ERRORLEVEL so BATUTIL subtracts 1980 from it. This creates an environmental variable containing the actual year.

`ECHO Date: %DATE%/%MONTH%/%YEAR%`	Display the date.

`SET DATE=`
`SET MONTH=`
`SET YEAR=`
	Reset the environmental variables.

`BATUTIL {WEEKDAY}`	Find the weekday.

`IF %RC%==0 ECHO Day:  Sunday`
`IF %RC%==1 ECHO Day:  Monday`
`IF %RC%==2 ECHO Day:  Tuesday`
`IF %RC%==3 ECHO Day:  Wednesday`
`IF %RC%==4 ECHO Day:  Thursday`
`IF %RC%==5 ECHO Day:  Friday`
`IF %RC%==6 ECHO Day:  Saturday`
	Display the weekday. Notice that testing on the contents of RC is easier than testing the ERRORLEVEL.

`BATUTIL {DOS}` `ECHO You Are Running DOS %RC%/10`	Display the version of DOS.

`BATUTIL {DRIVE}`
`IF %RC%==0 ECHO You Are Running This From A-Drive`
`IF %RC%==1 ECHO You Are Running This From B-Drive`
`IF %RC%==2 ECHO You Are Running This From C-Drive`
`IF %RC%==3 ECHO You Are Running This From D-Drive`
`IF %RC%==4 ECHO You Are Running This From E-Drive`
	Display the drive.

`BATUTIL {#MEM}`
`ECHO %RC%*4K Total Conventional Memory`
`BATUTIL {@MEM}`
`ECHO %RC%*4K Free Convention Memory`
`ECHO (Remember, BatUtil Takes Memory To Run)`
	Display the amount of installed and free conventional memory.

`BATUTIL {#LIM}`
`ECHO %RC%*64K Total Expanded (LIM) Memory`
`BATUTIL {@LIM}`
`ECHO %RC%*64K Free Expanded Memory`
	Display the amount of installed and free expanded (LIM) memory.

`BATUTIL {#XTENDED}`
`ECHO %RC%*16K Total Extended Memory`
`BATUTIL {@XTENDED}`
`ECHO %RC%*16K Free Extended Memory`
`ECHO (BatUtil May Have Problems Measuring`
`ECHO Extended Memory. This Is A DOS Problem.)`
	Display the amount of installed and free extended memory along with a warning.

`BATUTIL {#ENV}`
`ECHO %RC%*16 Total Environmental Memory`
`IF NOT ERRORLEVEL 10 ECHO Expanded Environment!`
`BATUTIL {@ENV}`
`ECHO %RC%*1 Free Environmental Memory`
	Display the amount of installed and free environmental memory. Warn the user if it is too small.

`BATUTIL {#DISK}`
`ECHO %RC%*(256K for hard disk or 8K for`
`    floppy) Total Disk Space`
`BATUTIL {@DISK}`
`ECHO %RC%*8K Free Disk Space`
	Display the free and total disk space for the default drive.

`ECHO `	Display a blank line by echoing ALT-255.
`PAUSE`	Pause the batch file.
`CLS`	Clears the screen.

Table 6-5   Continued.

Batch File Line	Explanation
BATUTIL {#TERMINAL} ECHO You Have %RC% Monitor(s) Attached	Tell the user how many monitors are attached.

BATUTIL {#WHICHMON}
IF %RC%==24 ECHO You Have An Unknown Monitor
IF %RC%==23 ECHO You Have An Hercules
    Incolor Monitor
IF %RC%==22 ECHO You Have An Hercules
    Plus Monitor
IF %RC%==21 ECHO You Have An Hercules Monitor
IF %RC%==12 ECHO You Have An MCGA Color Monitor
IF %RC%==11 ECHO You Have An MCGA Monochrome
    Monitor
IF %RC%==8 ECHO You Have An VGA Color Monitor
IF %RC%==7 ECHO You Have An VGA Monochrome
    Monitor
IF %RC%==6 ECHO You Have An PGC Monitor
IF %RC%==5 ECHO You Have An EGA Monochrome
    Monitor
IF %RC%==4 ECHO You Have An EGA Color Monitor
IF %RC%==2 ECHO You Have An CGA Color Monitor
IF %RC%==1 ECHO You Have An MGA Monitor
	Tell the user what type of monitor is installed.

BATUTIL [@ANSI] IF ERRORLEVEL 1 ECHO ANSI.SYS Attached IF NOT ERRORLEVEL 1 ECHO ANSI.SYS Not Attached	Tell the user if ANSI.SYS is attached.
BATUTIL [#KEYBOARD] IF ERRORLEVEL 1 ECHO Enhanced Keyboard Supported IF NOT ERRORLEVEL 1 ECHO Enhanced Keyboard Not Supported	Tell the user if the bios supports an enhanced keyboard.
BATUTIL [#RODENT] IF ERRORLEVEL 1 ECHO MS-Compatible Mouse Found IF NOT ERRORLEVEL 1 ECHO No Mouse Found	Tell the user if a mouse is attached.
BATUTIL {#INTEL} IF %RC%==0 ECHO You Have An 8088/8086 System IF %RC%==1 ECHO You Have An 80186 System IF %RC%==2 ECHO You Have An 80286 System IF %RC%==3 ECHO You Have An 80386/80486 System	Tell the user what type of computer they have.
BATUTIL [@INTEL] IF ERRORLEVEL 1 ECHO You Have A Math Coprocessor IF NOT ERRORLEVEL 1 ECHO You Do Not Have A Math Coprocessor	Tell the user if a math coprocessor is present.
BATUTIL {#PRN} ECHO You Have %RC% Printer(s) Attached	Tell the user how many printers are attached.
BATUTIL [@PRN] IF NOT ERRORLEVEL 1 ECHO The Printer Is Ready IF ERRORLEVEL 1 ECHO The Printer Is Not Ready	Tell the user if the printer is ready.
BATUTIL {#COMM} ECHO You Have %RC% Serial Port(s)	Tell the user how many serial ports are installed.
BATUTIL {#GAME} ECHO You Have %RC% Game Port(s)	Tell the user how many game ports are installed.
BATUTIL {#FLOPPY} ECHO You Have %RC% Floppy Disk Drive(s)	Tell the user how many floppy disk drives there are.

BATUTIL {EXIST COMMAND.COM}
IF ERRORLEVEL 0 IF NOT ERRORLEVEL 1
    ECHO COMMAND.COM In Current Subdirectory
IF ERRORLEVEL 1 IF NOT ERRORLEVEL 2
    ECHO COMMAND.COM In %FDIR% Subdirectory
IF ERRORLEVEL 2 ECHO COMMAND.COM Not Found
	Tell the user where COMMAND.COM was found.

SET FDIR=	Reset a variable.
BATUTIL [CHECK C:\BAT] IF ERRORLEVEL 9 ECHO C:\BAT Does Not Exist IF NOT ERRORLEVEL 9 ECHO C:\BAT Exists	Tell the user if the C:\BAT subdirectory exists.

Batch File Line	Explanation
`BATUTIL {NUMBERFILES C:\*.*}` `ECHO Your C-Drive Root Directory Has %RC% Files`	Tell the user how many files are in the root directory of the C-drive.

`ECHO`
`ECHO This Concludes Demonstration Of BATUTIL's`
`ECHO Ability To Find Information About The System`
`ECHO`
`ECHO Press Any Key To See The BATUTIL Screens!`
`PAUSE>NUL`
	Tell the user what will happen next and pause the batch file. The seemingly blank ECHO statements really echo an ALT-255.

`BATUTIL {CLS}`	Clears the screen.

`BATUTIL {ECHO The Screen Looks$S}`
`BATUTIL {ECHO Different Already$_}`
`BATUTIL {ECHO This$S}`
`BATUTIL {ECHO Was Printed$S}`
`BATUTIL {ECHO Using 5$S}`
`BATUTIL {ECHO Lines In$S}`
`BATUTIL {ECHO BATUTIL$_}`
`BATUTIL {ECHO While The$_Next 4-Lines$_Were`
`      Printed$_Using One Command$_}`
`BATUTIL {ECHO $_Now, Lets See Some Special`
`      Batutil$S}`
`BATUTIL {ECHO Metacharacters.$_Each Of The`
`      Following$S}`
	Use BATUTIL to print information on the screen. The "$S" prints a space (necessary at the end of a line to include a space) and the "$_" prints a carriage return. ECHO does not automatically generate a return.

`BATUTIL {ECHO Lines Uses Two Commands,$_A`
`      Single$S}`
`BATUTIL {ECHO Metacharacter And A Formfeed:$_}`
`BATUTIL {ECHO $E$_}`
`BATUTIL {ECHO $W$_}`
`BATUTIL {ECHO $Y$_}`
`BATUTIL {ECHO $_$_Press Any Key To Continue}`
`PAUSE>NUL`
	Display more information and pause the batch file.

`BATUTIL {CLS}`	Clears the screen.

`BATUTIL {BECHO Tab Books}`
`BATUTIL {BIGCHAR 255} {BECHO And Ronny}`
`BATUTIL {BECHO Richardson}`
	Print three lines of text in very large characters.

`BATUTIL {ECHO Press Any Key To Continue}` `PAUSE>NUL`	Print one line in normal-size characters and pause the batch file.
`BATUTIL {CLS}`	Clears the screen.

`BATUTIL {ROW 10} {COL 10} {ECHO Cursor At 10,10}`
`BATUTIL {ROW 20} {COL 10} {ECHO Cursor At 20,10}`
`BATUTIL {ROW 10} {COL 60} {ECHO Cursor At 10,60}`
`BATUTIL {ROW 24} {COL 65} {ECHO Cursor At 24,65}`
	Display messages at different positions on the screen.

`BATUTIL {ROW 24} {COL 01} {PRETTY @4F Press Any}` `BATUTIL {PRETTY @4F Key To Continue}`	Tell the user to press any key using alternative colors.
`PAUSE>NUL`	Pause the batch file.
`BATUTIL {CLS}`	Clears the screen.
`BATUTIL {ECHO Now..Music!$_}` `BATUTIL {ECHO Press Control-C To Bypass A Song$_}`	Tell the user what will happen next.
`BATUTIL {ECHO Dance of the Clowns$_}{SOUND 11}`	Play a song fragment and tell the user the name. Ten song fragments are built into BAT-UTIL.

`BATUTIL {ECHO Habana From Carmen$_}{SOUND 12}`
`BATUTIL {ECHO Sailor's Hornpipe$_}{SOUND 13}`
`BATUTIL {ECHO MapleLeaf Rag$_}{SOUND 14}`
`BATUTIL {ECHO Pomp And Circumstance$_}{SOUND 15}`
`BATUTIL {ECHO Porky Pig Theme$_}{SOUND 16}`
`BATUTIL {ECHO Pop Goes The Weasel$ }{SOUND 17}`
	Play some more songs. Notice the combination of two BAT-UTIL commands on a single line. You can combine as

Table 6-5 Continued.

Batch File Line	Explanation

`BATUTIL {ECHO William Tell Overture`
`        Part I$_}{SOUND 18}`
`BATUTIL {ECHO They Say You Are A Music`
`        Lover If$S}`
`BATUTIL {ECHO You Do Not Think Of The Lone`
`Ranger$_}`
`BATUTIL {ECHO William Tell Overture`
`        Part II$_}{SOUND 19}`
`BATUTIL {ECHO Yellow Rose Of Texas$_}{SOUND 20}`
`BATUTIL {ECHO These Songs Are Built In`
`        And Played$S}`
`BATUTIL {ECHO With A Single Command!$_$_}`
`BATUTIL {ECHO Press Any Key To Continue$ }`
	many commands as you like as long as the entire line does not exceed 127-characters. That is a DOS limitation.

`PAUSE>NUL`	Pause the batch file.
`BATUTIL {CLS}`	Clears the screen.
`BATUTIL {POP}{MHEADER First Menu}` `        {MENU option$SA option$SB option$SC}`	Display a menu by popping it onto the screen. Notice the $S spaces in the middle of the options. Since BATUTIL uses spaces to separate options, this is the only way to include a space in an option.

`IF ERRORLEVEL 1 IF NOT ERRORLEVEL 2`
`    ECHO A Selected`
`IF ERRORLEVEL 2 IF NOT ERRORLEVEL 3`
`    ECHO B Selected`
`IF ERRORLEVEL 3 IF NOT ERRORLEVEL 4`
`    ECHO C Selected`
	Tell the user which option was selected.

`BATUTIL {ECHO $_Press Any Key To Continue}` `PAUSE>NUL`	Pause the batch file.
`:MENU2`	Label marking the top of a menu loop.
`BATUTIL {CLS}`	Clears the screen.

`BATUTIL {SHADOW}{MHEADER $S$S$S$SSecond`
`    Menu$S$S$S$S}{MENU Lotus$S1-2-3 Microsoft$S`
`    Word dBASE$SIII Games Quit}`
	Display a menu with five options.

`IF ERRORLEVEL 1 IF NOT ERRORLEVEL 2`
`    ECHO Lotus 1-2-3 Selected`
`IF ERRORLEVEL 2 IF NOT ERRORLEVEL 3`
`    ECHO Word Selected`
`IF ERRORLEVEL 3 IF NOT ERRORLEVEL 4`
`    ECHO dBASE III Selected`
`IF ERRORLEVEL 4 IF NOT ERRORLEVEL 5`
`    ECHO Games Selected`
`IF ERRORLEVEL 5 IF NOT ERRORLEVEL 6`
`    ECHO Quit Selected`
	Tell the user what was selected. If this were an operational menu, these commands would be replaced with commands to run the programs.

`PAUSE`	Pause the batch file so the user can read the message.
`IF NOT ERRORLEVEL 5 GOTO MENU2`	If the user did not select quit, redisplay the menu.
`:MENU3`	Label marking the top of a menu.
`BATUTIL {CLS}`	Clears the screen.
`BATUTIL {FKEY}{MHEADER Third Menu}{MENU Lotus$S` `    1-2-3 Microsoft$SWord dBASE$SIII Games Quit}`	Display a menu similar to the one above only allow the user to select menu options with a function key.

Batch File Line	Explanation
| ```
IF ERRORLEVEL 1 IF NOT ERRORLEVEL 2
    ECHO Lotus 1-2-3 Selected
IF ERRORLEVEL 2 IF NOT ERRORLEVEL 3
    ECHO Word Selected
IF ERRORLEVEL 3 IF NOT ERRORLEVEL 4
    ECHO dBASE III Selected
IF ERRORLEVEL 4 IF NOT ERRORLEVEL 5
    ECHO Games Selected
IF ERRORLEVEL 5 IF NOT ERRORLEVEL 6
    ECHO Quit Selected
``` | Tell the user what was selected. If this were an operational menu, these commands would be replaced with commands to run the programs. |
`PAUSE`	Pause the batch file.
`IF NOT ERRORLEVEL 5 GOTO MENU3`	If the user did not select quit, redisplay the menu.
`:MENU4`	Label marking the top of a menu.
`BATUTIL {CLS}`	Clears the screen.
| ```
BATUTIL {MHEADER File-Based Menu}{FMENU
    SHOW-BU.BAT MENUTEXT}
``` | Read a more complex menu from a file--this file in this example. This is the only way to construct complex menus since DOS limits a command-line to 127-characters. |
| ```
IF ERRORLEVEL 1 IF NOT ERRORLEVEL 2
    ECHO Lotus V 2.3 Selected
IF ERRORLEVEL 2 IF NOT ERRORLEVEL 3
    ECHO Lotus V 3.2 Selected
IF ERRORLEVEL 3 IF NOT ERRORLEVEL 4
    ECHO dBASE III Selected
IF ERRORLEVEL 4 IF NOT ERRORLEVEL 5
    ECHO Word Selected
IF ERRORLEVEL 5 IF NOT ERRORLEVEL 6
    ECHO Windows Selected
IF ERRORLEVEL 6 IF NOT ERRORLEVEL 7
    ECHO Designer Selected
IF ERRORLEVEL 7 IF NOT ERRORLEVEL 8
    ECHO Crosstalk Selected
IF ERRORLEVEL 8 IF NOT ERRORLEVEL 9
    ECHO Games Selected
IF ERRORLEVEL 9 IF NOT ERRORLEVEL 10
    ECHO Exit Selected
``` | Tell the user which menu options was selected. |
| ```
ECHO Did You Notice The Help At the Bottom?
ECHO Press Any Key To Continue
``` | Give the user additional information. |
`PAUSE>NUL`	Pause the batch file.
`IF NOT ERRORLEVEL 9 GOTO MENU4`	If the user did not elect to quit, redisplay the menu.
`GOTO END`	Exit the batch file.
`:ERROR`	Label marking the section that tells the user there is not enough environmental space free to run the examples.
`CLS`	Clears the screen.
| ```
ECHO You Do Not Have Enough Free
ECHO Environmental Space To Run
ECHO This Demonstration.
ECHO
ECHO Expand Your Environment
``` | Explain the problem. Notice the use of ECHO ALT-255 to display blank lines. |
```

Table 6-5 Continued.

Batch File Line	Explanation
ECHO (The Batch File Utilities Book ECHO Tells You How) --or-- ECHO Delete Some Existing ECHO Environmental Variables Then ECHO Rerun This Demonstration ECHO ECHO Press Any Key To Exit Demonstration	
PAUSE > NUL	Pause the batch file.
GOTO END	Exit the batch file.
:END	Label marking the end of the batch file.

Conclusion

BATUTIL almost didn't make it into this book! Twice I tried to use the package and twice the manual left me so confused that I quit in frustration. In fact, I submitted the original draft of the book without BATUTIL. Luckily, the publisher called me back and asked me to add a few more pages to the book. Thus, bright and early the next Saturday, I sat down with two computers (one to experiment on, and one to take notes on) and BATUTIL.

I felt as if the manual was written from one programmer to another; the text is hard to read, harder to follow, and harder yet to understand. As I worked through the manual, however, I began to see the underlying structure of BATUTIL and found that the reading and following of the manual became less difficult. As I started to work on examples, I began to get excited, finally realizing just how powerful this package is.

I finished with BATUTIL late Saturday night—just in time for *Doctor Who*. By that point, I had become convinced that, with the possible exception of a few compilers in Chapter 8, BATUTIL was the single most powerful batch utility in this book. Instead of trying to put together a batch toolkit with five or ten other utilities, you can just use BATUTIL.

I can't think of a single thing you might want to do with a batch file that you can't do with BATUTIL! Find a copy and spend a day or two with it; you'll come away with one powerful toolkit.

Check

Name: Check
Version: 11-18-87
Price: Free
Category: Copyrighted
Summary: A program that can determine a great deal of information about the computer hardware and pass that information back to the batch file. It can also prompt the user for a single character response to a question. All information is passed using the ERRORLEVEL.

Author: Jeff Prosise, from *PC Magazine*

Availability: All *PC Magazine* files are available from that area on CompuServe. See any issue of *PC Magazine* for details.

Check is one of the many useful batch file utilities published by *PC Magazine* over the years. Although its most useful function is to ask the user a question and wait for a response, Check does much more.

Keywords

To communicate with the user, Check uses 16 keywords that follow the Check command. The keywords are as follows:

8087 and 80287 both check to see if a math coprocessor is present and set the ERRORLEVEL accordingly. Check was written some time ago and doesn't have a test for an 80387.

DAY sets the ERRORLEVEL to the day of the month.

DISKSPACE sets the ERRORLEVEL to indicate the amount of free disk space. To overcome the limitations of ERRORLEVEL, it reports the space in 16K blocks.

FILEFOUND sets ERRORLEVEL to indicate if the specified file exists.

FILESIZE returns the size of a file in kilobytes. All files 255K and larger are reported as 255.

FILETEXT checks the specified file to see if it contains the specified text. The text must match exactly, including capitalization. The 127-character limitation on the DOS command line limits the amount of text you can search for. Also, the command doesn't accept wildcards, so you can only search one file at a time unless you set up a FOR loop.

KEYBOARD checks the keyboard buffer to see if keystrokes are pending and then sets the ERRORLEVEL accordingly. Because Check can't clear the keyboard buffer, this keyword is of limited use.

KEYPRESS is a fairly standard ERRORLEVEL-asker that returns the ASCII value of the entered keystroke. It returns a 0 for all extended codes.

MEMORY returns the total installed conventional memory as an ERRORLEVEL value. To overcome the limitations of ERRORLEVEL, it reports memory in 16K blocks.

MODEL determines the model type of the computer and then sets ERRORLEVEL accordingly.

MONTH returns the month as an ERRORLEVEL value. It returns a 1 for January, a 2 for February, and so on.

TIME sets ERRORLEVEL equal to the current hour.

VERSION returns the first number of the version number (for example, DOS 3.0, 3.1, 3.2, and 3.3 all return a 3). Even though Check is fairly old, this feature still works for DOS 5.0.

VIDEOCARD checks the display card and then sets the ERRORLEVEL to indicate the type of display. Check is fairly old, so the highest display it supports is EGA; VGA and above are all returned as EGA.

VIDEOMODE returns a number between 1 and 6 to indicate the video mode.

Conclusion

The Check keywords are summarized in Table 6-6, while Table 6-7 presents CHECK 1.BAT, a long batch file using every Check keyword. It illustrates the use of the proper syntax, as well as techniques for branching and decision making based on the results of running Check.

Check is less useful than Batchman because it offers far fewer features. Still, you may find it useful.

Table 6-6   Available keywords for the Check program.

KEYWORD	SYNTAX	FUNCTION
8087 80287	CHECK 8087 CHECK 80287	Returns a 0 if there is a math coprocessor, a 1 if there is not a math coprocessor.
DAY	CHECK DAY	Returns the day of the month.
DISKSPACE	CHECK DISKSPACE	Returns the amount of free disk space on the default disk drive. Because of the limits of ERRORLEVEL, DISKSPACE can not simply report the disk space. Instead, it reports the number of full 16K blocks. So 200K is reported as 12. (200/16 = 12.5).
FILEFOUND	CHECK FILEFOUND file	Returns a 0 if the file exists and a 1 if it does not exist.
FILESIZE	CHECK FILESIZE file (No wildcards)	Returns the size of a file in K's. The maximum ERRORLEVEL value is 255 so all files 255K or larger return a value of 255.
FILETEXT	CHECK FILETEXT file "text" (No wildcards)	Returns a 0 if the text is found, a 1 if the text is not found or if the program encounters an error, such as the file does not exist. The text must match exactly, including capitalization.
KEYBOARD	CHECK KEYBOARD	Returns a 1 if there are keystrokes in the keyboard buffers, 0 if not.
KEYPRESS	CHECK KEYPRESS	Returns the ASCII value of any key that is pressed. If a key is pressed that produces an extended code (e.g. function key or cursor key) a 0 is returned. Note: lower- and uppercase keys return different values.

KEYWORD	SYNTAX	FUNCTION
MEMORY	CHECK MEMORY	Reports the total memory (not the free memory) in 16K blocks. So 40 corresponds to 640K (40*16). Not all this memory will be available.
MODEL	CHECK MODEL	Returns the computer model number on IBM machines. It may not work on some clones. The codes are: Code Machine 255 PC 254 XT and Portable PC 253 PCjr 252 AT 249 PC Convertible
MONTH	CHECK MONTH	Returns the month, Jan. = 1, Feb. = 2, and so on.
TIME	CHECK TIME	Returns the current hour in 24 hour format. So 1 PM to 1:59 PM returns a code of 13.
VERSION	CHECK VERSION	Returns the current version of DOS. Only the first number is reported. So 3.3, 3.2, 3.1, and 3.0 all return a 3. This is required because ERROR-LEVEL only supports whole numbers. DOS versions prior to 2.0 are not supported.
VIDEOCARD	CHECK VIDEOCARD	Returns a code the types of video displays. The codes are as follows: Code Display Type 0 MDA 1 CGA 2 EGA
VIDEOMODE	CHECK VIDEOMODE	Returns current video mode (1-16).

Table 6-7   CHECK1.BAT illustrates some of the capabilities of Check.

Batch File Line	Explanation
`ECHO OFF`	Turns command echoing off.
`REM CHECK1.BAT`	Remark giving the name of the batch file.

`CHECK 8087`
`IF ERRORLEVEL 1 ECHO No math coprocessor exists`
`IF ERRORLEVEL 1 GOTO 80287`
`IF ERRORLEVEL 0 ECHO Math coprocessor exists`
`IF ERRORLEVEL 0 GOTO 80287`
	Checks for 8087 math coprocessor. If found, tells user. Otherwise, looks for an 80287 coprocessor.

Table 6-7   Continued.

Batch File Line	Explanation

`:80287`
`CHECK 80287`
`IF ERRORLEVEL 1 ECHO No math coprocessor exists`
`IF ERRORLEVEL 1 GOTO DAY`
`IF ERRORLEVEL 0 ECHO Math coprocessor exists`
`IF ERRORLEVEL 0 GOTO DAY`
	Checks for 80287 math coprocessor. If found, tells user. Otherwise, skips to next section.

`:DAY`
`CHECK DAY`
`IF ERRORLEVEL 31 ECHO 31th of month`
`IF ERRORLEVEL 31 GOTO DISKSPAC`
`IF ERRORLEVEL 30 ECHO 30th of month`
 	
`The batch file continues in a similar fashion for days 29-3`
 	
`IF ERRORLEVEL 2 ECHO 2th of month`
`IF ERRORLEVEL 2 GOTO DISKSPAC`
`IF ERRORLEVEL 1 ECHO 1th of month`
`IF ERRORLEVEL 1 GOTO DISKSPAC`
	Runs Check to set the ERRORLEVEL equal to the day of the month, and then performs a series of ERRORLEVEL tests to echo the day. Note that after echoing the day, it jumps to the next test.

`:DISKSPAC`
`CHECK DISKSPACE`
`IF ERRORLEVEL 255 ECHO More than 4080K free on disk`
`IF ERRORLEVEL 255 GOTO FILEFOUN`
`IF ERRORLEVEL 200 ECHO More than 3200K and less than`
`    4080K free on hard disk`
`IF ERRORLEVEL 200 GOTO FILEFOUN`
 	
`The batch file continues in a similar fashion for 2400K-160K.`
 	
`IF ERRORLEVEL 10 ECHO More than 160K and less than`
`    800K free on hard disk`
`IF ERRORLEVEL 10 GOTO FILEFOUN`
`ECHO Less than 160K free`
`GOTO FILEFOUN`
	Runs Check to set the ERRORLEVEL equal to the amount of free space on the hard disk. Then performs a series of ERROR-LEVEL tests to echo the amount of space on the disk.

`:FILEFOUN`
`CHECK FILEFOUND NO-FILE.TXT`
`IF ERRORLEVEL 1 ECHO NO-FILE.TXT missing`
`IF ERRORLEVEL 1 GOTO FILEFOU2`
`IF ERRORLEVEL 0 ECHO NO-FILE.TXT found`
`IF ERRORLEVEL 0 GOTO FILEFOU2`
 	
`The batch file repeats this test for the file CHECK1.BAT in order to show what happens when the file exists.`
	Runs Check to check for file NO-FILE.TXT existing and sets the ERRORLEVEL accordingly. Then, uses a series of ERRORLEVEL tests to display the results.

`:FILESIZE`
`CHECK FILESIZE CHECKERR.BAT`
`IF ERRORLEVEL 255 ECHO File was 255K or larger`
`IF ERRORLEVEL 255 GOTO FILETEXT`
`IF ERRORLEVEL 200 ECHO File was 200-254k`
`IF ERRORLEVEL 200 GOTO FILETEXT`
 	
`The batch file continues in a similar fashion for 199K-2`
 	
`IF ERRORLEVEL 1 ECHO File was 1K`
`IF ERRORLEVEL 1 GOTO FILETEXT`
`IF ERRORLEVEL 0 ECHO File was 0K or did not exist!`
`IF ERRORLEVEL 0 GOTO FILETEXT`
	Runs Check to find the size of a specific file and places it in the ERROR-LEVEL. Then uses a series of ERRORLEVEL tests to echo that value.

`:FILETEXT`
`CHECK FILETEXT CHECK1.BAT 'CHECK'`
`IF ERRORLEVEL 1 ECHO Text not found in CHECK1.BAT or`
`    error encountered`
`IF ERRORLEVEL 1 GOTO FILETXT2`
`IF ERRORLEVEL 0 ECHO Text found in CHECK1.BAT`
`IF ERRORLEVEL 0 GOTO FILETXT2`
	Runs Check to see if the text "CHECK" exists in the file CHECK1.BAT and stores the results in the ERRORLEVEL. Then

Batch File Line	Explanation
The batch file performs the same test on a second set of text as an illustration.	uses a series of ERROR-LEVEL tests to display the results.

`:KEYBOARD`
`CHECK KEYBOARD`
`IF ERRORLEVEL 1 ECHO Keystroke waiting`
`IF ERRORLEVEL 1 GOTO KEYPRESS`
`IF ERRORLEVEL 0 ECHO Keystroke not waiting`
`IF ERRORLEVEL 0 GOTO KEYPRESS`
	Tests for a keystroke waiting and places the results into ERROR-LEVEL. A series of ERRORLEVEL tests displays the results.

`:KEYPRESS`
`CHECK KEYPRESS`
`IF ERRORLEVEL 122 ECHO z Pressed`
`IF ERRORLEVEL 122 GOTO MEMORY`
`IF ERRORLEVEL 121 ECHO y Pressed`
`IF ERRORLEVEL 121 GOTO MEMORY`
 	
`The batch file continues in a similar fashion for the remaining letters along with all the capital letters.`
	Runs Check to see which key was pressed and places the value in ERRORLEVEL. A series of ERRORLEVEL tests displays the value.

`:MEMORY`
`CHECK MEMORY`
`IF ERRORLEVEL 40 ECHO At least 640K RAM available`
`IF ERRORLEVEL 40 GOTO MODEL`
`IF ERRORLEVEL 39 ECHO 624K available`
`IF ERRORLEVEL 39 GOTO MODEL`
 	
`The batch file continues in a similar fashion for 608K-496K`
 	
`IF ERRORLEVEL 30 ECHO 480K available`
`IF ERRORLEVEL 30 GOTO MODEL`
`ECHO Less than 480K available`
	Runs Check to measure the amount of RAM and place the value into ERRORLEVEL. A series of ERRORLEVEL tests displays the value.

`:MODEL`
`CHECK MODEL`
`IF ERRORLEVEL 255 ECHO PC`
`IF ERRORLEVEL 255 GOTO MONTH`
`IF ERRORLEVEL 254 ECHO XT or Portable PC`
`IF ERRORLEVEL 254 GOTO MONTH`
`IF ERRORLEVEL 253 ECHO PCjr`
`IF ERRORLEVEL 253 GOTO MONTH`
`IF ERRORLEVEL 252 ECHO AT`
`IF ERRORLEVEL 252 GOTO MONTH`
`IF ERRORLEVEL 250 ECHO Unknown machine`
`IF ERRORLEVEL 250 GOTO MONTH`
`IF ERRORLEVEL 249 ECHO PC Convertible`
`IF ERRORLEVEL 249 GOTO MONTH`
`ECHO Unknown machine`
	Runs Check to find out the type of computer and place the value into ERROR-LEVEL. A series of ERRORLEVEL tests displays that value.

`:MONTH`
`CHECK MONTH`
`IF ERRORLEVEL 12 ECHO December`
`IF ERRORLEVEL 12 GOTO TIME`
`IF ERRORLEVEL 11 ECHO November`
`IF ERRORLEVEL 11 GOTO TIME`
 	
`The batch file continues in a similar fashion for October-February.`
 	
`IF ERRORLEVEL 1 ECHO January`
`IF ERRORLEVEL 1 GOTO TIME`
	Runs Check to find the month of the year and place it into the ERROR-LEVEL. A series of ERRORLEVEL tests displays the value.

Table 6-7 Continued.

Batch File Line	Explanation
| ```
:TIME
CHECK TIME
IF ERRORLEVEL 23 ECHO After 11PM
IF ERRORLEVEL 23 GOTO END
IF ERRORLEVEL 22 ECHO 10PM - 11PM
IF ERRORLEVEL 22 GOTO END

The batch file continues in a similar fashion for
10PM-3AM

IF ERRORLEVEL 1 ECHO 1AM - 2AM
IF ERRORLEVEL 1 GOTO END
IF ERRORLEVEL 0 ECHO Midnight - 1AM
IF ERRORLEVEL 0 GOTO END
``` | Runs Check to find the time and place it into the ERRORLEVEL. A series of ERRORLEVEL tests displays the value. |
| ```
:END
``` | Label marking the end of the batch file. |

CLUTIL

Name:	CLUTIL
Version:	1.3
Price:	$18.00
Category:	Shareware
Summary:	A collection of generally file-handling utilities.
Author:	William S. Mezian
	105½ 20th Avenue Apartment 2
	Saint Petersburg Beach, Florida 33706
Availability:	Many bulletin board systems carry CLUTIL.

CLUTIL [short for Command Line UTILities] is a collection of utilities designed primarily for use on the command line. However, some of the utilities are useful in batch files.

Programs

The programs included in CLUTIL are as follows:

CALLKEY is an excellent ERRORLEVEL-asker program. Rather than storing its results in the ERRORLEVEL like other programs, it converts the user's response to uppercase and then stores the ASCII value in an environmental variable called CALLKEY. This simplifies equality testing, using a line like IF %CALLKEY% = = 68 rather than dealing with the greater-than-or-equal tests of ERRORLEVEL.

If you must get more than a single character response from the user, running CALLKEY with an S option lets the user enter a multicharacter response. CALLKEY converts that to uppercase and stores the entire response in the CALLKEY environmental variable.

CALLKEY works under DOS 4.x and earlier, but it fails under DOS 5.0 in both the single- and multi-character response mode.

CLSHELL is a small DOS shell. Unlike more advanced shells, it doesn't show the disk visually, and you don't operate on files by tagging them. Rather, CLSHELL simply prompts you one piece at a time for the information the command needs. For example, to delete files, it asks you for the drive, subdirectory, and file specification; more likely, anyone knowing this information would find it easier to enter the information on the command line.

CDIR is a replacement for the DOS DIR command. It shows files in a multi-column format and displays different types of files in different colors.

CDIR displays the number of files, the size of the files, and the amount of free space—just like DOS 5.0. However, CDIR doesn't display any subdirectories, making it difficult to use to navigate the hard disk. If you display a file specification that doesn't exist (like CDIR *.NOT), CDIR states that only one file containing 0 bytes exists. In addition, CDIR displays a few characters of ANSI.SYS escape-sequences on the screen.

COLOR is a small utility that sets screen color. To change the color, you enter COLOR Foreground Background Attribute at the command line. For example, COLOR white red B would set the colors to a bright white text on a red background.

COLOR doesn't immediately change the color of the entire screen. Rather, it just changes the color flag ANSI.SYS uses. To change the color of the entire screen, you must issue a CLS command after running COLOR. Because other CLUTIL programs change the color of the display using ANSI.SYS, they can overwrite the color settings of COLOR.

FREE reports the amount of available disk space and memory. It doesn't set the ERRORLEVEL.

MBAK is a quasi-backup program. It copies the specified files to the specified drive. Unlike most backup programs, however, it leaves the files intact on the target disk and can't split large files across multiple disks. Like MOVE, it doesn't copy files to the disk unless they are newer than the backups already on the disk. Because MBAK expects to check the disk before backing up, MBAK is really useful only for small backups fitting on a single disk.

MDEL is a safer replacement for the DOS DEL/ERASE commands. You enter MDEL file specification at the command line, and it lists the files one at a time. You press Del to delete the file, Enter to skip it, or Escape to exit the program.

MERGE combines two or more files into one large file. The format of the command is MERGE first second output, but either the first or second set of files can be specified using wildcards. MERGE is cumbersome to use only because you must specify two sets of files to merge even if the first set is specified using wildcards. You can't fool it by giving an invalid specification for the second set because it checks before running. If your output file exists, the program asks if you want to overwrite it. You can't choose to append to the file.

MOVE performs the same function as NCOPY except that it deletes the source file after copying. MOVE actually copies and then deletes the files. Much better moving programs are available that only change the subdirectory information associated with the file without copying the file. Using that approach, you don't need twice the disk space as you do with MOVE.

MOVE has a flaw dangerous enough that you should never use this program to move files. When MOVE first tries to copy the files to the new location, it behaves exactly like NCOPY; if the target file is newer than the source file, it doesn't copy the file. However, it does delete the source file; and, as a result, the older file is lost. Normally, that wouldn't be a problem; but it would be if the newer files had mistakes and you wanted to replace it with the older file. Before deleting a file not copied first, MOVE should always ask the user.

NCOPY is a replacement for the DOS COPY command. It surpasses COPY by not overwriting files unless the file being copied is newer than the file being overwritten.

While not overwriting newer files with older files is an excellent safety feature, N-COPY's implementation is poor. The program doesn't tell you it's not overwriting the file. In fact, it only tells you when it has started copying and when it has finished. Although it doesn't overwrite the files unless the source file is newer, those copying messages could persuade you that the file had been overwritten. Especially troublesome would be when you actually wanted to overwrite the files.

TDD displays the day of the week, date, and time at the top of the screen, useful in a batch file for adding this information to the top of a menu.

VIEW displays an ASCII file one screen at a time and is far less useful than other programs of this type in that you can't scroll backwards. Once you start viewing a file, you must scroll to the file's end one screen at a time before you can stop. Also, VIEW doesn't accept wildcards. If you must view files, LIST.COM from Vernon D. Buerg (also shareware) is a much better program.

Conclusion

All of the CLUTIL programs require the computer to have ANSI.SYS loaded, without which most won't run. Even when the programs do run without ANSI.SYS, they tend to clutter the screen with escape sequences intended for ANSI.SYS. Therefore, you shouldn't consider CLUTIL unless you routinely load ANSI.SYS.

Except for CALLKEY and COLOR, the programs in CLUTIL aren't all that useful. They either operate dangerously (like MOVE), or other far superior shareware programs are available (like LIST.COM as a replacement for VIEW). ANSI.SYS users, however, will find CALLKEY and COLOR to be very useful.

DDDBATCH

Name:	DDDBATCH
Version:	1.0
Price:	$10 single user
	$30 site license
Category:	Shareware
Summary:	A collection of 12 utilities to improve batch files.
Author:	J. Barrett
Availability:	Included on the disk bound in this book.

While many of the other utility sets in this chapter try to be everything to everyone, DDD-BATCH is far less ambitious. Rather, it simply offers twelve useful utility programs. Like SEBFU (discussed later), each of the DDDBATCH utilities is a separate program. However, because DDDBATCH offers fewer utilities, the separate programs are more manageable.

0-9 is an ERRORLEVEL-asking program that only accepts the numbers 0-9 as a response; it sets the ERRORLEVEL equal to the number the user enters. Thus, it's useful as a menu selection program where you want to force the user to pick between a limited number of options on a menu. However, it doesn't beep if the user enters an invalid response, and it can't display a prompt. Both of these limitations can be overcome using clear messages in the batch file before running the program.

BEEP is a small program that sounds the speaker.

CLW clears a small user-specified portion of the screen, which makes it useful for managing windows within a batch file.

DAY returns the day of the week as an ERRORLEVEL value, where Sunday is 1, Monday is 2, and so on.

DR_BOX draws a box on the screen at the user-specified coordinates. Combined with the CLW program for clearing away a portion of the screen and the PRTAT program for locating the cursor and printing, DR_BOX makes possible complex-looking windows on the screen within batch files.

FCLS1 is a fancy way of clearing the entire screen by splitting the display across the middle. The top half of the screen scrolls up, while the bottom half scrolls down.

FCLS2 is another fancy way of clearing the entire screen by splitting it across the middle. This time, the top and bottom halves converge towards the center.

IS_TODAY compares the date entered after the command with today's date and then sets the ERRORLEVEL to indicate if they are the same.

MODE_NO checks for fifteen different display modes and then sets ERRORLEVEL to indicate which is being used.

PRT_ON checks the printer port and then sets the ERRORLEVEL to indicate if the printer is ready to use.

PRTAT locates the cursor at any position on the screen and then optionally prints text. This is how the batch file would print text once a window is drawn with DR_BOX or a section of the screen has been cleared with CLW.

YES_NO is a simple ERRORLEVEL-asker that only accepts the y or n key. It sets ERRORLEVEL to 1 for the y key and to 2 for the n key. which makes asking questions like "Do you really want to delete all the files?" easier in a batch file.

Table 6-8 briefly summarizes the DDDBATCH programs, while Table 6-9 shows a sample batch file illustrating many of the DDDBATCH programs.

Table 6-8 A summary of DDDBATCH programs.

Program	Function
0-9	Accepts only keystrokes 0-9 and sets ERRORLEVEL accordingly.
BEEP	Sounds the speaker.
CLW	Clears a portion of the screen.
DAY	Sets ERRORLEVEL corresponding to the day of the week.
DR_BOX	Draws a box on the screen.
FCLS1	Fancy way to clear the screen.
FCLS2	Another fancy way to clear the screen.
IS_TODAY	Compares the date against the date entered after the command and sets ERRORLEVEL accordingly.
MODE_NO	Sets ERRORLEVEL according to the display mode.
PRT_ON	Checks the printer and sets ERRORLEVEL accordingly.
PRTAT	Locates the cursor at a specified location on the screen and optionally displays text.
YES_NO	Accepts a y- or n-key and sets ERRORLEVEL accordingly.

Table 6-9 DDDBATCH.BAT illustrates many of the DDDBATCH commands.

Batch File Line	Explanation
`ECHO OFF`	Turns command echoing off.
`REM DDDBATCH.BAT`	Remark giving the name of the batch file.
`FCLS2`	Clears the screen.
`DR_BOX 8 5 12 78 2`	Draws a box on the screen.
`PRTAT 10 30 Do You Have A Color Display? (Y/N)`	Locates the cursor and display a message.
`YES_NO`	Runs a program that only accepts a y- or n-key.
`SET FORE=` `SET BACK=`	Resets two variables.
`IF ERRORLEVEL 2 GOTO SKIPCOLR`	If the user responds that the system is not color, skips setting the color variables.
`SET FORE=15` `SET BACK=1`	Sets the background to blue and the foreground to bright white.
`:SKIPCOLR`	Label marking the place to jump to for a black and white system.
`CLW 1 1 24 80 %FORE% %BACK%`	Clears the screen and sets the color.
`PRTAT 1 1`	Places the cursor at the top of the screen.
`PAUSE`	Pauses the batch file.
`FCLS1`	Clears the screen.

`ECHO The Next Line Will Only Accept 0-9`
`ECHO However, You Might Want To Experiment`
`ECHO With Other Characters First`
	Tells the user what will happen next.

Batch File Line	Explanation
`0-9`	Runs a program that only accepts a keystroke of 0-9.

`IF ERRORLEVEL 0 IF NOT ERRORLEVEL  1`
`   ECHO 0-Pressed`
`IF ERRORLEVEL 1 IF NOT ERRORLEVEL  2`
`   ECHO 1-Pressed`
 	
`Continues like this for 3-8`
 	
`IF ERRORLEVEL 8 IF NOT ERRORLEVEL  9`
`   ECHO 8-Pressed`
`IF ERRORLEVEL 9 IF NOT ERRORLEVEL 10`
`   ECHO 9-Pressed`
	Tells the user which key was pressed.

`DAY`	Sets the ERRORLEVEL according to the day of the week.

`IF ERRORLEVEL 1 IF NOT ERRORLEVEL 2`
`   ECHO Sunday`
`IF ERRORLEVEL 2 IF NOT ERRORLEVEL 3`
`   ECHO Monday`
`IF ERRORLEVEL 3 IF NOT ERRORLEVEL 4`
`   ECHO Tuesday`
`IF ERRORLEVEL 4 IF NOT ERRORLEVEL 5`
`   ECHO Wednesday`
`IF ERRORLEVEL 5 IF NOT ERRORLEVEL 6`
`   ECHO Thursday`
`IF ERRORLEVEL 6 IF NOT ERRORLEVEL 7`
`   ECHO Friday`
`IF ERRORLEVEL 7 IF NOT ERRORLEVEL 8`
`   ECHO Saturday`
	Displays the day.

`IS_TODAY 09/26/1992`	Tests to see if today is September 26, 1992.

`IF ERRORLEVEL 1 ECHO Today Is My Birthday`
`IF ERRORLEVEL 0 IF NOT ERRORLEVEL 1`
`   ECHO Today Is Not My Birthday`
	Displays the results of the above test.

`MODE_NO`	Tests the display mode.

`IF ERRORLEVEL 16 IF NOT ERRORLEVEL 17`
`   ECHO 640 x 350 64 Color Graphics`
`IF ERRORLEVEL 15 IF NOT ERRORLEVEL 16`
`   ECHO 640 x 350 Black and White Graphics`
`IF ERRORLEVEL 14 IF NOT ERRORLEVEL 15`
`   ECHO 640 x 200 16 Color Graphics`
`IF ERRORLEVEL 13 IF NOT ERRORLEVEL 14`
`   ECHO 320 x 200 16 Color Graphics`
`IF ERRORLEVEL 10 IF NOT ERRORLEVEL 11`
`   ECHO 640 x 200 4 Color Graphics (PC jr)`
`IF ERRORLEVEL  9 IF NOT ERRORLEVEL 10`
`   ECHO 320 x 200 16 Color Graphics (PC jr)`
`IF ERRORLEVEL  8 IF NOT ERRORLEVEL  9`
`   ECHO 160 x 200 16 Color Graphics (PC jr)`
`IF ERRORLEVEL  7 IF NOT ERRORLEVEL  8`
`   ECHO 80 x 25 Black and White Text`
`IF ERRORLEVEL  6 IF NOT ERRORLEVEL  7`
`   ECHO 640 x 200 2 Color Graphics`
`IF ERRORLEVEL  5 IF NOT ERRORLEVEL  6`
`   ECHO 320 x 200 4 Gray Graphics`
`IF ERRORLEVEL  4 IF NOT ERRORLEVEL  5`
`   ECHO 320 x 200 4 Color Graphics`
`IF ERRORLEVEL  3 IF NOT ERRORLEVEL  4`
`   ECHO 80 x 25 16 Color Text`
`IF ERRORLEVEL  2 IF NOT ERRORLEVEL  3`
`   ECHO 80 x 25 16 Gray Text`
`IF ERRORLEVEL  1 IF NOT ERRORLEVEL  2`
`   ECHO 40 x 25 16 Color Text`
`IF ERRORLEVEL  0 IF NOT ERRORLEVEL  1`
`   ECHO 40 x 25 No Color`
	Displays the results of the test.

`PRT_ON`	Tests the printer.

Table 6-9   Continued.

Batch File Line	Explanation

`IF ERRORLEVEL 2 ECHO Printer Is On`
`IF ERRORLEVEL 1 IF NOT ERRORLEVEL 2`
`   ECHO Printer Is Off`
	Displays the results of the test.

Conclusion

While DDDBATCH is too incomplete to serve as your only batch utility set, its programs are both helpful and simple to use and yet, at the same time, fairly powerful.

GET

Name:	GET
Version:	1.0
Price:	Free
Category:	Public Domain
Summary:	Passes information about the system to the batch file through the environment.
Author:	Bob Stephan
Availability:	Available on many bulletin board systems.

Get can obtain information in a number of ways, passing this information back to the batch file by either the environmental variable GET or sometimes ERRORLEVEL. The available GET options are as follows:

7 Checks for a math coprocessor and stores the results in the environmental variable GET and ERRORLEVEL.

A Checks for ANSI.SYS and stores the results in the environmental variable GET and ERRORLEVEL.

B Clears the screen.

C Accepts a single character response from the user, converts it to uppercase, and stores it in the environment. It also stores the ASCII value of the uppercase value in ERRORLEVEL. Storing the response in the environment makes batch files much more readable. (For example, look at the GET statement IF %GET% = = A GOTO Lotus compared to the standard IF ERRORLEVEL 65 IF NOT ERRORLEVEL 66 GOTO Lotus.)

D Gets the major DOS version (for DOS 4.01, 4 is the major version) and stores it in the environmental variable GET and ERRORLEVEL. You can also get the minor version rather than the major version.

E Gets the remaining environmental space and stores it in the environmental variable GET and ERRORLEVEL.

F Gets the size of a specified file in kilobytes and stores it in the environmental variable GET and ERRORLEVEL.

K Gets the free space on the specified drive in kilobytes and stores it in the environmental variable GET and ERRORLEVEL.

M Gets the free conventional memory and stores it in the environmental variable GET and ERRORLEVEL.

N Accepts a single y or n keystroke response from the user. It converts the response to uppercase, storing it in the environmental variable GET and ERRORLEVEL.

P Checks to see if a printer is attached and stores the results in the environmental variable GET and ERRORLEVEL.

S Accepts a full string from the user and stores it (*not* converted to uppercase) in the environmental variable GET. The ERRORLEVEL stores the length of this new variable.

T Accepts a single keystroke from the user just like the C option but displays a different prompt. C displays an optional prompt entered on the command line, while T reads a file containing up to 4096 bytes and displays that as a scrolling message at the bottom of the screen.

V Either gets the current video mode and stores it in the environmental variable GET and ERRORLEVEL or optionally changes the video mode.

Y Stores the current subdirectory in the environmental variable GET and the drive number in ERRORLEVEL.

GET is a very powerful program for getting information from the user and about the system—especially for being public domain.

IFF

Name: IFF
Version: 5.0
Price: $20.00
Category: Shareware
Summary: A utility set designed to ask different types of questions.
Author: John Knauer, Junior
              Post Office Box 747
              Brookfield, Connecticut 06804
Availability: Available on many bulletin board systems.

IFF is a batch toolkit designed around queries. All of IFF's options run by issuing the IFF question followed by an option letter and generally return information via ERRORLEVEL. In addition, many of the questions can display information on the screen—although this can be disabled for batch files. The IFF questions are as follows:

A Compares available RAM (conventional) against a number you enter on the command line and sets ERRORLEVEL to indicate if you have that much memory.

C Searches the entire drive to see if the specified file exists. It reports the results in ERRORLEVEL as well as changing to the subdirectory containing the file.

D Compares the system date against the date stored in the directory for IFF.EXE and reports its results in ERRORLEVEL. If the system date is later than the date for IFF.EXE, the IFF.EXE date is updated. Thus, a batch file can make a reasonable test to ensure the setting of the system date.

E Tests to see if a specified file exists but doesn't search all subdirectories or change to the subdirectory. Unlike the DOS IF EXIST command, this test doesn't trigger the DOS "Abort, Ignore, or Retry" error message if a problem exists with the drive.

F Searches the drive for a file (like the C option) but doesn't change to the subdirectory when it finds it.

I Prompts the user to enter a string, which is converted to uppercase and stored in the environment under the name IFF. Unlike similar routines, this option allows you to restrict the length of the information the user enters.

L Compares the disk label against a label entered on the command line.

M Reads a file from the disk, displays it, and then prompts the user to make a choice. You can restrict the user's choice but the method isn't very flexible. The choices go from 0-9 and then from A-Z, of which you can select the ending point but not the starting point. As a result, if your menu had eleven items, you would have to use 0-9 and A as your choices.

P Works just like the M option except that it doesn't read a file from the disk first. Thus, the batch file would have to handle displaying the menu.

Q Prompts the user for a y or n response and won't accept anything else.

R Searches the drive for up to ten names you've specified in a newly created file and sets ERRORLEVEL to indicate the first file found.

S Compares the available disk space against a number you enter on the command line and sets ERRORLEVEL to indicate if that much free space exists.

T Tests to see which drives are available and working on your system. For example, this option won't report an A drive without a disk in it because, although the drive's available, it isn't currently working.

W Pauses the batch file for the specified number of minutes or seconds.

X Tests to see if the specified number of LIM pages of memory (a page is 16K) is available.

IFF works well and is fairly easy to use.

Norton Batch Enhancer

Name:	Norton Utilities
Version:	5.0
Price:	$150.00
Category:	Commercial
Summary:	A full-featured DOS utility program that includes a number of batch file utilities.
Author:	Peter Norton Computing, Incorporated
	2210 Wilshire Boulevard
	Santa Monica, California 90403
Availability:	Available at any software store.

Norton includes the Batch Enhancer in his utilities. (Norton Utilities 4.0 had both a standard and advanced version, with only the advanced version containing the Batch Enhancer. With v5.0, that dual distinction of the utilities has been dropped.) Batch Enhancer began as a couple of small utilities like BEEP.COM. After a couple of rounds, these small utilities were compiled into a single program called BE.EXE. BE [short for Batch Enhancer] contains several different routines that you call up with a keyword after the BE. For example,

```
BE BEEP
```

would run the Beep program in exactly the same way as entering BEEP at the command line would with the older version. The features available with the Batch Enhancer are as follows:

Ask is an ERRORLEVEL-asker covered in detail in Chapter 1.

Beep sounds a tone on the speaker, of which you can control the pitch and duration. You can also repeat notes and control the delay between repeats. All this power gives the Batch Enhancer the ability to play simple songs on the speaker.

Box draws a box on the screen, the boxes being plain or fancy shadow-boxes in color. Once you draw a box, you can use the ROWCOL option to position the cursor to write inside the box for a fancy screen display.

Printchar repeats a single character a specified number of times and is useful for drawing a box.

Rowcol positions the cursor at a specific place on the screen. It can also write text to the screen, allowing much more specific handling of text than the ECHO command in DOS.

SA lets you change screen colors using English commands. The changes aren't permanent (CLS cancels them) unless you load ANSI.SYS.

Window works much like the BOX command except that you can zoom a window.

Those features are summarized in Table 6-10, while NORTON.BAT in Table 6-11 shows a batch file illustrating many of these commands.

Table 6-10   A summary of the Norton Utilities Batch Enhancer features.

Features	Function
Ask	Basically an ERRORLEVEL tester you use to get a single byte of information from the user and pass it back in as an ERRORLEVEL. Ask is one of the best ERRORLEVEL testers around. The syntax for the command is "BE ASK "prompt", keys, DEFAULT=key, TIMEOUT=#, ADJUST=n, color" and a typical batch line would be "BE ASK "Files will be deleted! Continue (y/n) " ny, DEFAULT=n, TIMEOUT=5". The Ask options are listed in the next table.
Beep	Sounds a tone on the speaker. There are numerous options to control the tone. They include specifying the tone duration, frequency, the number of times the tone is repeated and the delay between repeats. These options let you play a large variations of tones. In fact, prior versions of the Norton Utilities contains a sample batch file that uses the Beep function to play Mary Had a Little Lamp, and it does a good job.
Box	Draws a box on the screen. The syntax is "BE BOX top, left, bottom, right, line type, color" where top, left, bottom, and right specify box coordinates. Using the Batch Enhancer ROWCOL function, you can draw a box and then position the cursor to write text inside the box.
Printchar	Repeats a single character a specified number of times. It is a nice way to draw lines in a batch file.
Rowcol	Positions the cursor at a specific row and column on the screen and the optionally displays text.
SA	It lets you set the color of the screen and text using English names like Red and Bright. The changes are not permanent unless you have loaded ANSI.SYS in your CONFIG.SYS and will be reset by a CLS command.
Window	Much like the Box command except in includes options for zooming in the window and creating a shadow around the window. You specify the location and color just like the Box command.

Table 6-11   NORTON.BAT illustrates many
of the Norton Utilities Batch Enhancer commands.

Batch File Line	Explanation
`@ECHO OFF`	Turns command-echoing off.
`REM NORTON.BAT`	Remark giving the name of the batch file.
`REM This batch file illustrates`	Documentation remark.
`REM the Norton Batch Enhancer`	Documentation remark.
`CLS`	Clears the screen.
`BE ASK "Do you want to hear the computer beep (y/n) " ny`	Runs the Norton Utilities Batch Enhancer to get information from the user. The "ny" gives the responses it will accept. For the first acceptable response, it sets ERRORLEVEL to 1 and uses 2 for the second. This makes doing the tests easier than looking up

Batch File Line	Explanation
	ASCII values. It also ignores case.
`CLS`	Clears the screen.
`REM The above line with set ERRORLEVEL` `    to 2 for a y or Y`	Documentation remark.
`REM and 1 for a n or N`	Documentation remark.
`IF ERRORLEVEL 2 BE BEEP`	Sounds the speaker for a "y" response. No testing is required for a "n" because it has a lower ERRORLEVEL value.
`BE ASK "Do you want to hear a high pitch beep` `    (y/n) " ny DEFAULT=Y TIMEOUT=2`	Prompts the user again. This line sets a default if the user presses return or lets the program run out of time. The "TIMEOUT=2" says to use the default after two seconds.
`CLS`	Clears the screen.
`REM Notice that this will time out` `    after two seconds`	Documentation remark.
`REM with a default answer of y`	Documentation remark.
`IF ERRORLEVEL 2 BE BEEP /F5000 /D18`	If the user answered yes, sounds the speaker.
`REM The tone will sound at 5K Hertz for 1 sec.`	Documentation remark.
`REM Notice that duration is specified in` `    1/18 second intervals`	Documentation remark.
`CLS`	Documentation remark.
`REM Now let's draw boxes on the screen`	Documentation remark.
`BE BOX   0, 0, 5,15,DOUBLE,BOLD,BLUE`	Draws a blue, bold, double line on the screen from pixel 0,0 to 5,15.
`BE BOX   5,15,10,30,DOUBLE,BOLD,BLUE`	Draw a line.
`BE BOX  10,30,15,45,DOUBLE,BOLD,BLUE`	Draw a line.
`BE BOX  15,45,20,60,DOUBLE,BOLD,BLUE`	Draw a line.
`BE ROWCOL 23,0`	Positions the cursor for the prompt to come next.
`BE ASK "Press Any Key To Continue "TIMEOUT=10`	Asks the user a question, takes any answer or continues after ten seconds.
`CLS`	Clears the screen.

`BE BOX   0, 0, 0,10,SINGLE,BOLD,WHITE`
`BE BOX   0,10, 5,25,SINGLE,BOLD,WHITE`
`BE BOX   3,13, 8,28,SINGLE,BOLD,WHITE`
`BE BOX   9,19,14,34,SINGLE,BOLD,WHITE`
`BE BOX  12,22,17,37,SINGLE,BOLD,WHITE`
`BE BOX  15,25,20,40,SINGLE,BOLD,WHITE`
`BE BOX  18,28,23,43,SINGLE,BOLD,WHITE`
	Draws two boxes on the screen, one line at a time.

`BE ROWCOL 23,0`	Positions the cursor.
`BE ASK "Press Any Key To Continue "TIMEOUT=10`	Prompts the user.
`CLS`	Clears the screen.
`BE PRINTCHAR -,80`	Prints one character 80-times.

Table 6-11 Continued.

Batch File Line	Explanation
ECHO Warning: Something is about to happen	Tells the user something is going to happen.
ECHO This is just a test	Message to user.
ECHO If it were a real warning	Message to user.
ECHO instructions would follow	Message to user.
BE PRINTCHAR -,80	Prints one character 80-times.
BE ROWCOL 23,0	Positions the cursor.
BE ASK "Press Any Key To Continue "TIMEOUT=10	Prompts the user.
CLS	Clears the screen.
BE ROWCOL 0,0,"Cursor at top left of screen"	Positions the cursor and writes to the screen.
BE ROWCOL 10,40,"Cursor is in the middle of the screen"	Positions the cursor and writes to the screen.
BE ROWCOL 22,79,"X"	Positions the cursor and writes to the screen.
BE ROWCOL 23,0,"X was printed at bottom right"	Positions the cursor and writes to the screen.
BE ROWCOL 23,0	Positions the cursor.
BE ASK "Press Any Key To Set Screen Colors and Exit "TIMEOUT=10	Prompts the user.
CLS.	Clears the screen.
BE SA BOLD WHITE ON BLUE	Sets the screen colors.

Scanion Enterprises Batch File Utilities

Name:	Scanion Enterprises Batch File Utilities
Version:	2.2.0
Price:	$9.95
Category:	Shareware
Summary:	A collection of over 100 batch file utilities.
Author:	Paul Scanion
Availability:	Included on the disk bound in this book.

The Scanion Enterprises Batch File Utilities [SEBFU for short] is a collection of over 100 batch file utilities. Each command in SEBFU is a separate *.COM file. As a result, your disk can end up cluttered with quite a number of small program files. You might consider erasing the programs you aren't likely to use.

Programs

The programs included with SEBFU are as follows:

ADD adds a specified value to an environmental variable containing a numeric value. ADD combined with the SUB command forms an excellent way to do loops in a batch file.

BEEP sounds the speaker.

BIGLTR displays a large 10-character message on the screen and doesn't work with a VGA system.

CDCK checks to see if a CD-ROM drive is attached and then sets ERRORLEVEL accordingly. If you have a CD-ROM drive, you could use this in program-loading batch files to access the drive and ensure that you have turned it on. Some CD-ROM software locks up if the drive isn't turned on.

CDD moves down toward the root directory a specified number of levels.

CGABORDR changes the color of the border on a CGA display.

CHGC changes the color of the screen in a specific range, useful for printing a window on the screen in a color different from the rest of the screen.

CHGLOCK toggles the status of the CapsLock, NumLock, and ScrollLock keys.

CHKSUM computes a checksum for a specified file and can also test the results against a specified value. A batch file can use this to perform a quick-and-dirty test to see if a critical file had been specified by a virus.

CK101 checks to see if a 101-key keyboard is attached and then sets ERRORLEVEL accordingly.

CKCLK checks to see if the BIOS supports the year 1980 and then sets ERRORLEVEL accordingly. This is necessary for some other SEBFU utilities that work with the year.

CLR clears a specified portion of the screen, useful for erasing the text in a window on the screen.

CLRKEY clears the type-ahead buffer. A batch file might use this before asking a critical question to force the user to think twice about the answer.

COFF toggles the cursor off on some systems.

COLOR changes the screen colors.

CR pauses the batch file until the enter key is pressed. It ignores other keystrokes, although it beeps for invalid ones. Pressing escape will exit the program. CR really functions as a specialized PAUSE command.

CT toggles the cursor on and off.

CUON turns the cursor on.

CURKEY returns an ERRORLEVEL value for each cursor movement key and a 0 for any other key. CURKEY is primarily used to allow the user to move the cursor around a menu in a batch file rather than just accepting input.

DAYOFMO sets ERRORLEVEL to indicate the day of the month.

DBLBOX draws a box on the screen using a double line, useful for outlining a window on the screen.

DETANSI checks to see if ANSI.SYS was installed in the CONFIG.SYS file and then sets the ERRORLEVEL accordingly. This is a good way for the batch file to decide between plain screens and ANSI-formatted screens.

DFREE measures the amount of free space on the specified drive and either sets ERRORLEVEL or an environmental variable to report its results. A batch file could run DFREE prior to running a program requiring a lot of disk space.

DLINE draws a double line on the screen using the user-supplied coordinates.

DLST displays a list of all the files in the current subdirectory.

DRVCK checks to see if a drive exists and sets ERRORLEVEL accordingly. It can perform this task without triggering the DOS "Abort, Ignore, or Fail" error message.

DRVLST stores a list of logical drives in an environmental variable called VAR.

DSKRDY checks to see if a drive is ready to receive data and then sets ERRORLEVEL accordingly. It can perform this task without triggering the DOS "Abort, Ignore, or Fail" error message.

ENVSIZE checks to see how much free environmental space is available and then sets ERRORLEVEL accordingly. This is useful for batch files that use a number of environmental variables, as it allows them to make sure enough free space exists before running.

FCHR fills a selected area on the screen with a specified character.

FILES checks to see how many files exist in the current subdirectory and then sets ERRORLEVEL accordingly.

FREEM detects the amount of free memory and then sets ERRORLEVEL or an environmental variable accordingly. Thus, a batch file running a program needing a lot of memory can ensure that much memory exists before trying to run the program.

FSIZE checks to see how large a file is and then sets ERRORLEVEL accordingly. By combining this with DFREE, a batch file could test to see if a file would fit on a floppy disk before trying to copy it.

FUNKEY waits for the user to press F1-F10 and then sets the ERRORLEVEL accordingly. It ignores other keystrokes, although it beeps for invalid ones. Pressing escape will exit the program. Unfortunately, FUNKEY doesn't recognize the F11-F15 keys found on newer keyboards. Still, with more programs making use of function keys, this is an especially nice way to get input from the user.

GALF waits for the user to press a letter key, which is then converted to uppercase. ERRORLEVEL is set accordingly, with A=1, B=2, and so on, rather than using the ASCII values, making it easy to get an alphabetic response from the user.

GCURS finds the coordinates of the cursor and returns either the row or column as an ERRORLEVEL value or both as environmental variables. This is useful for finding the position of the cursor after the user has entered some information.

GDIR sets the environmental variable DIR equal to the current path, useful for writing batch files that return to their starting directory when finished.

GDRIVE sets ERRORLEVEL to indicate the current drive, useful for writing batch files that return to their starting drive when finished.

GETCC finds the column of the cursor and returns it as either an ERRORLEVEL or an environmental variable.

GETCOLR returns an ERRORLEVEL to indicate the current screen color, useful for restoring the screen to the appropriate color after a batch file has finished.

GETCR detects the cursor position and returns the row number as an ERRORLEVEL or environmental variable.

GETMCB displays a list of the current memory usage.

GETNUM waits for the user to press a number and sets the ERRORLEVEL accordingly. It ignores other keystrokes, although it beeps for invalid ones. Pressing escape will exit the program. Accepting only numbers makes GETNUM an excellent way for the user to select a menu option.

GETPG sets ERRORLEVEL to indicate the current video page.

GETVER sets ERRORLEVEL to indicate the major version of DOS in use.

GMEM returns the amount of free memory available as ERRORLEVEL or in an environmental variable.

GMODE sets ERRORLEVEL to indicate the video mode.

INKEY accepts a single keystroke from the user and sets the ERRORLEVEL to its ASCII value (thus, a typical ERRORLEVEL-asking type program).

INSTR searches an environmental variable and places a specified portion of that environmental variable into another environmental variable.

INVERT swaps the foreground and background colors, useful for developing eye-catching warning screens.

KEYSTAT sets ERRORLEVEL to indicate the status of the CapsLock, NumLock, or ScrollLock key.

LEN returns the length of a specified environmental variable.

LIMCK checks to see if an LIM (expanded memory) driver is attached and sets ERRORLEVEL accordingly.

LINE draws a line on the screen using the user-supplied coordinates.

LOCATE positions the cursor at a specific location on the screen.

LOGON can write a name, date, and time to a file, useful for recording who runs a program or for logging usage for taxes.

LPT1TO2 swaps the printer ports.

LST displays an ASCII file on the screen one page at a time.

MIDSTR places a portion of one environmental variable into another environmental variable.

MOUSECK checks to see if a mouse is attached and sets the ERRORLEVEL accordingly.

MOVCUR moves the cursor by a specified amount.

PAGE changes the video page.

PASSWORD gives the user three chances to enter the correct password. If the user succeeds, the batch file continues; otherwise, it locks up the computer and requires a cold reboot to continue. This version didn't work properly under DOS 4.0 or later: if the user entered a wrong password twice, it accepted the second password and prompted the user to enter a new password.

PATHCK checks to see if the specified subdirectory exists in the path, useful for a batch file to check if a program's subdirectory is in the path before trying to run that program.

PFF sends a form feed to the printer.

PRDY checks to see if the printer is ready and sets ERRORLEVEL accordingly.

PRINT displays a message.

PRINTC prints the ASCII character or characters corresponding to the numbers entered on the command line.

PRINTF prints any ASCII file up to 64K.

PRNSET performs a hardware reset of the printer.

RESPONSE accepts a multi-character response from the user and stores it under the environmental variable specified on the command line. This surpasses other programs because you can specify the environmental variable name to use.

Generally, you would only use this approach when a single character response isn't enough. Possible uses include asking the name of the user, a program to run, or a data file.

SAVEKEY places the specified key in the type-ahead buffer.

SCROLL moves a specified portion of the screen, useful for creating and maintaining windows within a batch file.

SCROLMSG displays a moving message at the bottom of the screen.

SETCUR changes the shape of the cursor.

SETDATE sets the date to the one specified on the command line.

SETERR sets ERRORLEVEL to the numeric value specified on the command line.

SETIME sets the time to the one specified on the command line.

SETMODE sets the video mode.

SETPG sets the video page.

SHOWVAR displays the contents of an environmental variable.

SKEY2 checks to see if keystrokes are pending in the type-ahead buffer and sets ERRORLEVEL accordingly.

SNGLBOX draws a box on the screen using a single line.

SOUND sounds the speaker.

SROWS sets the ERRORLEVEL to indicate the row the cursor is currently on.

STRING repeats a string a specified number of times.

SUB subtracts a specified value to an environmental variable that contains a numeric value. Combined with the ADD command, SUB forms an excellent way to implement loops in a batch file.

SWIDTH sets ERRORLEVEL to indicate the width of the display.

WAIT pauses the batch file a specified number of seconds.

WAITILL pauses the batch file until a specified time is reached, useful for writing batch files at the office to perform some network task (like a backup) after everyone has left.

WAITM pauses the batch file for the specified number of minutes.

WHATDAY sets ERRORLEVEL to indicate the day of the week, useful in the AUTOEXEC.BAT file to perform certain tasks (like a backup or an accounting closing) on a specific day.

WHATHR sets ERRORLEVEL to indicate the current hour. Combined with WHATMIN, this would be useful for timing activities.

WHATMIN sets ERRORLEVEL to indicate the current minute. Combined with WHATHR, this would be useful for timing activities.

WHATMO sets ERRORLEVEL to indicate the current month.

WHATYR sets ERRORLEVEL to indicate the number of years that have passed since 1980. It doesn't set it to the year directly because the maximum ERRORLEVEL value is 255.

WRITE displays a message on the screen.

WRITEF writes a small file to the screen, useful for displaying a menu or help text quickly.

XMCHK checks to see if extended memory is installed and sets ERRORLEVEL accordingly.

YN waits for the user to press either the y key or the n key and sets the ERRORLEVEL accordingly. It ignores other keystrokes, although it beeps for invalid ones. Pressing escape will exit the program. Thus, YN is perfect for questions like "Do you want to delete these files?" or "This takes three hours. Do you want to continue?"

YRSINCE calculates the number of years that have passed since a specified date and sets ERRORLEVEL accordingly.

YRSTILL calculates the number of years remaining until a specified date is reached and sets ERRORLEVEL accordingly.

Conclusion

Table 6-12 summarizes the programs that come in SEBFU, while Table 6-13 presents a batch file illustrating many of those programs.

Table 6-12   A summary of the SEBFU programs.

Program	Function
ADD	Increments the numeric contents of an environmental variable by a specified amount. Useful for performing loops in batch files.
BEEP	Sounds the speaker. This program can control the number of beeps.
BIGLTR	Displays a large 10-character message on the screen. Would not work on my VGA system.

Table 6-12 Continued.

Program	Function
CDCK	Checks to see if a CD-ROM drive is attached and sets the ERROR-LEVEL accordingly.
CDD	Moves down toward the root directory the specified number of subdirectory levels. Would not work under DOS 4.x or DOS 5.x.
CGABORDR	Changes the color of the border.
CHGC	Changes the screen colors for a selected range.
CHGLOCK	Toggles the state of Caps Lock, Num Lock, and Scroll Lock.
CHKSUM	Computes a checksum for the specified file and optionally tests it against a specified value and sets ERRORLEVEL to indicate the results. Would be useful for testing files for viral infection.
CK101	Checks to see if a 101-key keyboard is attached and sets ERROR-LEVEL accordingly. Did not work properly for a Northgate OmniKey Plus keyboard.
CKCLK	Checks to see if the BIOS supports the year 1980 and sets ERROR-LEVEL accordingly.
CLR	Clears a selected portion of the screen. Did not work under DOS 5.0.
CLRKEY	Clears the type-ahead buffer.
COFF	Toggles the cursor off on MGA and CGA systems.
COLOR	Sets the screen colors.
CR	Pauses until the enter key is pressed. All other keys just cause the computer to beep.
CT	Toggles the cursor on and off.
CUON	Turns the cursor on.
CURKEY	Returns an ERRORLEVEL value for each cursor key or zero for any other key.
DAYOFMO	Sets ERRORLEVEL to indicate the day of the month.
DBLBOX	Draws a box on the screen using a double line.
DETANSI	Checks to see if ANSI.SYS is installed and sets ERRORLEVEL accordingly. Did not work properly under DOS 5.0 or DOS 4.x.
DFREE	Either sets ERRORLEVEL to indicate the amount of free space of the specified drive or stores the value in an environmental variable. Did not work in DOS 4.0 and greater.
DLINE	Draws a line on the screen.
DLST	Lists the files in the current subdirectory.
DRVCK	Checks to see if the specified drive exists and set ERRORLEVEL accordingly.
DRVLST	Stores a list of the logical drives in the system in an environmental variable called VAR. Did not work under DOS 4.0 or greater.
DSKRDY	Checks to see if the specified drive is ready and sets ERRORLEVEL accordingly.
ENVSIZE	Checks to see how much environmental space is available and sets ERRORLEVEL accordingly.
FCHR	Fills a selected area on the screen with a specified character.
FILES	Checks to see how many files of the specified type exist in the current subdirectory and sets ERRORLEVEL accordingly.

Program	Function
FREEM	Either sets ERRORLEVEL to indicate the amount of free memory or stores the value in an environmental variable. Did not work in DOS 5.0.
FSIZE	Checks to see how large the specified file is and either sets ERROR-LEVEL accordingly or stores the information in an environmental variable.
FUNKEY	Waits for the user to press a function key and sets ERRORLEVEL accordingly. Any other key causes the computer to beep. Does not support F11-F15.
GALF	Waits for the user to press a letter key. All other keys are ignored and cause the computer to beep. It converts the letter the user presses to uppercase and returns an ERRORLEVEL of one for A, two for B, and so on.
GCURS	Checks either the row or column position of the cursor and returns that information in ERRORLEVEL or returns both in ROW and COL environmental variables.
GDIR	Sets the environmental variable DIR equal to the current subdirectory path. Did not work in DOS 5.0.
GDRIVE	Returns an ERRORLEVEL value to indicate the current drive.
GETCC	Detects the cursor position and returns the column number as an ERRORLEVEL. It can also place the cursor position in an environmental variable called CC, although this did not work with DOS 4.x or later.
GETCOLR	Returns a DOS ERRORLEVEL that indicates the current screen color.
CETCR	Detects the cursor position and returns the row number as an ERROR-LEVEL. It can also place the cursor position in an environmental variable called CR, although this did not work with DOS 4.x or later.
GETMCB	Displays a list of the current memory usage.
GETNUM	Accepts input from the user and sets ERRORLEVEL accordingly. It only accepts numbers. It sounds the speaker for any other keystroke.
GETPG	Sets ERRORLEVEL to indicate the current video page.
GETVER	Sets ERRORLEVEL or the environmental variable VER to indicate the current version of DOS. It returned incorrect values for DOS 4.0 or later.
GMEM	Returns the amount of memory available in ERRORLEVEL or in the environmental variable MEM. It sets values in 4K increments so 20=(28*4) or 112K. This did not work properly for DOS 4.0 or later.
GMODE	Returns an ERRORLEVEL to indicate the video mode.
INKEY	Accepts a single keystroke from the user and sets the ERRORLEVEL accordingly.
INSTR	Searches an environmental variable and outputs a substring to another variable.
INVERT	Swaps the foreground and background colors.
KEYSTAT	Returns an ERRORLEVEL to indicate the status of the Caps-Lock, Num-Lock, and Scroll-Lock keys.
LEN	Returns an ERRORLEVEL to indicate the length of a specified environmental variable.

Table 6-12   Continued.

Program	Function
LIMCK	Returns an ERRORLEVEL to indicate if a LIM driver is attached.
LINE	Draws a line on the screen at specified coordinates.
LOCATE	Positions the cursor at a specified point.
LOGON	Updates a file called LOGIN.LOG with a name, time and date.
LPT1TO2	Swaps printer ports.
LST	Displays a text file on the screen, one page at a time.
MIDSTR	Places a portion of one environmental variable into another variable. Under DOS 4.0 and larger, this did not work properly for most variable names. When used on the COMSPEC variable, it resets all the memory variables to nul.
MOUSECK	Returns an ERRORLEVEL value to indicate if a mouse is attached.
MOVCUR	Moves the cursor.
PAGE	Changes the active video page. It can also set ERRORLEVEL or the memory variable PAGE to indicate the current page.
PASSWORD	Requires the user to enter a password. If the user fails three time to enter the proper password, it locks the computer and requires the computer to be rebooted. PASSWORD did not work properly under DOS 4.0 and larger. If I entered the right password the first time, it worked. If I entered the wrong password twice in a row, it always accepted the second one and asked me to enter a new password.
PATHCK	Checks to see if a specified directory exists on the current path and sets ERRORLEVEL accordingly.
PFF	Sends a form feed to the printer.
PRDY	Checks the printer and sets ERRORLEVEL to indicate its status.
PRINT	Prints a message on the printer.
PRINTC	Prints the ASCII character or characters corresponding to the numbers entered on the command-line.
PRINTF	Prints any file up to 64K.
PRNSET	Performs a hardware reset of the printer.
RESPONSE	Accepts a multiple-character response from the user and places it in an environmental variable.
SAVEKEY	Places the specified keystroke into the type-ahead buffer.
SCROLL	Moves a specified portion of the screen.
SCROLMSG	Displays a moving message at the bottom of the screen.
SETCUR	Changes the shape of the cursor.
SETDATE	Sets the date to the one specified on the command-line.
SETERR	Sets the ERRORLEVEL to the specified value.
SETIME	Sets the time to the one specified on the command-line.
SETMODE	Sets the video mode.
SETPG	Sets the video page.
SHOWVAR	Displays an environmental variable. It does not work under DOS 5.0.
SKEY	Sets ERRORLEVEL to indicate if there are keystrokes in the type-ahead buffer.
SNGLBOX	Draws a box on the screen.
SOUND	Beeps the speaker using the specified tone and duration.

Program	Function
SROWS	Sets ERRORLEVEL to indicate the row the cursor is on.
STRING	Repeats a string a specified number of times.
SUB	Subtracts one or the specified amount from the specified environmental variable.
SWIDTH	Sets ERRORLEVEL to indicate the width of the display.
WAIT	Pauses the computer for the specified number of seconds.
WAITILL	Pauses the computer until the specified time is reached. Did not work under DOS 5.0.
WAITM	Pauses the computer for the specified number of minutes. Did not work under DOS 5.0.
WHATDAY	Sets ERRORLEVEL to indicate the day of the week.
WHATHR	Sets ERRORLEVEL to indicate the hour of the day in 24-hour format.
WHATMIN	Sets ERRORLEVEL to indicate the minute of the hour.
WHATMO	Sets ERRORLEVEL to indicate the month of the year.
WHATYR	Sets ERRORLEVEL to indicate the year. Because ERRORLEVEL values can not exceed 255, it starts counting from 1980 so 1991=11.
WRITE	Displays a message on the screen.
WRITEF	Displays a small file (under 4K) on the screen.
XMCHK	Sets ERRORLEVEL to indicate if extended memory is installed.
YN	Waits for either the y or n key to be pressed and sets ERRORLEVEL accordingly. No other keystrokes are accepted.
YRSINCE	Sets ERRORLEVEL to indicate the number of years that have passed since the specified year.
YRSTILL	Sets ERRORLEVEL to indicate the number of years until the specified year is reached.

Table 6-13   SEBFU.BAT illustrates many of the SEBFU programs.

Batch File Line	Explanation
`ECHO OFF`	Turns command echoing off.
`REM SEBFU.BAT`	Remark giving the name of the batch file.
`CLS`	Clears the screen.
`BIGLTR HELLO`	Prints HELLO in large letters.
`SCROLMSG Press Key To Start`	Prints "Press Key to Start" on the 25-line and scrolls it across the screen. This command automatically continues until a key is pressed.
`CLS`	Clears the screen.
`ECHO Sounding Speaker 10-Times`	Tells the user what will happen.
`BEEP 10`	Beeps the speaker ten times.
`CDCK`	Checks for a CD-ROM drive.

`IF ERRORLEVEL 1 ECHO You Have A CD-ROM Drive`
`IF NOT ERRORLEVEL 1 ECHO You Do Not Have A`
`    ROM Drive`
	Displays the results of the check for the CD-ROM drive.

`CK101`	Checks for a 101-key keyboard.

Table 6-13   Continued.

Batch File Line	Explanation

IF ERRORLEVEL 1 ECHO You Have A 101-Key
    Keyboard
IF NOT ERRORLEVEL 1 ECHO You Do Not Have
    A 101-Key Keyboard
	Displays the results of checking for the 101-key keyboard.

CKCLK	Checks to see if the bios supports 1980.
IF ERRORLEVEL 1 ECHO Your BIOS Supports 1980 IF NOT ERRORLEVEL 1 ECHO Your BIOS Does Not Support 1980	Displays results of the bios check.
DETANSI	Checks to see if ANSI.SYS is loaded.
IF ERRORLEVEL 1 ECHO ANSI.SYS Attached IF NOT ERRORLEVEL 1 ECHO ANSI.SYS Not Attached	Displays the results of checking for ANSI.SYS.

DRVCK D:
IF ERRORLEVEL 1 ECHO D-Drive Is Not A Valid
    Drive
IF NOT ERRORLEVEL 1 ECHO D-Drive Is A Valid
    Drive
	Checks to see if there is a D drive and displays the results.

DSKRDY B:
IF ERRORLEVEL 0 IF NOT ERRORLEVEL 1 ECHO
    B-Drive Ready
IF ERRORLEVEL 1 IF NOT ERRORLEVEL 2 ECHO
    B-Drive Exists But Not Ready
IF ERRORLEVEL 2 IF NOT ERRORLEVEL 3 ECHO
    B-Drive Unformatted
IF ERRORLEVEL 3 IF NOT ERRORLEVEL 4 ECHO
    B-Drive Does Not Exist
	Check to see if the B drive is ready and displays the results.

ENVSIZE	Checks to see how much environmental space is free.

FOR %%J IN (1 2 3 4 5 6 7 8 9 10) DO
    IF ERRORLEVEL %%J SET ENV=%%J
FOR %%J IN (11 12 13 14 15 16 17) DO
    IF ERRORLEVEL %%J SET ENV=%%J
FOR %%J IN (18 19 20 21 22 23 24) DO
    IF ERRORLEVEL %%J SET ENV=%%J
FOR %%J IN (25 26 27 28 29 30 31) DO
    IF ERRORLEVEL %%J SET ENV=%%J
FOR %%J IN (32 33 34 35 36 37 38) DO
    IF ERRORLEVEL %%J SET ENV=%%J
FOR %%J IN (39 40 41 42 43 44 45) DO
    IF ERRORLEVEL %%J SET ENV=%%J
FOR %%J IN (46 47 48 49 50 51   ) DO
    IF ERRORLEVEL %%J SET ENV=%%J
IF NOT %ENV%==51 ECHO You Have %ENV%-Bytes
    Of Free Environmental Space
IF %ENV%==51 ECHO You Have More Than 50-Bytes
    Of Free Environmental Space
	Displays the results of checking the environment.

SET ENV=	Resets the environmental variable.
FREEM MEMORY	Checks to see how much memory is available.
ECHO %MEMORY% Free Memory Remaining	Displays the results of checking the memory.
SET MEMORY=	Resets the environmental variable.
GCURS /V	Checks the cursor position.
ECHO Cursor At Row %ROW% And Column %COL%	Displays the results of checking the cursor position.
SET ROW= SET COL=	Resets environmental variables.

Batch File Line	Explanation
`GDIR`	Runs a program that stores the current subdirectory to an environmental variable.
`ECHO The Current Subdirectory Is %DIR%`	Displays the results.
`SET DIR=`	Resets the environmental variable.
`GDRIVE`	Checks the current drive.

`FOR %%J IN (1 2 3 4) DO IF ERRORLEVEL %%J`
`    SET DRIVE=%%J`
`IF %DRIVE%==1 ECHO A-Drive Is Current`
`IF %DRIVE%==2 ECHO B-Drive Is Current`
`IF %DRIVE%==3 ECHO C-Drive Is Current`
`IF %DRIVE%==4 ECHO D-Drive Is Current`
`SET DRIVE=`
	Displays the results and then reset the environmental variable.

`GETVER /V`	Checks the DOS version.
`ECHO The Current DOS Version Is %VER%` `SET VER=`	Displays the results and reset the environmental variable.
`LIMCK` `IF ERRORLEVEL 1 ECHO LIM Memory Installed`	Checks for expanded memory and displays the results.
`MOUSECK` `IF ERRORLEVEL 1 ECHO Mouse Connected`	Checks for a mouse and display the results.

`PRDY`
`IF ERRORLEVEL 0 IF NOT ERRORLEVEL 1`
`    ECHO Printer Ready`
`IF ERRORLEVEL 1 IF NOT ERRORLEVEL 2`
`    ECHO Printer Timed Out`
`IF ERRORLEVEL 2 IF NOT ERRORLEVEL 3`
`    ECHO General Printer Failure`
`IF ERRORLEVEL 3 IF NOT ERRORLEVEL 4`
`    ECHO Printer Needs Paper`
`IF ERRORLEVEL 4 IF NOT ERRORLEVEL 5`
`    ECHO Printer Busy`
`IF ERRORLEVEL 5 IF NOT ERRORLEVEL 6`
`    ECHO Printer Off-Line`
	Checks the printer and displays the results.

`PAUSE`	Pauses the batch file.
`CLS`	Clears the screen.
`ECHO Now Will Display Some Date Programs`	Tells user what will happen next.
`DAYOFMO`	Checks for the day of the month.

`FOR %%J IN (1 2 3 4 5 6 7 8 9 10) DO`
`    IF ERRORLEVEL %%J SET DAY=%%J`
`FOR %%J IN (11 12 13 14 15 16 17) DO`
`    IF ERRORLEVEL %%J SET DAY=%%J`
`FOR %%J IN (18 19 20 21 22 23 24) DO`
`    IF ERRORLEVEL %%J SET DAY=%%J`
`FOR %%J IN (25 26 27 28 29 30 31) DO`
`    IF ERRORLEVEL %%J SET DAY=%%J`
`ECHO The Day Of The Month Is %DAY%`
`SET DAY=`
	Displays the day of the month and then resets the environmental variable.

`DAYOFWK`
`IF ERRORLEVEL 7 ECHO Saturday`
`IF ERRORLEVEL 6 IF NOT ERRORLEVEL 7`
`    ECHO Friday`
`IF ERRORLEVEL 5 IF NOT ERRORLEVEL 6`
`    ECHO Thursday`
`IF ERRORLEVEL 4 IF NOT ERRORLEVEL 5`
`    ECHO Wednesday`
`IF ERRORLEVEL 3 IF NOT ERRORLEVEL 4`
`    ECHO Tuesday`
`IF ERRORLEVEL 2 IF NOT ERRORLEVEL 3`
`    ECHO Monday`
`IF ERRORLEVEL 1 IF NOT ERRORLEVEL 2`
`    ECHO Sunday`
	Displays the day of the week.

Table 6-13 Continued.

Batch File Line	Explanation

WHATHR
FOR %%J IN (1 2 3 4 5 6 7 8 9 10) DO
   IF ERRORLEVEL %%J SET HOUR=%%J
FOR %%J IN (11 12 13 14 15 16 17) DO
   IF ERRORLEVEL %%J SET HOUR=%%J
FOR %%J IN (18 19 20 21 22 23 24) DO
   IF ERRORLEVEL %%J SET HOUR=%%J
ECHO The Current Hour is %HOUR%
SET HOUR=
	Displays the hour of the day and then resets the environmental variable.

WHATMIN
FOR %%J IN (1 2 3 4 5 6 7 8 9 10) DO
   IF ERRORLEVEL %%J SET MIN=%%J
FOR %%J IN (11 12 13 14 15 16 17) DO
   IF ERRORLEVEL %%J SET MIN=%%J
FOR %%J IN (18 19 20 21 22 23 24) DO
   IF ERRORLEVEL %%J SET MIN=%%J
FOR %%J IN (25 26 27 28 29 30 31) DO
   IF ERRORLEVEL %%J SET MIN=%%J
FOR %%J IN (32 33 34 35 36 37 38) DO
   IF ERRORLEVEL %%J SET MIN=%%J
FOR %%J IN (39 40 41 42 43 44 45) DO
   IF ERRORLEVEL %%J SET MIN=%%J
FOR %%J IN (46 47 48 49 50 51 52) DO
   IF ERRORLEVEL %%J SET MIN=%%J
FOR %%J IN (53 54 55 56 57 58) DO
   IF ERRORLEVEL %%J SET MIN=%%J
FOR %%J IN (50 60) DO IF ERRORLEVEL %%J
   SET MIN=%%J
ECHO The Current Minute is %MIN%
SET MIN=
	Tests for the current minute, displays the results and resets the environmental variable.

PAUSE	Pauses the computer.
CLS	Clears the screen.

ECHO Now Will Show Keystroke Obtaining
   Programs
ECHO Press The Enter Key To Continue
ECHO Nothing Else Works But You Might Want
   To Experiment
	Tells the user what will happen next.

CR	Pauses until enter is pressed.

ECHO Press A Cursor Movement Key (e.g. The
   Up Arrow)
ECHO Nothing Else Works But You Might Want
   To Experiment
ECHO (Enter Also Accepted)
	Tells the user what will happen next.

CURKEY
IF ERRORLEVEL 4 IF NOT ERRORLEVEL 5 ECHO
   Right Arrow Pressed
IF ERRORLEVEL 3 IF NOT ERRORLEVEL 4 ECHO
   Left Arrow Pressed
IF ERRORLEVEL 2 IF NOT ERRORLEVEL 3 ECHO
   Down Arrow Pressed
IF ERRORLEVEL 1 IF NOT ERRORLEVEL 2 ECHO
   Up Arrow Pressed
	Runs a program that only accepts a cursor key and then tells the user what key was pressed.

ECHO Next, Only F1-F10 Will Be Accepted ECHO (Enter Also Accepted)	Tells the user what will happen next.
FUNKEY FOR %%J IN (1 2 3 4 5 6 7 8 9 10) DO IF ERRORLEVEL %%J SET FUNCTION=%%J ECHO F%FUNCTION% Pressed SET FUNCTION=	Runs a program that only accepts a function key, tells the user what happened, and resets the environmental variable.

Batch File Line	Explanation
`ECHO Now Will Accept Only Letter Keys`	Tells the user what will happen next.
`GALF`	Runs a program that only accepts a letter and sets ERRORLEVEL accordingly.

`IF ERRORLEVEL 1 IF NOT ERRORLEVEL 2`
`    ECHO A-Pressed`
`IF ERRORLEVEL 2 IF NOT ERRORLEVEL 3`
`    ECHO B-Pressed`
 	
`Continues in a similar fashion for C-X`
 	
`IF ERRORLEVEL 25 IF NOT ERRORLEVEL 26`
`    ECHO Y-Pressed`
`IF ERRORLEVEL 26 IF NOT ERRORLEVEL 27`
`    ECHO Z-Pressed`
	Displays which letter was pressed.

`ECHO Enter Any Text You Like, Up To` `    80-Characters`	Tells the user what will happen next.
`RESPONSE ENTERED`	RESPONSE will accept input from the user and store it in the environmental variable ENTERED.
`MOVCUR D`	Moves the cursor down because RESPONSE does not move the cursor.
`MOVCUR L 20`	Moves the cursor to the left 20-characters.
`ECHO You Entered %ENTERED%`	Displays what the user entered.
`SET ENTERED=`	Resets the environmental variable.
`PAUSE`	Pauses the batch file.
`CLS`	Clears the screen.
`ECHO SEBFU Demonstration` `ECHO I Will Now Loop Forwards 99-Times`	Tells the user what will happen next.
`PAUSE`	Pauses the batch file.
`SET COUNTER=00`	Sets the counter to zero.
`:ADDTOP`	Label marking the top of the loop.
`ADD COUNTER 1`	Adds one to the counter.
`ECHO %COUNTER%`	Echoes the current counter value.
`IF NOT %COUNTER%==99 GOTO ADDTOP`	Continues the loop if the counter has not yet reached 99.
`ECHO I Will Now Loop Backwards 99-Times`	Tells the user what will happen next.
`PAUSE`	Pauses the batch file.
`:SUBTOP`	Label marking the top of the batch file.
`SUB COUNTER 1`	Reduces the counter by one.

Table 6-13 Continued.

Batch File Line	Explanation
`ECHO %COUNTER%`	Displays the value of the counter.
`IF NOT %COUNTER%==00 GOTO SUBTOP`	If the counter has not reached zero, continues the loop.
`SET COUNTER=`	Resets the counter environmental variable.
`ECHO Inverting Colors`	Tells the user what will happen next.
`INVERT`	Inverts the colors.
`PAUSE`	Pauses the batch file.
`ECHO Inverting Colors Again`	Tells the user what will happen next.
`INVERT`	Inverts the colors again, returning them to their original variable.
`PAUSE`	Pauses the batch file.
`CLS`	Clears the screen.
`DBLBOX 5 5 20 75 1 15`	Draws a box on the screen.
`SET SPACE=`	Sets an environmental variable equal to a space.
`FCHR 6 6 19 71 1 15 %SPACE%`	Fills the box with spaces.
`LOCATE 10 10`	Locates the cursor.
`ECHO A Simple Window`	Displays a message in the box.
`LOCATE 22 01`	Locates the cursor near the bottom of the screen.

A few of the SEBFU utilities don't work properly under DOS 4.0 or later, although most do. Still, managing over one hundred small .COM files is difficult; SEBFU would work better if the many .COM files were collected into a single utility that used keywords to select the command to execute. Overall, though, many of the programs are very useful, and you simply can erase the unnecessary ones.

tBU

Name: tBU
Version: 3.0
Price: Free
Category: Copyrighted
Summary: A collection of very powerful functions for manipulating environmental variables.
Author: Todd R. Hill
             Claude N. Warren Jr.
Availability: Available on many bulletin board systems.

Most of the batch utilities in this book are programs run to perform some specific task. However, tBU (short for the Batch Utility) doesn't work that way; for the most part, it functions as an intermediary. You run tBU to perform some manipulation of an environmental variable, which you then use to perform some other task.

To run tBU, you provide it with a symbol telling it what to do, an environmental variable to manipulate, and optional parameters as required. tBU sometimes sets ERRORLEVEL, but the really useful information is stored in the environmental variable. As a result, you really should expand your environment while using tBU (see Appendix B).

The general format of the tBU command is

TBU − S VAR options

where S is the symbol used to tell tBU what to do. Please note that the symbol is case-sensitive. The VAR is the environmental variable where tBU stores the results, and options are the remaining symbol-specific parameters required by tBU.

The symbols supported by tBU and their general function are as follows:

A   Checks to see if ANSI.SYS is loaded.

b   Beeps the speaker.

C   Converts a value to a new radix.

c   Allows the user to enter a single keystroke from the keyboard.

D   Stores the date and/or time to the environmental variable.

d   Stores the date and/or time a file was created to the environmental variable.

E   Stores the size of the environment to the environmental variable.

e   Stores the amount of free space in the environment to the environmental variable.

F   Stores a formatted time stamp to the environmental variable.

f   Converts a string to uppercase.

h   Displays help.

I   Compares to strings to see if the first is less than, greater than, or equal to the second.

K   Stores the free disk space amount to the environmental variable.

k   Indicates if a specified amount of space is available on a disk.

L   Stores the current drive to the environmental variable.

M   Stores the amount of free memory to the environmental variable.

m   Finds the position of one string inside another string.

n   Stores just the filename portion of a file specification in the environmental variable.

o   Converts a string to lowercase.

P   Stores a substring to the environmental variable.

q   Sets one environmental variable equal to another.

R   Stores the DOS version to the environmental variable.

S   Strips out a portion of one string and replaces it with another.

s   Has the user enter a string for the keyboard and stores it in the environmental variable.

T   Checks to see if a file or subdirectory exists.

t   Checks to see if an extended keyboard is present and supported.

U   Converts a string to lowercase.

V   Checks to see if either Desqview or Topview is present.

W   Allows a batch file to loop several times.

w   Allows a batch file to loop as many times as necessary. The looping capabilities of tBU are so useful and powerful that I've shown an example batch file called LOOP.BAT in Table 6-14. While this example does nothing particular, I am sure you will find looping useful in your batch files.

Table 6-14   LOOP.BAT illustrates tBU's looping capacity.

Batch File Line	Explanation
@ECHO OFF	Turns command-echoing off.
REM NAME: LOOP.BAT REM PURPOSE: Illustrate Looping Capacity REM of tBU package. REM VERSION: 1.00 REM DATE: April 5, 1991	Documentation remarks.
CLS	Clears the screen.
ECHO -W Need Not Have Sequential Numbers	Gives the user some information about the tBU package.
:TOP1	Label marking the top of the first loop.
TBU -W LOOP 2 4 6 8 10 12 14 16 18	The -W option tells tBU to set the environmental variable LOOP equal to 2 the first time, 4 the second, and so on. When DOS reaches the command and LOOP=18, tBU sets ERRORLEVEL to one to indicate the looping has finished.
IF ERRORLEVEL 1 GOTO END1	IF ERRORLEVEL is one, the loop has finished and this line exits the loop. Without this exit-line, the loop would continue forever.
ECHO First Loop: Number %LOOP%	Tells the user what is happening.
GOTO TOP1	If it reaches this point, the looping has not finished, so continue looping.
:END1	Label marking the exit-point for the first loop.
CLS	Clears the screen.
ECHO -w Can Count With Numbers	Tells the user what will happen with the next tBU command.

Batch File Line	Explanation
:TOP2	Label marking the top of the next loop.
TBU -w LOOP 1 50	Starts off with LOOP=1 and continues in increments of one until LOOP=50, and then set ERRORLEVEL to one.
IF ERRORLEVEL 1 GOTO END2	Exits the loop when ERRORLEVEL is one.
ECHO Second Loop: Number %LOOP%	Tells the user what is happening.
GOTO TOP2	Continues looping.
:END2	Label marking the exit-point for the second loop.
CLS	Clears the screen.
ECHO -w Can Also "Count" With Letters	Tells the user what will happen next.
:TOP3	Label marking the top of the third loop.
TBU -w LOOP A AC	Starts off with LOOP=A and continues in increments of one until LOOP=Z. Continues looping with LOOP=AA until LOOP=50, and then sets ERRORLEVEL to one.
IF ERRORLEVEL 1 GOTO END3	Exits the loop if ERRORLEVEL is one.
ECHO Third Loop: Number %LOOP%	Tells the user what is happening.
GOTO TOP3	Continues the loop.
:END3	Label marking the exit-point for the third loop.

x   Stores a files extension to the environmental variable.

Y   Stores the current subdirectory to the environmental variable.

y   Stores the subdirectory portion of a file specification in the environmental variable.

z   Stores the size of a file in the environmental variable.

Table 6-15 summarizes the many tBU symbols, showing the syntax for each.

Unfortunately, tBU uses a complex syntax difficult to learn and terse documentation that makes learning tBU even more difficult. Fortunately, tBU is so powerful that you will soon wonder how you got along without it. In fact, after this book was finished, tBU is one of only a handful of utilities that found a permanent home on my crowded hard disk. I highly recommend tBU.

Table 6-15   A summary of tBU symbols and their meaning.

Symbol	ERRORLEVEL	Example	Description
A	0=No 1=Yes	TBU -A TEMP	Checks to see if ANSI.-SYS was loaded.
b		TBU -b 800 300	Beeps the speaker at a specified tone for a specified duration.
C	Length of new value.	TBU -C TEMP 15 10 16	Sets variable to value in new radix.
c	ASCII value of character entered.	TBU -c TEMP "Run?" yn	Allows the user to input a single keystroke. Can display a prompt, limit input to specific characters, and timeout after given period of time.
D	Length of string.	TBU -D TEMP "Date #D"	Sets variable to date and time. Can add optional text and control formatting.
d	Length of string.	TBU -d TEMP file "Time: #T"	Sets variable to date and time a file was created. Can add optional text and control formatting.
E	Environment size/10 in bytes.	TBU -E TEMP	Sets variable to total size of environment in bytes/10.
e	Amount of free Environment/10 in bytes.	TBU -e TEMP	Sets variable to size of free environment in bytes/10.
F	Length of string.	TBU -F TEMP 690000000 "Date: #D #T"	Sets variable to the formatted time stamp.
f	Length of string.	TBU -f C:\command.com	Sets variable to the upper-case filename, including period and extension. In other words, it strips off preceding path.
h	1 if keyword not found, 0 otherwise.	TBU -h help TBU.DOC	Locates a keyword and displays help on the screen.
I	0=Less Than 1=Equal 2=Greater Than	TBU -I TEMP "A" "d"	Compares two strings and sets variable to "LT", "GT" or "EQ" to indicate their relationship.
K	Bytes/Scale	TBU -K TEMP C: 1024	Sets variable to the free space on the specified drive divided by the scale value. (1024 in this example.)

Symbol	ERRORLEVEL	Example	Description
k	0=Yes 1=No	`TBU -k TEMP A: 102400`	Sets variable to indicate if the requested amount of free space (in bytes) is available on the indicated drive.
L	1=A: 2=B: 3=C: and so on	`TBU -L TEMP`	Sets variable to the current disk drive.
M	Free memory/scale in bytes.	`TBU -M TEMP 1024`	Sets variable to the amount of free memory in bytes divided by the optional scaling factor.
m	0 if not found, offset otherwise.	`TBU -m TEMP "B" "ABC"`	Finds one string in another and sets variable to the position where the string begins.
n	Length of string	`TBU -n TEMP C:\NO.BAK`	Sets variable to the filename portion of file. In other words, path, period, and extension are removed.
o	Length of string.	`TBU -o TEMP "UPPER"`	Sets variable to the lower-case value of the string.
p	Length of string.	`TBU -p TEMP` `"String" 1 3`	Sets variable to a substring of the input string beginning at the indicated position for the indicated length.
q	Length of string.	`TBU -q TEMP TEMP2`	Sets one variable equal to a second variable.
R		`TBU -R TEMP BOTH`	Sets variable to the major, minor, or both numbers of the DOS version.
S	Length of string.	`TBU -S TEMP "1st"` `"2nd" "Do It 1st"`	Sets variable to the third string with the portion of it containing the first string replaced by the second string.
s	Length of string.	`TBU -s TEMP "Enter` `your name: "`	Has the user enter a string from the keyboard.
T	0=Not Exists 1=Exists 2=Directory	`TBU -T TEMP word.exe`	Sets variable to "D" if it is a directory, "Y" if file exists and "N" if file does not exist.
t	0=No 1=Yes	`TBU -t TEMP`	Checks to see if an extended keyboard is both present and supported.

Table 6-15   Continued.

Symbol	ERRORLEVEL	Example	Description
U	Length of string.	TBU -U TEMP "lower"	Sets variable to uppercase of input string.
V	0=No 1=Yes	TBU -V TEMP	Sets variable to "N" if DesqView or Topview is not present, otherwise to the version number.
W	1=End of Loop 0=Otherwise	TBU -W TEMP 1 2 3 4	Sets variable to 1 on the first loop, 2 on the second, and so on.
w	1=End of Loop 0=Otherwise	TBU -w TEMP 1 9	Sets variable to 1 on the first loop, 2 on the second, and so on up to 9.
x	Length of string.	TBU -x TEMP word.com	Sets variable to the file's extension.
Y	Length of string.	TBU -Y TEMP	Sets variable to the current subdirectory.
y	Length of string.	TBU -y TEMP c:\wp\word\files	Sets variable to the subdirectory portion of a filename.
z	Size of file/scale.	TBU -z TEMP wp.com 10	Sets variable to the size of the file in bytes divided by the scale factor.

WHAT

Name: WHAT
Version: 1.47
Price: Free
Category: Public Domain
Summary: What can determine a great deal of information about the computer and pass that information back to the batch file. It can also prompt the user for a single character response to a question. Information is passed using the ERRORLEVEL and an environmental variable.
Author: Tom Peters
Availability: Available on many bulletin board systems.

Sometimes you can write a more effective batch file if you have some information about the environment under which the batch file is running. WHAT is an excellent program for obtaining that information.

The general format for the WHAT command is

WHAT X [E] Parameter-1 Parameter-2

where X is the option to run and E is the optional enhanced mode. Some of the WHAT options require additional parameters. Most of the WHAT options return a value in the environmental variable what and in ERRORLEVEL. The options available in WHAT are as follows:

7 tests to see if a math coprocessor is present. It sets ERRORLEVEL to 0 if a math coprocessor doesn't exist, to 1 if one does, and stores the same number in the environment. This proves useful if a program requires a math coprocessor or a command line switch to use the coprocessor.

A tests to see if ANSI.SYS is present. It sets ERRORLEVEL to 0 if ANSI.SYS is loaded, to 1 if not, and stores the result in the environment. This gives your batch file a way of altering its formatting depending on the status of ANSI.

C prompts the user for a single keystroke. You can limit the keystrokes the program will accept from the user to a specific list. The program is case-insensitive and treats all letters as uppercase. The actual uppercase version of the letter is stored in the environment, and the ERRORLEVEL is set to the ASCII value of the uppercase letter. Adding the E option keeps the program from echoing the keystroke to the user.

D returns the major version of DOS in the environment and (major*10) + minor in ERRORLEVEL. Adding the E option causes the program to store the minor version in the environment, which is useful when batch files must use DOS-specific commands. For example, a batch file might use the command CALL batch2 in DOS 3.3 and later and COMMAND/C batch2 in DOS 3.2 and earlier.

E returns the free space remaining in the environment and stores it in the environment and in ERRORLEVEL. Adding the E option divides the results by 10. Because WHAT makes extensive use of the environment, this helps ensure adequate environmental space.

F returns the size of a single file and stores it in the environment and in ERRORLEVEL. Wildcards aren't supported. Adding the E option divides the results by 10. When combined with the K option, this allows you to make sure enough free space exists to copy a file. You can also test a file's length to ensure that it's small enough for an editor with limited capacity to handle.

K returns the amount of free space on a drive and stores it in the environment and in ERRORLEVEL. Adding the E option divides the results by 10. Thus, you can check for adequate free space to install software or copy a file.

M returns the amount of free RAM and stores it in the environment and in ERRORLEVEL. Adding the E option divides the results by 10. Thus, you can ensure before running a program that adequate memory exists. It also would prevent the mistake of shelling out of one package, forgetting, and trying to run a second program.

P checks to see if a printer is attached and ready. It sets ERRORLEVEL to 0 if no printer is ready, to 1 if one is, and stores the same number in the environment. Because some programs will lock up the computer when trying to print without a ready printer, testing the printer first can prevent some problems.

S lets the user enter a string, such as a password or their name, storing the string in the environment and setting ERRORLEVEL equal to the length of the string. The E option disables screen echoing.

T stores the time in the environment and can be used to time-stamp a file. The E option changes the format.

V stores the video mode in both the environment and ERRORLEVEL, which can be useful when a program requires a specific video mode.

X stores the date in the environment and can be used to time-stamp a file. The E option changes the format.

Y stores the name of the current subdirectory in the environment. You can then write a batch file that returns to this subdirectory with a CD\ %WHAT% command. The E option stores the drive name rather than the subdirectory.

Table 6-16 summarizes the WHAT options, while SHOWWHAT.BAT in Table 6-17 is a batch file illustrating many of the SHOW options.

WHAT is extremely powerful and also easy to use; it belongs in everyone's batch file toolkit.

Table 6-16 A summary of WHAT options.

Option	Function	Returns
7	Tests to see if a math coprocessor is DesqView.	Stores one in environmental variable what and ERRORLEVEL if one is present, a zero otherwise.
A	Checks to see if ANSI.SYS was loaded when the computer was booted.	Stores one in environmental variable what and ERRORLEVEL if one is present, a zero otherwise.
C or CE	Prompts the user for a keystroke. The E option causes WHAT not to echo the keystroke to the screen.	Stores the keystroke in the environmental variable what and returns the ASCII value of the keystroke in ERRORLEVEL.
D	Test for the version of DOS.	Stores the major version in the environmental variable what and stores (major*10)+minor in ERRORLEVEL.
DE	Test for the version of DOS.	Stores the minor version in the environmental variable what and stores (major*10)+minor in ERRORLEVEL.
E or EE	Tests for the free bytes (E) or free bytes/10 (EE) of space in the environment.	Stores information in the environmental variable what and ERRORLEVEL.
F or FE *filename*	Tests for the files size in 1,000-bytes (F) or 10,000-bytes (FE).	Stores information in the environmental variable what and ERRORLEVEL.
K or KE *drive*	Tests for the free space on the drive in 1,000-bytes (K) or 10,000-bytes (KE) increments.	Stores information in the environmental variable what and ERRORLEVEL.

Option	Function	Returns
M or ME	Tests for free RAM in 1,000-bytes (M) or 10,000-bytes (ME) increments.	Stores information in the environmental variable what and ERRORLEVEL.
P	Checks for a printer.	Returns a one if a printer was found in the environmental variable what and ERROR-LEVEL, a zero otherwise.
S or SE	Accepts a string from the user. The E option causes WHAT not to echo the string to the screen.	Stores the string in the environmental variable what and the length of the string in ERRORLEVEL.
T or TE	Checks the time.	Returns the time in two formats in the environmental variable what.
V	Tests for the video mode.	Stores information in the environmental variable what and ERRORLEVEL.
X or XE	Checks the date.	Returns the date in two formats in the environmental variable what.
Y	Checks for the current subdirectory.	Returns the current subdirectory in the environmental variable what.
YE	Checks for the current drive.	Returns the current drive in the environmental variable what.

Table 6-17   SHOWWHAT.BAT illustrates many of the WHAT options.

Batch File Line	Explanation
`@ECHO OFF`	Turns command-echoing off.

`REM NAME:     SHOWWHAT.BAT`
`REM PURPOSE: Illustrate What V1.47`
`REM VERSION: 1.00`
`REM DATE:     April 3, 1991`
	Documentation remarks.

`CLS`	Clears the screen.
`WHAT A`	Runs WHAT and check to see if ANSI.SYS is present.
`IF %WHAT%==0 ECHO ANSI.SYS Not Found` `IF %WHAT%==1 ECHO ANSI.SYS Found`	Tells the user the results.
`WHAT CE "Press Any Letter   "` `   ABCDEFGHIJKLMNOPQRSTUVWXYZ`	Runs WHAT to accept any letter keystroke from the user.
`ECHO` `ECHO You Pressed %WHAT%`	Tells the user what key was pressed. The first ECHO line echoes an Alt-255 space because WHAT does not reset the cursor position after running this command.
`WHAT CE "Press Any Number"0123456789`	Asks the user for another keystroke and this time only accepts numbers.
`ECHO` `ECHO You Pressed %WHAT%`	Tells the user what keystroke was pressed.

Table 6-17   Continued.

Batch File Line	Explanation
`WHAT D`	Runs WHAT to test for the major DOS version.
`ECHO Your Major DOS Version` `   Is %WHAT%`	Tells the user the results.
`WHAT DE`	Runs WHAT to test for the major and minor DOS version.

`FOR %%J IN (0 1 2 3 4 5 6 7 8 9 10)`
`   DO IF ERRORLEVEL %%J SET WHAT=%%J`
`FOR %%J IN (11 12 13 14 15 16 17 18)`
`   DO IF ERRORLEVEL %%J SET WHAT=%%J`
 	
`Test continues for 19-50`
 	
`FOR %%J IN (51 52 53 54 55 56 57 58)`
`   DO IF ERRORLEVEL %%J SET WHAT=%%J`
	WHAT stores the combined version by multiplying the major version by ten and adding the minor version. By testing for ERRORLEVEL values up to 58, DOS through version 5.8 is covered. In these loops, the environmental variable what is continually updated as long as the counter %%J is less than or equal to ERRORLEVEL. Once %%J passes ERRORLEVEL, the if-test is false and the variable is not updated. Thus, when finished, the value of the environmental variable equals the ERRORLEVEL.

`ECHO You Complete DOS Version` `   Is %WHAT%/10`	Tells the user the results.
`WHAT E`	Runs WHAT to measure the free space in the environment.
`ECHO Your Environment Has %WHAT%` `   Free Bytes`	Tells the user the results.
`WHAT F SHOWWHAT.BAT`	Runs WHAT to measure the size of a file.
`ECHO SHOWWHAT.BAT Is %WHAT%K Large`	Tells the user the results.
`WHAT K`	Runs WHAT to measure the free disk space on the current drive.
`ECHO Current Drive Has %WHAT%K` `   Of Free Space`	Tells the user the results.
`WHAT M`	Runs WHAT to measure the free RAM.
`ECHO This Machine Now Has %WHAT%K` `   Free RAM`	Tells the user the results.
`WHAT P 1`	Runs WHAT to test for a printer on LPT1.
`IF %WHAT%==0 ECHO No Printer Found` `IF %WHAT%==1 ECHO Printer Found`	Tells the user the results.
`WHAT T`	Runs WHAT to get the time.
`ECHO Current Time Is %WHAT%`	Tells the user the results.
`WHAT TE`	Runs WHAT to get the time in another format.
`ECHO Also Known As %WHAT%`	Tells the user the results.
`WHAT V`	Runs WHAT to get the video mode.

Batch File Line	Explanation
`ECHO Video Mode is %WHAT%`	Tells the user the results.
`WHAT X`	Runs WHAT to get the date.
`ECHO Current Date Is %WHAT%`	Tells the user the results.
`WHAT XE`	Runs WHAT to get the date in another format.
`ECHO For Easy Sorting, Date Is` `   Also %WHAT%`	Tells the user the results.
`WHAT Y`	Runs WHAT to get the subdirectory.
`ECHO Current Subdirectory Is %WHAT%`	Tells the user the results.
`WHAT YE`	Runs WHAT to get the drive.
`ECHO Current Drive Is %WHAT%:`	Tells the user the results.
`WHAT 7`	Runs WHAT to test for a math coprocessor.

`IF %WHAT%==0 ECHO No Coprocessor`
`   Found`
`IF %WHAT%==1 ECHO Coprocessor Found`
	Tells the user the results.

X-BATCH

Name:	X-BATCH
Version:	1.0
Price:	$20.00
Category:	Shareware
Summary:	A collection of 13 useful utilities.
Author:	Gary R. Pannone
	9 Brady Road Ext.
	Westboro, Massachusetts 01581
Availability:	Available on many bulletin board systems.

X-BATCH is a collection of thirteen useful batch file utilities:

BOX draws a box on the screen. You can control the box size, location, and color, as well as even display it without erasing text already on the screen.

CHKENVIR checks to see if an environmental variable exists and (optionally) whether its contents match a specific value.

CHKSCRN checks to see if specific text is displayed on the screen and works only if the screen is in text mode.

CLRSCRN clears the screen and optionally changes the colors. Personally, I wish that it could just clear the screen inside a box, but that isn't possible.

COMPFILE compares the dates/sizes of two files to see which is earlier/larger.

CREATE creates a 0-length file if a file doesn't already exist with the given name. Of course, you can do the same thing using straight DOS. The command TYPE nofile > 0-LENGTH.TXT will create a 0-length file called 0-LENGTH.TXT if the file nofile *doesn't* exist.

CURSOR positions the cursor at a specific location on the screen, useful for controlling where DOS programs display their messages.

DISPFILE reads a file and displays it in a box on the screen. If the file is too large to fit, only the portion that fits is displayed. DISPFILE doesn't allow you to scroll around in the file.

DISPLAY displays text on the screen, allowing you to position the cursor first and control the color of the text.

GETCHAR allows you to accept a single keystroke from the user, either any character whatsoever or one from a specified list. Letters are converted to uppercase, and the ASCII value of the keystroke is returned.

SHOW displays the date, day, and time in a better format than DOS.

SOUND sounds the speaker, allowing you to control the frequency and duration.

WAIT pauses the batch file for a specific period of time or until a specific time is reached.

The X-BATCH commands are useful and easy to learn, with a sensible format that reads almost like English. Table 6-18 shows the X-BATCH commands, while SHOWX-BAT.BAT (Table 6-19) illustrates many of these commands.

Table 6-18   A summary of X-BATCH commands.

Command	Function
BOX	Draws a box on the screen and optionally changes colors inside the box.
CHKENVIR	Checks the contents of an environmental variable.
CHKSCRN	Checks the screen to see if it contains specified text.
CLRSCRN	Clears the screen and optionally changes colors.
COMPFILE	Compares the time/date and size of two files.
CREATE	Creates a 0-length file.
CURSOR	Positions the cursor.
DISPFILE	Displays a file on the screen.
DISPLAY	Displays text on the screen. Allows you to position the cursor and control colors.
GETCHAR	Obtains a single character from the user.
SHOW	Displays the time and date.
SOUND	Plays a sound on the speaker. You have control over the frequency and duration.
WAIT	Pauses the batch file for a specific period of time until a specific time is reached.

Table 6-19   SHOWXBAT.BAT
illustrates many of the X-BATCH commands.

Batch File Line	Explanation
`@ECHO OFF`	Turns command-echoing off.

`REM NAME:    SHOWXBAT.BAT`
`REM PURPOSE: Illustrate XBatch`
`REM VERSION: April 20, 1991`
`REM VERSION: 1.0`
	Documentation remarks.

`CLRSCRN COLORS 15 1`	Clear the screen to bright white letters on a blue background.
`DISPLAY "10 10" AT 10 10`	Display the text "10 10" at row-10 and column-10 on the screen.

`DISPLAY "20 20" AT 20 20`
`DISPLAY "10 50" AT 10 50`
`DISPLAY "20 50" AT 20 50`
`DISPLAY "15 38" AT 15 38`
	Display more text on the screen at different locations.

`DISPLAY "Press Any Key to Continue"` `    AT 24 2 COLORS 4 7`	Ask the user to press any key to continue. Display the text on row-24 starting at column-2 in red letters on a white background.
`CURSOR AT 1 1`	Position the cursor at the top of the screen.
`PAUSE>NUL`	Pause the batch file and pipe the DOS message to nul.
`CLRSCRN COLORS 4 7`	Clear the screen to red on white.
`BOX FROM  1  1 TO 24 80 SINGLE` `    COLORS 15 1 BRIGHT`	Draw a box on the screen that starts at row-1 and column-1 and goes to row-24 and column-80. Draw a single line around the box and color it white on a blue background.

`BOX FROM  1  1 TO 24 40 DOUBLE`
`    COLORS 15 1 BRIGHT`
`BOX FROM  1 40 TO 24 80 DOUBLE`
`    COLORS 15 1 BRIGHT`
`BOX FROM  5 20 TO 20 60 SINGLE COLORS  4 7`
`BOX FROM  1  1 TO  5 20 DOUBLE COLORS 14 1`
`BOX FROM 20 60 TO 24 80 DOUBLE COLORS  3 5`
	Draw more boxes on the screen.

`DISPLAY "Press Any Key to Continue"`
`    AT 24 2 COLORS 4 7`
`CURSOR AT 1 1`
`PAUSE>NUL`
`CLRSCRN COLORS 15 1`
	Clear the screen after the user presses a keystroke.

`DIR`	Perform a directory of the current subdirectory--just to get some text on the screen.
`BOX FROM  5 20 TO 20 60 DOUBLE NOCLEAR` `    COLORS  4 7`	Draw a box around the text without erasing any of the text inside the box.

`BOX FROM  5 20 TO 20 60 DOUBLE NOCLEAR`
`    COLORS  9 7`
`BOX FROM  5 20 TO 20 60 DOUBLE NOCLEAR`
`    COLORS 17 7`
`BOX FROM  5 20 TO 20 60 DOUBLE NOCLEAR`
`    COLORS  9 0`
`BOX FROM  5 20 TO 20 60 DOUBLE NOCLEAR`
`    COLORS  1 7`
	Draw more boxes in different colors around the text without erasing it.

Table 6-19 Continued.

Batch File Line	Explanation

`DISPLAY "Press Any Key to Continue"`
`    AT 24 2 COLORS 4 7`
`CURSOR AT 1 1`
`PAUSE>NUL`
	Wait for the user to press a keystroke.

`CHKENVIR PATH DEFINED`	Before erasing the screen, check to see if the PATH is defined.
`FOR %%J IN (0 1 2) DO IF ERRORLEVEL %%J` `    SET P=%%J`	Store the ERRORLEVEL as a variable so it can be reused by the next command.

`CHKENVIR COMSPEC EQUALS "C:\COMMAND.COM"`
`FOR %%J IN (0 1 2) DO IF ERRORLEVEL %%J`
`    SET C=%%J`
	Check for the COMSPEC variable's value and store the results.

`CHKSCRN "XBATCH"`
`FOR %%J IN (0 1) DO IF ERRORLEVEL %%J`
`    SET X=%%J`
	Read the screen to see if the text XBATCH appears anywhere and store the results.

`CLRSCRN COLORS 15 1`	Clears the screen.

`COMPFILE XBATCH.DOC WAIT.EXE BYDATE`
`FOR %%J IN (0 1 2) DO IF ERRORLEVEL %%J`
`    SET A=%%J`
	Check the dates of two files and store the results.

`COMPFILE XBATCH.DOC WAIT.EXE BYTIME`
`FOR %%J IN (0 1 2) DO IF ERRORLEVEL %%J`
`    SET B=%%J`
	Check the date and time of two files and store the results.

`COMPFILE XBATCH.DOC WAIT.EXE BYSIZE`
`FOR %%J IN (0 1 2) DO IF ERRORLEVEL %%J`
`    SET A=%%J`
	Check the size of two files and store the results.

`IF %X%==0 ECHO Before Erasing, XBATCH`
`        Found On Screen`
`IF %X%==1 ECHO Before Erasing, XBATCH`
`        Not On Screen`
`IF %P%==0 ECHO Path Defined`
`IF %P%==2 ECHO Path Not Defined!`
`IF %C%==0 ECHO COMSPEC=C:\COMMAND.COM`
`IF %C%==1 ECHO COMSPEC is not C:\COMMAND.COM`
`IF %C%==2 ECHO COMSPEC Not Found!`
`IF %A%==0 ECHO XBATCH.DOC And WAIT.EXE`
`        Have Same Date`
`IF %A%==1 ECHO XBATCH.DOC Has Later Date`
`        Than WAIT.EXE`
`IF %A%==2 ECHO XBATCH.DOC Has Earlier Date`
`        Than WAIT.EXE`
`IF %B%==0 ECHO XBATCH.DOC And WAIT.EXE`
`        Have Same Time`
`IF %B%==1 ECHO XBATCH.DOC Has Later Time`
`        Than WAIT.EXE`
`IF %B%==2 ECHO XBATCH.DOC Has Earlier Time`
`        Than WAIT.EXE`
`IF %B%==0 ECHO XBATCH.DOC And WAIT.EXE Have`
`        Same Size`
`IF %B%==1 ECHO XBATCH.DOC Is Larger Than`
`        WAIT.EXE`
`IF %B%==2 ECHO XBATCH.DOC Is Smaller Than`
`        WAIT.EXE`
	Display the results of these tests. Since these are not ERROR-LEVEL tests, the tests are not greater than or equal tests.

`SHOW DAY`
`SHOW DATE`
`SHOW TIME`
	Display some information using the built-in X-BATCH tests.

`SET A=`
`SET B=`
`SET C=`
`SET P=`
`SET X=`
`SET S=`
	Reset the environmental variables.

Batch File Line	Explanation

`DISPLAY "Do You Like the Demo So Far? (Y/N)"`
`    AT 24 2 COLORS 4 7`
`GETCHAR CHOICES "YN" AT 24 38`
	Display a prompt and ask a question.

`IF ERRORLEVEL 78 IF NOT ERRORLEVEL 79 GOTO NO` `IF ERRORLEVEL 89 IF NOT ERRORLEVEL 90 GOTO YES`	Branch depending on the user's response.

`CLRSCRN COLORS 15 1`
`ECHO INTERNAL ERROR!`
`ECHO EXITING PROGRAM`
`GOTO END`
	This section is a safety valve in case the logic is flawed. The batch file should never reach this point since the above branching should take care of all cases.

`:NO`	Label marking the beginning of the section for users who do not like the demo.
`CLRSCRN COLORS 15 1`	Clears the screen.
`SOUND FREQ 1000 FOR 5` `SOUND FREQ 5000 FOR 5`	Sound a 1 KHZ tone for 5-seconds and a 5 KHZ tone for 5-seconds.
`DISPLAY "Sorry, And I Worked So Hard" AT 10 30` `DISPLAY "I Will Leave You Alone Now!" AT 14 30`	Display a message.
`SOUND FREQ 10000 FOR 10`	Sound a higher pitch tone for 10-seconds. (Mean, aren't I?)
`GOTO END`	Exit the batch file.
`:YES`	Label marking the section of the batch file for those who liked the demo so far.
`CLRSCRN COLORS 15 1`	Clears the screen.
`DISPLAY "Thanks" AT 12 38`	Display a message.
`SOUND FREQ 1000 FOR 1`	Sound a brief tone.
`WAIT FOR 10`	Wait ten seconds.
`DISPFILE SHOWXBAT.BAT FROM  5 10` `    TO 20 60 DOUBLE COLORS 15 4`	Display the top of the batch file on the screen.
`WAIT FOR 10`	Leave it on the screen for ten seconds.
`CLRSCRN COLORS 15 1`	Clears the screen.
`DISPLAY "Thanks For Your Attention" AT 12 30`	Display a final message.
`CURSOR AT 24 1`	Position the cursor.
`:END`	Label marking the end of the batch file.

7

Other batch utilities

BATCH.EXE

Name:	BATCH.EXE
Version:	Unknown
Price:	Unknown
Category:	Unknown
Summary:	Converts ASCII files to batch files.
Author:	Unknown
Availability:	Available on some bulletin board systems.

BATCH.EXE comes without any documentation or identification. The first time you run it, a small batch file and a few lines of instructions are created. After that, you run BATCH .EXE to convert ASCII files to batch files for display. The resulting batch files are a series of ECHO commands that display the text with a PAUSE and CLS command at the end of each screen of information.

BATCH.EXE can't deal properly with ASCII files without a carriage return and line feed at the end of each line. It creates one lone ECHO statement for each line. For a typical word processing document with a carriage return and line feed only at the end of each paragraph, this can result in ECHO statements several hundred or even thousands of characters long. On some versions of DOS, the computer locks up when a command line in a batch file exceeds the 127-character limit set by DOS.

Because no documentation for BATCH.EXE exists, I was unable to determine if it's shareware or public domain and thus available for posting on bulletin board systems. While it's available on many bulletin boards, you should avoid it because of its lack of documentation and poor performance.

Batch Maker

Name:	Batch Maker
Version:	1.0
Price:	Free
Category:	Public Domain
Summary:	Automates writing simple batch files.
Author:	Robert L. Miller
Availability:	Available on many bulletin board systems.

Robert L. Miller has written a public domain program called Batch Maker to automate creating batch files. Batch Maker takes advantage of DOS replaceable parameters, which can be used both as commands and switches. The command to start Batch Maker is

```
C>BATMAKER FILES – Switch
```

where FILES are the files Batch Maker should use. Only one type of file can be used, but you can use wildcards. The switches are listed in Table 7-1.

Table 7-1   Batch Maker can make several different types of batch files depending on the switches you use.

OPTION	FUNCTION
-A	%1 FILENAME.EXT %2 %3
-B	%1 %2 FILENAME.EXT %3 %4
-C	%1 %2 FILENAME.EXT %3 %4
-D	%1 < FILENAME.EXT > %2 %3
-E	%1 < FILENAME.EXT > > %2 %3
-F	%1 < FILENAME.EXT | %2 > %3 %4
-G	%1 < FILENAME.EXT | %2 > > %3 %4
-H	PRINTS HELP MESSAGE
-I	%1 %2 %3 FILENAME.EXT %4 %5

Batch Maker reads in the list of file defined by FILES. It then sorts the list and constructs a batch file with one line per file, with the number and arrangement of replaceable parameters being controlled by the switch. The resulting batch file is always named NAMES.BAT. Using the command

```
C>BATMAKER *.ARC – A
```

you can generate the NAMES.BAT file shown in Fig. 7-1.

```
%1 BATMAKER.ARC %2 %3
%1 REBOOT21.ARC %2 %3
```

7-1   NAMES.BAT is a batch file produced by Batch Maker.

I use Batch Maker as the first of a two step process. After Batch Maker creates NAMES.BAT, I rename the batch file and edit it. If you want to copy most of your batch files to the A drive, you'll find it much easier to edit NAMES.BAT than to issue the copy command for each file. If I am planning to reuse the batch file, I rename it to prevent it from being overwritten the next time I run Batch Maker.

BatDay

Name:	BatDay
Version:	1.0
Price:	Free
Category:	Copyrighted
Summary:	Executes a different batch file based on the day of the week.
Author:	Tony Tortonelli
Availability:	Available on many bulletin board systems.

Certain tasks exist that you want the computer to run automatically but only occasionally. For example, you might want to run your disk optimizer once a week, make an incremental backup once a week, make a full backup once a month, and run a program to save an image of your file allocation table [FAT] once a day. Under DOS, you have only two very limited choices: put the command in the AUTOEXEC.BAT file and perform it every time you reboot, or remember to run the program manually. BatDay offers a third choice.

When you run BatDay, it executes one of seven batch files (SUN.BAT, MON.BAT, TUES.BAT, and so on) depending on the day of the week. You would put the commands for that day in the individual batch files.

In order to run its batch files, BatDay loads a second copy of COMMAND.COM. That process passes a copy of the environment to MON.BAT—or whichever batch file is running that day. When the batch file terminates and control passes back to the original batch file that ran BatDay (generally the AUTOEXEC.BAT file), that copy of the environment is lost. As a result, you can't use BatDay to set the PATH or control any other environmental variables.

Rebooting, however, does cause problems with BatDay (although DO-ONCE, covered next, is immune to this). Generally, you would include the BatDay command in your AUTOEXEC.BAT file. Unfortunately, as a result, every time you reboot on Monday, BatDay will run MON.BAT even if you only want to run it once. In addition, if you don't use the computer on Monday, then MON.BAT won't execute until next Monday—another problem also avoided with DO-ONCE. If neither problem concerns you, then BatDay is a good solution to running some routines occasionally. Otherwise, you will want to look at DO-ONCE.

BATDEL

Name:	BATDEL
Version:	1.0
Price:	Free
Category:	Copyrighted
Summary:	Automatically deletes a batch file after running.
Author:	Bill Wingate
	XenneX Enterprises
	2870 East 33rd Street
	Tulsa, Oklahoma 74105
Availability:	Available on many bulletin board systems.

Sometimes you create a special batch file to automate a long process. If you don't ever plan to repeat the process, you might want to have the batch file delete itself when finished. You can actually do this with DOS by adding the command DEL BATCH.BAT as the last line of the batch file. Of course, you would replace BATCH.BAT with the actual name of the batch file. If you make this the last line of the batch file and follow the command immediately with an EOF marker, everything will work fine. If you follow the command with a return, DOS will delete the batch file properly but give you a "Batch file missing" error message.

Of course, if you put the DEL BATCH.BAT command in the middle of the batch file, none of the rest of the batch file will execute. DOS reads batch files one line at a time and once the batch file is deleted, nothing remains to be read.

BATDEL overcomes all of the minor problems associated with having a batch file delete itself. You can add the command BATDEL BATCH.BAT anywhere in the batch file, again replacing BATCH.BAT with the actual name of the batch file to delete. This command loads a small memory resident program (about 6K) that watches the batch file run. When control returns to DOS, the memory resident program deletes the batch file and removes most of itself from memory.

The documentation claims that all of BATDEL is removed from memory. However, under DOS 5.0, about 449 bytes remained in memory. This small reduction in memory isn't very significant, but it does keep you from unloading any other memory resident programs.

Because the only side effect of having a batch file delete itself is an error message, I don't find BATDEL a very useful program (especially because I rarely need a batch file to delete itself).

BOOTLOG

Name:	BOOTLOG

Version:	1.0
Price:	Free
Category:	Copyrighted
Summary:	Displays the date and time in a convenient format.
Author:	Brian E. Smith
	59 Main Street
	Piedmont, South Carolina 29673
Availability:	Included on the disk bound in this book.

You can track the usage of any program you start with a batch file by piping the date and time you start and stop to a log file. Normally, this is still a little difficult because you must pipe a return to the DATE and TIME commands, putting them on different lines.

BOOTLOG overcomes this problem. It displays both the date and time on the same line without the need to press return. You can then pipe that information to a log file to track your usage of a program.

Brkstate

Name:	Brkstate
Version:	1.0
Price:	Free
Category:	Public Domain
Summary:	Sets the ERRORLEVEL to indicate the status of BREAK.
Availability:	Included on the disk bound in this book.

When you run Brkstate, it sets the ERRORLEVEL to 1 if BREAK is on and to 0 if BREAK is off. Because you can change the status of BREAK in a batch file, its current status might be handy to know. Of course, you could just set BREAK to the value you need, which would probability be faster than running Brkstate and then testing the status of ERRORLEVEL.

CALL

Name:	Call
Version:	Unknown
Price:	Unknown
Category:	Unknown
Summary:	Allows batch files running under DOS 3.21 and earlier to run a second batch file and have control return to the calling batch file.
Author:	George Palecek

Availability: Available on many bulletin board systems.[1]

Prior to DOS 3.3, if one batch file called another, control would never return to the original batch file. With the CALL command, one batch file could run another one and still regain control after it had finished. The command to run the second batch file is CALL batch2.

The CALL program from George Palecek adds the same capabilities to DOS 2.0 through DOS 3.21 using the exact same syntax. However, the program documentation doesn't indicate if the program is public domain or shareware, so you can't tell whether or not you are violating the author's copyright by using and sharing the program.

You don't need the program in any case. If you add the EXIT command as the last line of the batch file you want to call, then the command COMMAND/C batch2 works just as well.

Check

Name:	Check
Version:	11-18-87
Price:	Free
Category:	Copyrighted
Summary:	A program that can determine a great deal of information about the computer hardware and pass that information back to the batch file. It can also prompt the user for a single character response to a question. All information is passed using the ERRORLEVEL.
Author:	Jeff Prosise, from *PC Magazine*
Availability:	All *PC Magazine* files are available from their area on CompuServe. See any issue of *PC Magazine* for details.

Check is one of the many useful batch file utilities published by *PC Magazine* over the years. Although its most useful function is to ask the user a question and wait for a response, Check does much more. To communicate with the user, Check uses 16 keywords that follow the Check command (see Table 7-2).

Check is best learned through use. Table 7-3 shows CHECK1.BAT, a long batch file using every keyword of Check. It illustrates proper syntax use, as well as techniques for branching and decision making based on the results of running Check.

Check can be used in numerous ways:

- When you start your word processor, you can erase all the *.BAK files if your B drive is cramped for space.

---

[1]The documentation doesn't indicate the status of this software, so no way exists to identify the program as public domain, shareware, or commercial.

- The MIS department can distribute a new program that will install itself only if enough space exists for all the files.
- A batch file can decide which version of a program to run depending on whether the system has a color or monochrome monitor or whether a math coprocessor is installed.

Of course, this is just a short list of suggestions. I am sure you will have numerous uses for Check.

Table 7-2   A summary of keywords for the Check program.

KEYWORD	SYNTAX	FUNCTION
8087 80287	CHECK 8087 CHECK 80287	Returns a 0 if there is a math coprocessor, a 1 if there is not a math coprocessor.
DAY	CHECK DAY	Returns the day of the month.
DISKSPACE	CHECK DISKSPACE	Returns the amount of free disk space on the default disk drive. Because of the limits of ERRORLEVEL, DISKSPACE can not simply report the disk space. Instead, it reports the number of full 16K blocks. So 200K is reported as 12. (200/16 = 12.5).
FILEFOUND	CHECK FILEFOUND file	Returns a 0 if the file exists and a 1 if it does not exist.
FILESIZE	CHECK FILESIZE file (No wildcards)	Returns the size of a file in K's. The maximum ERRORLEVEL value is 255 so all files 255K or larger return a value of 255.
FILETEXT	CHECK FILETEXT file "text" (No wildcards)	Returns a 0 if the text is found, a 1 if the text is not found or if the program encounters an error, such as the file does not exist. The text must match exactly, including capitalization.
KEYBOARD	CHECK KEYBOARD	Returns a 1 if there are keystrokes in the keyboard buffers, 0 if not.
KEYPRESS	CHECK KEYPRESS	Returns the ASCII value of any key that is pressed. If a key is pressed that produces an extended code (e.g. function key or cursor key) a 0 is returned. Note: lower- and uppercase keys return different values.
MEMORY	CHECK MEMORY	Reports the total memory (not the free memory) in 16K blocks. So 40 corresponds to 640K (40*16). Not all this memory will be available.

Table 7-2 Continued.

KEYWORD	SYNTAX	FUNCTION
MODEL	CHECK MODEL	Returns the computer model number on IBM machines. It may not work on some clones. The codes are: Code Machine 255 PC 254 XT and Portable PC 253 PCjr 252 AT 249 PC Convertible
MONTH	CHECK MONTH	Returns the month, Jan. = 1, Feb. = 2, and so on.
TIME	CHECK TIME	Returns the current hour in 24 hour format. So 1 PM to 1:59 PM returns a code of 13.
VERSION	CHECK VERSION	Returns the current version of DOS. Only the first number is reported. So 3.3, 3.2, 3.1, and 3.0 all return a 3. This is required because ERROR-LEVEL only supports whole numbers. DOS versions prior to 2.0 are not supported.
VIDEOCARD	CHECK VIDEOCARD	Returns a code the types of video displays. The codes are as follows: Code Display Type 0 MDA 1 CGA 2 EGA
VIDEOMODE	CHECK VIDEOMODE	Returns current video mode (1-16).

Table 7-3 CHECK1.BAT illustrates some of the capabilities of Check.

Batch File Line	Explanation
`ECHO OFF`	Turns command echoing off.
`REM CHECK1.BAT`	Remark giving the name of the batch file.

`CHECK 8087`
`IF ERRORLEVEL 1 ECHO No math coprocessor exists`
`IF ERRORLEVEL 1 GOTO 80287`
`IF ERRORLEVEL 0 ECHO Math coprocessor exists`
`IF ERRORLEVEL 0 GOTO 80287`
	Checks for 8087 math coprocessor. If found, tells user. Otherwise, looks for an 80287 coprocessor.

`:80287`
`CHECK 80287`
`IF ERRORLEVEL 1 ECHO No math coprocessor exists`
`IF ERRORLEVEL 1 GOTO DAY`
`IF ERRORLEVEL 0 ECHO Math coprocessor exists`
`IF ERRORLEVEL 0 GOTO DAY`
	Checks for 80287 math coprocessor. If found, tells user. Otherwise, skips to next section.

Batch File Line	Explanation
| ```
:DAY
CHECK DAY
IF ERRORLEVEL 31 ECHO 31th of month
IF ERRORLEVEL 31 GOTO DISKSPAC
IF ERRORLEVEL 30 ECHO 30th of month

The batch file continues in a similar fashion for
days 29-3

IF ERRORLEVEL 2 ECHO 2th of month
IF ERRORLEVEL 2 GOTO DISKSPAC
IF ERRORLEVEL 1 ECHO 1th of month
IF ERRORLEVEL 1 GOTO DISKSPAC
``` | Runs Check to set the ERRORLEVEL equal to the day of the month, and then performs a series of ERRORLEVEL tests to echo the day. Note that after echoing the day, it jumps to the next test. |
| ```
:DISKSPAC
CHECK DISKSPACE
IF ERRORLEVEL 255 ECHO More than 4080K free on disk
IF ERRORLEVEL 255 GOTO FILEFOUN
IF ERRORLEVEL 200 ECHO More than 3200K and less than
    4080K free on hard disk
IF ERRORLEVEL 200 GOTO FILEFOUN

The batch file continues in a similar fashion for
2400K-160K.

IF ERRORLEVEL 10 ECHO More than 160K and less than
    800K free on hard disk
IF ERRORLEVEL 10 GOTO FILEFOUN
ECHO Less than 160K free
GOTO FILEFOUN
``` | Runs Check to set the ERRORLEVEL equal to the amount of free space on the hard disk. Then performs a series of ERROR-LEVEL tests to echo the amount of space on the disk. |
| ```
:FILEFOUN
CHECK FILEFOUND NO-FILE.TXT
IF ERRORLEVEL 1 ECHO NO-FILE.TXT missing
IF ERRORLEVEL 1 GOTO FILEFOU2
IF ERRORLEVEL 0 ECHO NO-FILE.TXT found
IF ERRORLEVEL 0 GOTO FILEFOU2

The batch file repeats this test for the file
CHECK1.BAT in order to show what happens when the
file exists.
``` | Runs Check to check for file NO-FILE.TXT existing and sets the ERRORLEVEL accordingly. Then, uses a series of ERRORLEVEL tests to display the results. |
| ```
:FILESIZE
CHECK FILESIZE CHECKERR.BAT
IF ERRORLEVEL 255 ECHO File was 255K or larger
IF ERRORLEVEL 255 GOTO FILETEXT
IF ERRORLEVEL 200 ECHO File was 200-254k
IF ERRORLEVEL 200 GOTO FILETEXT

The batch file continues in a similar fashion for
199K-2

IF ERRORLEVEL 1 ECHO File was 1K
IF ERRORLEVEL 1 GOTO FILETEXT
IF ERRORLEVEL 0 ECHO File was 0K or did not exist!
IF ERRORLEVEL 0 GOTO FILETEXT
``` | Runs Check to find the size of a specific file and places it in the ERROR-LEVEL. Then uses a series of ERRORLEVEL tests to echo that value. |
| ```
:FILETEXT
CHECK FILETEXT CHECK1.BAT 'CHECK'
IF ERRORLEVEL 1 ECHO Text not found in CHECK1.BAT or
    error encountered
IF ERRORLEVEL 1 GOTO FILETXT2
IF ERRORLEVEL 0 ECHO Text found in CHECK1.BAT
IF ERRORLEVEL 0 GOTO FILETXT2

The batch file performs the same test on a second
set of text as an illustration.
``` | Runs Check to see if the text "CHECK" exists in the file CHECK1.BAT and stores the results in the ERRORLEVEL. Then uses a series of ERROR-LEVEL tests to display the results. |
```

Table 7-3 Continued.

Batch File Line	Explanation

`:KEYBOARD`
`CHECK KEYBOARD`
`IF ERRORLEVEL 1 ECHO Keystroke waiting`
`IF ERRORLEVEL 1 GOTO KEYPRESS`
`IF ERRORLEVEL 0 ECHO Keystroke not waiting`
`IF ERRORLEVEL 0 GOTO KEYPRESS`
	Tests for a keystroke waiting and places the results into ERROR-LEVEL. A series of ERRORLEVEL tests displays the results.

`:KEYPRESS`
`CHECK KEYPRESS`
`IF ERRORLEVEL 122 ECHO z Pressed`
`IF ERRORLEVEL 122 GOTO MEMORY`
`IF ERRORLEVEL 121 ECHO y Pressed`
`IF ERRORLEVEL 121 GOTO MEMORY`
 	
`The batch file continues in a similar fashion for the remaining letters along with all the capital letters.`
	Runs Check to see which key was pressed and places the value in ERRORLEVEL. A series of ERRORLEVEL tests displays the value.

`:MEMORY`
`CHECK MEMORY`
`IF ERRORLEVEL 40 ECHO At least 640K RAM available`
`IF ERRORLEVEL 40 GOTO MODEL`
`IF ERRORLEVEL 39 ECHO 624K available`
`IF ERRORLEVEL 39 GOTO MODEL`
 	
`The batch file continues in a similar fashion for 608K-496K`
 	
`IF ERRORLEVEL 30 ECHO 480K available`
`IF ERRORLEVEL 30 GOTO MODEL`
`ECHO Less than 480K available`
	Runs Check to measure the amount of RAM and place the value into ERRORLEVEL. A series of ERRORLEVEL tests displays the value.

`:MODEL`
`CHECK MODEL`
`IF ERRORLEVEL 255 ECHO PC`
`IF ERRORLEVEL 255 GOTO MONTH`
`IF ERRORLEVEL 254 ECHO XT or Portable PC`
`IF ERRORLEVEL 254 GOTO MONTH`
`IF ERRORLEVEL 253 ECHO PCjr`
`IF ERRORLEVEL 253 GOTO MONTH`
`IF ERRORLEVEL 252 ECHO AT`
`IF ERRORLEVEL 252 GOTO MONTH`
`IF ERRORLEVEL 250 ECHO Unknown machine`
`IF ERRORLEVEL 250 GOTO MONTH`
`IF ERRORLEVEL 249 ECHO PC Convertible`
`IF ERRORLEVEL 249 GOTO MONTH`
`ECHO Unknown machine`
	Runs Check to find out the type of computer and place the value into ERROR-LEVEL. A series of ERRORLEVEL tests displays that value.

`:MONTH`
`CHECK MONTH`
`IF ERRORLEVEL 12 ECHO December`
`IF ERRORLEVEL 12 GOTO TIME`
`IF ERRORLEVEL 11 ECHO November`
`IF ERRORLEVEL 11 GOTO TIME`
 	
`The batch file continues in a similar fashion for October-February.`
 	
`IF ERRORLEVEL 1 ECHO January`
`IF ERRORLEVEL 1 GOTO TIME`
	Runs Check to find the month of the year and place it into the ERROR-LEVEL. A series of ERRORLEVEL tests displays the value.

`:TIME`
`CHECK TIME`
`IF ERRORLEVEL 23 ECHO After 11PM`
`IF ERRORLEVEL 23 GOTO END`
`IF ERRORLEVEL 22 ECHO 10PM - 11PM`
`IF ERRORLEVEL 22 GOTO END`
 	
`The batch file continues in a similar fashion for 10PM-3AM`
	Runs Check to find the time and place it into the ERRORLEVEL. A series of ERRORLEVEL tests displays the value.

Batch File Line	Explanation

`IF ERRORLEVEL 1 ECHO 1AM - 2AM`
`IF ERRORLEVEL 1 GOTO END`
`IF ERRORLEVEL 0 ECHO Midnight - 1AM`
`IF ERRORLEVEL 0 GOTO END`	

`:END`	Label marking the end of the batch file.

Checkerr

Name: Checkerr
Version: 1.0
Price: Free
Category: Public Domain
Summary: Creates a batch file to check ERRORLEVEL values.
Author: Marek Majewski
Availability: Available on many bulletin board systems.

Checkerr contains a program you run once. The program creates a long batch file checking all possible ERRORLEVEL values and displaying its current value on the screen. Of course, you easily can create this batch file yourself, although running Checkerr is much faster.

The documentation suggests that you should add the command to start a program at the top of the batch file. However, the batch file works fine if you run it separately once you have run a program with an ERRORLEVEL value you want to check.

CTRL-P

Name: CTRL-P
Version: 1.0
Price: Free
Category: Copyrighted
Summary: Simulates pressing Ctrl-PrintScreen.
Author: Keith P. Graham
Availability: Available on many bulletin board systems.

You can send a copy of the text DOS sends to the display by pressing Ctrl-PrintScreen. You turn this off by pressing Ctrl-PrintScreen again. This can help log the process of a long batch file, especially if you don't want to stay and watch it run. CTRL-P is a tiny program allowing you to issue the Ctrl-PrintScreen command from within the batch file. Thus, you can skip the logging on paper-wasting sections that already work.

Unfortunately, CTRL-P didn't work under DOS 5.0.

DATETIME

Name: DATETIME
Version: 4.4
Price: Free
Category: Copyrighted
Summary: A nice way to set the clock on a machine without a built-in clock.
Author: Paul S. Burney
              10800 Alpharetta Highway
Availability: Available on many bulletin board systems.

If your older machine lacks a clock, your clock has failed, or your battery is dead, then you probably often skip setting the date and time. Oh sure, you've added the DATE and TIME commands to your AUTOEXEC.BAT file; but you usually just press return to bypass them.

DATETIME resolves this problem and is especially helpful for the date. Just replace the DATE and TIME commands in your AUTOEXEC.BAT file with a DATETIME command. When DATETIME runs, it reads the date and time from its directory entry; and, most often, the date is either correct or just one day off. The date is displayed in big letters. The up and down arrows change the month, while the left and right arrows change the day. Because the date is rarely off by more than a day, setting the date is almost as quick as just pressing return.

Next, DATETIME displays the time it found on its file. Unfortunately, the time isn't as likely to be as correct as the date was; but because you already have the date right, you might as well go ahead and set the time. The up and down arrows change the hour, while the left and right arrows change the minute. Interestingly, while DATETIME generally significantly decreases the keystrokes necessary to change the date, it generally increases those required to set the time.

Once you press return to accept the time, DATETIME updates the date and time of its file entry to reflect this new information. Then the information is ready the next time you reboot.

DDATE.COM

Name: DDATE.COM
Price: Unknown
Category: Unknown
Summary: Allows the user to set the date using the cursor arrows.
Author: Hal Sampson
Availability: Available on many bulletin board systems.

DDATE.COM reads the date from its own directory entry to estimate the date and then displays that on the screen. You change the day by using the left and right arrows, while you change the month by using the up and down arrows. When you press return, DDATE .COM changes the date and resets its file date in the directory.

DDATE.COM simplifies date setting on machines without a clock. You would generally use DDATE.COM in the AUTOEXEC.BAT file.

DDATE.COM is available on many bulletin board systems but doesn't have a documentation file, so you can't determine if the file is shareware, public domain, or commercial (although the code does contain a 1982 copyright notice by Hal Sampson). Because you can't determine whether DDATE.COM is public domain, you may want to ignore it to avoid violating copyright.

DISSOLVE.COM

Name:	DISSOLVE.COM
Version:	Unknown
Price:	Unknown
Category:	Unknown
Summary:	A fancy way to clear the screen.
Author:	Unknown
Availability:	Available on many bulletin board systems.

DISSOLVE.COM has the same goal as the CLS command: it clears the screen. However, rather than simply clearing it, DISSOLVE.COM dissolves the screen images until the screen is blank.

DO-ONCE

Name:	DO-ONCE
Version:	2.20
Price:	Free
Category:	Copyrighted
Summary:	Runs programs once a day/week/month.
Author:	Glenn Snow
	1 Carmel Parkway
	Mundelein, Illinois 60060
Availability:	Available on many bulletin board systems.

Like BatDay, DO-ONCE gives you an alternative way to occasionally run commands. To run DO-ONCE, type

```
DO-ONCE keyword command
```

The keywords are as follows:

@DAY runs the command/program the first time the computer is booted each day, e.g., @MONDAY, @TUESDAY, etc. (whatever day of the week you choose). Thus, @MONDAY would run the command/program the first time the computer is booted each Monday.

@#, where # is a date, runs the command/program the first time the computer is booted on that day of the month. Thus, @1 would run a command/program (say an account closing program) the first of the month.

Unfortunately, if you don't use your computer on the first, then the account closing program isn't run when you boot on the second. Adding a plus sign after the @ (e.g., @ + 1) causes DO-ONCE to run the command/program on either that day/date if possible or otherwise on the first day/date the computer is finally booted up after that.

Unlike similar programs, DO-ONCE isn't limited to controlling a single program. Rather than using the date on a file to record the last time it ran, DO-ONCE creates a data file in the root directory to store the date on which it runs each command or program. Thus, you can use DO-ONCE on as many separate lines as you like and have it handle each one of them properly. If you don't want the data file in the root directory, you can set an environmental variable to point to wherever you'd like DO-ONCE to store it.

DO-ONCE includes a nifty utility for editing its data file. You would use the editor if you had set the clock to an invalid data (like 1-1-1999) and then ran your AUTOEXEC .BAT file. In that case, DO-ONCE would reset all the dates in the data file to 1-1-1999 and wouldn't run any programs until after that date.[2]

You might also want to edit the file to remove lines where you have dropped a DO-ONCE command. For example, if you had a line in your AUTOEXEC.BAT file saying DO-ONCE @MONDAY CHKDSK/F, then DO-ONCE created a line in its data file to track that command. Even if you remove the command from your AUTOEXEC.BAT file, the line remains in the DO-ONCE data file. The more lines you have in the data file, the slower DO-ONCE runs; removing extra lines can speed it up.

The editor is limited to editing data files tracking no more than 256 different DO-ONCE commands. Still, because each command has only one line (no matter how many times DO-ONCE checks or runs that line), this is hardly a significant limitation.

Overall, DO-ONCE is an extremely well thought-out and useful program for expanding the power of your AUTOEXEC.BAT file.

---

[2]The logic behind this takes a little thought. Consider an example where you want to run a program every Monday and you use the @MONDAY keyword. When DO- ONCE examines its data file, it checks to see if today is both a Monday and later than the last time the command/program was run. When you boot on Monday, it would pass the first criteria but wouldn't pass the second until after 1-1-1999.

Drvrdy

Name:	Drvrdy
Version:	1.0
Price:	Free
Category:	Copyrighted
Summary:	Tests a drive and sets ERRORLEVEL to indicate if the drive is ready.
Availability:	All *PC Magazine* files are available from their area on CompuServe. See any issue of *PC Magazine* for details.

In a batch file, you can have trouble determining the readiness of a drive (especially a floppy one). You can try a command like IF EXIST A:*.*, but this will result in a DOS "Not ready reading drive A: Abort, Retry, Fail" error message if the drive contains no disk.

Drvrdy overcomes this problem: it can test a disk drive without triggering an error message, even if the drive isn't ready. Drvrdy returns an ERRORLEVEL of 7 if the drive is ready and a 2 if the drive isn't ready. You run Drvrdy with the command DRVRDY A:, although the color is optional.

Drvrdy malfunctions if you specify the letter of a nonexistent drive. On my system, I have two floppy drives and two hard drives, so my system uses drives A-D. The command DRVRDY F returns an ERRORLEVEL of 1, the command DRVRDY F: locks up the computer, and the command DRVRDY X: reboots the computer. However, you shouldn't encounter problems if you only use Drvrdy on the two floppy drives most computers have.

Emschk

Name:	Emschk
Version:	1.0
Price:	Free
Category:	Public Domain
Summary:	Checks to see if EMS memory is installed and, if so, what type.
Author:	Christopher J. Dunford
	The Cove Software Group
Availability:	Available on many bulletin board systems.

Emschk checks to see if EMS memory is installed and, if so, what type. It sets ERRORLEVEL to 0 if none is installed, to 1 if there is EMS memory being controlled by a pre-4.0 memory manager, to 2 if there is Enhanced EMS memory, to 3 if there is LIM 4.0 memory, and to 255 if it encounters an error. Some programs require EMS memory to run; this program gives a batch file the ability to check the memory before running an applications. This is especially important with the newer memory manager, like QEMM or 386Max, that give you the ability to use one type of memory for another.

Errlevel

Name:	Errlevel
Version:	1.0
Price:	Free
Category:	Copyrighted
Summary:	Tests on several types of information and sets ERRORLEVEL accordingly.
Author:	Paul M. Sittler
Availability:	Available on many bulletin board systems.

Errlevel solves the problem of how to make general information available to a batch file. It runs tests on things like the date and then places the results in the ERRORLEVEL. The batch file can then test the ERRORLEVEL and take different actions depending on what it finds.

The general form of an Errlevel command is ERRLEVEL switch, where switch determines what Errlevel tests for. The available switches are as follows:

\# When you enter a number 0-255 rather than a switch, Errlevel sets the ERRORLEVEL value to that number, giving you an easy way to set the ERRORLEVEL to a specific value for batch file testing.

d Tells Errlevel to test the date and return an ERRORLEVEL value of 1-31.

h Tells Errlevel to test the hour and return an ERRORLEVEL value of 0-23.

j Tells Errlevel to test the Julian date and return an ERRORLEVEL value of 1-366.

m Tells Errlevel to test the month and return an ERRORLEVEL value of 1-12.

w Tells Errlevel to test the weekday and return an ERRORLEVEL value of 1-7. It returns Sunday as 1, Monday as 2, and so on.

y Tells Errlevel to test the year and return an ERRORLEVEL value of around 200. It returns 1991 as 199, 1992 as 200, and so on.

Between all of these switches, Errlevel is extremely useful in getting specific information to the batch file for testing.

EX

Name:	EX
Version:	1.0
Price:	Free
Category:	Copyrighted
Summary:	Lets one batch file run another and then return control to the original batch file.

Author: Doctor Debug
          Steel City Software
Availability: Available on many bulletin board systems.

Prior to DOS 3.3, if you included the command to run a batch file in another batch file, control never returned to the original file. For example, if FIRST.BAT runs SECOND .BAT, FIRST.BAT wouldn't start running again when SECOND.BAT terminated.

The CALL command in DOS 3.3 changed all this. If FIRST.BAT had a CALL SEC-OND command, then FIRST.BAT would resume at the line following the CALL SECOND line. EX replicates that ability for earlier versions of DOS: just replace the CALL SEC-OND line with an EX SECOND line.

EX would be priceless if it were the only way to accomplish this function: being able to nest batch files this way makes easier the building of subroutines simplifying complex batch files. However, a certain DOS trick accomplishes the same thing without needing an additional program: the command COMMAND/C SECOND will load a second copy of the command processor and run the second batch file. If the last line of that batch file is EXIT, then the second command processor will unload and the original batch file will resume.

Because you can accomplish the same thing with a DOS trick prior to DOS 3.3 and you don't need the program since DOS 4.0, you have little reason to acquire EX.

Flip

Name: Flip
Version: Unknown
Price: Unknown
Category: Unknown
Summary: Changes the state of several togglable operations.
Author: Unknown
Availability: Available on many bulletin board systems.

A number of operations on your computer are toggled; that is, they toggle between two settings (for example, your CapsLock, NumLock, and ScrollLock keys are either on or off). Flip is designed to control the status of these keys. To use Flip, you issue the command FLIP toggle setting where toggle is a keyword and setting is its status. The supported keywords are as follows:

CAPS sets the CapsLock on or off.

NUM sets the NumLock on or off.

SCROLL sets the ScrollLock on or off.

MONO toggles the monitor into monochrome mode. There is no setting after the keyword.

COLOR toggles the monitor into color mode. There are two settings after the keyword—40 or 80—that are used to select the desired display mode.

EJECT ejects a page on the printer. There is no setting after the keyword.

PRTSC prints the screen on the printer like a Print Screen. There is no setting after the keyword.

LOGGING toggles sending a copy of the screen display to the printer on or off.

Flip works and works well. However, the documentation doesn't give the status of the software, so you can't be sure if you are violating anyone's copyright by using the software. For that reason, I suggest you avoid using the software.

Fly

Name:	Fly
Version:	1.0
Price:	A few dollars[3]
Category:	Shareware
Summary:	Fly creates a temporary batch file, runs it, and then deletes it.
Author:	Bob Halsall
Availability:	Available on many bulletin board systems.

Have you ever wanted to run several commands taking a long time to execute but didn't want to take the time to create a batch file? If you have, Fly can help you. It presents a line editor allowing you to enter the commands one line at a time (although once you go to the next line, you can't return to the preceding lines to make changes). Once you have entered all the lines, Fly creates a temporary batch file containing your commands, runs that batch file, and then deletes it.

Of course, you can do the same thing without a program. The batch file SHOW-FLY .BAT in Table 7-4 works exactly the same way as Fly, except that you must press the F6 key and return when you finish rather than just pressing the return key.

Table 7-4   SHOWFLY.BAT performs
the same function as Fly without a program.

Batch File Line	Explanation
`@ECHO OFF`	Turns command-echoing off.

`REM NAME:      SHOW-FLY.BAT`
`REM PURPOSE: Demonstrate The Ability`
`REM          Of A Batch File To Do`
`REM          Same Thing As FLY.EXE`
`REM VERSION: 1.00`
`REM DATE:      March 25, 1991`
	Documentation remarks.

`CLS`	Clears the screen.

---

[3]The author asks that, if you like the program, you donate a few dollars to the American Cancer Society.

Batch File Line	Explanation
IF EXIST JUNK.BAT GOTO ERROR	If the temporary work file exists, skip it. You could have the batch file pick a new number or just go ahead and delete the file, depending on your preferences.
ECHO Enter Batch File Commands One ECHO Line At A Time ECHO ECHO When Done, Press Return To Get ECHO To A Blank Line Then Press ECHO The F6-Key and Return Again	Explains how to use this batch file. The third line creates a blank line by echoing Alt-255, a non-printing character.
COPY CON JUNK.BAT	Causes DOS to copy the keyboard input to the file JUNK.BAT. This line can be used from the DOS prompt to create batch files.
CALL JUNK.BAT	Calls the batch file JUNK.BAT where control returns to SHOW-FLY.BAT. If you have a version of DOS that does not support this command, this line should look like this: COMMAND/C JUNK
DEL JUNK.BAT	Deletes the temporary batch file.
GOTO END	Exits the batch file.
:ERROR	Section marking the error-handling routine.
ECHO Working File JUNK.BAT Exists ECHO Delete Or Rename And Rerun SHOW-FLY.BAT	Tells the user about the problem.
GOTO END	Exits the batch file.
:END	Label marking the end of the batch file.

GENEL

Name: GENEL
Version: 1.0
Price: Free
Category: Copyrighted
Summary: Sets the ERRORLEVEL
Author: Brian E. Smith
              59 Main Street
              Piedmont, South Carolina 29673
Availability: Included on the disk bound in this book.

DOS's ERRORLEVEL feature is nice; however, in writing and testing batch files, I have found two problems with it. First, when trying to test error handling routines, I sometimes find it very difficult to force a specific ERRORLEVEL value in order to test what a batch file does when that condition exists. Second, I know of no easy way to reset the ERRORLEVEL to 0. I found this problem in abundance while writing batch files needing a lot of error checking. Basically, I would run them once and force an error to see how they worked. (For example, I originally did things like copying to a disk drive with the drive door open to force an error.) Once I had run the test, the batch file would stop the next time because I hadn't reset the value.

GENEL is a small program correcting this problem. The syntax is

```
GENEL #
```

where # is any integer from 0 to 255. The program sets the ERRORLEVEL to the number you specify and then exits.

Isit

Name:	Isit
Version:	1.0
Price:	Free
Category:	Copyrighted
Summary:	Compares the real day with a day entered on the command line and sets ERRORLEVEL accordingly.
Author:	Brian E. Smith
	59 Main Street
	Piedmont, South Carolina 29673
Availability:	Included on the disk bound in this book.

You only want to perform some tasks, like full backups or accounting closure, on certain days. As a general rule, checking in a batch file for the day of the week is difficult; however, Isit makes it simple. You enter a command like

```
ISIT Friday
```

and Isit sets ERRORLEVEL to 1 if it's and 0 otherwise. That way, you could have your AUTOEXEC.BAT file perform an incremental backup on Friday. You could also have another batch file that closes the accounting books on Friday.

Of course, if you put Isit in your AUTOEXEC.BAT file and you reboot in the middle of a day, the same task could be performed twice. To avoid this problem, I like the idea of a shutdown batch file you run just before turning off the computer. That batch file could perform an incremental backup every day but Friday—when it performs a full backup. It could also perform the weekly book closing.

Isit runs without problems under DOS 4.x or earlier. While I capitalized Friday above, Isit's case-insensitive. Unfortunately, Isit won't run properly under DOS 5.0—it always sets ERRORLEVEL to 0 whether the days match or not.

Key-Fake

Name:	Key-Fake
Price:	Free
Category:	Copyrighted
Summary:	Feeds keystrokes into an application from a batch file.
Author:	Charles Petzold
Availability:	All *PC Magazine* files are available from their area on CompuServe. See any issue of *PC Magazine* for details.

Once some programs are loaded, you still end up entering the same keystrokes. For example, with Lotus, you generally select 123 if you load the Lotus shell. Batch files can't help you avoid having to make these selections. Once the program starts, the batch file remains inactive until the program terminates.

Key-Fake overcomes this problem. It is memory-resident and requires about 1K of memory. Prior to running a program, you simply load Key-Fake and tell it which characters to feed into the application (up to the 124-character limit). Once the program starts, the characters are fed automatically.

A special character tells the program the buffer is empty, thus fooling programs that flush the buffer prior to execution. You can enter characters either directly or as their ASCII value. (With some characters, like Return, you must enter the ASCII value).

While Key-Fake will be useful for only a few programs, it's very helpful for those programs.

Lptchk

Name:	Lptchk
Version:	1.0
Price:	Free
Category:	Public Domain
Summary:	Checks the specified printer port and sets ERRORLEVEL to indicate its status.
Author:	R. Vander Kinter
Availability:	Available on many bulletin board systems.

Printing in a batch file is always a little dangerous. You never know if the printer is ready; and, in addition, if the batch file is for general distribution, you don't even know if a printer exists and for which port it would be attached.

Lptchk solves this problem by checking the printer port and setting ERRORLEVEL to indicate its status. While it defaults to checking LPT1, you can have it check LPT2 as well. Because Lptchk sets ERRORLEVEL, you can have the batch file skip over the printing if Lptchk doesn't find a printer or finds a problem.

Menuware Batch File Utilities

Name:	Menuware Batch File Utilities
Version:	1.0
Price:	$10.00[4]
Category:	Shareware
Summary:	A collection of utilities primarily for counting.
Author:	Interfaces, People, and Magic
	Post Office Box 4496
	Middletown, Rhode Island 02840
Availability:	Available on many bulletin board systems.

Menuware Batch File Utilities [MWBAT2 for short] is a collection of utilities primarily designed to allow counting in batch files and to measure time. MWBAT2 stores the time and a single counter in a low memory address not normally used, thus not increasing the memory usage of these programs. The programs have no memory resident component.

The manual warns that "the batch and timer variables are stored in a low memory address that may be used by other applications. If problems are encountered or erroneous results reported, please consult your application manual." I encountered no problems using MWBAT2, so I expect the implementation is quite stable. If you do have problems, the manual offers no other help for resolving them.

The utilities included with MWBAT2 are as follows:

ADD adds the specified amount to the batch variable. This variable is limited from -127 to $+127$, so you are limited when using this variable as a counter.

AMIAT checks to see if the batch file is currently in the subdirectory specified on the command line and sets ERRORLEVEL accordingly.

CHTIMER reports the number of minutes that have passed (up to 120) since ST-TIMER was last run, thus giving you a way to time batch file executions.

CMP compares the amount specified on the command line to the current value of the batch variable and sets ERRORLEVEL accordingly.

CMPDS compares the amount of free disk space on the default drive with the amount specified on the command line and sets ERRORLEVEL accordingly.

DEC subtracts 1 from the batch variable.

GDRIVE sets ERRORLEVEL to indicate the current drive.

STORE2 stores the specified value in the batch variable.

STTIMER resets the timer variable to 0 or starts it counting if it hasn't been accessed before.

---

[4]The author adds a strange extension to shareware called menuware. Under this, the author allows you to register only those programs you want to use, with the individual registration fee being one dollar. However, many of the utilities (especially the system variable ones) work together, so it seems to me you would be better off just registering all of them.

SUB subtracts the amount specified on the command line from the batch variable.

VALUE copies the value stored in the batch variable to ERRORLEVEL so a batch file can use it.

Table 7-5 summarizes these programs, while Table 7-6 shows a batch file using many of the MWBAT2 features.

The batch and timer variables are excellent implementations of these concepts that you won't find in any other batch utility. If you must handle loops or time in a batch file, you will find them very worthwhile.

Table 7-5   A summary of the Menuware Batch File Utilities programs.

Utility	Function
Add	Menuware can maintain a single "system variable" in low memory. This variable is not stored in the ERRORLEVEL value but has the same limitation. It must be an integer between -127 and 127. This variable stays in memory until the system is reset. Add increases the value of this variable by a specified amount.
AMIAT	Uses ERRORLEVEL to report if the current subdirectory matches the subdirectory listed after the AMIAT command.
CHTIMER	Reports the time since the STTIMER utility was run. The report is through the DOS ERRORLEVEL although the time is not stored there.
CMP	Compares the system variable to a specified value and reports via the DOS ERRORLEVEL if it is larger, smaller, or equal to the specified value.
CMPDS	Compares disk space to a specified value and reports via the DOS ERRORLEVEL if it is larger, smaller, or equal to the specified value.
DEC	Subtracts one from the system variable.
GDRIVE	Returns the current drive via the DOS ERRORLEVEL. For example, A:=1, B:=2, and so on.
INC	Increases the system variable by one.
STORE	Stores a specified value to the system variable.
STTIMER	Sets/resets the timer to zero.
SUB	Subtracts a specified amount from the system variable.
VALUE	Returns the value of the system variable via the DOS ERRORLEVEL. Because ERRORLEVEL is limited to integers from -127 to 127, the system variable is similarly limited.

**Table 7-6   MWBAT2.BAT illustrates many
of the features of Menuware Batch File Utilities.**

Batch File Line	Explanation
`@ECHO OFF`	Turns command-echoing off.

`REM NAME:      MWBAT2.BAT`
`REM PURPOSE: Demonstrate MWBAT2`
`            Package`
`REM VERSION: 1.00`
`REM DATE:     March 25, 1991`
	Documentation remarks.

Table 7-6 Continued.

Batch File Line	Explanation
STTIMER	Stores the current time in low memory. This uses an area of memory not normally used and so does not reduce the memory available to other application.
STORE 0	Stores zero to the batch variable. Like the time, this value is stored in low memory.
:TOP	Label marking the top of a loop.
INC	Increments the batch variable by one.
VALUE	Copies the batch variable to ERRORLEVEL.
FOR %%J IN (1 2 3 4 5 6 7 8 9 10) DO IF ERRORLEVEL %%J SET LOOP=%%J	Stores the ERRORLEVEL value to a variable.
ECHO Loop Number %LOOP% of 10	Tells the user its value.
IF NOT ERRORLEVEL 10 GOTO TOP	If this is not the tenth loop, continues looping.
:TOP2	Label marking the top of a second loop.
ECHO Loop Number %LOOP% of 10 Going Down	The first time through, LOOP has a value of ten. After that, its value is determined below.
DEC	Decreases the batch variable by one.
VALUE	Transfers the batch variable to ERRORLEVEL.
FOR %%J IN (1 2 3 4 5 6 7 8 9 10) DO IF ERRORLEVEL %%J SET LOOP=%%J	Transfers the ERRORLEVEL to a variable.
IF ERRORLEVEL 1 GOTO TOP2	If less than ten loops, continues looping.
AMIAT C:\BAT	Checks to see if the current subdirectory is C:\BAT.
IF ERRORLEVEL 1 ECHO I Am In C:\BAT Subdirectory IF NOT ERRORLEVEL 1 ECHO I Am Not In C:\BAT Subdirectory	Tells the user the results of that test.
GDRIVE	Tests to see what the current drive is.
IF ERRORLEVEL 1 IF NOT ERRORLEVEL 2 ECHO Running From A-Drive IF ERRORLEVEL 2 IF NOT ERRORLEVEL 3 ECHO Running From B-Drive IF ERRORLEVEL 3 IF NOT ERRORLEVEL 4 ECHO Running From C-Drive IF ERRORLEVEL 4 IF NOT ERRORLEVEL 5 ECHO Running From D-Drive IF ERRORLEVEL 5 IF NOT ERRORLEVEL 6 ECHO Running From E-Drive	Tells the user the results of that test.

Batch File Line	Explanation
`CHTIMER`	Transfers the contents of the timer to ERRORLEVEL.

`FOR %%J IN (0 1 2 3 4 5 6 7 8 9 10)`
`   DO IF ERRORLEVEL %%J SET TIME=%%J`
`FOR %%J IN (11 12 13 14 15 16 17) DO`
`   IF ERRORLEVEL %%J SET TIME=%%J`
`FOR %%J IN (18 19 20 21 22 23 24) DO`
`   IF ERRORLEVEL %%J SET TIME=%%J`
`FOR %%J IN (25 26 27 28 29 30 31) DO`
`   IF ERRORLEVEL %%J SET TIME=%%J`
	Transfers the contents of ERROR-LEVEL to a variable.

`ECHO Demonstration Took %TIME%` `   Minutes`	Gives the user this information.
`IF ERRORLEVEL 31 ECHO Or Longer!`	If ERRORLEVEL was 31, then the demonstration may have taken longer because this is the highest ERRORLEVEL value tested for.

NoBoot

Name: NoBoot
Version: 1.0
Price: Free
Category: Copyrighted
Summary: A small memory-resident program disabling Ctrl-Alt -Del.
Author: Ethan Winer
Availability: All *PC Magazine* files are available from their area on CompuServe. See any issue of *PC Magazine* for details.

A batch file can be stopped in three ways:

- You can turn off the computer.
- You can press Ctrl-Break or Ctrl-C.
- You can reboot the computer.

NoBoot is a small (672 byte) memory-resident program that protects against the third option of rebooting the computer. With NoBoot loaded, the Ctrl-Alt-Del sequence is disabled and won't reboot the computer. Of course, that means you also can't use Ctrl-Alt-Del if a program causes your computer to lock up. Not only is Ctrl-Alt-Del disabled, the tiny reboot switch appearing on the back of some keyboards will be disabled as well.

ONBOOT

Name: ONBOOT

Version:	1.01
Price:	Free
Category:	Copyrighted
Summary:	Performs a task the first time the computer is booted or after any warm or cold boot.
Author:	Christopher J. Dunford
	The Cove Software Group
	Post Office Box 1072
	Columbia, Maryland 21044
Availability:	Available on some bulletin board system.[5]

You might like for your computer to perform certain tasks only the first time it boots for the day. For example, you might make an incremental backup or run a hard disk testing program. If you just included the commands in your AUTOEXEC.BAT file, you'd end up performing the task every time the computer rebooted, especially troublesome when you're having trouble with software and are forced to reboot often.

ONBOOT overcomes this problem. You add the command ONBOOT DAILY command to your AUTOEXEC.BAT. When the computer boots, ONBOOT checks the date of its program file against the system date. If they are the same, ONBOOT skips the command; if its date is earlier, it updates the date on the program file and then performs the specified command. If you have multiple commands, you can put them in a batch file and have ONBOOT execute the batch file. ONBOOT also has switches to perform a specified task only during a warm or cold boot, although those switches would be less useful than the daily switch.

PALRUN

Name:	PALRUN
Version:	1.0
Price:	$20.00
Category:	Shareware
Summary:	Allows you to run a batch file or program stored inside an archive file.
Author:	PAL Software New York, Incorporated
	51 Cedar Lane
	Ossining, New York 10562
Availability:	Available on many bulletin board systems.

Although batch files are a very nice way to automate routine tasks, they require a lot of

---

[5]The author has restricted the software to distribution by noncommercial bulletin board system and users groups, so you may find it difficult to locate.

room. The cluster size on my system is 2K, so every file (no matter how small) requires 2K of space. On some systems, the cluster size (and therefore the minimum batch file size) can be as large as 8K! Using that much space to store a tiny batch file can be a real drawback to using a lot of batch files.

On my computer, I have 56 batch files that should only take up 53K. Because of the 2K minimum, however, they use 143K of disk space.

Your small utilities situation can be just as bad. The SEBFU 2.2 utilities (covered in Chapter 6) from Scanlon Enterprises has 104 small programs. They should require only 25K of disk space; but, because of the 2K minimum, they take up 213K of disk space.

PALRUN provides a solution to this problem, working with PKzip to let you store your batch files and programs in an archive file.

Archiving began on PC systems with a program called ARC from System Enhancement Associates [SEA]. ARC compressed files into a single file with an .ARC extension. That gave you savings from the compression action of the program; and, by having one file instead of two, you limited the amount of space wasted due to the limitation of every file using a full cluster.

Soon after ARC was developed, a company called PKware developed the program PKARC to compete with ARC. PKARC used the same file format as ARC but ran much faster. Of course, SEA sued PKware. The case was settled with PKware agreeing to no longer use the ARC file format. Thus, PKware developed their own file format called ZIP and placed it in the public domain for public use, although their specific archiving program—now called PKZip—was copyrighted.

Because the ZIP format was in the public domain and because of the bad feeling that the computing community had toward SEA (resulting from the lawsuit), PKZip supplanted ARC as the dominate archiving program. Like ARC and PKARC, PKZip compresses multiple files into a single archive file.

PALRUN uses that archive file to store batch files and programs for running. To use PALRUN, you first use PKZip to archive your batch files and small programs into a single file called PALHOUSE.ZIP. Because you need PKZip to use PALRUN, you must register both programs. (PKZip is also shareware.) After you store your batch files and programs in PALHOUSE.ZIP, you erase the uncompressed versions.

Now you no longer run your batch files by issuing their name at the DOS command line; rather, you precede their name with PALRUN. Thus, to run MENU.BAT, you would enter

PALRUN MENU

PALRUN unarchives MENU.BAT for you and then executes it. When MENU.BAT terminates, PALRUN automatically erases it. (Remember, because it's stored in the archive file, you don't need to keep the uncompressed version when it's not running.) PALRUN works the same with programs as it does with batch files.

Using PALRUN will take some planning and some work. To begin with, unarchiving a file takes time. You must decide for yourself if you are willing to wait. The delay is noticeable even on my 386/25, and readers with slower machines may find the delay intolerable.

In addition, you must make some intelligent decisions about which programs to run under PALRUN. Large programs take longer to unarchive and save proportionally less space, so you may want to only use PALRUN on smaller programs and batch files. Remember, PALRUN wants all the files stored in PALHOUSE.ZIP; as that file becomes larger from adding either more or longer files, the unarchiving becomes progressively slower.

Finally, you will have to perform a massive system conversion to use PALRUN. Every batch file running a program stored in PALHOUSE.ZIP must be rewritten to issue the command PALRUN program rather than just the program command to run the program; for example, 123 becomes PALRUN 123. In addition, every batch file calling another batch file with the command CALL batch must be rewritten as PALRUN batch.

Also, every batch file depending on environmental variables must be rewritten. When DOS loads the PALRUN program to run, it is passed a copy of COMMAND.COM with the copy of the environment. While the batch file is running, it makes changes to that copy of the environment. When the batch file terminates, PALRUN unloads from memory after cleaning up. When that happens, its copy of the environment—along with all the changes made by the batch file—are discarded and thus unavailable for other batch files. If one batch file calls a second batch file, yet another copy of COMMAND.COM is loaded with its own copy of the environment. When the called batch file terminates, its environment is also lost, so its changes aren't available to the batch file calling it.

You can load PALRUN permanently into memory so that it processes each command without having to precede the command with the PALRUN command. This also allows you to maintain a common environment for primary batch files (those run from the DOS prompt), although you still have a problem with losing the changes made by called batch files.

This mode also allows you to enter longer (253-character) command lines than DOS (127-character) and lets you enter multiple commands on the command line by separating them with a caret. (A *caret*, the ^ symbol, is entered by pressing Shift-6.)

In addition to the extensive required reconfiguration, PALRUN has a significant flaw causing most users to avoid it: it won't run under DOS 4.0. PALRUN tries to have PKZip extract the file you request, but somehow the process doesn't work—even though PKZip works perfectly under DOS 4.0—so PALRUN can't find the file to run. DOS 5.0 causes even more problems. The file is extracted and runs properly; but PALRUN bypasses DOS to delete the files in a manner not compatible under DOS 5.0, resulting in a "Sector not found reading drive *" error message.

The first time I got that error message, I was concerned that my flaky Seagate hard disk had failed once again. However, I ran the Norton Disk Doctor on it and discovered it to be fine—for the moment. Just to be sure, I tried PALRUN on another computer and half a dozen floppy disks—all with the same results.

The space required for small batch files can be painfully large on a system with limited hard disk space. Because of the problem with DOS 4.0 and DOS 5.0 and the overall difficulty in using PALRUN, however, I can't recommend it. Still, I am glad that someone's trying to find a solution to this problem, and I hope that PALRUN is at least the start of a workable solution.

PED

Name:	PED
Version:	Unknown
Price:	Unknown
Category:	Unknown
Summary:	An excellent program for modifying your path interactively. It can write the results back to the AUTOEXEC.BAT file.
Author:	Unknown
Availability:	Available on many bulletin board systems.

When you start PED, it allows you to either add a subdirectory to your path or delete an existing subdirectory from the path. When you select the option to add a path, it reads the current drive and presents you with a numbered list of every subdirectory. You scroll through the list and input the number of the subdirectory to add to the path. You must be logged onto the drive containing the subdirectory to add.

When you select the option to delete a subdirectory, PED presents you with a numbered list of all the subdirectories currently in the path. You input the number of the subdirectory to delete from the path.

If you make changes and then exit, PED gives you the option of writing the new path to your AUTOEXEC.BAT file. PED is the best program I have seen for modifying your path interactively but unfortunately comes with no documentation and lacks any indication of its status. I therefore recommend ignoring it to avoid possible copyright infringement.

Prnstate

Name:	Prnstate
Version:	1.0
Price:	Free
Category:	Public Domain
Summary:	Checks the status of the printer and sets ERRORLEVEL accordingly.
Author:	Mike Gribble
Availability:	Available on many bulletin board systems.

Prnstate will test to see if a printer is attached and ready and then set the ERRORLEVEL accordingly. In its default mode of operation, it displays a lot of text on the screen at the same time; however, a switch exists to avoid this. Prnstate only checks LPT1, so avoid it if you have a printer connected to LPT2.

ProBat

Name:	ProBat
Version:	1.0
Price:	$35 American
	$45 Canadian
Category:	Shareware
Summary:	A batch file development environment.
Author:	Mark Tigges
	2925 Altamont Circle
	West Vancouver B.C. Canada V7V 3B9
Availability:	Available on many bulletin board systems.

ProBat is both a combination word processor for writing batch files and screen processor for designing the screens shown within the batch file. The word processor is a small editor using Wordstar keystrokes. For users who have learned those Wordstar keystrokes, this can be a handy editor. However, Wordstar keystrokes aren't very logical, and better editors with a more logical command structure are available (such as the DOS 5.0 editor).

The ProBat wordprocessor has a nasty "gota" that can cause serious data loss. In several sections, you press F10 to get statistical information. During batch file editing, however, pressing F10 immediately exits to DOS without saving the batch file being edited and without asking if you really want to lose your batch file.

The screen processor function brings up a screen where you can move the cursor around, draw boxes, or enter text at any point on the screen. You also can change colors for different areas, although you may have to experiment because often the background color you select from the menu isn't the one ProBat uses.

Once you have finished your screens, ProBat includes a separate utility you can use to display them. Because you don't display your menus using DOS, every machine using your batch files must have a copy of ProBat.

When developing screens, trying to edit a nonexistent screen can cause the program to terminate with a "Runtime Error" without saving data.

Also, a menu function is built into ProBat. You use the ProBat editor to edit the menu options. Next, you edit the CUSTMENU.BAT file included with ProBat so that it contains all the commands necessary to run the menu options. If you use DOS 3.3 or later, this batch file can also CALL other batch files to run the menu options (even though the author hasn't explained this). This menu system isn't very flexible, unable to call up another ProBat menu (e.g., nested menus), and you can't change the name of the batch file running the menu system.

All in all, ProBat isn't very user friendly. As discussed above, pressing F10 at the wrong time can cause you to instantly lose everything you've worked on since the last save. This unfortunate lack of verification is carried through to other ProBat functions. For example, one menu option can delete files. Once you press enter, those files disappear without any sort of verification.

RUN

Name:	RUN
Version:	1.0
Price:	Free
Category:	Copyrighted
Summary:	Executes programs or batch files from any subdirectory without changing directories or specifying a path on the command line.
Author:	Unknown
Availability:	Available from the *PC Magazine* forum on CompuServe.

Prior to DOS 3.0, you couldn't run a program or batch file by specifying the full path on the command line. Thus, a command like

```
\ BATCH \ TEMP \ PROGRAM /S
```

was invalid. Thus, users wanting to run certain programs were forced to either include their subdirectory in the path or write a batch file to change to the program's subdirectory first. RUN fixes all this.

Run executes programs or batch files from any subdirectory without changing directories or specifying a path on the command line. The format for the command is

```
RUN [/C|/S][d:][subdirectory]filename [program arguments]
```

Of course, RUN.COM must be in your PATH. If you don't specify a subdirectory on the command line, RUN searches the entire disk for the program. You can have RUN look on an alternative drive rather than the current one by specifying that drive on the command line. The program arguments are those arguments passed on to the program once RUN finds and runs it.

If you specify the /C switch, RUN changes to the subdirectory containing the program before running it. Batch files require this, as do some programs (such as early releases of Wordstar). The /S switch causes RUN not to change subdirectories. The default mode is /S, and the documentation contains instructions to change the default to /C and back to /S. During its search, pressing any key will abort the operation of RUN.

Users with DOS 3.0 or later have little use for RUN because DOS will allow you to specify a full path to a program or batch file on the command line. However, because DOS 2.x doesn't do this, users of DOS 2.x will find RUN a very handy program.

SetError

Name:	SetError
Version:	1.0
Price:	Free

Category: Copyrighted (You may use the program on all of the machines you own,
               but you may not give copies of the program to anyone else.)
Summary: Sets the ERRORLEVEL to the value specified on the command line.
Author: Ronny Richardson
Availability: Included on the disk bound in this book.

DOS's ERRORLEVEL feature is nice; however, in writing and testing batch files, I have
found two problems with it. First, when trying to test error handling routines, I sometimes
find it very difficult to force a specific ERRORLEVEL value in order to test what a batch
file does when that condition exists. Second, I know of no easy way to reset the
ERRORLEVEL to 0. I found this problem in abundance while writing batch files needing
a lot of error checking. Basically, I would run them once and force an error to see how
they worked. (For example, I originally did things like copying to a disk drive with the
drive door open to force an error.) Once I had run the test, the batch file would stop the
next time because I hadn't reset the value.

    SetError is a small program I wrote to correct this problem. The syntax is

    SETERROR #

where # is any integer from 0 to 255. The program sets the ERRORLEVEL to the number
you specify and exits. If you enter anything other than an integer between 0 and 255, the
program gives you an error message and exits without setting ERRORLEVEL. You can
add the command

    SETERROR 0

as one of the first commands (after @ECHO OFF) to any batch file where you use the
ERRORLEVEL value for error trapping, ensuring that the batch file starts with a clean
ERRORLEVEL value.

Spy

Name: Spy
Version: 1.1
Price: Free
Category: Copyrighted
Summary: Logs the time a batch file is run.
Author: Danny Walters
Availability: Available on many bulletin board systems.

You add the command SPY file to a batch file, and Spy logs every time the batch file is run.
It creates no screen display, so if you have echo turned off, the user doesn't know the
usage is being logged. It doesn't store the name of the batch file in the log, so you will
need to use a different log for each batch file. The log continues to accumulate times and
dates each time the batch file runs, necessitating that you clear out the files occasionally
before they become very large.

If you must log batch usage, Spy works well. You might want to change the name to something like GETREADY so that the user doesn't know you are spying on him/her. If you added the Spy command before and after running your programs, you would have an elementary usage log.

STACKEY

Name:	STACKEY
Version:	3.0
Price:	$39.00 (Includes BATUTIL)
Category:	Shareware
Summary:	A memory resident program that lets you stack keystrokes in the keyboard buffer.
Author:	The Support Group
	Lake Technology Park
	Post Office Box 130
	McHenry, Maryland 21541
	(800) 872-4768
Availability:	Available on many bulletin board systems.

You just can't do some things with batch files. For example, you can't load a file into Lotus 1-2-3; even if you somehow get the keystrokes into the buffer using DOS, Lotus flushes the buffer while loading.

STACKEY is a powerful tool for putting keystrokes into the keyboard buffer while working around all sorts of problems (like Lotus). STACKEY itself is a 2K memory resident program. You can't load it into high memory using a memory manager like 386Max because it won't work there.

To run STACKEY in its simplest form, you issue a command like

    STACKEY "DIR"CR

which tells STACKEY to issue a DIR command and then press return. For the above example, you might tell STACKEY to issue the commands /FRMYFILE"CR to load a file. STACKEY has commands that delay issuing the command until after Lotus flushes the buffer.

You can actually perform some fairly complex tasks using STACKEY. Practically anything you can do typing from the keyboard, you can do using STACKEY.

While STACKEY performs the task of managing the typeahead keyboard buffer extremely well, I just don't see a big advantage in it. Most programs, including Lotus, can be automated with macros. For example, while loading, Lotus can automatically run a macro (a \0 macro in the worksheet AUTO123.WK1) that performs far more than STACKEY can. In fact, every program I regularly use can automatically process a macro when loading; and, in all cases, that macro can outperform STACKEY.

STACKEY has keywords and switches allowing it to perform tasks beyond managing the typeahead buffer, such as the following:

- delaying a batch file until a specific time is reached or for a specified period of time. Of course, BATUTIL (included with STACKEY) does this as well.
- switching monitors and ports.
- changing display modes.
- modifying the cursor. BATUTIL performs this as well.
- beeping the speaker. BATUTIL performs this as well.
- printing a screen "dump."
- rebooting the computer. BATUTIL can perform this as well.
- immediately halting a batch file. If necessary, it can turn break on before issuing the Ctrl-Break command.
- get a single keystroke from the user—a task BATUTIL performs exceptionally well.
- waiting for the user to press Enter, y, or n—all tasks.

After reading the STACKEY manual, I felt that it was written by the same person who wrote the BATUTIL manual (see Chapter 6). While complete, the STACKEY manual is difficult to read and hard to follow. However, unlike BATUTIL, the rewards are far less for wading through it.

If you need a program to manage the typeahead buffer, STACKEY is a good choice. However, in most cases, you will find yourself better off using a program's built-in macros or looking for another approach to a problem.

State

Name:	State
Price:	Free
Category:	Copyrighted
Summary:	Checks to see if a file exists and sets ERRORLEVEL accordingly.
Author:	Keith P. Graham
Availability:	Available on many bulletin board systems.

When you issue the command STATE path \ file, the program checks to see if the file exists. If it does, it sets ERRORLEVEL to 0; otherwise, it sets it to 1. Then you can use the ERRORLEVEL value for branching in a batch file.

You can do the same using an IF EXIST statement in the batch file; and, in many cases, State has no advantage over IF EXIST. One case where State works differently is for 0-length files. IF EXIST says they exist, while State sets ERRORLEVEL to indicate they don't exist. Which approach you use depends on your application.

Time Runner

Name:	Time Runner

Version:	1.0
Price:	$25.00
Category:	Shareware
Summary:	A utility that will run up to five programs at preselected times. These programs can be .COM, .EXE, or .BAT.
Author:	Brian Albright
	Allsoft Computer Products
	2404 Sugar Maple Court
	Monmouth Junction, New Jersey 08852
Availability:	Available on many bulletin board systems.

When you first run it, Time Runner displays a single screen. You select the box to modify and then enter the date and time to run the program. When finished with that, you select OK and Time Runner prompts you for the batch file to run. You enter the filename without the extension, which could also be a .COM or .EXE program filename. You can enter up to five programs to be run at a predetermined time. This information can be saved for repeated use.

Time Runner is excellent for running a communications script to log on a remote database late at night in order to download information and only pay the lowest rate possible. It could also be used to run your backup program late at night if your method doesn't require you to change diskettes.

Using the above method, you would have to change the date every day you ran Time Runner. You can also start Time Runner with the command

    TIMERUN [1,2,3,4,5 or A]

You place the cells to run inside angle brackets (or A, for all cells); and Time Runner uses the time in those cells, running them today regardless of the date in the cell. Thus, you can easily use Time Runner to perform a repetitive task or tasks every day.

The major limitation of Time Runner isn't a program limitation but rather a DOS one. DOS only provides for feeding keystrokes to a program through piping, and many programs ignore piped information. If a program requires keystrokes to run and won't accept piped ones or use a script file, you can load the keystrokes with Stackey.

Every now and then, I must run a complex dBASE reporting program that takes about four hours to run even compiled with Clipper. However, it easily runs at night using Time Runner. In general, any application that can run unattended can be run using Time Runner, which makes Time Runner a very useful program.

Time Runner uses 129K, so the memory available to the application is reduced by that amount.

Ultimate Screen Manager

Name:	Ultimate Screen Manager
Version:	1.20
Price:	$39.00

Category:	Shareware
Summary:	Creates, modifies and displays advanced screens.
Author:	MDFlynn Associates
	Post Office Box 5034
	Redwood City, California 94063
Availability:	Included on the disk bound in this book.

The Ultimate Screen Manager [USM for short] is a jack-of-all-trades (at least when dealing with the screen). USM allows you to design simple screens giving the user information, menus allowing the user to make a choice, and data entry screens allowing the user to enter information similar to entering information into a database front-end. This information is then stored in environmental variables for use as the batch file sees fit.

Your first task in using USM is to design the actual screen. USM has a number of tools that help you draw out the screen. You can easily draw boxes, lines, and control the color of various sections of the screen. In fact, you can quite realistically think of USM as a screen processor.

With all the tools USM offers for designing screens, learning how to use them can be daunting. The manual doesn't make that any easier, only briefly describing the function of each tool. Really needed with a tool this powerful are a few examples that the new user can follow. As it is now, you should plan to spend a couple of afternoons learning how to use USM.

The screens you design in USM are displayed using a second USM program called DSPLY. Because you can't display USM screens from DOS, every machine where you plan on using a batch file must have a copy of USM.

USM screens can do more than simple display information for the user; they can also function as a menu and can obtain information from the user. The menus can be made to look very impressive, given USM's ability to control every aspect of the screen. Once the user makes a selection, that information is passed back to the batch file using ERRORLEVEL. It is then up to the batch file author to take care of handling the selection.

Finally, USM can be used as a quasi-database front-end. The USM screen can prompt the user for any type of information and store that information in environmental variables. I was able to fairly quickly develop a screen that would prompt users for their name, address, and phone number. A USM screen can handle both character and numeric input.

Of course, once you get this sort of information from the user, you are fairly limited in what you can do with it (DOS simply doesn't have the batch file power to process this information). You can use it for branching to different sections of a batch file, or you can pipe it into a file for logging purposes, but that's about it.

Because USM works so closely with the environment, it includes several tiny utilities to perform specific tasks on the environment. They are as follows:

RMVVAR removes any environmental variable matching the partial string entered after the command. Thus, the command RMVVAR RO would remove the variables RONNY, RONNIE, and ROTATE. Notice that you don't use wildcards with the command. USM starts all environmental variables with a dollar sign, making it easy to use RMVVAR to delete them when you exit USM.

LOGTIME takes the time and date, in the format of "Sun, Apr-07-1991, 14:33:20," and places it in the environmental variable you specify. You can use the variable as is for time stamping or process it with the next function for other purposes like performing a backup every time you boot on Sunday.

SUBSTR takes a portion of one environmental variable and stores it in another. For example, if you used LOGTIME to store the time and date in the variable COMBINE, then the command SUBSTR DAY = COMBINE(1,3) would take three characters beginning with the first and place them in the variable DAY. (In this case, that would be the day of the week).

ENVSIZE reports on the total size of the environment, the free space remaining, and the DOS version. You can display this information on the screen or place it in an environmental variable.

ENVPATCH patches DOS 2.0 through 3.1 to increase the size of the environment. It is NOT needed for DOS 3.0 and later because DOS builds in a mechanism for doing this (see Appendix B for details). DOS 2.x, however, needs this patch to expand the environment.

The Ultimate Screen Manager is a complex tool and, like any complex tool, takes time to learn. The manual could have shortened this learning time by including a couple of tutorials the user could follow, but it fails to do this. In any case, the time you spend learning USM is time well spent because USM is an extremely powerful screen and information management tool for batch files.

Wait10

Name:	Wait10
Version:	1.0
Price:	Free
Category:	Public Domain
Summary:	Pauses the batch file for 10 seconds.
Availability:	Included on the disk bound in this book.

WAIT10.COM is a tiny (37-byte) program. When you add the Wait10 command to your batch file, the batch file pauses for 10 seconds. That gives the reader time to read the screen without having to press a key to continue. Need more time? Just run Wait10 twice in a row. Any key the user presses while Wait10 is running is passed to the batch file once Wait10 terminates. Wait10 waits a true 10 seconds no matter what the normal speed of the computer running it.

Zerobat

Name:	Zerobat
Price:	Free

Category:	Copyrighted
Summary:	A batch file to create 0-length files, a program to accept a y or n input, and a replacement for the PAUSE command.
Author:	John C. Van Lund
Availability:	Available on many bulletin board systems.

Zerobat actually consists of three different programs:

CALLYN sets ERRORLEVEL to 255 for a y key, 254 for an n key, 1 for a function key, and 0 for anything else. CALLYN requires ANSI.SYS to operate properly. In addition, it doesn't work under DOS 5.0 (it sets ERRORLEVEL to 34 no matter which key is pressed).

CONTINUE displays a flashing red "Continue with any key" message at the top right of the screen and waits for the user to press any key to continue. CONTINUE doesn't need ANSI.SYS to run.

ZERO.BAT uses the other two programs while creating a 0-length file for the user. You can easily create a 0-length file for yourself using the command TYPE file > 0-LENGTH where file is the name of a file that does NOT exist and 0-length is the name you plan to give the 0-length file. Because it's so easy to create a 0-length file yourself, you hardly need a complex batch file to do it for you.

CALLYN's inability to run under DOS 5.0 and its need for ANSI.SYS make it less useful than similar programs. ZERO.BAT isn't terribly useful because you can do the same thing yourself with one line of code (plus its use of CALLYN means it requires ANSI.SYS as well).

8
Alternative batch languages interpreters/compilers

Some few readers need more power than DOS offers. For those readers, two packages are available that allow the writing of even more powerful batch files: the Extended Batch Language Plus [usually just called EBL Plus], and Beyond.Bat.

Both of these programs add a great deal of power to your batch files, but both also have several drawbacks that you seriously should consider before purchasing one of them:

- *Portability.* An EBL Plus or Beyond.Bat batch file requires EBL Plus or Beyond .Bat to run, so you must purchase a copy of the program for every machine you plan to use.

- *Learning difficulty.* One reason for the ease of DOS batch files is that most of the commands are "regular" DOS commands that you already know how to use. Unfortunately, this isn't true with the commercial batch languages: they are very much a programming language and, like any other programming language, require study and practice to learn.

- *DOS compatibility.* When using any package that functions as a superset of DOS, you always must be concerned that it won't be compatible with the next DOS release.

- *Memory resident problems.* Both of these programs have memory resident modules and thus the potential for conflicting with other memory resident programs.

- *Price.* You can write DOS batch files without purchasing any other program; also, you can purchase the utilities in this book for a small fee. However, Beyond.Bat is a commercial package with a significant price tag; and EBL Plus is a shareware package with a less expensive but still significant price.

Both EBL Plus and Beyond.Bat resemble Basic. They have a full range of programming features including mathematical operations and string operations. Although difficult to learn, they offer batch file power not available otherwise.

Beyond.Bat

Name:	Beyond.Bat
Version:	1.0
Price:	$99.00
Category:	Commercial
Summary:	Beyond.Bat is a program completely replacing the DOS batch language with a more powerful version.
Author:	VM Personal Computing, Inc.
	41 Kenosia Avenue
	Danbury, Connecticut 06810
	(203) 798-3800
Availability:	Order directly from VM Personal Computing. They are no longer actively marketing Beyond.Bat and have no plans to upgrade the program. Copies are still available for sale, though.

Beyond.Bat has two modes of operation: nonresident and resident mode. Nonresident mode operates Beyond.Bat without the need to load a memory resident module. In this mode, each Beyond.Bat command in your batch file must start with a BB, which invokes the Beyond.Bat processor BB.COM. The Beyond.Bat commands following the BB are passed to BB.COM as the variables %1, %2, and so on. Beyond.Bat can also process the entire batch file if no DOS command lines exist.

Operation

Beyond.Bat has three methods of operation:

- *Fully memory resident.* Beyond.Bat loads everything it needs into memory so that no command requires it to read the disk. This method requires 165K of RAM, which is enough to make this mode only useful for someone running Beyond.Bat from a floppy disk system.

- *Partially memory resident.* Beyond.Bat loads a 5K kernel into RAM that examines every command entered at the DOS prompt. If it's a Beyond.Bat script, that script is run; otherwise, the command is passed to DOS. Memory requirements for semi-memory resident are similar to stand-alone except for the additional 5K of RAM for the memory resident program.

- *Stand-alone.* In this mode, Beyond.Bat isn't active until called. To call Beyond .Bat, you precede the script file name with a BB. This mode requires 128K to run a script and an additional 65K to run an application.

Beyond.Bat reads the entire script into memory prior to execution, which is much faster than DOS's method of reading the batch file one line at a time. Beyond.Bat applications aren't compiled, which means that everyone you develop an application for must have Beyond.Bat to execute that application—an expensive proposal.

Beyond.Bat comes with a simple ASCII editor. You can use this editor to create and modify both Beyond.Bat and DOS batch files. The editor is very similar to the VM editor found on many mainframe computers and, as such, is more cumbersome than many small editors without mainframe roots.

You use Beyond.Bat commands to write Beyond.Bat batch files, which makes Beyond.Bat a programming language. Users of Relay Gold or Relay Silver will have a head start in learning this language: Beyond.Bat comes from the same company, and its language is almost identical to the script language used in the Relay products.

Beyond.Bat can read and write files. It can create and use variables far beyond the %0-%9 and environmental variables (e.g., %PATH%) offered by DOS. The variable names can be up to nine characters long and can contain information with up to 258 characters. System variables (like &Date) store global information.

In addition to branching based on variable values (as with DOS), you can use mathematical or string operations on these variables. Prior to v3.3, DOS couldn't branch from one batch file to another and return (without the COMMAND/C trick). Beyond.Bat handles this and other types of branching with ease.

In addition to subroutines, Beyond.Bat allows all the batch files for a specific application to be collected into libraries for easy management, which makes it easier to develop complex applications the way you should (i.e., in pieces).

Beyond.Bat simplifies the development of screens that can be used to provide the user with information or request information from the user. Beyond.Bat can perform input validation on information requested from the user. One of the sample applications is a restaurant reservation system written in Beyond.Bat code.

Some of the Beyond.Bat commands/keywords are listed in Table 8-1. I have left out much of the input/output commands and some of the less useful commands, as I merely want to demonstrate the power of the language and not document it. As you can see from this partial list, Beyond.Bat offers a wealth of features, with the more useful ones being listed in Table 8-2. Beyond.Bat also defines special variables, such as the date, DOS version, the type of monitor, the number of replaceable parameters entered, the time, and much more useful information.

Table 8-1   A summary of Beyond.Bat keywords and commands.

Keyword	Operation
*	Identifies a comment just like the REM in DOS. In fact, some versions of DOS allow you to use the asterisk to signal a comment.
-	Identifies a label just like a colon in a DOS batch file.
ARGSTRING	Beyond.Bat sets the variable ARGSTRING to the string you entered when you started the script file. This command lets you change it.
BEEP	Beeps the speaker.
CANCEL	Cancels a function such as printing.
CHAIN	Jumps to another script file without returning to the original script file when the new one terminates.
CHDIR	Changes subdirectories just like the DOS command of the same name. (It can be abbreviated to CD in DOS.)
CLEAR	Clears the screen like the DOS CLS command.
CLOSE	Closes any files Beyond.Bat has opened.
CMSG	Writes text to the editor's command line.
COMMAND	Runs a command separately and not as part of the current script file.

Table 8-1   Continued.

Keywords	Operation
CURSOR	Moves the cursor to the specified location.
DISPLAY	Shows a panel.
DOSDIR	Accesses files in another directory.
EXIT	Leaves the script processor.
GLOBAL	Defines a variable where other script files can use it.
GOSUB	Calls a subroutine within a script file.
GOTO	Just like the DOS GOTO command, it branches to a label.
IF	Compares two conditions, just like the DOS IF command.
LOCAL	Defines a variable so that other script files can not use the value.
LOOP	Allows a section of code to be repeated.
ON	Monitors a condition and performs a specified command when that condition is true.
OPEN	Gets a file ready for manipulation by Beyond.Bat.
PARSE	Breaks a command string down into its component parts.
PRINT	Prints a file.
PRIVATE	Keeps the value of a variable within a subroutine.
PRINTSCREEN	Prints the screen.
QUIET	Suppresses output just like piping to NUL.
RETURN	Returns to the main portion of a script file from the subroutine.
RUN	Performs a DOS command or run a program.
RUN DOS	Shells to DOS.
SET	Used to configure script options. Beyond.Bat does not use the SET command to establish values for environmental variables as DOS does.
SMSG	Shows a message on the status line.
STACK	Places a character into the keyboard buffer. Not related to the DOS 3.3 CONFIG.SYS STACK command.
STOP	Terminates a script file.
WAIT	Pauses a script file for a specified time much like a timed PAUSE would.

Table 8-2   A summary of Beyond.Bat functions.

Function	Operation
&ARGNUMBER	The number of arguments in a string.
&ASCII	Returns the hexadecimal value of a character.
&CALCULATE	Calculates an expression.
&CHARACTER	Returns the ASCII value of a hexadecimal number.
&DATATYPE	Tells you what type of data a variable contains.
&DAYOFWEEK	Returns the day of the week.
&DAYOFYEAR	Returns the day of the year.
&DECIMAL	Returns the decimal value of a hexadecimal number.
&DEFINED	Returns information on how a script variable is defined.
&DISKSIZE	Returns the size of the disk.
&DISKSPACE	Returns the amount of free space.

Function	Operation
&DOS-ENVIRONMENT	Returns a DOS environmental variable.
&DOS-ENVMASTER	Returns a DOS environmental variable from the master copy of the environment.
&GDATE	Returns a Georgian date for a Julian date.
&HEXA-DECIMAL	Returns a hexadecimal number for a decimal number.
&HOURS	Converts time to Hours:Minutes:Seconds format.
&INSTRING	Returns a portion of a string.
&JDATE	Converts a Georgian date to a Julian date.
&LEFT	Left-justifies a string.
&LENGTH	Returns the length of a string.
&LOWER	Converts a string to all lowercase.
&MASK	Converts a string to all X's.
&REPLACE	Exchanges one string for another.
&REVERSED	Reverses the order of a string.
&RIGHT	Right-justifies a string.
&SECONDS	Converts time to seconds.
&SUBSTRING	Returns a portion of a longer string.
&TRIM	Removes extra spaces from a string.
&UPPER	Converts a string to all uppercase.

VM Personal Computing sells an Advanced Development Kit for $25. This kit allows the user to

- add memory resident help to existing applications.
- add a learn mode to Beyond.Bat.
- use Beyond.Bat as a keyboard macro program.
- access the editor in pop-up mode.

Some examples

One real problem with DOS is controlling how many loops a batch file performs. With Beyond.Bat, it's as easy as setting up a loop counter. BB-1.BAT in Table 8-3 does just that; the loop counter is &COUNTER and it's increased by 1 using the built in mathematics of Beyond.Bat. When the counter reaches 10, the batch file drops out of the loop using an IF statement. Although it can't perform advanced mathematics, Beyond.Bat can at least perform adding, subtracting, multiplying, and dividing. BB-2.BAT in Table 8-4 illustrates this.

Table 8-3   BB-1.BAT will loop a specified number of times just like a Basic program.

Batch File Line	Explanation
`*BB-1.BAT`	Remark giving the name of the batch file.
`&Counter=0`	Sets the counter equal to zero.
`-TOP`	Marks the top of a loop.

Table 8-3   Continued.

Batch File Line	Explanation
`&Counter=&Counter+1`	Increments the counter by one.
`ECHO Counter is currently` `     &Counter`	Echoes the value of the counter.
`IF (&Counter=10) THEN GOTO OUT`	If the counter equals ten, jumps out of the loop.
`GOTO TOP`	Goes back to the top of the loop and continues processing.
`-OUT`	Label used to jump out of the loop.
`ECHO Loop has finished`	Message indicating the loop has finished.

Table 8-4   BB-2.BAT illustrates beyond a doubt that Beyond.Bat has no trouble with mathematics.

Batch File Line	Explanation
`* BB-2.BAT`	Remark line giving the name of the batch file.
`* Mathematics Demonstration`	Remark line documenting the purpose of the batch file.
`&ADD=1+1`	Beyond Bat command that adds two numbers and stores the results in a variable named ADD.
`ECHO 1+1=&ADD`	Echoes the equation and the results.
`&MULTIPLY=2*2`	Multiplies two numbers and stores the results in a variable.
`ECHO 2*2=&MULTIPLY`	Echoes the equation and the results.
`&SUB=10-5`	Subtracts two numbers and stores the results in a variable.
`ECHO 10-5=&SUB`	Echoes the equation and the results.
`&DIVIDE= 100/20`	Divides two numbers and stores the results in a variable.
`ECHO 100/20=&DIVIDE`	Echoes the equation and the results.
`&COMPLEX=(100+37)*(8-5)/3`	Evaluates a complex equation and stores the results in a variable.
`ECHO (100+37)*(8-5)/3=&COMPLEX`	Echoes the equation and the results.

Screen design remains one of the most time-consuming parts of writing batch files. You're stuck with high-ordered ASCII characters; and, unless you have a special screen design program, entering them can be difficult. Beyond.Bat simplifies this task. BB-3.BAT in Table 8-5 displays a screen (called a *panel* by Beyond.Bat). PANEL.PNL in Fig. 8-1 is the script file used to define the panel. This example even has code built in for the user to enter their name and have it stored in an environmental variable.

Table 8-5   BB-3.BAT displays a screen that Beyond.Bat helps to create.

Batch File Line	Explanation
*BB-3.BAT	Remark giving the name of the batch file.
*DEMONSTRATE A PANEL	Remark documenting the purpose of the batch file.
&SUBJECT="Batch Files"	Defines a variable.
&NAME=	Defines a variable.
DISPLAY PANEL PANEL.PNL	Displays a menu.
-TOP	Label.
DISPLAY INPUT &RESPONSE	Waits for an input from the user.
IF (&RESPONSE=ENTER) GOTO END	If the user presses return, exits the batch file.
SMSG KWhat?	Displays a message.
GOTO -TOP	Jumps to the top of the batch file.
DISPLAY END	End of the display portion of the batch file.

```
)ATTR
_             INPUT REVERSED HIGH
$             OUTPUT HIGH
+             OUTPUT LOW
^             TEXT REVERSED
)BODY
+


                                TAB Books Presents...

                        A Beyond.Bat Demonstration Panel



        This Book is About..... ^                +

        Please Enter Your Name: _                     +
)INIT
FIELD TEXT 1 VARIABLE &SUBJECT
FIELD INPUT 1 VARIABLE &NAME
```

8-1 This file defines a Beyond.Bat panel.

Technical support

VM Personal Computing is no longer actively marketing Beyond.Bat, although they still currently have copies for sale. As a result, technical support is sketchy at best. Beyond.Bat is difficult to learn, and the sketchy technical support means that only users very interested in Beyond.Bat or very technically proficient should consider purchasing it.

Bugs

Beyond.Bat memory resident applications wouldn't run from a DOS memory resident shell, although the stand-alone applications ran without any problem. On some clones, running an application with a BB command when Beyond.Bat is loaded as a memory resident program will cause the computer to lock and force a cold reboot.

While Beyond.Bat is powerful, it suffers from a number of frustrating bugs. For example, in setting up the BB-2.BAT example batch file back in Table 8-4, I couldn't get the division operation to work. After laboring over it for longer than half an hour, I changed the numbers in the example and suddenly it worked perfectly. I often hit such minor, but frustrating, bugs.

Documentation

The authors of the Beyond.Bat documentation failed to remember they were writing documentation for a programming language not documented elsewhere. Explanations include all the necessary information but are often brief with few examples. No quick reference card exists.

Conclusion

Beyond.Bat is an extremely powerful replacement for DOS batch files, with its main drawback simply being VM Personal Computing's decision to stop both actively marketing and upgrading it. As a result, you should consider Beyond.Bat only for very unique situations. Addition problems include the lack of a compiler, poor documentation, and poor technical support.

Extended Batch Language Plus

Name:	Extended Batch Language Plus
Version:	4.02
Price:	$79.00
Category:	Shareware
Summary:	A complete replacement for the DOS batch language that greatly extends the power of batch files.
Author:	Frank Canova, Seaware Corporation
	Post Office Box 1656
	Delray Beach, Florida 33444
Availability:	Order directly from Seaware or download from any major bulletin board.

Extended Batch Language Plus [EBL Plus] is a shareware program and is available from many computer bulletin boards. EBL Plus is available for $79.00 from the author, Frank Canova. Write to him in care of Seaware Corporation at the above address. If you order the program from the author, you also will need to include $3.00 for shipping. Because of the long lead time involved in producing a book, you should write to check the price before sending money.

Unlike most shareware programs, EBL Plus doesn't have an ASCII file manual on the disk. If you want documentation, you must pay the registration fee. You'll need it—the information in the chapter isn't enough to use EBL Plus without the manual.

Operation

Before a batch file can run an EBL Plus command, it must have a BAT line (which loads the EBL Plus command processor). The command processor requires about 48K, remaining in memory until the batch file terminates or the batch file specifically unloads it. This EBL Plus command processor gives EBL Plus all its power.

With EBL Plus, all of your batch files are created identically to DOS batch files, and a batch file can contain a mixture of DOS and EBL Plus commands. EBL Plus only passes those commands to DOS that it doesn't understand, unless you use the SHELL command to force EBL Plus to turn a command over to DOS.

Like DOS, EBL Plus has a number of keywords, shown in Table 8-6. EBL Plus adds a number of functions to batch files (see Table 8-7). EBL.BAT in Table 8-8 is a sample batch file illustrating many of the Extended Batch Language Plus keywords and functions.

EBL Plus is very much a complete batch language. It performs most of the commonly needed enhancements batch file authors need—all in one package. It is clearly one of the better batch file enhancements.

Table 8-6   A summary of keywords for Extended Batch Language Plus.

Keyword	Operation
*	Identifies an EBL Plus comment.
-	Identifies a name for a GOTO statement.
BEEP	Sounds the speaker.
BEGSTACK	EBL Plus can stuff characters into the keyboard stack for use by applications using the BEGSTACK command.
BEGTYPE	Marks the beginning of lines to be typed to the screen. Typing continues until EBL Plus encounters an END statement.
CALL	Calls a batch file subroutine.
CALL.PURGE	Clears all pending returns.
CLS	Clears the screen just like the DOS command.
COLORCHAR	Changes the color of text.
EXIT	Leaves a batch file and returns to DOS.
GOTO	Jumps to a label, just like the DOS GOTO command.
IF	Similar to the DOS IF statement, it makes decisions based on conditions. Unlike DOS, EBL Plus can make greater than, less than, or case-sensitive comparisons. It can also perform an IF-THEN-ELSE test, and the actions taken as the result of passing an IF-statement can continue over multiple lines.
INKEY	Reads a single keystroke from the keyboard.
INTERPRET	Evaluates an expression and runs EBL Plus command(s) contained in that expression.
LEAVE	Stops EBL Plus and returns control of the batch file to DOS.
LOCATE	Positions the cursor on the screen.
-ON.ERROR-	Marks a special section that is executed if EBL Plus encounters an error.
PARSE	Breaks down an expression into its parts.
READ	Prompts the user for an input and stores that input in a variable or variables(s). READ can accept values in excess of a single character.

Table 8-6 Continued.

Keyword	Operation
READ.PARSED	Prompts the user for an input, parses that input, and stores it in variables.
READSCRN	This reads characters off the screen and can act based on what it reads.
READSCRN.-PARSED	Reads characters off the screen, parses them, and stores them in variables.
REPEAT	Process an action more than once.
RESUME	Returns control to a program after an error.
RETURN	Causes EBL Plus to exit from a subroutine and resumes processing the main batch file.
SHELL	Temporarily exits to DOS to run a single command. EBL Plus remains in memory.
SKIP	Jumps forward a specified number of lines.
STACK	Stuffs keystrokes into the keyboard buffers.
STACK.ON/ STACK.OFF	Turns on and off the flow of characters from the stack.
STACK.PURGE	Clears out all the characters in the stack.
STATEOF	Checks to see if a file exists.
TYPE	Displays text on the screen. It works very similar to the DOS ECHO command.
WAIT	Pauses the batch file.

Table 8-7 A summary of functions for Extended Batch Language Plus.

Function	Operation
ABS	Returns the absolute value of the number or calculation specified inside the parenthesis. Absolute value is a mathematical term. It means that zero or a number above zero is not affected and a number below zero is made positive.
C2H	Converts an ASCII string to hexadecimal.
CENTER	Centers a text string on the screen. It requires two inputs, the string to center, and the width in which to center that text. Normally the width will be the screen width of eighty. In a bow to the British, you can also spell the function "CENTRE."
CHARIN	Accepts a single keystroke just like INKEY, except the keystroke always comes from the keyboard even if characters have been placed into the buffer.
CHDIR	Just like the DOS CD or CHDIR commands, it changes the current drive and/or subdirectory.
COLOR	Allows the use of colors in menus and text.
COPIES	Returns multiple copies of a string.
CURSOR.ROW CURSOR.COL	Returns the current position of the cursor.
D2H	Converts a decimal (base ten) number into a hexadecimal (base sixteen) number.
DATE	Returns the system date. EBL Plus gives you a great deal of flexibility in how this is displayed.

Function	Operation
DELWORD	Removes a portion of a string.
DIR	Returns the specified files.
EDIT	Allows text on the screen to be edited, much like the data entry function of a database.
FIELD	Returns the contents of a field on the screen.
FIND	Locates a phrase in a string.
FLOAT	Returns the value of a calculation with the fractional portion of the number intact.
FRAC	Returns just the fractional part of a number.
GETDIR	Returns the current subdirectory. The real power of this function is you can store it in a variable for later use.
H2C	Converts hexadecimal values to ASCII values.
H2D	Converts hexadecimal values to decimal values.
INT	Returns the integer (non-fraction) part of a number.
INT86	Executes an 8086 software interrupt and is only for very advanced users. Misusing it can cause you to lose data, crash the system, or even destroy disk files.
KEY	Places the named keystroke into the keyboard stack.
KEYPRESSED	Returns a "T" if a key has been pressed and a "F" otherwise. Normally, you would use this with functions discussed later to give the user a certain amount of time to respond to a prompt.
LEFT	Returns part of a string of variables. It requires two inputs: the string and the number of characters to return. It returns characters from the left.
LENGTH	Returns the length of a string.
LOCATE x y	Positions the cursor on the screen at a specific location. Generally, you would follow this command with a TYPE command to write information to the screen at that location.
LOWER	Converts all characters in a string to lowercase. Only letters are effected.
MKDIR	Makes a subdirectory.
NOT	Reverses a logical decision just like the DOS NOT function.
PEEK	Like the Basic Peek statement, this returns the value of the byte of memory in hex at the specified location. This is for advanced users only.
PLAY	Plays a note on the speaker.
POKE	Like the Basic Poke statement, this writes the specified value to memory at the specified location. This is for advanced users only.
REBOOT	Reboots the computer just like pressing Control-Alternate-Delete.
REVERSE	Transposes a string.
RIGHT	Returns the right-most specified number of characters from a character string.
RMDIR	Removes a subdirectory.
SEEK	Finds the position in a file that is being written to.
SELECT	Picks an item from a list on the screen using the cursor control keys.
SPACE	Changes the spacing of a string.

Table 8-7 Continued.

Function	Operation
STRIP	Removes extra characters (usually spaces) from both sides of a character string. An optional parameter causes it to only strip extra characters from one side.
SUBWORD	Returns a portion of a string.
TIME	Like DATE(), this returns the system time and like DATE(), there are a number of parameters to control how it is formatted.
TRACE	A debugging aid that causes addition information to be displayed while the batch file is running.
UPPER	Converts a string to all uppercase.
VERIFY	Checks to be sure that one string is made up of only the characters in another string.
VERSION	Returns the current EBL Plus version.
WHATFUNC	EBL Plus loads its functions separately from the main package because they take up memory all the time. To minimize memory, they are broken down into three partial packages and one full package. That way, if you do not need all the functions, you can only load one or two parts. This functions returns a value indicating which functions are loaded.
WINDOW	Draws a window on the screen.
WORD	Returns the specified word.
WORDS	Returns the specified words.

Table 8-8 EBL.BAT illustrates usage of Extended Batch Language Plus.

Batch File Line	Explanation
`@ECHO OFF`	Turns command-echoing off.

`REM EBL.BAT`
`REM Sample Extended Batch`
`REM Language Batch File`
	Documentation remarks.

`BAT * Load EBL Into Memory`	The "BAT" loads the Extended Batch Language Plus [EBL Plus] program into memory. It requires about 48K and will automatically unload itself when the batch file terminates. The rest of the line is a comment.
`CLS`	Clears the screen.
`ECHO Sound Speaker`	Displays a message.
`BEEP`	An EBL Plus command that sounds the speaker.

`BEGSTACK`
`Now is the time for all ;`
`good men to come to the ;`
`aid of their country.`
`Now is the time for all ;`
`good men to come to the ;`
`aid of their country.`
`Now is the time for all ;`
	Everything between the "BEG-STACK" and "END" is loaded into the keyboard buffer and supplied to the first program that reads the buffer. The semicolon on the end of some lines causes EBL Plus to ignore the return at

Batch File Line	Explanation

`good men to come to the ;`
`aid of their country.\1A`
`END`
	the end of those lines. The \1A is hexadecimal for a Control-Z.

`COPY CON NUL`	Copies from the keyboard to NUL, thus using the keystrokes loaded into the buffer above.
`PAUSE`	Pauses the batch file until a key is pressed.
`CLS`	Clears the screen.
`COLORCHAR @ AS COLOR(RED)`	Sets "@" as a switch that toggles characters between standard color and red. In addition, EBL Plus prints a space when this character is used to change colors.

`BEGTYPE`
`  This line is typed to the screen.`
`@So is this one.@`
`  Only the second line was red.`
`@This line is red too.@`
`END`
	Everything between "BEGTYPE" and "END" is typed directly to the screen, with the "@" acting as a color-toggle as described above.

`COLORCHAR @ AS COLOR(YELLOW)`	Changes the color-toggle to yellow.

`BEGTYPE`
`  This line is plain.`
`@But this line is yellow.@`
`END`
`PAUSE`
	Displays more information on the screen.

`GOTO -SKIP`
`ECHO This Lines Will Be Skipped`
`ECHO This Lines Will Be Skipped`
`ECHO This Lines Will Be Skipped`
`-SKIP`
	Jumps to a label. Works just like a DOS "GOTO" command except labels are treated differently.

`READ Do You Want To Exit (Y/N) > %A`	Gets a character from the user. The "READ" command is not limited to a single character.
`IF %A=Y EXIT`	If the user enters "Y", exits the batch file. Dual testing avoids capitalization problems.
`IF %A=y EXIT`	If the user enters "y", exits the batch file. Dual testing avoids capitalization problems.
`CLS`	Clears the screen.
`READ Enter 1 To See Special Screen >%B`	Gets more information from the user. Asking for a number avoids capitalization problems.
`IF %B=1 THEN`	While EBL Plus supports a standard IF-statement, this form is far more powerful. The "THEN" tells EBL Plus that everything between the "BEGIN"

Table 8-8 Continued.

Batch File Line	Explanation
	and "END" is to be executed only if the IF-statement is true.

BEGIN
COLORCHAR @ AS COLOR(BLUE)
BEGTYPE
@
11111111111111111111111111111111111111
          One Screen
11111111111111111111111111111111111111
@
END
PAUSE
END if
	This screen is displayed only if the above IF-statement is true. Notice the use of the color-toggle.

CLS	Clears the screen.
REPEAT WITH %I = 1 to 80	Sets I=1, and continues until reaching an "END". Then, increments I by one and goes through the loop again. Continue this until I equals 80.
REPEAT WITH %J = 1 to 20	Sets J=1, and continues until reaching an "END". Increments J by one and goes through the loop again. Continues until J is 20.
LOCATE %I %J	Positions the cursor on the screen.
TYPE "O"	Prints an "O" on the screen at the cursor position from above.
END Repeat	Marks the bottom of the J-loop.
END Repeat	Marks the bottom of the I-loop.
PAUSE	Pauses the batch file.
CLS	Clears the screen.
READ Enter Your Name > %1 %2	Requests information from the user. Here the " > " marks the end of the prompt and not the normal DOS pipe.
TYPE "Welcome" %1 %2	Types "Welcome" and then the user's name as entered above.
TYPE "All Batch Files Are"	Displays a message on the screen.

%B=DIR("*.BAT")
REPEAT WHILE %B IS NOT ""
    TYPE %B
    %B=DIR("*.BAT",i)
END REPEAT
	Loops through all the *.BAT files in the current subdirectory and displays their name one at a time.

PAUSE	Pauses the batch file.
CLS	Clears the screen.
SKIP 10	Skips the next ten lines.
TYPE This Is Line 1 TYPE This Is Line 2 TYPE This Is Line 3 TYPE This Is Line 4 TYPE This Is Line 5	Because of the "SKIP 10" command, all of these lines are skipped and not executed.

Batch File Line	Explanation

`TYPE This Is Line  6`
`TYPE This Is Line  7`
`TYPE This Is Line  8`
`TYPE This Is Line  9`
`TYPE This Is Line 10`	

`TYPE This Is Line 11`	This is the next line after the "SKIP 10" line that is executed.
`TYPE`	Displays a blank line on the screen.
`TYPE Now I Will Pause` `TYPE For 10-Seconds`	Tells the user what will happen next.
`WAIT UNTIL TIME(10)`	Pauses the batch file for 10-seconds.
`TYPE Finished Waiting`	Lets the user know the wait is over.
`PAUSE`	Waits for the user to press a key.
`TYPE "I'm Thinking of a 2-Digit No."`	Tells the user what is happening.
`TYPE "Enter Your Guess"`	Tells the user to enter a guess.
`%1 = 27`	Sets up the value.
`REPEAT WITH %A = 5 DOWN TO 0`	Loops through and give the user up to six guesses.
`        READ %2`	Reads the users guess.

`        IF %2 = %1`
`        BEGIN`
`                TYPE "Good Guess!!!!!"`
`                EXIT REPEAT`
`        END`
	Performs these steps if the user guesses the number. The "EXIT REPEAT" breaks out of the loop early.

`        IF %A = 0`
`        BEGIN`
`                TYPE "The Number Was " %1`
`                TYPE "This Number Doesn't"`
`                TYPE "Change When This Is"`
`                TYPE "Run Again"`
`                EXIT REPEAT`
`        END`
	IF %A=0, then the user is out of guesses, so tell him/her what the number was.

`        IF %2 > %1 TYPE "Lower:"  %A "More Tries"`	If the guess was too high, tells the user to guess lower and lets him/her how many guesses remain.
`        IF %2 < %1 TYPE "Higher:" %A "More Tries"`	If the guess was too low, tells the user to guess higher and lets him/her how many guesses remain.
`END REPEAT`	End of the repeat-loop.

Drawbacks

The biggest drawback is, of course, the lack of portability discussed above. Extended Batch Language Plus won't run at all under DOS 5.0: as soon as BAT.COM tries to load, the computer locks up. EBL Plus also won't run reliably on an IBM Model 80 running

IBM DOS 4.0. In fact, under DOS 4.0, neither the installation program nor the demonstration program would finish running. Both of them would terminate in mid-course but without locking the computer. The sample batch file EBL.BAT back in Table 8-8 does run successfully under DOS 4.0.

Conclusion

If you are running DOS 3.3 or earlier and you want to extend your batch files, Extended Batch Language Plus 1.1 offers a good way to do that; you get most of the utilities you need packaged in a single program. However, if you run DOS 4.0 or later, you will want to wait until a more compatible version of EBL Plus is released.

SCR

Name:	SCR
Version:	1.0
Price:	$30.00
	Registration of SCR includes registration of BQ, the author's other shareware program.
Category:	Shareware
Summary:	A replacement for the DOS batch language with strong looping and screen control.
Author:	T. G. Browning
	MorganSoft
	2170 Baynor Street
	SE Salem, Oregon 97302
Availability:	Included on the disk bound in this book.

Using SCR, you create an ASCII file containing a mixture of SCR commands and a few supported DOS commands. SCR is a mixture of the worst aspects of an interpretive and compiled language. It runs slowly and requires users to have a copy of SCR, just like an interpretive language. In addition, you can't enter a single command on the command line to test its effect, as with a compiler.

SCR has over seventy keywords that you can use in your SCR scripts (see Table 8-9). Table 8-10 shows a sample script using many of these keywords.

Table 8-9   A summary of SCR keywords that help you construct complex scripts.

SCR Command	Explanation
//	Remark, just like REM in DOS.
BACK	Changes the background color.
BLOCKATTR	Change the display characteristics for a block on the screen.
BLOCKCLR	Clears a block on the screen.
BOX	Draws a box on the screen.
CASE	Run one of several alternatives using a case construction.

SCR Command	Explanation
CD or CHDIR	Change subdirectories.
CHDRV	Change drives.
CLEARSCREEN	Clears the screen without resetting the color as CLS does.
CLREOL	Clears a line beginning at the cursor position and extended to the right of the screen.
COMLOAD	Load a copy of COMMAND.COM then run a program.
CONCAT$	Merge two variables into a single variable.
COPY	Copies files the same as the DOS COPY command.
CURSBLOCK CURSNORM CURSHALFBLOCK	Changes the shape of the cursor.
CURSOROFF CURSORON	Turn the cursor on and off.
DATE	Same as the DOS DATE command.
DEBUG	Causes SCR to invoke the editor when it encounters an error.
DEL ERASE	Erase files, just like the DOS commands of the same name.
DELETELINE	Deletes an entire line.
DIR	Same as the DOS DIR command.
UP DOWN LEFT RIGHT	Move the cursor in the indicated direction.
ECHO ON/OFF	Control command echoing, just like DOS.
ELSE	Part of an IF/THEN/ELSE/ENDIF statement, it defines what to do if an IF-statement is false.
END	Marks the end of a command file.
ENDCASE	Marks the end of a CASE command.
ENDIF	Marks the end of an IF-statement.
EXIST	Checks to see if a parameter exists.
FOR/NEXT	Defines a loop, just like in Basic.
FORE	Sets the foreground color.
GOTOXY	Positions the cursor on the screen.
IF	Marks the top of an IF/THEN/ELSE/ENDIF statement. It tells SCR to perform a task only if a statement is true.
INPUT	Define a variable.
INSERTLINE	Insert a line on the screen at the indicated position.
JUMP	Go to another position in the batch file and continue processing. Like the GOTO command in DOS.
LEFT$	Retain only some of the characters from the left side of a string variable.
LINEPATTERN	Fill a line with a given pattern.
LOAD	Load and run a program.
LOADSCR	This loads a second SCR file and begins processing it.
MID$	Retain only some of the characters from the middle of a string variable.
MKDIR	Creates a subdirectory.

Table 8-9   Continued.

SCR Command	Explanation
PATTERN	Clears the entire screen and fills it with a specified character.
PAUSE	Pause a batch file for a specified period of time.
POPDIR PUSHDIR	Save and recall the current subdirectory.
RIGHT$	Retain only some of the characters from the right of a string variable.
RELOAD	Loads another SCR file and starts processing it from the top.
RENAME	Changes the name of a file.
REPEAT/UNTIL	Loops through some commands until a specified condition is reached.
RET	When loading another SCR file, this stores the name of the current SCR file and the position in that file.
RESTARTON/ RESTARTOFF	A debugging command that controls whether or not to restart the current file after running the editor.
RMDIR	Removes a subdirectory.
SCROLLDN SCROLLUP	Scroll the cursor up or down one line.
SEND	Sends a form feed to the printer.
SENDPRINTER	Sends information to the printer.
SET	Stores information to a variable.
SHELL	Shells out of SCR to DOS.
SOUND	Plays a note on the speaker.
SNOWON SNOWOFF	Controls the status of snow checking when running a CGA monitor.
TIME	Sets the time.
TYPE	Sends text to the screen.
WAITKEY	Flushes the keyboard buffer and waits for a key to be pressed.
WHILE/ENDWHILE	Forms a loop that continues until a condition is met.
WRITE AT	Write a string to the screen at specified coordinates.
WRITEBETWEEN	Write a message between the specified columns.
WRITEVERT	Write a text string vertically.
WRT	Write a text string at the current cursor position and do not advance the cursor to the next line when done.
WRITIN	Write a text string at the current cursor position and advance the cursor to the next line when done.

Table 8-10   RONNY.SCR illustrates many of the SCR commands.

Batch File Line	Explanation
@ECHO OFF	Turns command-echoing off.
// RONNY.SCR	Remark giving the name of the SCR-file.
// Draw Some Boxes	Documentation remark.
BACK BLUE FORE WHITE	Sets the background and foreground colors. These will stay in effect until changed.
CURSOROFF	Turns the cursor off.
CLEARSCREEN	Clears the screen.

Batch File Line	Explanation
BOX SINGLE-LINE 1 1 10 80 BOX SINGLE-LINE 1 1 24 10 BOX SINGLE-LINE 30 10 10 20	Draws three boxes on the screen.
GOTOXY 1 1	Positions cursor at top left corner of screen.
CLREOL	Clears this row to the end of the line.
PAUSE 10	Waits .1 seconds.
GOTOXY 1 2 CLREOL PAUSE 10	Clears the second row.
This continues for rows 3-23	
GOTOXY 1 24 CLREOL PAUSE 10	Clears the 24-line.
GOTOXY 1 25 CLREOL	Clears the 25-line.

WRTLN "Now I will ask you for some
    information."
WRTLN "While answering, you can use
    the following:"
WRTLN "CTRL-Y: Delete entire
    answer"
WRTLN "CTRL-J Enter: Delete to end
    of answer"
WRTLN "INSERT: Insert a space"
WRTLN "DELETE: Delete a
    character"
WRTLN "HOME: Go to the first
    character"
WRTLN "END: Go to the last
    character"
WRTLN "BACKSPACE: Delete a
    character to left"
WRTLN "RIGHT ARROW: Move to the
    right"
WRTLN "LEFT ARROW: Move to the
    left"
	Displays information for the user.

SCROLLUP 10	Scrolls the text up 10-lines.
GOTOXY 1 22	Positions the cursor.
WRT "Enter Your Name:"	Asks a question.
INPUT 20 22 30 S1	Has the user enter information in row-22, column-20. There is room for 30-characters and is stored in variable S1.
GOTOXY 1 23	Positions the cursor.
WRT "Enter Your City:"	Asks a question.
INPUT 20 23 20 S2	Gets information from the user.
GOTOXY 1 24	Positions the cursor.
WRT "Enter Your State:"	Asks a question.
INPUT 20 24 2 S3	Gets information from the user.
CLEARSCREEN	Clears the screen.
SCROLLUP 2	Scrolls up to lines.
SET S4=S1	Stores the users name in another variable.
WRT "The First Five Characters Of Your Name Are: "	Tells the user what will be displayed next.
LEFT$ S4 5	Strips off all but the five left characters of the user's name.

Table 8-10   Continued.

Batch File Line	Explanation
WRTLN S4	Displays those five characters. The contents of the variable was copied to another variable to keep from affecting the original contents.
WRT "The Last Ten Characters Of Your City Are: "	Tells the user what will be displayed next.
SET S4=S2	Stores the city under another name.
RIGHT S4 10	Strips out all but the right 10-characters of the city.
WRTLN S4	Displays the stripped down city.
WRT S1	Displays the user's name.
WRT " of "	Displays a message.
WRT S2	Displays the city.
WRT ", "	Displays a comma.
WRTLN S3	Displays the state.
PAUSE 200	Waits .2 second.
PATTERN 219 PATTERN 177 PATTERN 176 PATTERN 255	Alternatively fills the screen with four different patterns.
PUSHDIR	Stores the current subdirectory.
WRT "Current Subdirectory Is: " CD	Tells the user the current subdirectory.
CHDIR \	Changes to the root directory.
WRTLN	Displays a blank line.
WRTLN "Changing To Root"	Tells the user about the change.
POPDIR	Returns to the original subdirectory.
WRT "Returning To: "	Tells the user.
CD	Displays the resulting subdirectory.
PAUSE 100	Pauses for .1 second.
CLEARSCREEN	Clears the screen.
FOR J = 1 to 80	Marks the top of a loop that will be repeated 80-times.
WRITEVERT AT J 1 "Ronny Richardson"	Writes my name vertically on the screen.
NEXT	Marks the bottom of the loop.
CURSORON	Turns the cursor back on.
END	Marks the end of the file.

SCR comes with a Wordstar-like editor to help you construct your scripts. It doesn't do any syntax checking, nor does its online help have any information about SCR. As a result, you aren't much better using this editor than any other program editor. Its one advantage over other editors is in debugging mode, where SCR can automatically load the editor and move it to the first line with an error.

Distributing SCR scripts

With the other interpreters, your distribution alternatives are quite limited; you must purchase a copy for every computer where you want to be able to run the program. With SCR, you have a better alternative.

The documentation explains how to lock a program name into SCR.EXE so that it can only run one script. You can then distribute your script and SCR.EXE for a one-time fee of only five dollars, no matter how many copies of SCR.EXE you plan to distribute. This is extremely reasonable.

Drawbacks

Because SCR simplifies loop manipulation, you easily can get stuck in an "endless-loop" while trying to write a complex one. (This happened to me a couple of times while evaluating the program.) When that happens, you must reboot because neither Ctrl-Break, Ctrl-C, nor Escape will stop SCR.

The documentation is scarce, giving each keyword only a few lines of explanation. As a result, you easily can construct a script that should work—at least according to the manual—but doesn't. When that happens, you can't do much but experiment. In order to do justice to this program, the manual should be much larger with more examples.

Conclusion

SCR is a massive program still on its first release, so naturally it will have bugs. Once those bugs are shaken out, SCR will be a very impressive program.

The ability to distribute unlimited operational copies of SCR scripts for only $5.00 gives SCR a major advantage over EBL Plus or Beyond.Bat.

Batch file compilers

DOS reads a batch file one line at a time, executing each line and then reading the next one. This takes a long time—especially with a slow computer or slow hard disk. A batch file compiler corrects this program by converting a batch file into a stand-alone program.

The process of compiling a batch file introduces a unique problem. Batch files have direct access to the DOS master copy of the environment; in essence, when a batch file changes the environment, it stays changed when the batch file terminates. Programs, however, only get a copy of the environment. When they terminate, this environmental copy is erased and any changes are lost. Thus, if the environmental change is only for use inside the compiled batch file, then you won't have a problem. If you want the change to remain after the compiled batch file finishes, however, too bad.

Although compiling a batch file introduces environmental problems, it eliminates another and perhaps more bothersome problem. Because DOS reads and processes batch files one line at a time, batch files run very slowly. When compiled, however, they are converted into programs; and, when DOS runs programs, it loads them entirely into memory. Of course, by loading the entire program into memory, less memory is available for loading memory resident software. However, loading the entire program into memory means that your compiled batch files will run very quickly.

In addition to speed, a compiler offers the additional advantage that any available enhancements are built into the resulting program. As a result, you can distribute the program without worrying about other users needing copies of the utilities referenced in the batch file.

Bat2Exec

Name:	Bat2Exec
Version:	1.3
Price:	Free
Category:	Copyrighted
Summary:	Converts batch files into .COM programs that run much faster but doesn't add any new features to batch files.
Author:	Doug Boling
Availability:	All *PC Magazine* files are available from their area on CompuServe. See any issue of *PC Magazine* for details.

PC Magazine introduced their Bat2Exec batch file compiler in the August 1990 issue (Volume 9, Number 14) in the Utilities column. Bat2Exec is strictly a batch file compiler—it will compile existing DOS batch files—but it adds no new features to the language. Thus, you get additional speed and security without the overhead of learning new commands and working with a new environment. You can completely write and debug your batch files using DOS and then compile them when finished.

Compiling a batch file

To compile a batch file, you enter

```
BAT2EXEC file
```

at the DOS prompt. You must include the .BAT extension even though Bat2Exec only compiles .BAT files.

Once you have compiled a batch file, the resulting .COM file generally operates just like the original batch file, only much faster. The increase in speed is due to the differences in the way DOS handles .COM programs and batch files. As mentioned before, when running a program, DOS loads the entire program into memory and generally doesn't need to access the disk again to execute the program. When running a batch file, however, DOS reads the batch file from the disk one line at a time, thus reading the disk many times for a large batch file. Because the disk is generally the slowest component in a system, DOS is slowed down a great deal.

You shouldn't compile any program that loads a memory-resident program. When a batch file loads a memory resident program, the program doesn't take up any more room than it would if it were loaded from the command line. When a program loads a memory-resident program, DOS can't reclaim the memory used by the original program (the compiled batch file), resulting in the memory-resident program taking up much more room. In addition, the AUTOEXEC.BAT file should never be compiled, as DOS will only run it as a batch file. Finally, pressing Ctrl-Break while running a batch file causes a DOS "Terminate batch job (Y/N)" message, while pressing Ctrl-Break during a compiled program run simply terminates the program.

Problems

Earlier versions of Bat2Exec, including the one printed in *PC Magazine*, required an End-Of-File [EOF] marker on the last line of the batch file. This is a holdover from CP/M, a pre-PC operating system. CP/M required an EOF because it only stored the number of clusters in the file and didn't know where in the last cluster the file ended. Thus, the EOF marker told it where the file ended. DOS stores the actual length of the file, so an EOF marker would be redundant. Because most programs don't require an EOF marker and ignore one if it's present, most editors don't add one to the end of a file. If your editor doesn't, add a blank line to the bottom of the batch file and enter Alt−26 (you must use the numbers on the keypad) on that line. This should enter a right-pointing arrow—the EOF marker. The latest version available for downloading from CompuServe corrects this problem.

While the latest version corrects the problem with End-Of-File markers, it introduced a larger problem. When this version compiles a batch file with a line like FOR %%J IN (*.DOC) DO ECHO %%J, the file doesn't work properly. Sometimes the command echoes correctly, and other times it only echoes a few characters—which may not even be characters that the batch file should be echoing.

When Bat2Exec successfully compiles a batch file, it creates a .COM program performing the same task. You will want to keep the batch file in case you ever need to modify it. Because DOS executes .COM programs over batch files, you can store both in the same directory and DOS will also run the compiled program.

Because Bat2Exec doesn't add any new features to DOS, the best candidates for compiling are those batch files taking a long time to run. Bat2Exec compiled batch files don't respond properly to the ERRORLEVEL if it's set prior to running the compiled program because DOS resets the ERRORLEVEL for each program it runs. Bat2Exec also resets the ERRORLEVEL to 0 when it exits or calls an external batch file. If your batch files use the CLS command to clear the screen, you will have to rework them before compiling because Bat2Exec ignores the CLS command. You can clear the screen by using a series of 24 ECHO Space Alt−255 commands in place of the CLS command. The Alt−255 looks like a space on the screen, but DOS treats it differently and the compiled batch file ends up echoing 24 blank lines.

These problems are significant but not fatal, merely forcing you to scan your batch files to ensure suitability for Bat2Exec. After compiling your batch file, you should test it extensively to make sure it still works properly. These errors suggest that possibly other bugs lurk out there, as yet undiscovered.

Conclusion

Batch files compiled with Bat2Exec run much faster and are immune from modification by others without access to the source code in the .BAT file. Because Bat2Exec adds no new features to batch file, it's best used only for those batch files taking a long time to run or needing protection from modification by others.

The diskette includes a copy of FANCYECH.COM. It is FANCYECH.BAT compiled by Bat2Exec. Batch files that put a lot of information on the screen are excellent candidates for compiling with Bat2Exec.

Batcom

Name:	Batcom
Version:	2.45
Price:	$59.95 (including shipping and handling)
Category:	Commercial
Summary:	A batch file compiler.
Author:	Wenham Software Company
	5 Burley Street
	Wenham, Massachusetts 01984
	(508) 774-7036
Availability:	Order Batcom directly from Wenham Software.

If you're running your batch files through DOS, you're probably using a number of batch file enhancement programs. With Batcom's range and diversity, you probably can discard almost all of those utilities.

Operation

Batcom works with two types of files: standard batch files and Batcom enhanced files. A standard batch file has a .BAT extension and runs under DOS as well as Batcom. A Batcom file has a .BC extension and only runs after being compiled with Batcom.

For the most part, you will want to create custom Batcom files that take advantage of all the enhancements Batcom offers.

When you simply want to compile an existing file, Batcom lets you work with it without having to modify the source code as Builder and Son of a Batch do. This nicely allows you to run your batch file under DOS until you have it debugged and then compile it with Batcom without worrying about any errors or differences introduced by translating it to an intermediate file.

Of course, when you want to use any of the many Batcom enhancements, you can no longer debug your batch files first using DOS. You must go through the edit-compile-run debugging cycle.

Table 8-11 summarizes the many keywords Batcom adds to the language. Table 8-12 shows SHOW-BC.BS, a Batcom file utilizing many of the Batcom keywords. The enclosed diskette contains a copy of SHOW-BC.EXE.

Problems

While compiling a batch file, Batcom will display the lines on the screen and try to find errors; however, its error spotting ability is very poor. Most syntax problems with Batcom keywords are simply passed off as a program to run.

Table 8-11 A summary of Batcom keywords.

OPTION	FUNCTION
ABS	Returns the absolute value of a variable.
ADD	Adds two variables together.
ANSI	Causes the compiler to compile the batch file using ANSI.SYS support. This requires the user to have ANSI.SYS loaded and is generally not a good idea.
BEEP	Sounds the speaker.
BIOS	Causes the compiler to compile the batch file using BIOS screen drivers, the default mode.
BOX	Draws a box on the screen using single lines.
BREAK	Turns Batcom support for Ctrl-Break on and off.
CLEAR_BOX	Erases a section of the screen.
CLEARBUF	Clears keystrokes from the keyboard buffer.
COPYD	Copies a file onto an existing file but only if the file being erased is older than the one replacing it.
DAY_OF_MONTH	Returns the day of the month.
DAY_OF_WEEK	Returns the day of the week.
DIV	Divides one variable into another.
DO_IF	Marks the top of a block of commands to be executed if the statement is true.
DO_WHILE	Marks the top of a block of statements to continue performing as long as a statement remains true.
DOUBLE_BOX	Draws a box on the screen using double lines.
ECHONOLF	ECHO command that does not issue a line feed.
ELSE	Used in the middle of a DO_IF statement to mark the statements to execute if the statement is false.
EMMFREE	Returns the amount of LIM memory.
EMMSTATUS	Returns the status of LIM memory.
END_IF	Marks the end of a DO_IF block.
END_WHILE	Marks the bottom of a DO_WHILE block.
ERROR_LEVEL	Converts ERRORLEVEL to a Batcom variable.
EXIT	Causes the program to immediately terminate.
FILEDATE	Indicates which of two files has the earlier date.
FILESIZE	Returns the size of a file of total for a group of files.
FILETIME	Indicates which of two files has the earlier time.
FIND_STRING	Locates one string inside another string.
FORMFEED	Sends a formfeed to the printer.
FREEDISK	Returns the amount of free disk space.
FREEMEM	Returns the amount of free memory.
GET_VIDEO_MODE	Returns the video mode.
GETDIR	Returns the current subdirectory.
GETDRIVE	Returns the current drive.
GETKEY	Waits for the user to press a keystroke and returns that code as an ERRORLEVEL.
GOSUB	Passes control to a subroutine.
GOSUB_PARAMETER	An optional parameter that is passed to a subroutine.

Table 8-11 Continued.

OPTION	FUNCTION
HOUR_HOUR	Returns the hour.
KEYBUF	Places keystrokes in the keyboard buffer.
KEYPRESSED	A logical test to see if a keystroke is in the keyboard buffer.
LABEL	Marks a label the same as a colon in a batch file. You can also use the colon.
LOCATE	Positions the cursor on the screen.
LOWER	Converts a string to all lowercase.
LTRIM	Removes the leading spaces from a string.
MINUTE_MINUTE	Returns the minute.
MOD	Returns the modulus (integer remainder) two variables.
MONTH_MONTH	Returns the month.
MUL	Multiplies one variable times another.
PARSE	Strips a string down into individual words.
PAUSENOLF	PAUSE command that does not issue a line feed.
READ	Reads a line of text from the user and places it in a variable.
READ_FILE	Reads text from a file and places it in user defined variables.
READ_SCREEN	Reads text from the screen and places it into a variable.
RETURN	Exits a subroutine and resumes the calling program.
RTRIM	Removes the trailing spaces from a string.
SECONDS_SECONDS	Returns the seconds.
SET_BACKBROUND_COLOR	Controls the background color.
SET_COLOR	Controls the foreground color.
SET_VIDEO_MODE	Changes the video mode.
SPACES	Sets a Batcom variable equal to a given number of spaces. This function does not work properly. Rather than just spaces, it leaves the leading and trailing quotes in the variable.
STRING_LENGTH	Returns the length of a string.
SUB	Subtracts one variable from another.
SUBSTRING	Extracts any portion of a variable and stores it in another variable.
UPPER	Converts a string to all uppercase.
WAIT	Pauses the batch file for a specific amount of time.
WAITKEY	Pauses the batch file for a specific amount of time but aborts the timing and continues if the user presses a key.
YEAR_YEAR	Return the year.

Table 8-12 SHOW-BC.BAT illustrates many of Batcom's enhancements.

Batch File Line	Explanation
@ECHO OFF	Turns command-echoing off.
REM NAME: SHOW-BC.BC REM PURPOSE: Illustrate Batcom REM VERSION: 1.00 REM DATE: April 5, 1991	Documentation remarks.
CLS	Clears the screen.
ECHO Let's Do Some Math (Ugh!) ECHO We Need Some Numbers First	Tells the user what will happen.

Batch File Line	Explanation
LET %!A = 20 LET %!B = 25 LET %!C = -5 LET %!D = 102	Assigns values to four Batcom variables.
ECHO A = %!A ECHO B = %!B ECHO C = %!C ECHO D = %!D	Displays those values for the users.
LET %!Z = %!A	Transfers the value of A to an unused variable.
ADD %!Z %!B	Adds the values of Z and B and stores the answer in Z. Because the math functions can not store the answer in a separate variable, you must use a temporary variable (Z) or you lose the original value.
ECHO A + B = %!Z	Tells the user the answer.
LET %!Z = %!B ADD %!Z %!C ECHO B + C = %!Z	Performs another addition.
LET %!Z = %!C SUB %!Z %!D ECHO C - D = %!Z	Performs a subtraction.
LET %!Z = %!D DIV %!Z %!A ECHONOLF D / A = %!Z ECHO (Notice The Integer Math)	Performs division. Note the ECHONOLF. That is the same as ECHO except it does not move the cursor to the next line. As a result, the next ECHO is printed on the same line.
LET %!Z = %!C MUL %!Z %!B ECHO B * C = %!Z	Performs multiplication.
LET %!Z = %!C ABS %!Z ECHO Absolute Value of C is %!Z	Computes an absolute value.
ECHO ECHO ECHO ECHO Now, Let's Do A Screen ECHO Press Any Key To Start	Displays some blank lines and a message. In Batcom, an ECHO command by itself displays a blank line, unlike DOS.
PAUSE > NUL	Pauses the batch file.
CLS	Clears the screen.
BOX 4 4 10 64	Draws a box on the screen beginning at row-4 and column-4 and continuing to row-10 and column-64.
LOCATE 7 30	Positions the cursor.
ECHONOLF This Is A Simple Box	Displays text.
DOUBLE_BOX 1 66 23 80 LOCATE 10 68 ECHONOLF Another Box	Draws another box, this time with double lines and writes more text inside it.
BOX 15 4 23 40 LOCATE 18 15 ECHONOLF Yet Another Box LOCATE 20 7 ECHONOLF I'll Let You Look A Few Seconds	Draws a third box and write text inside it.

Table 8-12 Continued.

Batch File Line	Explanation
WAITKEY 10	Waits for ten seconds.
BEEP	Beeps the speaker.
CLEAR_BOX 2 67 22 79 CLEAR_BOX 5 5 9 63 CLEAR_BOX 16 5 22 39	Clears the inside of the boxes.
LOCATE 18 15 ECHONOLF Notice That I LOCATE 20 7 ECHONOLF Erased The Contents Of The Boxes	Writes text inside one of the boxes.
WAITKEY 10	Waits ten seconds.
CLS	Clears the screen.
ECHO Now I Will Count For You! ECHO Press Any Key To Begin	Tells the user what will happen next.
PAUSE > NUL	Pauses the batch file.
CLS	Clears the screen.
LET %!A = 1	Defines a variable.
DO_WHILE NOT %!A = 20	Defines the top of a loop. Continues with this loop until A equals 20.
ECHONOLF %!A	Displays the variable.
ECHONOLF	Display a space by echoing ALT-255. Batcom had trouble with spaces, see text for details.
ADD %!A 1	Increases A by one.
END_WHILE	Marks the end of the loop.
ECHO ECHO	Displays two blank lines.

DO_WHILE NOT %!A = 0
    ECHONOLF %!A
    ECHONOLF
    SUB %!A 1
END_WHILE
ECHO
ECHO
	Uses an identical loop to count down from 20.

ECHO Neat -- Don't You Think! ECHO Next Let's Look At Some Of ECHO The Information Batcom Can ECHO Figure Out ECHO ECHO ECHO Press Any Key To Begin	Tells the user what is happening.
PAUSE > NUL	Pauses the batch file.
CLS	Clears the screen.
ECHO --------- DATES ----------	
GOSUB MONTH	Runs a subroutine called MONTH. Subroutines are user code that performs a task. They are used when the same task needs to be performed several times. You write the code once and call it as needed. Here, they are used simply for illustration.

Batch File Line	Explanation
GOSUB DAY GOSUB DATE GOSUB YEAR ECHO -----------TIME----------- GOSUB HOUR GOSUB MINUTE GOSUB SECOND ECHO Press Any Key To Continue	Runs several more subroutines.
PAUSE > NUL	Pauses the batch file.
CLS	Clears the screen.
ECHO --------- SYSTEM --------- GOSUB VIDEO GOSUB DIRECTORY GOSUB SPACE GOSUB MEMORY GOSUB FILES	Runs more subroutines
EXIT	The EXIT command causes the program to immediately terminate. If followed by a number 0-255, it sets ERRORLEVEL to that value. All subroutines must be below the EXIT command.
:DAY DAY_OF_WEEK IF ERRLEVEL = 0 ECHO It Is Sunday IF ERRLEVEL = 1 ECHO It Is Monday IF ERRLEVEL = 2 ECHO It Is Tuesday IF ERRLEVEL = 3 ECHO It Is Wednesday IF ERRLEVEL = 4 ECHO It Is Thursday IF ERRLEVEL = 5 ECHO It Is Friday IF ERRLEVEL = 6 ECHO It Is Saturday ECHO RETURN	Finds the day of the week using the Batcom DAY_OF_WEEK function. Notice the ERRLEVEL function. This is the same as IF ERRORLEVEL except it only test for equality unlike the DOS greater-than-or-equal test.
:DATE DAY_OF_MONTH ERROR_LEVEL %!A ECHO The Date is %!A ECHO RETURN	Finds the day of the month using the Batcom DAY_OF_MONTH function. Notice the ERROR_LEVEL function. This function transfers the ERRORLEVEL to a Batcom function without a lot of testing.
:YEAR YEAR_YEAR ERROR_LEVEL %!A ECHO The Year Is %!A ECHO RETURN	Finds the year using the Batcom YEAR_YEAR function. The manual claims to return the year as an ERRORLEVEL. However, DOS limits the ERRORLEVEL to 0-255. Batcom handles the year properly internally but actual sets ERRORLEVEL to 199 for 1991, 200 for 2000, 201 for 2001, and so on.
:MONTH MONTH_MONTH IF ERRLEVEL 1 ECHO It Is January IF ERRLEVEL 2 ECHO It Is February IF ERRLEVEL 3 ECHO It Is March IF ERRLEVEL 4 ECHO It Is April IF ERRLEVEL 5 ECHO It Is May IF ERRLEVEL 6 ECHO It Is June IF ERRLEVEL 7 ECHO It Is July IF ERRLEVEL 8 ECHO It Is August IF ERRLEVEL 9 ECHO It Is September IF ERRLEVEL 10 ECHO It Is October	Finds the day of the month using the Batcom MONTH_MONTH function.

Table 8-12   Continued.

Batch File Line	Explanation

```IF ERRLEVEL 11 ECHO It Is November```
```IF ERRLEVEL 12 ECHO It Is December```
```ECHO```
```RETURN```	

```:FILES```	Label marking the top of a subroutine to get file information. Note that subroutines do not have to be written in the same order they are used.
```LET %!F = SHOW-BC.EXE```	Stores a filename to a Batcom variable.
```FILESIZE %!F```	Uses a Batcom function to find the size of the file stored in %!F, replacing the value of %!F in the process.
```ECHO SHOW-BC.EXE Is %!F-Bytes```	Tells the user the results.
```ECHO```	Displays a blank line.
```RETURN```	A RETURN is always the last line of every subroutine.

```:SPACE```
```LET %!F = C:```
```FREEDISK %!F```
```ECHO C-Drive Has %!F-Bytes Free```
```ECHO```
```RETURN```
	Finds the free space on the C drive using the Batcom FREEDISK function.

```:MEMORY```
```FREEMEM %!F```
```ECHO You Have %!F-Bytes Of```
```   Free Memory```
```ECHO Remember, This Program```
```   Uses RAM```
```ECHO```
```RETURN```
	Finds the amount of free memory using the Batcom FREEMEM function.

```:DIRECTORY```
```GETDIR %!F```
```ECHO Current Directory Is %!F```
```ECHO```
```RETURN```
	Finds the current subdirectory using the Batcom GETDIR function.

```:VIDEO```
```GET_VIDEO_MODE %!F```
```ECHO Current Video Mode Is %!F```
```ECHO```
```RETURN```
	Finds the video mode using the Batcom GET_VIDEO_MODE function.

```:HOUR```
```HOUR_HOUR```
```ERROR_LEVEL %!A```
```ECHO The Hour Is %!A```
```ECHO```
```RETURN```
	Find the hour using the Batcom HOUR_HOUR function.

```:MINUTE```
```MINUTE_MINUTE```
```ERROR_LEVEL %!A```
```ECHO The Minute Is %!A```
```ECHO```
```RETURN```
	Find the minute using the Batcom MINUTE_MINUTE function.

Batch File Line	Explanation

`:SECOND`
`SECONDS_SECONDS`
`ERROR_LEVEL %!A`
`ECHO The Second Is %!A`
`ECHO`
`RETURN`
	Find the second using the Batcom SECOND_SECOND function.

While writing one program, I started a loop with the command DO__WHILE__NOT rather than DO__WHILE NOT and Batcom missed it entirely. It assumed DO__WHILE __NOT was a DOS program and simply passed the command to DOS, which then gave me a "Bad command or filename" error message.

Batcom must walk a fine line between assuming something is an error and assuming it's a DOS program. After all, if I had a batch file to run a program called DOT__WHIL .EXE, I wouldn't want it to generate an error message when it reached that line because that would be a valid program. As is, Batcom seems to err too much on the side of assuming every invalid keyword is a DOS command or program.

Batcom has a great deal of difficulty generating spaces. I first tried to generate a space using the command

    LET %!A = " "

That didn't work as I had planned because it included the quotes in the variable. Next, I tried

    LET %!A = 1
    SPACES %!A

The manual claims this converts A into a string variable padded with as many spaces as its prior numeric variable. It does that but also adds a quote mark to the left and right of the variable. Next I tried echoing the space I needed using the DOS commands

    SET SPACE =
    ECHO %SPACE%

with a space after the equal sign. Batcom ignored the space after the equal sign and assigned SPACE as empty. I finally gave up and used Alt−255 whenever I needed a space.

Conclusion

Except for the problem with the spaces, Batcom is a very nice compiler. It offers less enhancements than Builder but creates much smaller and tighter code.

Builder

Name: Builder
Version: 1.5

Price:	$149.95
Category:	Commercial
Summary:	A batch file compiler.
Author:	Hyperkinetix, Incorporated
	666 Baker Street
	Suite 405
	Costa Mesa, California 92626
	(714) 668-9234
Availability:	Order Builder directly from the vendor.[1]

Like Batcom, Builder offers enough enhancements that you will rarely need any other batch utility.

Operation

Builder has two modes of operation: interactive and batch. In the interactive mode, Builder combines the compiler with a simple editor. If you load an existing batch file, Builder does a good job of converting it into a Builder file with necessary changes made automatically. Some of those changes include the following:

- Commands to run a program have a RUN command inserted in front of them: thus, WORDSTAR becomes RUN WORDSTAR. This applies not only to programs but to commands like CD \ and D:5, which are DOS commands but not batch commands.

- A few commands like FOR use a slightly different syntax under Builder than they do under DOS. For example, the command FOR %%J IN (*.*) DO ECHO %%J becomes FOR %%J IN "*.*" DO ECHO %%J under Builder. Builder makes all these conversions automatically.

- The "@" is stripped off the beginning of commands. Under DOS, "@" turns off command echoing for a single line. Because commands don't echo in Builder, it doesn't need this.

- A few label names are converted. For example, Builder objects to "END" as a label name but converts it automatically.

All of these conversions are less of a problem than they first seem. The main reason for using Builder is to take advantage of all the neat enhancements it offers. Because those enhancements have no counterpart under DOS, you can't debug your batch files under DOS.

It would be nice if the editor in Builder would monitor the lines as you type them and flag any errors it finds; however, it doesn't do that. When you finish writing the code, you press F9 to compile it. You can also press Alt−C to bring up the pull-down menu.

---

[1]A crippled version of Builder is included on the disk bound in this book so that you can try it out before purchasing the "real" one. This version of Builder works just like the original except that no help is available, and it also adds a comment in any files it compiles reminding you to purchase the program.

Strangely, while menus compiled under Builder support a mouse, Builder itself doesn't.

If Builder finds errors while trying to compile a program, it opens a smaller window below the main window. In that window, it gives the line number for each line with an error and a brief error message. Often, the error message is simply "syntax error." If too many errors exist to fit on the screen, you can use the menu to switch to that window and scroll around. Once you have corrected all the errors, Builder compiles, links, and writes the disk file automatically when you press F9.

While compiled batch files run faster than do regular batch files, Builder will mainly be used for its many enhancements (see Table 8-13). As you can see, Builder offers a wealth of enhancements that will do almost anything any other program listed in this book can do. Table 8-14 shows a sample Builder program also contained and compiled on the enclosed diskette so you can see Builder perform its tricks.

To compile a batch file in batch mode, you enter

BLD file

on the command line. If the file is a batch file, Builder automatically converts it to a Builder file and then tries to compile it. If it's successful, it creates the program file automatically. If not, it creates a file containing all the error messages, prints a brief error message to the screen, and then exits to DOS.

Table 8-13 A summary of Builder keywords. In addition to these, Builder supports all DOS batch commands and can run any stand-alone program.

New Commands	Function
'	Adds a comment to the batch file, just like REM in DOS.
BEEP	Sounds the bell.
BOX	Draws a box of the screen. You can set colors at the same time.
CALL	Runs a DOS batch file and then returns control to the Builder compiled batch file. This is the default mode of operation. The command exists only to provide compatibility with DOS batch files that use the CALL command to run another batch file and then regain control.
CASE	Allows batch files to be written in case-format. You define a test and then have a series of CASE statements that define one possible outcome. The statements under a CASE statement are executed only when that CASE is true.
CANCELED	A built-in variable that has a value of one if the last keyboard input ended with the user pressing escape.
CLOSE	Closes a file and releases the memory associated with that file.
CLOSEALLFILES	Closes all open files and releases all the memory associated with those files.
CLS	Clears the screen, just like in DOS.

Table 8-13   Continued.

New Commands	Function
CURRENTDRIVE	Places the current drive in a string variable.
DOSERRORLEVEL	Assigns the value of the DOS ERRORLEVEL to a variable for easy storage and easier testing.
DISKFREE	Assigns the amount of free space on a specified drive to a variable.
DISKLABEL	Assigns the volume label to a variable.
DISKREADY	Assigns a value to a variable to indicate if the specified drive is read to use.
DROPDOWN	Creates a drop-down menu for the user to select items from.
ECHO	Works just like the DOS ECHO command. Builder has the more powerful SAY command so the only purpose of the ECHO command is to maximize compatibility with DOS.
ELSE	Defines commands to be performed if a statement is false.
EMSAVIL	Assigns the amount of EMS memory that is available to a variable.
EMSINSTALLED	Assigns a one to a variable if EMS is available, a zero otherwise.
EMSMAJOR	Assigns the major (e.g. 3 or 4) EMS version number to a variable.
EMSMINOR	Assigns the minor EMS version number to a variable.
EMSTOTAL	Assigns the total installed EMS memory amount to a variable.
EMSVERSION	Assigns the complete EMS version number to a variable.
ENVAVAIL	Assigns the amount of free environmental space to a variable.
ENVTOTAL	Assigns the total amount of environmental space to a variable.
EOF	Assigns a zero to a variable if the file being read is not yet to the end of the file.
EXIT	Stops the batch file and returns control to DOS.
FILE	Configures Builder to begin writing to the specified file.
FILESIZE	Assigns the size of a file to a variable.
FOR	Just like DOS, the FOR command loops through a series of items and performs a single action on each item. Like DOS, FOR commands can not be nested.
GETKEY	Gets a single keystroke from the user. It works better than programs like Norton's Ask that place their values in ERRORLEVEL because you can test with an equality test rather than the greater than or equal tests DOS uses with ERRORLEVEL.
GETYN	Gets a single keystroke from the user but only accepts a "y" or "n". Like Norton's Ask program, it sets ERRORLEVEL to 0 for a "n" and 1 for a "y".
GOTO	Jumps to another part of the batch file and resumes processing, just like DOS.
GOTOXY	Locates the cursor at a specific location on the screen.
IF	Determines if a command or series of commands is to be executed based on a logical test, just like DOS.

New Commands	Function
INPUT	Accepts multiple characters from the user and assign them to a variable.
INTEGER	Allocates an integer variable for Builder to use.
LASTKEY	Stores the value from the Getkey command.
LONGINT	Allocates an integer variable for Builder to use. LONGINT integers accept larger numbers than do INTEGER ones.
LIGHTBAR	Chooses an item from a moving lightbar menu.
MAXCOLS	Assigns the current width of the screen to a variable.
MAXROWS	Assigns the current length of the screen to a variable.
MOVE	Copies a file from one location to another (possibly with a new name) and then deletes the original version. This actually copies the file; it does not work like some move commands that simply rewrite the directory information without copying it.
ONPATH	Assigns a value to a variable to let you know if the specified file is somewhere in the path.
OPEN	Opens a file so Builder can work with it.
OSMAJOR	Assigns the major DOS version number to a variable.
OSMINOR	Assigns the minor DOS version number to a variable.
OSVERSION	Assigns the entire DOS version number to a variable.
PARAMCOUNT	A keyword used in an IF-test to represent the number of parameters entered on the command line.
PASSWORD	Accepts input from the user and compares it to a password you enter on the command line. If the two are the same, it sets ERRORLEVEL to 0; otherwise it sets ERRORLEVEL to 1.
PAUSE	Like DOS, it causes the batch file to wait until a key is pressed. However, there is no "Strike a key to continue" message.
POPUP	A general menu creation tool.
READLINE	Gets a single line of text from a file and assigns it to a variable.
REBOOT	Performs a warm reboot. This is very useful if you have a batch file modify a CONFIG.SYS or AUTOEXEC.BAT file.
REM	Flags a line as a comment that is ignored by Builder. Builder also uses the apostrophe to mark comments.
RENSUB	Renames a DOS subdirectory.
REPEAT	Repeats a command the indicated number of times.
REWIND	Returns to the top of a file.
ROWCOL	Moves the cursor to a specific location.
RUN	Passes a command out of the compiled batch file to DOS.
SAVEFILE	Saves an open file without closing it.
SAY	Similar to ECHO, except you can control the text location and color.
SET	Creates or changes environmental variables.
SHIFT	Just like the DOS SHIFT commands, it moves the contents of %2 into %1, %3 into %2 and so on.
STRING	Allocates space for string variables.

Table 8-13 Continued.

New Commands	Function
SUB	Marks a section of batch file cost as a subroutine.
SYSTEM	Passes the contents of a string variable to DOS as a command.
UNSHIFT	The opposite of a DOS SHIFT command. %0 becomes %1, %1 becomes %2, and so on.
USE BIOS/DOS	Selects how the compiled batch file handles text.
WHEREX	Returns the column containing the cursor.
WHEREY	Returns the row containing the cursor.
WHILE	Repeats a command or series of commands until a specific condition takes place.
WRITELINE	Writes a string to a file.

Table 8-14   ZBUILD.BAT is a sample Builder file compiled and included on the disk bound in this book.

Batch File Line	Explanation

`' REM Builder Example`
`' This Batch File Must Be Compiled To Run`
`' Set Up Variables`
	Documentation remarks. Builder can use either a REM or an apostrophe to indicate a remark.

`STRING   Drive`
`LONGINT  FreeSpace`
`INTEGER  IsThereEMS`
`LONGINT  EMSFree`
`LONGINT  EMSThere`
`INTEGER  Major`
`INTEGER  Minor`
`STRING   All`
`INTEGER  E_Available`
`INTEGER  E_Total`
`INTEGER  F_Size`
`STRING   First`
`STRING   Last`
`STRING   Title`
`INTEGER  Rows`
`INTEGER  Columns`
`INTEGER  Lotus123`
`INTEGER  Parameters`
	These statements "declare" variable names and types. Builder requires you to do this prior to using the variables.

`CLS`	Clears the screen.
`' Draw Some Boxes`	Documentation remark.

`DOUBLE BOX   1, 1,80,24 BRIGHT WHITE    ON RED`
`SINGLE BOX   5, 5,20,10 BRIGHT RED      ON BLACK`
`SINGLE BOX  10,10,20,10 BRIGHT RED      ON BLACK`
`SINGLE BOX  10,20,20,10 BRIGHT MAGENTA ON WHITE`
`SINGLE BOX   1,35,15,20 BRIGHT CYAN     ON RED`
	Draws five boxes on the screen.

`SAY @ 10,34 "<BRIGHT WHITE>Press Any Key` `       To Continue"`	Tells the user the batch file has paused until a key is pressed.
`PAUSE`	Pauses the batch file. Unlike DOS, this command by itself does not display any message.
`CLS`	Clears the screen.

`DROPDOWN "Select Your Title"`
`     ITEM "        MS          "`
`          Title:="MS. "`
	Puts a drop-down menu on the screen for the user to select a title

Batch File Line	Explanation

``
    ITEM "   MR   "
        Title:="MR. "
    ITEM "   MRS   "
        Title:="MRS. "
    ITEM "   DR   "
        Title:="Doctor "
END
``
	from. Once the user selects a title, set a variable to the appropriate title.

`CLS`	Clears the screen.
`SAY "Please Enter Your First Name: ";` `INPUT First`	Requests the user's first name and places the response into a variable called FIRST.
`SAY`	Skips a line. Unlike the DOS ECHO command, SAY alone prints a blank line.
`SAY "Please Enter Your Last  Name: ";` `INPUT Last`	Obtains the user's last name and stores it in a variable.
`CLS`	Clears the screen.
`SAY "<BRIGHT WHITE>Hello "; Title; First;` `    " "; Last`	Tells the user hello. Notice the use of user-inputted variables and the TITLE variable set using the menu.
`SAY "<BRIGHT WHITE>Sounding Speaker"`	Tells the user what will happen next.
`BEEP`	Sounds the speaker.
`Drive:=CURRENTDRIVE`	Stores the drive letter to a variable.
`SAY "<BRIGHT RED>The Current Drive Is "; Drive`	Tells the user which drive is the current drive.
`FreeSpace:=DISKFREE Drive`	Stores the amount of free space to a variable.
`SAY "<BRIGHT GREEN>The "; Drive; "-Drive Has` `    "; FreeSpace; "-Bytes of Free Space"`	Tells the user how much space is available.
`IsThereEMS:=EMSINSTALLED`	Performs a logical test to see if EMS-memory is installed and stores the results in a variable.
`IF NOT IsThereEMS SAY "<BRIGHT MAGENTA>EMS` `    Not Installed"`	If no EMS-memory is installed, tells the user.
`IF NOT IsThereEMS GOTO NOEMS`	If no EMS-memory is installed, skips the remaining tests.
`EMSFree:=EMSAVAIL`	Stores the amount of available EMS-memory to a variable.
`SAY "<BRIGHT MAGENTA>There is "; EMSFree;` `    "-Bytes of EMS Available"`	Tells the user how much EMS-memory is available.
`EMSThere:=EMSTOTAL`	Stores the total amount of EMS-memory to a variable.
`SAY "<BRIGHT MAGENTA>There is "; EMSThere;` `    "-Bytes of EMS Installed"`	Tells the user.
`Major:=EMSMAJOR`	Stores the major EMS version to

Table 8-14   Continued.

Batch File Line	Explanation
	a variable. If you were running version 4.0, this would store the "4" to the variable. Both this and MINOR are numeric variables, while ALL is a string variable.
`Minor:=EMSMINOR`	Stores the minor EMS version to a variable. In the above example, this would be a "0".
`All:=EMSVERSION`	Stores the EMS version number to a string variable. In the above example, this would be a "4.0".

`SAY "<BRIGHT MAGENTA>The EMS Major Number`
`   is "; Major`
`SAY "<BRIGHT MAGENTA>The EMS Minor Number`
`   is "; Minor`
`SAY "<BRIGHT MAGENTA>The EMS        Number`
`   is "; All`
	Gives the EMS information to the user.

`:NOEMS`	Label marking the end of the EMS testing section.
`E_Available:=ENVAVAIL`	Stores the amount of free environmental space to a variable.
`E_Total:=ENVTOTAL`	Stores the amount of total environmental space to a variable.

`SAY "<BRIGHT GREEN>You Have "; E_Total;`
`   "-Bytes of Environmental Space ";`
`SAY "<BRIGHT GREEN>of That, ";E_Available;`
`   "-Bytes is Free"`
	Gives the environmental information to the user.

`F_Size:=FILESIZE "ZBUILD.COM"`	Stores the size of ZBUILD.COM in a variable.
`SAY "<BRIGHT BLUE>The Size of ZBUILD.COM is` `   "; F_Size; "-Bytes"`	Tells the user.
`SAY "Only A Y or N Key Will Be Accepted"` `SAY "But Try Other Keys First"`	Tells the user what will happen next.
`GETYN`	Gets a "Y" or "N" keystroke from the user.
`SAY "-Pressed"`	Tells the user what key was pressed. GETYN displays the keystroke itself so this simply completes the message.
`SAY "Next, Only A Q Will Be Accepted"` `SAY "Note that A Lowercase q Will NOT Work"`	Tells user what will happen next.
`:TOPKEY`	Label marking the top of a loop where the only character that will be accepted is a "Q".
`GETKEY`	Gets any keystroke from the user.
`IF LASTKEY IS {Q} GOTO DONEKEY`	If that keystroke was a "Q", exits the loop.
`BEEP`	The batch file reaches this line only if the user presses an invalid key so the batch file beeps.

Batch File Line	Explanation
`GOTO TOPKEY`	Loops back to the top of the loop.
`:DONEKEY`	Label marking the loop exit point.
`Columns:=MAXCOLS`	Stores the maximum number of columns in a variable.
`Rows:=MAXROWS`	Stores the maximum number of rows in a variable.
`SAY "You Display Can Show "; Columns;` `SAY " Columns and "; Rows; " Rows"`	Tells the user.
`Lotus123:=ONPATH "LOTUS.EXE"`	Performs a logical test to see if LOTUS.EXE is in the path.
`IF Lotus123 IS 1 SAY "LOTUS.EXE In Path"` `IF Lotus123 IS 0 SAY "LOTUS.EXE Not In Path"`	Tells the user.

`Major:=OSMAJOR`
`Minor:=OSMINOR`
`All:=OSVERSION`
	Stores the major, minor, and entire DOS version in variables.

`SAY "Your Major DOS Version Is "; Major;`
`SAY " Your Minor DOS Version Is "; Minor`
`SAY "Your DOS Version Is "; All`
	Tells the user.

`Parameters:=PARAMCOUNT`	Stores the number of parameters entered on the command line in a variable.

`SAY "Including The ZBUILD Command, ";`
`SAY "You Entered "; Parameters`
`SAY "Parameters When You Started This Program"`
	Tells the user.

`SAY "<BRIGHT CYAN>Press Any Key To` `     Continue Demonstration"`	Tells the user to press any key to continue the batch file.
`PAUSE`	Pauses the batch file until a key is pressed.
`:MENUTOP`	Label marking the top of a menu loop. The loop is required so the user will return to the menu after running a non-exit option.
`CLS`	Clears the screen.
`DROPDOWN "Sample Menu"`	Command that displays the menu. Each line below this until the END-line that starts with an ITEM keyword will become a menu option.
`    ITEM "          Run Lotus          "`	This line marks the first item in the menu. Notice the spaces around the text, this makes the menu wider.

`        CLS`
`        SAY "I Would Run Lotus Here"`
`        SAY "Then I Would Reload Menu"`
`        SAY "Notice The Mouse Support"`
`        SAY "Press Any Key To Continue"`
`        PAUSE`
`        GOTO MENUTOP`
	All of the command between the above ITEM-line and the next ITEM-line are executed when this item is selected. Notice the last line goes to the top of the loop to redisplay the menu.

`    ITEM "          Run dBASE          "`
`        CLS`
`        Say "I Would Run dBASE Here"`
`        SAY "Then I Would Reload Menu"`
`        SAY "Notice The Mouse Support"`
`        SAY "Press Any Key To Continue"`
	Next menu option.

Table 8-14   Continued.

Batch File Line	Explanation
PAUSE GOTO MENUTOP	
ITEM " QUIT Menu " SAY "Exiting Menu"	Last menu item. Because this is the option to exit the menu, it does not redisplay the menu.
END	Keyword marking the end of the menu.
:MENUTOP2	Label marking the top of a second menu. A LIGHTBAR menu works just like a DROPDOWN menu, only the display mode is different.

CLS
LIGHTBAR
   ITEM "Run Lotus "
     CLS
     SAY "I Would Run Lotus Here"
     SAY "Then I Would Reload Menu"
     SAY "Press Any Key To Continue"
     PAUSE
     GOTO MENUTOP2
   ITEM "Run dBASE "
     CLS
     Say "I Would Run dBASE Here"
     SAY "Then I Would Reload Menu"
     SAY "Press Any Key To Continue"
     PAUSE
     GOTO MENUTOP2
   ITEM "QUIT Menu"
     SAY "Exiting Menu"
END
	A moving lightbar menu.

CLS	Clears the screen.
SAY "Next,I'm Going To Ask You For A Password" SAY "Remember, The Password Is:" SAY SAY "<BLINK><BRIGHT WHITE>Tab Books" SAY SAY "Capitalization Is Not Critical" SAY SAY "Press Any Key When You Are Ready" PAUSE CLS	Tells the user what will happen next.
:NOPASS	Label marking the top of the section requiring a password.
SAY @ 12,30 "<BRIGHT WHITE>Enter Your Password: ";	Tells the user to enter a password.
PASSWORD "Tab Books"	Command that accepts the password and tell Builder the password so it can set the ERRORLEVEL accordingly.
IF ERRORLEVEL 0 IF NOT ERRORLEVEL 1 GOTO YESPASS	If ERRORLEVEL is zero, the user entered the proper password, so it exits the loop.
SAY @ 20,01 "<BLINK><BRIGHT RED>Wrong Password! Try Again"	If the batch file reaches this line, an invalid password was entered, so it tells the user.

Batch File Line	Explanation
`GOTO NOPASS`	Goes to the top of the loop.
`:YESPASS`	Label marking the exit point of the password loop.

`CLS`
`SAY "This Concludes The Demonstration"`
`SAY "Thank You For Taking The Time To View It"`
`SAY`
`SAY "Ronny Richardson"`
`SAY "Copyright 1991"`
	Exits the batch file.

Problems

Builder displays less-than-clear error messages when it finds an error: all you get is a line number and the message. The error messages are made even more cryptic because they aren't listed or explained in the manual. Also, while compiled Builder menus support a mouse, Builder itself doesn't.

The manual for Builder isn't that good. It starts off with an introduction to compilers, presents a reference section on all of the Builder commands, and then quits. No tutorial on using the Builder-specific commands is included, nor is a list of error-message explanations. I have heard that later editions of the manual will have a tutorial, but I haven't yet seen it.

Conclusion

Builder is a fantastic product. It is powerful enough to replace all your batch file utilities; and because the resulting files are compiled, you can distribute them without paying royalties or worrying about other users needing copies of utilities. In fact, the SetError and SkipLine included on the disk were written with Builder.

PowerBatch

Name: PowerBatch
Version: 1.4
Price: $30
Category: Shareware
Summary: A batch file compiler.
Author: Computing Systems Design, Incorporated
6712 East 102nd Street
Tulsa, Oklahoma 74133
(913) 299-8202
Availability: Available on many bulletin board systems.

Unlike the other compilers in this chapter, PowerBatch isn't able to compile most DOS batch files without modification. PowerBatch can't even compile simple, common batch lines like ECHO Hello without user modifications! While the major reason for using a batch compiler is to expand the power of your batch files, you shouldn't have to go back and make extensive modifications to existing, debugged batch files in order to compile them.

Because of PowerBatch's inability to handle even the simplest batch file, it's best to think of PowerBatch as a programming language like Pascal or C that happens to create batch-like programs.

Operation

If you want to use PowerBatch to compile existing batch files, you first need to make extensive modifications to them. Those modifications include the following:

- ECHO. You must enclose the text after an ECHO command in quotes so that ECHO Hello becomes ECHO "Hello". When this won't work, you should avoid this conversion and instead use a PowerBatch command like WRITELINE Hello. PowerBatch compiles the program in such a way that it accesses the disk drive and loads COMMAND.COM every time it executes an ECHO command. I compiled a two-line batch file that had two ECHO statements. When I ran it, extensive disk activity took place and the compiled batch file took several seconds to run.

- REM. PowerBatch doesn't recognize the REM command as a valid batch command, and it generates an error message for every word following the REM command. You must change all REMs to semicolons.

- DOS. Simple DOS commands like COPY A:*.* B: don't work. These commands must be changed to COPY "A:*.* B:" with quote marks surrounding everything after the DOS command.

Much of PowerBatch's problems in handling standard batch files result from it wanting to treat each line as a command followed by a variable. On the COPY A:*.* B: line, it recognizes COPY as a DOS command but thinks A:*.* and B: are variables. Similarly, PowerBatch accepts the CD \ command as valid and compiles it properly because there is nothing after the command.

If you think of PowerBatch as a program language with many of the features of a batch file, this begins to make more sense. Like many programming languages (but no other batch compiler), PowerBatch requires you to define variables before you use them. Its syntax also more closely matches that of other languages than do the other batch compilers.

PowerBatch adds a number of new commands to the batch language (see Table 8-15). Table 8-16 shows SHOW-PB.PWR, a batch file using many of the PowerBatch commands. The enclosed disk contains a copy of the resulting program file.

Table 8-15   A summary of new batch commands added by PowerBatch.

New Commands	Function
?COLOR	Retrieves the current color setting from the system.
?CURRDIR	Retrieves the current drive and subdirectory from the system.
?DATE	Retrieves the current date from the system.
?DIREXIST	Checks the system to see if a directory exists.
?DISKSPACE	Retrieves the current disk size and free space from the system.

New Commands	Function
?DRIVEEXIST	Checks to see if a given letter is a valid drive.
?ENVSTR	Retrieves the contents of any environmental variable.
?FILEEXIST	Checks the system to see if a file exists.
?INPATH	Checks to see if a file exists in the system path.
?TIME	Reads the system time.
ADD	Adds to variables together.
BEEP	Sounds the speaker.
BLINK	Causes the text on the screen to blink.
BOX1	Draws a box on the screen.
BREAKON/BREAKOFF	Controls the status of break within a compiled PowerBatch program.
CENTER	Centers text on the screen.
CLEAR	Erases the screen.
CLEARBOX	Erases the text within a given set of coordinates.
CLEARLINE	Erases a single line.
COLOR	Sets the default colors.
COMPARE	Compares the contents of two variables.
CONCAT	Combines two strings.
GOTO	Jumps to a label and continues processing.
GOTOXY	Positions the cursor on the screen.
HALT	Immediately stops the PowerBatch program and exits to DOS. Optionally sets ERRORLEVEL on exit.
LABEL	Marks a PowerBatch label.
LENGTH	Calculates the length of a string.
LOWER	Converts a string to all lowercase.
MIDSTRING	Strips out part of the string in one variable and stores it in another variable.
NORMAL	Resets the display mode.
PROMPT	Changes the setting of the prompt.
READKEY	Gets a single keystroke from the user.
READSTR	Gets an entire string from the user.
READUPKEY	Gets a single keystroke from the user and converts it to uppercase.
READYN	Gets a single keystroke from the user and only accept a y- or n-key. Converts it to uppercase.
REVERSE	Switches the screen to inverse video.
SETENV	Places a variable into the environment.
SETPATH	Changes the path.
SETVAR	Stores the contents of one variable in another variable.
SUBTRACT	Subtracts one variable from another.
UPPER	Converts a string to uppercase.
VARIABLE	Defines a variable.
WAIT	Pauses the batch file for a given period of time.
WRITE	Displays text on the screen at the current cursor position.
WRITEAT	Displays text on the screen at the given cursor position.
WRITELINE	Displays text on the screen at a given line.

Batch File Line	Explanation
; NAME: SHOW-PB.PWR ; PURPOSE: Illustrate PowerBatch ; VERSION: 1.25 ; DATE: April 6, 1991	Documentation remarks.

VARIABLE Tone1 4 800 ; Define Tone
VARIABLE Tone2 2 10 : Define Duration
VARIABLE Tone3 1 2   ; Define Number of
                     ; Repeats
VARIABLE Junk 1 "A" ; Define A Data Input
                     ; Variable
VARIABLE Delay 2 50 ; Define Delay Between
                     ; Screens
VARIABLE SDelay 2 20 ; Define Short Delay
VARIABLE First,8   ; Variable For Name
VARIABLE Last,20   ;
VARIABLE Upper1,8   ; Case Change Variable
VARIABLE Upper2,20   ;
VARIABLE Lower1,8   ;
VARIABLE Lower2,20   ;
VARIABLE Drive,1   ; Query Variables
VARIABLE Sub,65   ;
VARIABLE Day,9   ;
VARIABLE Month,2   ;
VARIABLE Date1,2   ;
VARIABLE Year,4   ;
VARIABLE Space1,20   ;
VARIABLE Space2,20   ;
VARIABLE Time1,11   ;
VARIABLE RedOnGray,3,116 ; Define
                         ; Colors
VARIABLE RedOnBlack,3,4   ;
VARIABLE YelOnBlue,3,30   ;
VARIABLE BlueOnGray,3,113   ;
	PowerBatch requires that all variables be defined before they are used. This section defines the variables used in this program. It is a good programming practice to define all the variables at the top of the program, although PowerBatch does not require that.

CLEAR YelOnBlue	Clears the screen using the colors defined in the variable YelOnBlue
CENTER "PowerBatch Demonstration",1	Centers text on the screen on line one.
CENTER "Written by Ronny Richardson",3	Centers text on the screen on line three.
BEEP Tone1,Tone2,Tone3	Beeps the speaker using the frequency, , and number of repeats defined by these variables.
CENTER "Press Any Key To Begin",12	Centers text on the screen.
GOTOXY 1,24	Position the cursor in column-1 on row-24.
READKEY Junk	Gets a keystroke from the user and store it in variable Junk.
CLEARLINE 12,YelOnBlue	Clears line-12 on the screen using the color defined by YelOnBlue.
GOTOXY 10,20	Positions the cursor.
WRITE "Enter Your First Name: ",YelOnBlue	Writes text to the screen.
READSTR First	Reads a string from the user and stores it in a variable. It was defined

Batch File Line	Explanation
	as an 8-character variable, so the user can only enter eight characters.
`GOTOXY 10,22`	Positions the cursor.
`WRITE "Enter Your Last Name:` `   ",YelOnBlue`	Writes text to the screen.
`READSTR Last`	Reads information from the user.
`CLEAR`	Clears the screen using default colors.

`MIDSTRING Upper1,First,1,8`
`MIDSTRING Lower1,First,1,8`
`MIDSTRING Upper2,Last,1,20`
`MIDSTRING Lower2,Last,1,20`
	Stores the user's first name under Upper1 and Lower1 and his/her last name under Upper2 and Lower2.

`UPPER Upper1`
`UPPER Upper2`
`LOWER Lower1`
`LOWER Lower2`
	Creates all upper- and lowercase versions of the users name.

`WRITEAT 30,01 First`
`WRITEAT 30,03 Upper1`
`WRITEAT 30,05 Lower1`
	Writes the user's first name to the screen at three locations. The first number is the column and the second is the row.

`WAIT SDelay`	Waits for the period of time defined by the variable.

`WRITEAT 30,08 First`
`WRITEAT 30,10 Upper1`
`WRITEAT 30,12 Lower1`
`WAIT SDelay`
	Writes the user's first name again and waits.

`WRITEAT 30,15 First`
`WRITEAT 30,17 Upper1`
`WRITEAT 30,19 Lower1`
`WAIT SDelay`
	Writes the user's first name again and waits.

`WRITEAT 36,01 Last`
`WRITEAT 36,03 Upper2`
`WRITEAT 36,05 Lower2`
`WAIT SDelay`
	Writes the user's last name and waits.

`WRITEAT 36,08 Last`
`WRITEAT 36,10 Upper2`
`WRITEAT 36,12 Lower2`
`WAIT SDelay`
	Writes the user's last name again.

`WRITEAT 36,15 Last`
`WRITEAT 36,17 Upper2`
`WRITEAT 36,19 Lower2`
`WAIT Delay`
	Writes the user's last name one more time.

`CLEAR YelOnBlue`	Clears the screen.
`?CURRDIR Drive,Sub`	Gets the current subdirectory from the system.
`?DATE Day,Month,Date1,Year`	Gets the current date from the system.
`?DISKSPACE,Drive,Space1,Space2`	Gets the amount of space on the current drive from the system.
`?TIME,Time1`	Gets the current time from the system.

Table 8-16   Continued.

Batch File Line	Explanation

WRITEAT 10,01,"Current Drive And
       Subdirectory Is: "
WRITEAT 10,05,"The Day Of The Week Is:"
WRITEAT 10,02,"The Date Is:"
WRITEAT 10,03,"The "
WRITEAT 14,03,Drive
WRITEAT 15,03,"-Drive Has This Much Space:"
WRITEAT 10,04,"It has This Much Space
       Remaining:"
WRITEAT 10,06,"The Current Time Is:"
WRITEAT 50,01,Drive
WRITEAT 51,01,":"
WRITEAT 52,01,Sub
WRITEAT 50,05,Day
WRITEAT 50,02,Month
WRITEAT 52,02,"/"
WRITEAT 53,02,Date1
WRITEAT 55,02,"/"
WRITEAT 56,02,Year
WRITEAT 50,03,Space1
WRITEAT 50,04,Space2
WRITEAT 50,06,Time1
	Writes this information to the screen.

WAIT Delay	Pauses the batch file.
CLEAR RedOnGray	Clears the screen.
BOX1 01,01,20,05,RedOnGray	Draws a box from column-1, row-1 to column-20, row-5 using the color defined by RedOnGray.
BOX1 21,01,40,05,RedOnGray BOX1 41,01,60,05,RedOnGray BOX1 61,01,80,05,RedOnGray BOX1 01,06,20,10,RedOnGray BOX1 21.06,40.10,RedOnGray BOX1 41,06,60,10,RedOnGray BOX1 61,06,80,10,RedOnGray BOX1 01,11,20,15,RedOnGray BOX1 21,11,40,15,RedOnGray BOX1 41,11,60,15,RedOnGray BOX1 61,11,80,15,RedOnGray BOX1 01,16,20,20,RedOnGray BOX1 21,16,40,20,RedOnGray BOX1 41,16,60,20,RedOnGray BOX1 61,16,80,20,RedOnGray BOX1 01,21,20,25,RedOnGray BOX1 21,21,40,25,RedOnGray BOX1 41,21,60,25,RedOnGray BOX1 61,21,80,25,RedOnGray	Draws more boxes on the screen.
WAIT Delay	Pauses the batch file.
CLEAR YelOnBlue	Clears the screen.
BOX1 01,01,20,05,YelOnBlue BOX1 21,01,40,05,YelOnBlue BOX1 41,01,60,05,YelOnBlue BOX1 61,01,80,05,YelOnBlue BOX1 01,06,20,10,YelOnBlue BOX1 21,06,40,10,YelOnBlue BOX1 41,06,60,10,YelOnBlue BOX1 61,06,80,10,YelOnBlue BOX1 01,11,20,15,YelOnBlue BOX1 21,11,40,15,YelOnBlue BOX1 41,11,60,15,YelOnBlue	Draws more boxes on the screen.

Batch File Line	Explanation
BOX1 61,11,80,15,YelOnBlue BOX1 01,16,20,20,YelOnBlue BOX1 21,16,40,20,YelOnBlue BOX1 41,16,60,20,YelOnBlue BOX1 61,16,80,20,YelOnBlue BOX1 01,21,20,25,YelOnBlue BOX1 21,21,40,25,YelOnBlue BOX1 41,21,60,25,YelOnBlue BOX1 61,21,80,25,YelOnBlue	
WAIT Delay	Pauses the batch file.
WRITEAT 08,03,"Boxes" WRITEAT 28,03,"Can" WRITEAT 48,03,"Have" WRITEAT 68,03,"Text" WRITEAT 29,13,"In" WRITEAT 48,13,"Them"	Writes text in some of the boxes.
WAIT SDelay	Pauses the batch file.
WRITEAT 08,23,"But" WRITEAT 28,23,"You" WRITEAT 48,23,"Knew" WRITEAT 67,23,"That!"	Writes more text in the boxes.
WAIT Delay	Pauses the batch file.
CLEARBOX 01,01,20,05,BlueOnGray CLEARBOX 21,01,40,05,BlueOnGray CLEARBOX 41,01,60,05,BlueOnGray CLEARBOX 61,01,80,05,BlueOnGray CLEARBOX 01,06,20,10,BlueOnGray CLEARBOX 21,06,40,10,BlueOnGray CLEARBOX 41,06,60,10,BlueOnGray CLEARBOX 61,06,80,10,BlueOnGray CLEARBOX 01,11,20,15,BlueOnGray CLEARBOX 21,11,40,15,BlueOnGray CLEARBOX 41,11,60,15,BlueOnGray CLEARBOX 61,11,80,15,BlueOnGray CLEARBOX 01,16,20,20,BlueOnGray CLEARBOX 21,16,40,20,BlueOnGray CLEARBOX 41,16,60,20,BlueOnGray CLEARBOX 61,16,80,20,BlueOnGray CLEARBOX 01,21,20,25,BlueOnGray CLEARBOX 21,21,40,25,BlueOnGray CLEARBOX 41,21,60,25,BlueOnGray CLEARBOX 61,21,80,25,BlueOnGray	Erases the insides of the boxes. Even though you give the same coordinates here as you do to create the boxes, PowerBatch is intelligent enough to only erase the inside of the box while maintaining the lines in place.
WAIT Delay	Pauses the batch file.
CLEAR YelOnBlue	Clears the screen before exiting.

Problems

The major problem with PowerBatch is its inability to compile DOS batch files without extensive modifications, as discussed above. It suffers from other problems as well.

You must be very careful about syntax. For example, the command

```
CENTER "message",n
```

will center a message on line n of the screen as written. However, if you add a space after the comma for readability, the command won't execute properly, always writing to the first line. PowerBatch refuses to compile the same line when a space exists between the CD and the backslash because it will consider the backslash to be a variable.

The compiler locks up the computer fairly often. In fact, I had to reboot more than twenty times while writing the sample batch file that illustrates PowerBatch! At one point, it locked up simply because I had quotes around a number in a variable definition statement, even though the manual claims that's acceptable. Once I removed the quotes, it compiled normally. Another time, it repeatedly refused to compile a file for no apparent reason, working finally when I removed a blank line.

Conclusion

The authors have done well in extending the batch language with PowerBatch. In the process, however, they seem to have forgotten their roots. Batch files that would compile under every other compiler required extensive modifications to compile at all under Power-Batch. In many cases, it was quicker to rewrite a working batch file using PowerBatch commands than to undertake the daunting task of converting an existing batch file for PowerBatch. This might be acceptable to someone just starting out with batch files, but someone with a large library of working batch files is going to find this to be a very high price for PowerBatch. Because you must use nonstandard syntax for standard batch commands under PowerBatch, it's going to be tough to mentally adjust between working under DOS and working under PowerBatch.

Son of a Batch

Name:	Son of a Batch
Version:	1.01
Price:	$69.95
Category:	Commercial
Summary:	A simple batch file compiler.
Author:	Hyperkinetix, Incorporated
	666 Baker Street
	Suite 405
	Costa Mesa, California 92626
	(714) 668-9234
Availability:	Order Son of a Batch directly from the vendor.

The president of Hyperkinetix calls Son of a Batch "the batch compiler from hell." Hyperkinetix originally released Son of a Batch as an interim solution while working on Builder, their premium compiler. However, Son of a Batch has remained popular, perhaps because of the fantastic name. Hyperkinetix won't be improving Son of a Batch, but current versions are available for sale. I recommend purchasing Builder instead; the price isn't much higher, and Hyperkinetix will be supporting Builder in the future.

Of course, if you hold the name "Son of a Batch" close to your heart, you always could rename BUILDER.EXE as SOB.EXE.

Compiling a batch file

Compiling a batch file is a three-step process:

1. *Convert the batch file into Son of a Batch format.* The compiler does much of this for you when it first reads in the batch file.

2. *Compile the batch file.* This reads the Son of a Batch format file and begins the process of creating the program file. As part of the process, it checks for errors. When the compiler finds an error, it writes the line number to the screen but doesn't tell you what the error is.

3. *Link the batch file.* This actually creates the program file.

The first step converts FILE.BAT to FILE.SOB while converting the batch file to its own format. Differences include the following:

- The batch file commands IF EXIST file IF string = = string SET variable = something must have quotation marks around portions of them, so they become IF EXIST "file" IF "string" = = "string" SET "variable" = "something"; the conversion program does some of this automatically. The conversion didn't convert SET statements, so I had to change all these manually.

- Nonbatch commands must be preceded by a RUN command. It makes this conversion automatically.

- The parentheses in a FOR statement must be replaced with quotation marks.

New commands

Son of a Batch adds to the batch language new commands that are a subset of the commands listed for Builder. Other programs add commands to batch files like Son of a Batch. The major problems with all these utilities is portability. You can only share batch files using these programs with someone who owns the programs. The advantage of Son of a Batch is that while you can't share the compiler, you can freely share your compiled batch files. That also means you can share the extensions Son of a Batch adds to the batch language!

However, these extensions and nonstandard syntax do raise a problem. Once you begin using them, you can't debug your program as a batch file under DOS because DOS doesn't have these extensions. Thus, writing the extended batch files becomes more difficult.

Problems

I ran into four problems using Son of a Batch that were fairly minor once you figure them out.

First, every time I ran Son of a Batch, it gave me a linker error message saying "Unable to create program due to linker error." The manual doesn't mention the linker or linker error messages at all. As a result, I didn't even have a clue about what to do next. It turned out that the linker would go ahead and create the program.

Second, Son of a Batch batch files can't modify the DOS prompt (even temporarily) while a program is running. If a compiled batch file has a PROMPT command in it, Son of a Batch seems to compile it properly but runs it unpredictably.

Third, compiled batch files can't start Lotus. The compiler does something to the batch file that causes Lotus to become confused and tell you a driver is missing. While all the other programs I use worked with Son of a Batch compiled batch files, I expect that some other programs might cause problems.

Fourth, Son of a Batch ignores the CTTY NUL and CTTY CON commands. Because Son of a Batch gives you more control over masking commands sent to the screen, this isn't a major problem. However, you can't mask all screen messages with Son of a Batch, so some extra ones will slip through.

The manual for Son of a Batch isn't all that great. It starts off with an introduction to compilers, presents a reference section on all of the Son of a Batch commands, and then quits. No tutorial on using the Son of a Batch-specific commands is presented, nor is a listing of error message explanations.

Conclusion

Because Hyperkinetix will be supporting Builder instead of Son of a Batch in the future, you would be better served purchasing Builder. In addition, Son of a Batch offers less control over your batch files. Also, there are no ELSE, CASE, or WHILE functions in Son of a Batch like in Builder. However, for speeding up fairly simple batch files, Son of a Batch is quite adequate.

Compiler comparison

One test of a compiler is how small and tight the generated code is. To test the compilers, I created a very tiny 4-byte batch file containing the command @DIR followed immediately by an End-Of-File marker. Bat2Exec did the best job, the resulting .COM file required only 430 bytes. Batcom did almost as well, its .EXE file requiring only 930 bytes. Builder and Son of a Batch did much worse, their .COM programs requiring almost 8.5K. However, PowerBatch was totally horrible, creating a 31,791-byte file!

To see if the results changed for large batch files, I took a massive 5,433-byte batch file I use every day and compiled it. Bat2Exec created a 6,860-byte program, Batcom created a 10,080-byte program, and Builder and Son of a Batch created 15,688-byte programs. PowerBatch wasn't able to even compile this file without extensive modifications that rendered this test meaningless. Clearly, if size is critical, then you want either Bat2Exec if you need no features beyond DOS or Batcom if you need enhancements.

In terms of speed, DOS is surprisingly the fastest program when running straight DOS commands. I created SPEED.BAT (shown in Table 8-17) to test the various compil-

**Table 8-17   SPEED.BAT runs a number of
DOS commands that time various compiled programs.**

Batch File Line	Explanation
@ECHO OFF	Turns command-echoing off.
TIME < C:\RETURN > C:\TIMER.TXT	Pipes the starting file into a file called TIMER.TXT. The file RETURN contains a single return to supply the return TIME expects.

Batch File Line	Explanation
REM NAME: SPEED.BAT REM PURPOSE: Speed Test of Compilers REM VERSION: 1.00 REM DATE: April 5, 1991 REM Will Use Only DOS Commands For REM Test So I Do Not Have To Worry REM About Different In Enhancements REM And Because Bat2Exec Offers REM No Enhancements	Documentation remarks.
C:	Changes to the C drive.
CD\	Changes to the root directory.
DIR C:\WORD DIR C:\123R3 DIR C:\DBASE3	Performs several directories.
CHKDSK C:	Runs CHKDSK.
COPY C:\AUTOEXEC.BAT C:\TEMP COPY C:\CONFIG.SYS C:\TEMP	Copies some files.
CD\TEMP CD\ CD\TEMP	Changes directories several times.
DEL AUTOEXEC.BAT DEL CONFIG.SYS	Deletes some files.
CD\	Changes back to the root directory.
TIME < C:\RETURN >> C:\TIMER.TXT	Pipes the ending time to a file.

ers. Because the syntax of the enhancements is different and because Bat2Exec offers no enhancements, SPEED.BAT contains only DOS commands. DOS runs SPEED.BAT in 12.41 seconds, Bat2Exec takes 14.45 seconds, Batcom takes 19.23 seconds, Builder and Son of a Batch take 18.18 seconds, and PowerBatch takes 25.10 seconds.

In terms of features, Builder clearly is the best, with Batcom and PowerBatch tied for second. Bat2Exec comes in a distant fourth because it adds no features.

Table 8-18 shows a comparison of the results of the different test.

**Table 8-18   Performance comparison
of some common batch file compilers.**

Test	DOS	Bat2Exec	Batcom	Builder	Power-Batch
Size of small batch file (bytes)	4	430	930	8,815	31,791
Size of large batch file (bytes)	5,433	6,860	10,080	15,688	NA[1]
Time to run SPEED.BAT (seconds)	12.41	14.45	19.23	18.18	25.10[2]

1   The modifications required for this batch file to compile under PowerBatch were so extensive as to render the resulting size of the file invalid for comparison.

2   PowerBatch required most of the parameters to the commands to be enclosed in quotes in order to run. These changes were made. The other three compilers handled SPEED.BAT unmodified.

So, which one should you buy? If you just want to protect existing batch files against modification, Bat2Exec will do that and the price (i.e., free) is certainly right. If you want to create batch files exceeding the power of DOS, then Batcom has a nice combination of power and low price. If you want absolutely the most powerful batch files going, then you want Builder.

9

Using the environment booting programs

All of these programs are designed to reboot your computer. They all work on most close clones; but some combinations of hardware, software, and a slightly nonstandard clone may cause one or more of these programs to fail. For that reason, I have included several of them; you can try them all and see which one works for you.

A program can cause two types of reboots: warm or cold. A warm reboot is the same as pressing Ctrl-Alt-Del key combination. The computer doesn't go through its memory tests and certain other power-on tests. In contrast, a cold reboot is just like turning the machine off and back on. You will see the computer go through its memory test as it reboots.

You may be wondering exactly why anyone would want to have a program that reboots the computer. Two applications come to my mind immediately:

- You must change the configuration of your computer, so you write a set of batch files to copy different versions of your AUTOEXEC.BAT and CONFIG.SYS files to the root directory. After doing that, the batch file reboots the computer so the new configuration can take effect.

- You have a batch file that requires a password. As extra protection, it reboots the computer if the user enters the wrong password three times.

I'm sure you can think of other uses.

Batchman

Name: Batchman
Version: 1.0
Price: Free

Category: Copyrighted
Summary: Batchman is an incredibly powerful collection of 48 batch utilities in one
               tiny program.
Author: Michael Mefford
Availability: All *PC Magazine* files are available from their area on CompuServe. See
               any issue of *PC Magazine* for details.

Batchman is a collection of numerous useful batch commands in one program. Having all
the commands in one program keeps it small because, otherwise, each command would
need one cluster of disk space. To run a command, you enter

    BATCHMAN command [options]

The full set of commands available in Batchman are covered in Chapter 6. However,
the Batchman commands that simply reboot the computer are as follows:

    COLDBOOT, to perform a cold reboot of the computer.
    WARMBOOT, to perform a warm reboot of the computer.

Again, for complete Batchman coverage, see Chapter 6.

Reboot1

Name: Reboot1
Version: 1.0
Price: Free
Category: Copyrighted
Summary: Performs a cold reboot.
Availability: All *PC Magazine* files are available from their area on CompuServe. See
               any issue of *PC Magazine* for details.

Reboot1 performs a cold reboot of the computer.

Reboot2

Name: Reboot2
Version: 1.0
Price: Free
Category: Copyrighted
Summary: Performs a warm reboot.
Availability: All *PC Magazine* files are available from their area on CompuServe. See
               any issue of *PC Magazine* for details.

Reboot2 tries to perform a warm reboot. On the several computers I tested it on, it appeared to work the first time; but if you ran it again without a cold reboot, it locked up. I only recommend you try this program only if the others fail to work for you.

Warmboot

Name:	Warmboot
Version:	1.0
Price:	Free
Category:	Copyrighted
Summary:	Reboots the computer.
Availability:	All *PC Magazine* files are available from their area on CompuServe. See any issue of *PC Magazine* for details.

WARMBOOT.COM is a 20-byte program that performs a warm reboot of the computer.

AUTOEXEC.BAT programs

BOOTEXEC

Name:	BOOTEXEC
Version:	1.0
Price:	$10.00
Category:	Shareware
Summary:	A small 496-byte device driver that lets you change the name of your AUTOEXEC.BAT file to any legal file name.
Author:	Tom R. Donnelly
	Computer Software and Consulting
	Post Office Box 3856
	San Dimas, California 91773
Availability:	Included on the disk bound in this book.

A lot of programs want to modify your AUTOEXEC.BAT file during their installation process, which leads to various methods of protecting your AUTOEXEC.BAT file. Some of the more common ones are as follows:

- Making your AUTOEXEC.BAT file read-only.
- Renaming your AUTOEXEC.BAT file to another name and then making a fake one-line AUTOEXEC.BAT file that calls the "real" one.

Unfortunately, these methods have problems, so there's no fool-proof method of protecting your AUTOEXEC.BAT file using DOS.

BOOTEXEC can help you. Using BOOTEXEC, you add one line to your CONFIG.SYS that looks like this:

DEVICE = C: \ DRIVERS \ BOOTEXEC.SYS C: \ BAT \ REALAUTO.BAT

You must specify the full path to both the BOOTEXEC.SYS file and the AUTOEXEC .BAT file you want to use. The name for the AUTOEXEC.BAT file can be any legal DOS file name and doesn't need to have a .BAT extension. Loading the BOOTEXEC.SYS driver uses 496 bytes of memory, and that memory isn't released.

BOOTEXEC doesn't give you the option of selecting different AUTOEXEC.BAT files on boot up. However, if you use CONFIG.CTL, you can add multiple BOOTEXEC lines to your CONFIG.SYS and then select the one you want to use as the computer boots.

BOOTEXEC is a handy program with a tiny appetite for RAM.

Environmental programs

Chapter 8 covers programs designed to interact directly with the CONFIG.SYS file. This section covers programs designed to evaluate or work with the environment after booting.

ENV

Name:	Environmental Editor (ENV)
Version:	1.00b
Price:	$5.00
	$15.00 to also receive the next upgrade.
Category:	Shareware
Summary:	Allows you to expand your PATH beyond 127 characters and edit your other environmental variables.
Author:	Thuan-Tit Ewe
	Post Office Box 1016
	Capitola, California 95010
Availability:	Included on the disk bound in this book.

ENV is an environmental editor, displaying the current environmental variables one at a time in a small window at the screen bottom. If the contents exceed 80 characters, they scroll off the screen to the right. You can move the cursor to the portion of the variable not showing on the screen.

Using ENV, you can edit any of the variables, although you can only see one at a time. One nice feature of ENV is that it lets you expand your PATH beyond the 127-character limit of DOS. (The actual PATH is limited to 122 characters because the PATH = portion requires the first five characters.)

This limit comes about not because DOS limits the PATH statement but because DOS limits command lines to 127 characters. Using ENV, you can go in and expand your PATH statement to the length you need, within the constraints of your free environmental space. Because ENV works in batch mode as well, you can build the ENV commands necessary to build a long PATH into your AUTOEXEC.BAT file.

A PATH exceeding 122 characters works just fine; however, DOS isn't configured to deal with it. As a result, only the first 122 characters are displayed when you issue a SET or ECHO %PATH% command.

ENV won't allow you to edit any other environmental variable so that it exceeds 127 characters, including its name. This is appropriate because any batch testing or echoing of an environmental requires that the entire statement—not just the environmental variable— be less than 127 characters.

In addition to editing and expanding your PATH, ENV works much like an intelligent SET command. You can edit any of the variables currently in the environment. ENV is limited only in that it can't add new variables to the environment.

ENV can edit variables both interactively and in batch mode. However, other than expanding the PATH, ENV offers little advantage in batch mode. It can add text to the front or back of an existing environmental variable, but so can DOS.

In interactive mode, ENV is a very nice way to edit environmental variables. It also gives you the option of saving your environment by writing out a batch file that will re-make your current environment. If you have expanded your PATH to beyond 122 characters, ENV writes out a batch file with a SET command exceeding 127 characters. Under some versions of DOS, a batch file line exceeding 127 characters locks up the computer.

Overall, ENV is a nice interactive environmental editor and a great way to expand your PATH beyond 122 characters.

ENVCOUNT

Name:	ENVCOUNT
Version:	1.0
Price:	Free
Category:	Copyrighted
Summary:	Displays the amount of information stored in the environment.
Author:	Richard Hale
Availability:	All *PC Magazine* files are available from their area on CompuServe. See any issue of *PC Magazine* for details.

When you enter ENVCOUNT on the command line, it tells you how much information in bytes is stored in the environment. However, it doesn't tell you how much free space the environment has.

FindEnv

Name:	FindEnv
Version:	1.0
Price:	Free
Category:	Copyrighted
Summary:	Displays summary information about the environment.
Availability:	All *PC Magazine* files are available from their area on CompuServe. See any issue of *PC Magazine* for details.

When you run FindEnv, it displays the starting address of the environment, its size, the amount used, and its free space. This is useful if you are trying to adjust the size of your environment so that you have enough room for environmental variables.

ISDEV.COM

Name:	ISDEV.COM
Price:	Free
Category:	Copyrighted
Summary:	A small program that can check to see if a device driver is loaded into memory.
Author:	Chris DeVoney
Availability:	A short script to create ISDEV.COM was printed in the February 1991 issue of *PC/Computing* magazine.

ISDEV.COM is a small program that will check memory to see if a specified device driver is loaded. If it finds that device driver, it sets ERRORLEVEL to 0; otherwise, it returns a value of 1. This allows your batch file to perform different tasks depending on memory configuration. This logically allows for the changing of the CONFIG.SYS file and a reboot if a program requiring a specific configuration doesn't find it.

Table 9-1 shows a batch file that will check to see if HIMEM.SYS is loaded. If it is, the batch file loads Windows. If not, it replaces the current CONFIG.SYS with one that loads HIMEM.SYS and reboots the computer. The user is left to expand WINDOWS.BAT to automatically load Windows after rebooting.

Table 9-1   WINDOWS.BAT uses ISDEV.COM
to determine if HIMEN.SYS is loaded and acts accordingly.

Batch File Line	Explanation
`@ECHO OFF`	Turns command-echoing off.
`REM WINDOWS.BAT`	Remark giving the name of the batch file.
`ISDEV XMSXXXX0`	Text to see if HIMEM.SYS is loaded.

Batch File Line	Explanation
`IF ERRORLEVEL 0 IF NOT ERRORLEVEL 1 GOTO OK`	If HIMEM.SYS is loaded, jumps to the section that starts Windows.
`REM Assume CONFIG.001 Loads HIMEN.SYS` `REM Assume CONFIG.002 Does Not`	Documentation remarks.
`C:` `CD\`	Makes sure the user is in the root directory of the C drive.
`COPY CONFIG.001 CONFIG.SYS`	Replaces the current CONFIG.SYS file with one that loads HIMEM.SYS
`REBOOT`	Reboots the computer. This requires a rebooting program. This batch file uses one called REBOOT.
`:OK`	Label marking the section that loads Windows.
`C:` `CD\WINDOWS`	Changes to the Windows subdirectory.
`WIN`	Starts Windows.

As you can see from this batch file, you don't test for HIMEM.SYS with the name HIMEM. Rather, you use XMSXXXX0. Most device drivers have different names in memory than they do on the command line. The article that accompanies ISDEV.COM points out that PC$MOUSE is the name for a Logitech or Mouse Systems mouse driver, EMSXXXX0 is for LIM memory, SMARTAAR is for SMARTDRV, EMMXXXX0 is for QEMM-386, and MS$MOUSE is for a Microsoft mouse. The reader is left to figure out names for the remaining device drivers. The article suggests a couple of programs to help find the names. I also found out that with many device drivers, you will find the name listed very near the top of the code so that you can often find it with a command like

TYPE DEVICE.SYS | MORE

As the article also points out, ISDEV.COM can't test for all device drivers because of the name they use. ANSI.SYS and DISPLAY.SYS use CON, while PRINTER.SYS uses PRN. These exist even without the device driver being loaded, so ISDEV.COM can't test for them.

Right after I saw ISDEV.COM, I found another interesting use for it. My computer developed an intermittent fault that kept it from recognizing COM ports. If I rebooted several times, however, it would finally recognize them. I added the following lines to my AUTOEXEC.BAT file:

ISDEV MS$MOUSE
IF ERRORLEVEL 1 REBOOT

Because I have a serial mouse, MOUSE.SYS wouldn't load if the computer didn't recognize the serial ports. These two lines caused the computer to reboot over and over until it recognized the serial ports. After a week or so, of course, the problem went away by itself. Go try and figure that one out.

Ronset

Name:	Ronset
Version:	2.1
Price:	$20.00
Category:	Shareware
Summary:	A very powerful tool for manipulating environmental variables. Unfortunately, it doesn't work with newer versions of DOS.
Author:	Ron Bemis 9601 Forest Lane Apartment #222 Dallas, Texas 75243
Availability:	Available on many bulletin board systems.

Under DOS, you can do very little with environmental variables. You can create and erase them using the SET command, or print and test them in batch files by surrounding their names with percent signs; but beyond that, DOS has little use for them.

All that changes under Ronset. Using Ronset, there is little you can't do with environmental variables. The basic command to use Ronset is

```
RONSET A = XYZ(n,m)
```

In this command, A represents the environmental variable that the results will be stored in when the command finishes. The XYZ represents one of almost one hundred functions you can perform. (For example, the ADD function sums two numbers.) The n and m represent the parameters being passed to the function.

Table 9-2 lists most of the functions available in Ronset. A few additional functions working with a FidoNet node aren't of general interest.

Table 9-2   Ronset contains several important functions for inputting data.

Mathematical Function	Syntax Usage
ABS	RONSET A=ABS(n) Stores the absolute value (positive value) of n in the environmental variable A.
ADD	RONSET A=ADD(n,m) Adds two numbers and stores the results in the environmental variable A.
DIV	RONSET A=DIV(n,m) Computes the product of n/m and stores the results in the environmental variable A.
EQ	RONSET A=EQ(n,m) Stores a one in the environmental variable A if n=m, a zero otherwise.

Mathematical Function	Syntax / Usage
GE	RONSET A=LE(n,m) Stores a one in the environmental variable A if n is greater than or equal to m, a zero otherwise.
GT	RONSET A=GT(n,m) Stores a one in the environmental variable A if n is greater than m, a zero otherwise.
LE	RONSET A=LE(n,m) Stores a one in the environmental variable A if n is less than or equal to m, a zero otherwise.
LT	RONSET A=LT(n,m) Stores a one in the environmental variable A if n is less than m, a zero otherwise.
MOD	RONSET A=MOD(n,m) Stores n modulo m (the remainder of repeatedly computing n/m until the remainder is less than n) in the environmental variable A.
MULT	RONSET A=MULT(n,m) Multiples n times m and stores the results in the environmental variable A.
NE	RONSET A=NE(n,m) Stores a one in the environmental variable A if n is not equal to m, a zero otherwise.
NEG	RONSET A=NEG(n) Stores n times negative one in the environmental variable A.
POW	RONSET A=POW(n,m) Stores n to the m power in the environmental variable A.
SQR	RONSET A=SQR(n) Stores n squared in the environmental variable A.
SQRT	RONSET A=SQRT(n) Stores the square root of n in the environmental variable A.
SUB	RONSET A=SUB(n,m) Subtracts m from n and stores the results under the environmental variable A.

Binary Function	Syntax / Usage
AND	RONSET A=AND(n,m) Stores the bitwise AND of n and m in the environmental variable A.
BIN	RONSET A=BIN(n) Stores the binary conversion of n in the environmental variable A.
HEX	RONSET A=HEX(n) Stores the hexadecimal conversion of n in the environmental variable A.

Table 9-2   Continued.

Binary Function	Syntax Usage
NOR	RONSET A=NOR(n,m) Stores the bitwise NOR of n and m in the environmental variable A.
NOT	RONSET A=NOT(n) Store the ones compliment of n in the environmental variable A.
OCT	RONSET A=OCT(n) Stores the octal conversion of n in the environmental variable A.
OR	RONSET A=OR(n,m) Stores the bitwise OR of n and m in the environmental variable A.

String Function	Syntax Usage
ALPHA	RONSET A=ALPHA(string) Stores a one in the environmental variable A if the string is comprised entirely of letters, a zero otherwise.
ASC	RONSET A=ASC(string) Stores the ASCII value of the first character of the string in the environmental variable A.
CONCAT	RONSET A=CONCAT(a,b,c) Stores the concatenation (combination) of several strings in the environmental variable A.
EQS	RONSET A=EQS(string1,string2) Compares the two strings and stores a one to environmental variable A if they are the same, a zero otherwise.
GES	RONSET A=GES(character1,character2) Stores a one in the environmental variable A if character1 comes after character2 in the alphabet or is the same character, a zero otherwise.
GTS	RONSET A=GTS(character1,character2) Stores a one in environmental variable A if character1 comes after character2 in the alphabet, a zero otherwise.
ITS	RONSET A=ITS(character1,character2) Stores a one in environmental variable A if character1 comes before character2 in the alphabet, a zero otherwise.
LEFT	RONSET A=LEFT(n,string) Stores the n-left characters of the string in the environmental variable A.
LEN	RONSET A=LEN(string) Stores the length of the string in the environmental variable A.
LES	RONSET A=LES(character1,character2) Stores a one in environmental variable A if character1 comes before character2 in the alphabet or is the same character, a zero otherwise.

String Function	Syntax Usage
LOW	RONSET A=LOW(string) Converts the string to all lowercase and stores it in the environmental variable A.
MID	RONSET A=MID(m,n,string) Stores the n-characters of the string beginning with the m-th character in the environmental variable A.
NES	RONSET A=NEW(character1,character2) Stores a one in the environmental variable A if the two characters are the same, a zero otherwise.
NUM	RONSET A=NUM(string) Stores a one in the environmental variable A if the string is comprised entirely of numeric characters, a zero otherwise.
NUMBER	RONSET A=NUMBER(string) Stores a one in the environmental variable A if the string is comprised entirely of numbers, a zero otherwise.
POS	RONSET A=POS(string1,string2) Searches string2 for the first occurrence of string1 and stores its position in environmental variable A.
REPLACE	RONSET A=REPLACE(old,new,string) Searches string for old and replaces it with new storing the result in environmental variable A.
RIGHT	RONSET A=RIGHT(n,string) Stores the n-right characters of the string in the environmental variable A.
UP	RONSET A=UP(string) Converts the string to all uppercase and stores it in the environmental variable A.

Input Function	Syntax Usage
CHAR	RONSET A=CHAR(prompt,allowed,seconds) Displays a prompt and waits the specified number of seconds for the user to enter a character contained in allowed. That character is stored in the environmental variable A.
LEVEL	RONSET A=LEVEL(n) Causes the program to exit and set ERRORLEVEL to n. No environment variable is created.
STRING	RONSET A=STRING(prompt,length) Displays a prompt and waits for the user to enter a character string. That character string is stored in the environmental variable A. The length restricts the length of the string the user may enter. The default length is 80-characters.

Table 9-2 Continued.

Filename Function	Syntax Usage
DIR	RONSET A=DIR(file) Strips off the filename of the file and stores the drive letter, colon, and path in the environmental variable A.
DRIVE	RONSET A=DRIVE(file) Strips off the path and filename of the file and stores just the drive letter and colon in the environmental variable A.
EXIST	RONSET A=EXIST(file) Stores a one in the environmental variable A if the specified file exists, a zero otherwise.
EXPAND	RONSET A=EXPAND (file) Stores the full path, including drive, to the specified file in the environmental variable A. Wildcards are expanded and the name of the first file is the one used.
EXT	RONSET A=EXT(file) Strips off the drive, path, and name of the file and stores just the extension in the environmental variable A. Wildcards are not expanded.
FILE	RONSET A=FILE(file) Strips off the drive and path of the file and stores just the filename in the environmental variable A. Wildcards are not expanded.
FULL	RONSET A=FULL(file) Stores the full path, including drive, to the specified file in the environmental variable A. Wildcards are not expanded.
NAME	RONSET A=NAME(file) Strips off the drive, path, and extension of the file and stores just the name in the environmental variable A. Wildcards are not expanded.
PATH	RONSET A=PATH(file) Strips off the drive and filename of the file and stores just the path in the environmental variable A.
BYTE	RONSET A=BYTE(n,file) Stores the ASCII value of the character in the n-th position of the specified file in the environmental variable A.
LONG	RONSET A=LONG(location,file) Stores the 32-bit value at the specified location in the indicated file in the environmental variable A.
WORD	RONSET A=WORD(location,file) Stores the 16-bit value at the specified location in the indicated file in the environmental variable A.

Miscellaneous Function	Syntax Usage
DATE	RONSET A=DATE() Stores the date in the environmental variable A.
ECHO	RONSET A=ECHO(string) Displays the specified string on the console.
ENV	RONSET A=ENV() Stores the amount of free environmental space in the environmental variable A.
EXEC	RONSET A=EXEC(command) Runs a DOS command and stores its ERRORLEVEL termination value in the environmental variable A.
FREE	RONSET A=FREE(drive) Stores the amount of free space on the specified drive in the environmental variable A.
IF	RONSET A=IF(test,true,false) Stores the value of the true statement if the test if true and the value of the false statement if the test if false.
MEM	RONSET A=MEM() Stores the amount of free memory in the environmental variable A.
PRN	RONSET A=PRN() Stores a number representing the status of the printer in the environmental variable A.
RAND	RONSET A=RAND(max) Stores a random number between zero and max-1 in the environmental variable A.
SOUND	RONSET A=SOUND(length,tone) Plays the specified tone without setting a value in the environmental variable A.
TENV	RONSET A=TENV() Stores the total amount of environmental space in the environmental variable A.
TIME	RONSET A=TIME() Stores the time to the environmental variable A.
TOTAL	RONSET A=TOTAL(drive) Stores the total amount of space on the specified drive in the environmental variable A.
VER	RONSET A=VER(type) Stores the DOS version number in the environmental variable A. The type indicates if the major, minor, or both numbers are stored.

As you can see, Ronset gives you the ability to do almost anything you can imagine with environmental variables. Were it not for one flaw, Ronset would be one of the most powerful and useful batch utilities available. Unfortunately, it can't run under any current version of DOS. I tested it under IBM DOS 3.3, 4.0, and Microsoft DOS 5.0; it wouldn't work under any of them. I finally located a copy of DOS 2.1, however, and then it worked perfectly. Once Ronset is upgraded to work with more modern versions of DOS, I will highly recommend it.

Scanion Enterprises Batch File Utilities

Name: Scanion Enterprises Batch File Utilities
Version: 2.2.0
Price: $9.95
Category: Shareware
Summary: A collection of over 100 batch file utilities.
Author: Paul Scanion
Availability: Included on the disk bound in this book.

The Scanion Enterprises Batch File Utilities [SEBFU for short] is a collection of over 100 batch file utilities. The programs that work with the environment are discussed here.

Each of the commands in SEBFU is a separate *.COM file. As a result, your disk can end up cluttered with quite a number of small program files. You might consider erasing those program files you aren't likely to use.

ADD adds a specified value to an environmental variable containing a numeric value. Combined with the SUB command, ADD forms an excellent way to implement loops in a batch file.

DETANSI checks to see if ANSI.SYS was installed in the CONFIG.SYS file and then sets the ERRORLEVEL accordingly. This is a good way for the batch file to decide between plain screens and ANSI-formatted screens.

ENVSIZE checks to see how much free environmental space is available and then sets ERRORLEVEL accordingly, useful for batch files using a number of environmental variables because it allows them to ensure enough free space before running.

FREEM detects the amount of free memory and sets ERRORLEVEL or an environmental variable accordingly. This allows a batch file running a program requiring a lot of memory to ensure that much memory exists before execution begins.

GETMCB displays a list of the current memory usage.

INSTR searches an environmental variable and places a specified portion of that environmental variable into another environmental variable.

LEN returns the length of a specified environmental variable.

LIMCK checks to see if an LIM (expanded memory) driver is attached and sets ERRORLEVEL accordingly.

MIDSTR places a portion of one environmental variable into another environmental variable.

MOUSECK checks to see if a mouse is attached and sets the ERRORLEVEL accordingly.

SHOWVAR displays the contents of an environmental variable.

SUB subtracts a specified value to an environmental variable containing a numeric value. Combined with the ADD command, SUB forms an excellent way to implement loops in a batch file.

XMCHK checks to see if extended memory is installed and sets ERRORLEVEL accordingly.

All SEBFU programs are described in detail in Chapter 6.

Showerr

Name:	Showerr
Version:	1.0
Price:	Free
Category:	Public Domain
Summary:	A memory resident program that displays the ERRORLEVEL when it changes.
Author:	Ken Hipple
Availability:	Available on many bulletin board systems. Generally distributed as part of the Getkey package.

No programs exist that can find out the current ERRORLEVEL value because running a program resets ERRORLEVEL to 0. As a result, the common way to find out the ERRORLEVEL is to run a slow batch file.

Showerr is an ERRORLEVEL display program that avoids both problems by loading itself as memory resident. That way, when Showerr runs later, DOS isn't loading a program and doesn't reset the ERRORLEVEL. Because it stays in memory, Showerr reduces your available memory by about 900 bytes. Showerr monitors the ERRORLEVEL and pops up a message any time it changes. You must press a key to continue.

This approach works and is useful when working on a batch file or other application where ERRORLEVEL must be closely monitored. However, you can't unload Showerr; and, in general use, the ERRORLEVEL changes fairly often. As a result, Showerr is always popping up, displaying the ERRORLEVEL value and waiting for you to press a key. It will soon start to annoy you; and not long after that, it will get downright irritating.

Showerr would have been a much better program if it stayed in the background and then you pressed a hotkey to get a report on the ERRORLEVEL. Still, it's the only program I know to monitor the ERRORLEVEL.

Other programs

COMMENT.SYS

Name: COMMENT.SYS
Price: Free
Category: Copyrighted
Summary: A device driver for entering comments and ANSI.SYS escape sequences in the CONFIG.SYS file.
Author: Skip Gilbrech
Availability: Available on many bulletin board systems.

Up until DOS 4.0, there wasn't a convenient way to enter a comment or display a message from within the CONFIG.SYS file. That changed in DOS 4.0 with the addition of the REM command. While intended as a way to document the CONFIG.SYS file, it also displayed during its execution, so it also became a way of displaying messages.

COMMENT.SYS adds those abilities to earlier versions of DOS. To display a message, you enter a DEVICE = COMMENT.SYS message command to your CONFIG.SYS file. Normally, DOS will print the message in all uppercase; but with COMMENT.SYS, you can add a backslash to the text to toggle between upper- and lowercase. If ANSI.SYS has already been loaded, you can also send escape sequences using COMMENT.SYS. After displaying the message, COMMENT.SYS removes all traces of itself from memory so you don't use additional memory by adding COMMENT.SYS comments to your CONFIG.SYS file.

HITAKEY.SYS

Name: HITAKEY.SYS
Version: 3.0
Price: Free
Category: Copyrighted
Summary: Pauses CONFIG.SYS execution until a key is pressed.
Author: Raymond P. Tackett
Availability: Available on many bulletin board systems.

You have installed a new board, and it required a new device driver. Now nothing seems to work right. You see several new messages on the screen while the computer boots, but they go by too quickly for you to read. What are you going to do?

Rather than trying to hit Ctrl-Break to stop the booting so you can read the messages before they scroll off the screen, you can install HITAKEY.SYS. Just add the line DE-VICE = HITAKEY.SYS message to your CONFIG.SYS file. (The message is optional.) HITAKEY.SYS pauses the execution of the CONFIG.SYS until you press a key. It clears the keyboard buffer while loading, so you must press a key after it loads. This pause gives you a chance to read the messages on the screen. After you press a key, HITAKEY.SYS aborts its loading so that it uses no memory, and the CONFIG.SYS file continues execution.

Nobrk

Name:	Nobrk
Version:	1.0
Price:	Free
Category:	Copyrighted
Summary:	A small device driver that prevents Ctrl-Break from stopping a batch file.
Author:	John Pulliam
	Walter Cox
	Benjamin Diss
Availability:	Available on many bulletin board systems.

Nobrk consists of two parts: a small device driver and a control program. The device driver is loaded in the CONFIG.SYS configuration file and requires about 300 bytes. NOBRK.SYS works by intercepting all keypresses and looking for the Ctrl-Break and Ctrl-C key combinations. If break is off, it resets the keyboard controller and exits. If break is on, it passes the keypress to the appropriate handler.

The default mode for Nobrk is Break Off, meaning a Ctrl-Break isn't passed on. The second portion of Nobrk is a small control program that toggles the status of Break. When Break is On, Ctrl-Break and Ctrl-C will stop a batch file in their normal fashion.

Nobrk is most useful in systems where the AUTOEXEC.BAT file loads a password or security program and you must prevent the user from aborting the AUTOEXEC.BAT file before the security program has run. However, Nobrk can't prevent the user from booting from a floppy disk and completely avoiding the problem.

THRASHER

Name:	THRASHER
Version:	1.0
Price:	Free
Category:	Public Domain
Summary:	Tests the computer at multiple BUFFERS= to find the optimum setting.
Author:	Monte Ferguson
	833 W. Highland
	Ravenna, Ohio 44266
Availability:	Available on many bulletin board systems.

If you don't have a CONFIG.SYS configuration file or you don't have a BUFFERS=
statement in it, the buffers defaults to some low setting like 2 or 3 depending on your
machine and version of DOS. If you are trying to find the proper setting for your computer, the manual isn't much help. It suggests experimenting. Right! We haven't anything
better to do than play with our buffers.

THRASHER is a one-shot program that takes care of testing multiple buffers for you.
Format a bootable disk and then copy all the THRASHER files to it. Finally, reboot and
let THRASHER run all night.

THRASHER's AUTOEXEC.BAT file takes care of rerunning a test for buffer values
1-32. It reports its results in seconds and stores them in a file. You view the file in the
morning and set the buffers statement on your hard disk to equal the lowest time in the
report file. Nothing could be easier. Figure 9-1 shows the report for my computer.

THRASHER really grinds the A drive while running. However, if you follow my
instructions above, you will be asleep and it won't bother you. In any case, you only have
to run THRASHER once per machine unless you make major changes to your computer.

```
Tested drive A:. With BUFFERS=01, elapsed time is 1579 seconds.
Tested drive A:. With BUFFERS=02, elapsed time is 1119 seconds.
Tested drive A:. With BUFFERS=03, elapsed time is 885 seconds.
Tested drive A:. With BUFFERS=04, elapsed time is 380 seconds.
Tested drive A:. With BUFFERS=05, elapsed time is 253 seconds.
Tested drive A:. With BUFFERS=06, elapsed time is 250 seconds.
Tested drive A:. With BUFFERS=07, elapsed time is 247 seconds.
Tested drive A:. With BUFFERS=08, elapsed time is 244 seconds.
Tested drive A:. With BUFFERS=09, elapsed time is 241 seconds.
Tested drive A:. With BUFFERS=10, elapsed time is 239 seconds.
Tested drive A:. With BUFFERS=11, elapsed time is 237 seconds.
Tested drive A:. With BUFFERS=12, elapsed time is 234 seconds.
Tested drive A:. With BUFFERS=13, elapsed time is 232 seconds.
Tested drive A:. With BUFFERS=14, elapsed time is 229 seconds.
Tested drive A:. With BUFFERS=15, elapsed time is 227 seconds.
Tested drive A:. With BUFFERS=16, elapsed time is 237 seconds.
Tested drive A:. With BUFFERS=17, elapsed time is 248 seconds.
Tested drive A:. With BUFFERS=18, elapsed time is 246 seconds.
Tested drive A:. With BUFFERS=19, elapsed time is 245 seconds.
Tested drive A:. With BUFFERS=20, elapsed time is 241 seconds.
Tested drive A:. With BUFFERS=21, elapsed time is 239 seconds.
Tested drive A:. With BUFFERS=22, elapsed time is 236 seconds.
Tested drive A:. With BUFFERS=23, elapsed time is 234 seconds.
Tested drive A:. With BUFFERS=24, elapsed time is 231 seconds.
Tested drive A:. With BUFFERS=25, elapsed time is 230 seconds.
Tested drive A:. With BUFFERS=26, elapsed time is 227 seconds.
Tested drive A:. With BUFFERS=27, elapsed time is 225 seconds.
Tested drive A:. With BUFFERS=28, elapsed time is 223 seconds.
Tested drive A:. With BUFFERS=29, elapsed time is 221 seconds.
Tested drive A:. With BUFFERS=30, elapsed time is 219 seconds.
Tested drive A:. With BUFFERS=31, elapsed time is 237 seconds.

Tested drive A:. With BUFFERS=32, elapsed time is 237 seconds.
```

9-1 THRASHER generates a
report for each BUFFERS=
setting.

10

Multiple configurations

It is becoming more and more difficult to develop one single configuration that works with all your programs. If you have a network, it eats up so much memory that some memory-hogging programs won't run. If you want to run Windows 3.0, you may find that the configuration it wants is less than optimal for your non-Windows software. In addition, the old problem still exists of some programs wanting extended memory and other programs wanting you to use a memory manager to turn your extended memory into expanded memory. What is a poor user to do?

For a quick solution, you can develop a custom configuration for each needed environment. This involves creating two configuration files: the AUTOEXEC.BAT, and CONFIG.SYS files. On my machine at home, I have four configurations:

- DOS 5.0 several device drivers loaded and DOS loaded into high memory. These device drivers are a CD-ROM driver and a mouse driver. I also load DOSKEYS, a small DOS memory resident program for recalling keystrokes.

- DOS 5.0 with nothing extra loaded. I load DOS into high memory and nothing else, which gives me over 630K for very large programs!

- DOS 4.01 with nothing extra loaded. I use this configuration to test software that won't run under DOS 5.0. This configuration is more complex than just swapping AUTOEXEC.BAT and CONFIG.SYS files because the DOS files must also be swapped. Only MultiBoot can handle this.

- Windows. This is a DOS 5.0 system optimized for Windows 3.0.

My machine at the office needs three different configurations: Windows, maximum memory, and Novell network.

Except for swapping operating systems, you can do all this with batch files. All you really need to do is

- tell the batch file which configuration to use.
- have the batch file copy the appropriate configuration files to the root directory of the C drive.
- have the batch file reboots.

As batch file applications go, this one isn't even that complicated. Developing this type of application is covered in my *MS-DOS Batch File Programming* book (TAB Book #3916). I even discuss how the batch file can check the environment before running a specific program, perform these steps automatically if the wrong configuration is in place, and then automatically start the application after rebooting.

For the most part, these utilities perform the same actions as these batch files would. However, the utilities generally are easier to set up and have a nicer interface.

BOOT.SYS

Name:	BOOT.SYS
Version:	1.27
Price:	$39.00
Category:	Shareware
Summary:	Allows your computer to boot from multiple configurations.
Author:	Hans Salvisberg Froeschmattstr
	40 CH-3018 Berne Switzerland[1]
Availability:	Available on many bulletin board systems.

With the possible exception of MultiBoot, BOOT.SYS is the most powerful and flexible program available for booting in multiple configurations. To install BOOT.SYS, you begin by creating a special CONFIG.SYS configuration file. The first line should be DEVICE = BOOT.SYS, while the last line controlled by BOOT.SYS is DEVICE = BOOT.END. You construct the first menu option by entering the line DEVICE = BOOT.1 text where text describes this option. Below this line, you enter the CONFIG.SYS commands to be executed if the user selects this option.

A simple menu for optionally loading a caching program would look like this:

```
DEVICE = C: \ BOOT \ BOOT.SYS
DEVICE = BOOT.1 Skip Loading Cache
DEVICE = BOOT.2 Load Small Cache
DEVICE = C: \ CACHE \ CACHE.SYS 128
DEVICE = BOOT.3 Load Large Cache
DEVICE = C: \ CACHE \ CACHE.SYS 1024
DEVICE = BOOT.END
```

The default display for the CONFIG.SYS menu is fairly plain, but BOOT.SYS offers several switches described in the manual to improve its appearance.

---

[1] To register with the author, you have two choices. You either can send him your credit card number, and he'll charge it with the Swiss registration (70 Francs); or you can send him a postal money order for 70 Francs. Luckily, an easier way exists: you can send $39 in US funds to this address:

Public Software Library
Post Office Box 35705
Houston, Texas 77235.

The displayed code is a simple example, but BOOT.SYS can construct much more complex menus and present up to 25 different ones. You could first query the user about loading the cache, then a RAM disk, and finally network support. Menus can even be nested: you could simply have the user choose between loading and not loading the cache, and then go to a new menu to have the user select between a number of different sizes.

DOS processes the CONFIG.SYS file when it contains BOOT.SYS in an interesting fashion. DOS first processes everything in the file up to the DEVICE = BOOT.SYS statement. At that point, BOOT.SYS takes over and has the user work through all the menus without returning control to DOS. The user's choices will determine which lines of the CONFIG.SYS file get processed; BOOT.SYS passes only those lines back to DOS for processing. After that, DOS processes any statements that follow the DEVICE = BOOT.END line.

You should understand this because DOS processes some drivers immediately if it finds them anywhere in the CONFIG.SYS file. If you want BOOT.SYS to handle these, then you must rename them so DOS won't recognize them. Also, this algorithm complicates using a memory manager like 386Max with BOOT.SYS. If you were using a manager like MultiBoot that simply boots from multiple sets of CONFIG.SYS and AUTOEXEC.BAT files, then you have 386Max optimize each set individually. However, with BOOT.SYS, you use it to pick the lines to execute from one common CONFIG.SYS file. Unless you severely limit the number of choices the user can make under BOOT.SYS, then it will be difficult or impossible to optimize those choices for the memory manager.

This isn't a problem as long as you only have one menu in BOOT.SYS because each choice really relates to an individual CONFIG.SYS file—where they just happen to be stored in a common file. You probably are starting with several CONFIG.SYS files already optimized by your memory manager and then just importing them into the common file for BOOT.SYS to manage. They will work just as well here.

Now, consider three different menus each with four choices. This means twelve (3*4=12) possible configurations, with each possibly requiring different switches for the memory manager to optimize them.

BOOT.SYS can manage your AUTOEXEC.BAT file as well. BOOT.SYS remembers the choices the user makes in the CONFIG.SYS file. A separate program called BOOT.COM can access those choices and feed it back to the AUTOEXEC.BAT file using ERRORLEVEL. If the CONFIG.SYS file has multiple menus, then BOOT.SYS can grab the response for each menu individually. The AUTOEXEC.BAT file can then follow different branches for different menu choices.

If you must make a choice that affects only the AUTOEXEC.BAT file, you still must make it in the CONFIG.SYS file. You just construct the CONFIG.SYS file so the action is the same no matter which option the user selects. Then the AUTOEXEC.BAT file can access those choices and branch accordingly.

BOOT.SYS contains a couple of extensions that go beyond its menuing system. They are as follows:

EDIT performs the same function as CONFIG.CTL. It lets you edit individual lines of the CONFIG.SYS file while the computer is booting, subject to the limitation that you can't increase the length of any line.

BOOTASSIST allows the computer to boot without BOOT.SYS staying in memory, as well as allowing you to control whether or not the user can reboot the computer.

COLOR lets you control the color BOOT.SYS uses to display its menu.

EXTMON in a dual monitor system lets you control which monitor BOOT.SYS uses. Currently, only a few computers are supported for this option.

PAUSE.SYS is a separate utility included with BOOT.SYS that pauses the CONFIG.SYS file until you press a keystroke. This is useful if your CONFIG.SYS file has error messages that scroll off the screen too fast for you to read.

If you just want to choose between a couple of configurations, then BOOT.SYS is too powerful for you. Because of its power, configuring BOOT.SYS is more difficult than the other programs in this chapter. However, if you must load a large number of different configurations or control the loading of a number of device drivers individually, then BOOT .SYS offers the ultimate in CONFIG.SYS power.

CHENV

Name:	Change Environment
Version:	1.0
Price:	Free
Category:	Public Domain
Summary:	Copies the specified AUTOEXEC.BAT and CONFIG.SYS configurations files and reboots.
Author:	Pedro P. Polakoff III
Availability:	Available on many bulletin board systems.

CHange ENVironment [or CHENV for short] simplifies the storing of multiple configurations. You create as many versions of your AUTOEXEC.BAT and CONFIG.SYS configuration files as you need, with the AUTOEXEC.BAT files stored under the name AEB.*xxx* and the CONFIG.SYS files stored under the name CFS.*xxx*. The *xxx* must match for each pair.

To change the configuration, you issue the command CHENV xxx where xxx is the extension of the configuration files you want to use. If you used the command CHENV 007, the program would issue the commands COPY AEB.007 AUTOEXEC.BAT and COPY CFS.007 CONFIG.SYS, and then it would reboot the system. All of the AEB.*xxx* and CFS.*xxx* files must be in the root directory of the C drive.

CHENV is a simple, straightforward program that works well. Its only drawback is it doesn't check to see if the current AUTOEXEC.BAT and CONFIG.SYS configuration files have been modified before overwriting them. If you forget that you have modified these files, you could lose your modifications.

CONFIG.CTL

Name:	CONFIG.CTL
Version:	1.0
Price:	Free
Category:	Copyrighted
Summary:	A program that allows you to edit the CONFIG.SYS file while the computer is booting.
Author:	Michael J. Mefford
Availability:	All *PC Magazine* files are available from their area on CompuServe. See any issue of *PC Magazine* for details.

Some commands in your CONFIG.SYS must be included there, while others are there only because you use them occasionally. For example, I often find myself editing my CONFIG.SYS file to add ANSI.SYS because I am working with a program requiring it. Also, I normally use a FILES = 20 statement, but one program I use regularly requires a FILE = 50 statement.

DOS provides only two ways to deal with these problems:

- Edit your CONFIG.SYS file as required and reboot.
- Keep multiple copies of your CONFIG.SYS file and have either you or a batch file copy the version you need over top of CONFIG.SYS and then reboot.

CONFIG.CTL is a very powerful way for handling the need of dealing with multiple CONFIG.SYS files. Using CONFIG.CTL, you mark the items you want to change. When you reboot, CONFIG.CTL lets you modify the marked items. The specific steps for using CONFIG.CTL are as follows:

1. Rearrange your CONFIG.SYS file so that all the files you want to possibly change are grouped together. On some systems, some device drivers must be loaded: be sure not to include them in this batch. As much as possible, these commands should be at the end of your CONFIG.SYS file.

2. Place a DEVICE = CONFIG.CTL n statement above this group of statements. If CONFIG.CTL isn't in your root directory, you will have to specify the full path to the device driver. The n represents the number of seconds CONFIG.CTL should wait before assuming you are not going to modify the commands, which allows the computer to run completely unattended.

3. Place a DEVICE = CONFIG.END statement below the last command you want to be able to modify, effectively marking the files. Still, no CONFIG.END file actually exists, so when DOS finally processes this line, you will get an error message. Just ignore it.

When you reboot, DOS processes all the lines up to the DEVICE = CONFIG.CTL line. It then stops and asks you if you want to edit the marked lines in your CONFIG.SYS file. Pressing Escape causes DOS to process the remaining lines as originally written. Pressing any other key brings up the marked lines for editing.

Your ability to edit the lines is fairly limited. Pressing F1 toggles the line under the cursor between active and unactive. Lines marked unactive aren't processed when booting continues.

You can't edit the portion of the command prior to the equal sign. For a line like FILE = 20, you could edit the 20 but not the FILE = portion of the line. You can make the editable portion shorter but not longer. Thus, you could only increase the FILES = 20 line up to FILES = 99 and no more.

The real trick to using CONFIG.CTL is how you specify the command lines. For example, if you anticipate needing more than 99 files, you should specify the line as FILES = 020. The extra zero doesn't normally affect booting, but it gives you extra room for booting. If you anticipate occasionally needing a special device driver, add a line like DEVICE = Not Used At This Time in the area marked for editing. Normally, this line just results in an error message; but it does give you room to add the occasionally necessary device driver. When adding this line, make sure you leave enough room to specify a full path to the device driver.

Once you finish editing the CONFIG.CTL file, press F2 to finish booting. The changes you make are only in effect for this booting; the CONFIG.SYS file on the disk is unaffected.

For situations where you occasionally must modify your CONFIG.SYS file, CONFIG.CTL provides an extremely powerful means.

DynaBoot

Name:	DynaBoot
Version:	1.1
Price:	$15
Category:	Shareware
Summary:	Boots from up to 100 different configurations.
Author:	Matthew J. Palcic
	MJP Enterprises
	1030 Dayton-Yellow Springs Road
	Xenia, Ohio 45385
Availability:	Unknown

DynaBoot and its configuration file must first be installed in the root directory. Next, you edit the DynaBoot configuration file to indicate your different configurations. For each configuration, you provide a DOS filename, a short description, and a long description.

Next, you create a CONFIG.SYS and AUTOEXEC.BAT file for each configuration. If one of your configurations had the name EMPTY, then the configuration files for

EMPTY will be named EMPTY.SYS and EMPTY.BAT. These must also be stored in the root directory.

DynaBoot simplifies the creation and modification of configuration files because it has a built-in editor. The editor presents a split screen, where the top half is the AUTO-EXEC.BAT file for that configuration and the bottom half is the CONFIG.SYS file for that configuration. This presentation takes a little getting used to but turns out to be convenient when you're trying to script a new configuration.

As the only real drawback to this arrangement, your root directory usually ends up very cluttered. If you pushed DynaBoot to its limit of 100 different configurations, Dyna-Boot would have 202 files in the root directory! (i.e., 100 CONFIG.SYS files, 100 AUTOEXEC.BAT files, DYNABOOT.EXE, and the DynaBoot configuration file.) DynaBoot would be better off keeping its files in a subdirectory, even if it forced you to use a specific name as does Reset.

DynaBoot is simple to use, once configured. To select a new configuration, you either can enter DynaBoot on the command line and scroll down its menu to select the configuration, or you can enter DYNABOOT name where name corresponds to one of the configuration names. DynaBoot copies NAME.BAT to AUTOEXEC.BAT, NAME.SYS to CONFIG.SYS, and then does a warm reboot. Like other programs of this type, any modifications you've made to the existing configuration files are lost when DynaBoot copies over them. Once you have DynaBoot up and running, however, it works flawlessly.

EZ-EXEC

Name:	EZ-EXEC
Version:	1.0
Price:	$10
Category:	Shareware
Summary:	Allows you to change your AUTOEXEC.BAT file while the computer is booting.
Author:	T.H.E. SoftWareHouse
	Post Office Box 34246
	Omaha, Nebraska 68134
Availability:	Available on many bulletin board systems.

While most of the other utilities in this chapter allow you to run with multiple CON-FIG.SYS and AUTOEXEC.BAT files, EZ-EXEC limits itself to the AUTOEXEC.BAT file. As a result, you only can have one CONFIG.SYS file while using EZ-EXEC.

EZ-EXEC doesn't work the same as the other utilities. You use only one copy of your AUTOEXEC.BAT file and have it load EZ-EXEC. EZ-EXEC then brings up a menu of the booting options you've configured it to use. The shareware version is limited to 6 options, while the registered version will work with 19 options.

To configure EZ-EXEC, you assign a title to each of the options; you then switch to a separate screen and assign DOS commands and/or programs to each menu option. EZ-EXEC allows you to assign a number of commands to each option. You can assign even more by placing the commands in a batch file and telling EZ-EXEC to run that batch file. You can set the default for each option so that it runs unless toggled off or doesn't run unless toggled on.

For my system, I configured the following options:

- *SET variables.* This sets up the handful of environmental variables required by the various programs I use. I had EZ-EXEC run a batch file to do this and set the default to run it automatically.

- *Set path and prompt.* I had EZ-EXEC issue the DOS commands to do this and set the default to run it automatically.

- *Load TSR Software.* I normally use only one memory resident program, DOSKEYS. I had EZ-EXEC issue the DOS command to start DOSKEYS and I set the default to not run this.

When the computer boots, it processes the CONFIG.SYS file normally and then runs the AUTOEXEC.BAT file. The AUTOEXEC.BAT file loads EZ-EXEC. You move the cursor around, select the options to run on this booting, and then press F10 to continue booting. Although EZ-EXEC is a program, it's able to properly place environmental variables and the path in the master copy of the environment.

EZ-EXEC's inability to modify the CONFIG.SYS file makes it far less useful than the other utilities in this chapter. However, if you use only one CONFIG.SYS file and just want to be able to control which memory resident packages load, then EZ-EXEC works adequately. Of course, you could also use one of the ERRORLEVEL-asker programs in Chapter 1 and have the AUTOEXEC.BAT ask you before loading each memory resident program.

MultiBoot

Name:	MultiBoot
Version:	1.0
Price:	Free
Category:	Copyrighted
Summary:	A small program that allows you to boot with multiple environments.
Author:	Douglas Boling
Availability:	All *PC Magazine* files are available from their area on CompuServe. See any issue of *PC Magazine* for details.

MultiBoot is an exciting program from *PC Magazine* that allows you to boot your computer in up to four different configurations. Those four configurations can consist of different versions of your CONFIG.SYS and AUTOEXEC.BAT files or even of different operating systems. For example, one session could be DOS 3.3, another could be DOS

4.0, another could be 4DOS, and the last could be OS/2! Alternately, you could have one session configured for Windows, another for maximum memory, and a third for network use.

After installation and configuration, MultiBoot replaces the DOS boot record with its own boot record. Then every time you reboot, MultiBoot can pop up and ask you which of four possible sessions you want to run. You pick your session, and MultiBoot performs the work necessary to configure the computer for that session. After that, MultiBoot gets out of the way and lets the computer boot normally, thus requiring no memory during operation.

Interestingly, MultiBoot loads and runs before DOS. As a result, it can't use DOS features to help it load and run, so MultiBoot handles everything itself. The February 26, 1991 issue of *PC Magazine* gives complete details on its operation, so I won't review them here. In any case, if you get a copy of MultiBoot, you will want a copy of this issue for the detailed instructions on how to configure and run MultiBoot.

Configuration

Prior to running the MultiBoot configuration program, you must create a CONFIG.SYS and AUTOEXEC.BAT file for each of the sessions you plan on adding (up to the maximum of four). If you are planning on booting from multiple operating systems or different DOS versions, MultiBoot will need access to floppy disks with their system files during configuration.

I installed MultiBoot on my office computer for what will be a common use of Multi-Boot. The first session loads all the Novell network drivers so I can use the network. The second session bypasses all the Novell network drivers to maximize my memory. Creating the second copy of the CONFIG.SYS and AUTOEXEC.BAT files was as easy as copying the original files to another name and stripping out the network-loading lines. MultiBoot has no editing facilities, so you must edit outside of MultiBoot.

When I installed MultiBoot at home, I installed one session with DOS 5.0, a second with DOS 4.0, and a third with DOS 5.0 combined with 386Max, which was a more difficult configuration. DOS 4.0 needs its own DOS utilities because most of them check the version number before running. I created a second DOS directory and copied the DOS 4.0 files to that subdirectory. My original PATH included the \ DOS50 subdirectory, so I edited the PATH in the AUTOEXEC.BAT file I was using for that session to include \ DOS40 instead.

Creating the AUTOEXEC.BAT and CONFIG.SYS files for 386Max proved to be more difficult. I copied my DOS 5.0 CONFIG.SYS and AUTOEXEC.BAT files to another name to save them and then started the 386Max installation program. However, I had already installed MultiBoot for the first two sessions. 386Max must reboot the computer several times during the installation process, and MultiBoot interfered with that. I finally ended up disabling MultiBoot until I had 386Max configured.

One nice aspect of MultiBoot is that it doesn't overwrite the AUTOEXEC.BAT and CONFIG.SYS configuration files with alternate versions. Rather, it renames the existing configuration files to their original names and then renames the new set to AUTOEXEC .BAT and CONFIG.SYS. This way, you can modify the configuration files without losing your modifications when you reboot.

A significant problem

Some formatting programs, most notably the Safe Format program from the Norton Utilities, don't format system floppy diskettes the same way DOS does. Norton takes a shortcut and just transfers the boot record from the hard disk to the floppy disk. Of course, that's the boot record modified by MultiBoot. However, Norton doesn't transfer the other files MultiBoot needs to operate. Thus, when you try to boot from the floppy diskette, you get two nasty error messages saying "Can't find file MBOOT SYSBoot Failure" and "Can't find file LASTBOOT.BIN." After that, the computer quits booting.

Thus, the system disk created by the Norton Safe Format program isn't bootable, even when used on a machine with MultiBoot loaded. This could be nasty if the unbootable disk were a recovery disk and you either were trying to correct a problem or had created a boot disk for a floppy drive with only laptop and no other system disks handy.

Still, this problem is avoidable. Anytime you create a system floppy disk on a machine running MultiBoot, just boot from it to ensure that it boots properly. Also, because the DOS FORMAT program works properly with MultiBoot, just use it to format your system diskettes.

Conclusion

I had a few minor problems running the MultiBoot configuration program on an IBM Model 80 in a fairly standard configuration. At one point, the program dropped me to DOS for no reason and filled the screen with high-ordered characters. Because all you do in the configuration program is specify the CONFIG.SYS and AUTOEXEC.BAT files to use and copy system files for multiple operating systems, I didn't lose a lot of work when dropped to DOS. Still, this is a minor drawback to an otherwise excellent program.

If you must run under multiple configurations, MultiBoot is an excellent choice. In addition, it's free (after the downloading costs), making the price right too.

Reset

Name:	Reset
Version:	1.2
Price:	Free
Category:	Public Domain
Summary:	Manages multiple AUTOEXEC.BAT and CONFIG.SYS configuration files.
Author:	Bruce Travers
Availability:	Available on many bulletin board systems.

Reset is a small program allowing you to boot using multiple sets of AUTOEXEC.BAT and CONFIG.SYS configuration files. To use Reset, you first create a \ BOOT subdirectory on your C drive—the program is inflexible and won't use any other subdirectory or drive.

In the \BOOT subdirectory, you create a set of configuration files for each configuration you will boot with. The two files must have the same name, with the AUTOEXEC .BAT file having an .AUT extension and the CONFIG.SYS file having a .CON extension. To Reset the computer in a new configuration, you enter the command RESET filename, where filename is the name of the configuration files to use. Reset copies those files to the root directory of the C drive and then reboots.

Reset has the following several switches to control its operation:

/A   Normally, Reset hides the configuration files and makes them read-only. This switch causes it to skip this step.

/C   This switch causes Reset to also reset an All Charge Card.

/P#   This switch causes Reset to pause after copying the configuration files for the indicated number of seconds. Thus, machines with a cache that waits to write to the disk have time to finish writing the configuration files to disk.

/Q   This switch causes Reset not to display its normal progression messages.

/W   This switch causes Reset to use a warm rather than cold reboot.

You can combine switches where needed. The documentation also includes a number of patches you can make to change the default operation of Reset.

Reset simplifies the handling of multiple configuration files. I had only one small problem using it: the /W (warm reboot) option wouldn't work on my PS/2 computer. Otherwise, the program worked flawlessly.

SYSCFG

Name:	SYStem ConFiGuration database or SYSCFG for short.
Version:	3.0[2]
Price:	$19.95
Category:	Shareware
Summary:	Maintains a database of multiple configuration files for easy reconfiguration of the computer.
Author:	Masterware
	2442 Tilghman Street #1
	Allentown, Pennsylvania 18104
Availability:	Included on the disk bound in this book.

Like Batmenu, from the same author, SYSCFG is an extremely clever database application used to tackle a DOS problem. Using SYSCFG, you create as many CONFIG.SYS and AUTOEXEC.BAT configuration files as you need for your system. You might create one configuration for Windows, another for straight DOS, and a third that loads a memory manager to maximize available memory.

---

[2]The version I discuss here is v2.5; v3.0 arrived too late for me to include in the discussion. However, I was able to include v3.0 on the disk rather than v2.5.

SYSCFG stores each individual configuration file in a database. You don't have to create the files using SYSCFG: it can import any configuration files you already have from any ASCII file. Once the file is in SYSCFG, you can delete the original ASCII file if you like.

SYSCFG has a built-in editor for creating new configuration files or for modifying existing ones. It also has the usual database functions that allow you to view the files, sort them, and then delete them. You can also list just the titles of the files rather than the entire files. You assign the titles in SYSCFG so they aren't part of the configuration file itself.

SYSCFG isn't memory resident and doesn't affect the normal operation of the system in any respect. When you must change configurations, you start SYSCFG and select boot from the Main menu. It then asks you for the set of configuration files you want to use. (The pairs of CONFIG.SYS and AUTOEXEC.BAT files are stored as a set, so you can't select one from each set.) Once you make your selection, SYSCFG replaces the existing configuration files on the C drive with the configuration file you selected from its database and then reboots the system.

SYSCFG works very well. It has two minor drawbacks, only one of which will affect most users. First, SYSCFG automatically writes its records to the C drive no matter which disk you boot from. This generally isn't a problem because most computers boot from the C drive and you normally wouldn't need SYSCFG when booting from a floppy disk.

Unfortunately, SYSCFG also doesn't check the configuration files as it writes to them just prior to rebooting. If you've made changes to the files, SYSCFG should give you the opportunity to incorporate those changes into SYSCFG but doesn't. Rather, it simply overwrites the existing configuration files with the ones from its database. Because an overwrite rather than an erase occurs, you generally can't recover the lost information using an unerasing program.

Both of these drawbacks are very minor; and, overall, SYSCFG is an excellent package. You should give it strong consideration if you must boot under multiple configurations.

Hints

After working with all these programs to set up multiple configurations for testing, I finally understand the difficulty of maintaining multiple configurations. When I upgraded from Word 5.0 to Word 5.5, the name of the subdirectory with my word processor changed from \ WORD50 to \ WORD55. Normally, that isn't a big deal—you just edit your AUTOEXEC.BAT file and change your path statement. However, it suddenly becomes a big deal when you have twenty different versions of the AUTOEXEC.BAT file!

I finally realized that you do essentially four different things with your AUTOEXEC .BAT file:

- Create system variables using the SET and MODE commands.
- Create a path (really part of creating system variables, but I decided to keep it separate).
- Perform setup tasks, like writing a format-protection file or checking to see if you must perform a backup.
- Load any memory-resident software you plan on using.

As a general rule, the first three uses are the same for most versions of your AUTOEXEC.BAT files. I put them into SETS.BAT, SETPATH.BAT, and SETUP.BAT, respectively; and now I just have every one of my AUTOEXEC.BAT files call these three batch files. Thus, when my path changes or I must add an environmental variable, I only must make the change in one place.

Appendix A
Modifying InKey

InKey has a very nice dual-personality. If you simply need a program to include in a batch file to ask the user questions, you can use one of the InKey programs off the diskette without worrying about how it works. If you plan on using InKey in this fashion, you probably don't need to read this appendix. However, if you need a specialized program, you can modify InKey to fit your needs. An especially nice feature of InKey is that you need only the Debug program (usually included with any version of DOS) to construct and modify it.

If you plan on modifying InKey, you should begin by building your own version. In the process of doing that, you add in your own modifications. This appendix describes how to construct InKey and then how to modify it.

What InKey does

Before releasing control of the computer to a COM-format user program, DOS first constructs in memory a 256-byte work area called the Program Segment Prefix [PSP]. Beginning at offset 81h in the PSP is a replica of the command line that called the program, lacking only the program name itself and any DOS redirection operators that might have been present; the length (in bytes) of the command string appears at offset 80h. InKey simply reaches back into the command-line area of the PSP and writes whatever it finds to the screen.

A few characters can't be used in an InKey prompt line. The four redirection operators— < , > , |, and > > —aren't allowed, nor is the carriage return (because it's the universal command-line terminator in DOS). In addition, the dollar sign—$—isn't allowed. Many of the DOS screen-handling routines require the dollar sign as an end-of-string marker; InKey respects this convention, so any user-embedded $ characters will truncate the prompt.

Constructing InKey

The first portion of InKey is the same for all keyboards and all upshift values. Table A-1 shows the keystrokes necessary to start the program. After completing the work there, the

Table A-1 The first part of the DEBUG script for entering INKEY.COM.

Debug Response	Enter	Purpose
	C>DEBUG INKEY.COM	Start Debug and specifies file to create.
File not found		Debug's message to let you know this is new file.
-		Debug's prompt.
-	A 100	Assemble a new program.
xxxx:0100		The xxxx will be different for each computer and is not important. The numbers after the colon are the numbers listed in this figure.
xxxx:0100	JMP 0124	Skip over the data area.
xxxx:0100	DB ' INKEY.COM 3.0 - (C)1987 S. Moore',1A	Copyright notice. (Enter all on one line, not broken.)
xxxx:0124	MOV BX,0080	Point BX to command-line length byte in PSP.
xxxx:0127	CMP Byte Ptr [BX],01	Is there a meaningful string?
xxxx:012A	JBE 0139	If not, get a keystroke.
xxxx:012C	ADD BL,[BX]	Else point BX to last character of string.
xxxx:012E	INC BX	Next character is the <cr>.
xxxx:012F	MOV Byte Ptr [BX],24	Change it to end-of-string marker "$".
xxxx:0132	MOV AH,09	Select DOS "display a string" service.
xxxx:0134	MOV DX,0082	Point DX to beginning of string
xxxx:0137	INT 21	And write the prompt.
xxxx:0139	MOV AH,00	Select BIOS "get next keybd char" service.
xxxx:013B	INT 16	Wait for the keystroke.
xxxx:013D	CMP AL,00	Is it an extended key code?
xxxx:013F	JNZ 014F	No, so process it normally.
xxxx:0141	XCHG AH,AL	Yes, clear AH and prepare to pass it back.
Find your keyboard in the following figures and continue entering INKEY.COM		

program diverges depending on the keyboard or upshift value you plan on using. Table A-2 shows the program for a regular keyboard, Table A-3 shows it for an enhanced keyboard, and Table A-4 shows it for an old Tandy 1000 keyboard. If you are using a custom upshift value—as described later—your program would be similar to these but would use different values. After this, the work to complete the program is the same for all versions (see Table A-5).

Table A-2 The second part of the DEBUG script for entering INKEY.COM (regular keyboard).

Debug Response	Enter		Purpose
xxxx:0143	ADD	AX,007B	Add an "upshift" value to eliminate aliases. You may want to change this
xxxx:0146	NOP		Keyboard Modification Area.
xxxx:0147	NOP		Keyboard Modification Area.
xxxx:0148	NOP		Keyboard Modification Area.
xxxx:0149	NOP		Keyboard Modification Area.
xxxx:014A	NOP		Keyboard Modification Area.
Find the rest of the script and finish entering INKEY.COM			

Table A-3 The second part of the DEBUG script for entering INKEY.COM (enhanced keyboard).

Debug Response	Enter		Purpose
xxxx:0143	ADD	AX,0059	Add an "upshift" value to eliminate aliases. You may want to change this.
xxxx:0146	CMP	AX,0080	Is upshifted code valid, e.g. >= 128?
xxxx:0149	JB	0139	No? Reject and go wait for another
Find the rest of the script and finish entering INKEY.COM			

Table A-4 The second part of the DEBUG script for entering INKEY.COM (Tandy keyboard).

Debug Response	Enter		Purpose
xxxx:0143	ADD	AX,0048	Add an "upshift" value to eliminate aliases. You may want to change this.
xxxx:0146	CMP	AX,0080	Is upshifted code valid, e.g. >= 128?
xxxx:0149	JB	0139	No? Reject and go wait for another.
Find the rest of the script and finish entering INKEY.COM			

Table A-5 The third and last part of the DEBUG script for entering INKEY.COM.

Debug Response	Enter		Purpose
xxxx:014B	MOV	DL,7F	Echo as "home plate" character, ASCII 127.
xxxx:014D	JMP	0157	And go spit it out.
xxxx:014F	CMP	AL,61	Is it lowercase "a" or above?.
xxxx:0151	JB	0155	If not, let it alone.
xxxx:0153	AND	AL,DF	Else force it to uppercase.
xxxx:0155	MOV	DL,AL	Echo it as a normal character.
xxxx:0157	PUSH	AX	Save AX (Int 21 Fn 2 alters AL).
xxxx:0158	MOV	AH,02	Select DOS "display a character" service.
xxxx:015A	INT	21	Write character to the screen.
xxxx:015C	POP	AX	Restore the code in AL.

Table A-5 Continued.

Debug Response	Enter	Purpose
xxxx:015D	MOV AH,4C	Select "terminate with return code".
xxxx:015F	INT 21	And exit.
xxxx:0161	R CX	Modify register.
0000		Current value of register.
:		Register modification prompt.
:	0061	Write size of .COM file to register.
-	W	Write .COM file to disk.
Writing 0061 bytes		Debug message.
-	Q	Quit Debug.

Modifying InKey

The keystroke reporting function

An important concept in keystroke retrieval programs is that of *aliasing* (i.e., the reporting of a keystroke under something other than its actual ASCII identity). Aliasing can be both desirable and undesirable.

One useful form of aliasing is case-insensitivity. In a menu of alphabetic choices, for example, it's inefficient to test each keystroke twice for both the lowercase and uppercase forms of a character. However, removing case sensitivity must be done carefully. Otherwise, undesirable aliases can be introduced. Depending on the strategy chosen, the numeric keys 0-9 might not be reported accurately.

InKey converts lowercase alphabetic characters to uppercase but lets the rest pass through almost untouched. Because anti-aliasing was InKey's main design goal, only four characters are rendered inaccessible because of aliases, and those are at the very top of the standard ASCII set. The pipe symbol, the tilde, and the braces are reported as their unshifted counterparts: the backslash, the grave accent, and the square brackets.

Because even a slightly complex batch file might need a few seconds to determine the correct course of action, InKey displays a character acknowledging the keystroke so that the user isn't tempted to press it again. If the key represents an ASCII character, InKey displays it. For codes below ASCII 32 (the space), the symbol assigned by the IBM-PC firmware is displayed (if one exists). The only exceptions to this are the tab, backspace, carriage return, line feed, and bell. The returned ERRORLEVEL value is accurate; but, rather than displaying the symbol, the cursor obeys the code. If a non-ASCII key is pressed, InKey displays the "home plate" character—ASCII 127.

The second kind of undesirable aliasing deals with the *extended key codes*. The computer's built-in keystroke retrieval services (DOS Interrupt 21h Function 8, and BIOS Interrupt 16h Function 0) report a code for the character that the key represents (its ASCII code), as well as a code representing a number assigned to the key itself based on its keyboard position and the status of the Ctrl, Alt, and Shift keys.

If a key doesn't represent an ASCII character—such as the function keys F1 through F10, or the cursor pad keys—only the extended code is reported. If this happens to coincide with an ASCII character code, an alias could occur. Thus, the F10 key (extended code 68) could alias as uppercase D (ASCII code 68) and report the same ERRORLEVEL. To avoid this problem and make available both regular and extended keys, InKey adds a numeric upshift value to extended codes, so that they are reported with ERRORLEVEL values from 128 to 255—where there are no "official" ASCII keyboard characters.

Modification notes

The choice of an upshift value is somewhat critical. To preserve the anti-aliasing feature, it must produce an ERRORLEVEL code not lower than 128 (hex 80). Because the computer allocates only one byte for a return code (the lower half of the accumulator, register AX), the maximum value of ERRORLEVEL—code plus upshift—can't exceed 255 (hex FF). Using an upshift of 123 (hex 7B), InKey can handle the full range of extended codes supported by the BIOS for the "traditional" and "early AT" 83/84-key keyboards. A full list of extended ERRORLEVEL codes is given in Appendix D.

Here's how the upshift is calculated. From 255, subtract the highest extended code available:

```
   255
 - 132   (Ctrl-PgUp)
 ------
   123
```

Then subtract the upshift value from 128 to find the lowest code that can be reported:

```
   128
 - 123
 ------
     5   (Shift-Tab is at code 15)
```

Adapting InKey to accommodate the 101-key IBM Enhanced Keyboard or the older Tandy keyboards (such as the 1000)—and still preserve anti-aliasing—isn't difficult. The set of acceptable extended key codes must be restricted by lowering or raising the upshift value, which creates the possibility of aliases on the lower end and exceeding ERRORLEVEL 255 on the upper end. A few additional lines of program code must be introduced to prevent this from happening.

Moreover, the Tandy and IBM keyboards access the "enhancement" keys (such as F11 and F12) in different ways, requiring further modification of InKey's code. IBM added an additional function call (10h) to BIOS Interrupt 16h for the enhancement keys; the Tandy BIOS gets them all from Function 0, which InKey normally uses. The Tandy extended key codes also are markedly different from their IBM counterparts.

Except for very specialized applications, the lowest non-ASCII key likely to be offered the user will be unshifted F1, code 59, so it's probably best to chop off extended keys from the bottom of the range. First, calculate a new upshift value as demonstrated earlier:

IBM Enhanced Keyboard		Tandy 1000 keyboard	
255		255	
− 166	*(Alt-Enter)*	− 183	*(Alt-F12)*
89	*(hex 59)*	72	*(hex 48)*

With these upshifts, calculate the lowest codes that won't be rejected:

128	128
− 89	− 72
39	56

The lowest available key for the IBM Enhanced Keyboard will be Alt-Z, code 44; for the Tandy, it will be F1 at code 59.

To plug in these new values (which must be in hexadecimal notation):

```
DEBUG INKEY.COM          <Return>
−E 144 new-upshift-value  <Return>
```

For the IBM Enhanced Keyboard only, you must also change the Int 16h function call from 0h to 10h:

```
−E 13A 10   <Return>
```

Finally, you will replace the five NOP instructions beginning at offset 0146 with two program lines that will enforce your new lower bound on extended codes:

```
−A 146                    <Return>
xxxx:0146   CMP AH,80     <Return>
xxxx:0149   JB 0139       <Return>
xxxx:014B                 <Return>
```

Although it isn't necessary, you may want to rename the program before you save and quit so that you'll have both versions:

```
−N new-name.COM   <Return>
−W                <Return>
Writing 0061 bytes
−Q                <Return>
```

Chopping from the bottom of the range is trickier. To calculate the upshift, subtract from 128 the lowest code you wish to report. For example,

128	
− 16	*(Alt-Q)*
112	*(hex 70)*

To find the highest reportable code, subtract the new upshift from 255:

```
  255
- 112
-----
  143   (IBM Ctrl-5 or Tandy Alt-Enter)
```

Use DEBUG as before to plug in the new value, being sure to change the IBM function call if necessary. The enforcement code also differs slightly because you would be checking for an upper bound rather than the lower:

```
- A 146                   <Return>
xxxx:0146   CMP AX,FF     <Return>
xxxx:0149   JA 0139       <Return>
xxxx:014B                 <Return>
```

Rename the program if you wish, and then be sure to Write before you Quit.

_____Appendix B_____
The DOS environment

Using the DOS environment, you can create a set of variables that can be accessed by any batch file and by any program. This environment is useful for passing parameters between programs and batch files, as well as for supplying batch files with often used information without having to enter it on every command line.

In spite of these advantages, the DOS environment is under-utilized, for a couple of reasons. First, the DOS environment is poorly documented. In fact, the %variable% was undocumented until just recently. While undocumented, it works with DOS 2.0 and later. A second limitation is limited space. Using a long PATH and a complex PROMPT will fill up your environment! Don't worry; this appendix will show you how to expand the size.

A final problem is that programs only have access to a copy of the environment, not the original one. Thus, a program can use the environment as temporary storage or as a source of direction, but it can't use it to pass information to other programs. While programs (.COM and .EXE files) only have access to a copy of the environment, batch files have access to the original and these limitations don't apply to them. In addition, a few of the utilities presented in this book will search through memory to find the master copy of the environment and make the changes there.

What is it?

The DOS environment is a section of RAM (Random Access Memory) that DOS sets aside for specific information. (For your information, this area is called the Master Environment Block.) Three pieces of information are always stored in the environment. They are

- the location of COMMAND.COM.
- the PATH, if one has been set.
- the PROMPT, if it has been changed from the default.

You can see the contents of your environment by entering the command SET followed by an Enter. Note that some of the information can be so wide that it wraps to a second line of the screen.

This original copy of the environment is "owned" by COMMAND.COM, and COMMAND.COM is the only program that can modify its contents. Users can modify its contents from the DOS prompt and batch files can do the same, but other programs generally can't modify this original environment. Any time you run a program, that program gets a copy of the environment either from the COMMAND.COM if it's run from the DOS prompt or from another program if you shell out of one program to run another.

This has important implications for memory resident (TSR or terminate and stay resident) software. When you load the TSR software, it gets a copy of the environment from COMMAND.COM; however, that copy is static. If you update the original environment with a SET command, the copies of that environment attached to TSR software aren't updated. This can create problems if the TSR software depends on environmental variables to function properly.

When a program terminates, its copy of the environment is also terminated. Any changes to the environment made to that copy are lost forever. For example, if you are running Lotus 1-2-3 and you use the /System to shell to DOS to change your prompt, the new prompt will be lost as soon as you return to Lotus. (Lotus loads a second copy of COMMAND.COM to let you shell out. That copy of COMMAND.COM has an environment attached and your new prompt is stored there. You use the EXIT command to return to Lotus and that EXIT command unloads this copy of COMMAND.COM and terminates its environment.)

The SET command

DOS stores each piece of information in the environment as a string. As you will see later, this allows you to enter absolutely anything you want into the environment. The general syntax for placing information into the environment is

```
SET variable = value
```

The only space should be between the SET and the variable name. DOS will actually accept other spaces (for example, before or after the equal sign). These are treated as part of the variable name or the value and thus makes working with them difficult. The command

```
SET TEMP = C:\JUNK%
```

will actually create a variable named "TEMP<Space>" containing the value "<Space> C:\JUNK" (with <Space> obviously representing a space—" "). You will avoid a lot of problems by avoiding extra spaces in the SET command.

The keywords COMSPEC, PATH, and PROMPT have special meaning in DOS. You can use them to change default values in the environment. The general syntax for these is

```
SET COMSPEC = value
SET PATH = value
SET PROMPT = value
```

However, DOS allows you to drop the SET in front of these.

Warning: Changing COMSPEC is dangerous and can cause your computer to lock up. If the command isn't just right, you will get the dreaded "Cannot load COMMAND, system halted" error message. You must reboot when you get this message. You must change COMSPEC to increase the environment, which this chapter shows you how to do safely. When experimenting, make sure you save everything first.

In addition to the three entries DOS places into the environment automatically, DOS allows you to store your own information in the environment. This custom information can be accessed by programs, as well as accessed and modified by batch files. The GOHOME.BAT batch file in Table B-1 always moves you to a default directory defined at the beginning of the session. You set or change the home subdirectory with the command

**Table B-1   GOHOME.BAT allows the user
to dynamically change the home directory.**

Batch File Line	Explanation
REM GOHOME.BAT	Remark giving the name of the batch file.
IF NOT (%HOME%)==() CD\%HOME%	If the environmental variable HOME has been set, changes to that subdirectory.

SET HOME = C: \ SUBDIRECTORY. By setting HOME at the beginning of the session, I can readily move back to HOME. Unlike a hard-wired batch file, I can change HOME on the fly as my needs change.

You can remove a variable from memory using the

SET VARIABLE =

command. Be sure not to enter any spaces after the equal sign, or you will SET the variable equal to spaces. You can check to be sure the variable was removed by entering the SET command by itself.

SET PROMPT

The default DOS prompt is a C>, which tells you almost nothing. The C indicates the default drive. The PROMPT command can be used to change the DOS prompt to a wide range of prompts and is normally used in the AUTOEXEC.BAT file. When used by itself, PROMPT resets the prompt to C>.

Any printable character string can be included in the PROMPT command. In fact, one of the first tricks most computer users learn is to include their name or company name in the prompt. Special characters can be included in the prompt using the commands in Table B-2. Any other character following a dollar sign is ignored.

The most popular prompt is

SET PROMPT = pg

This command adds the current subdirectory to the default disk display.

Table B-2   A summary of the
metacharacters you can use
in a PROMPT statement.

Command	Action
$$	Displays a dollar sign
$t	Displays the time
$d	Displays the date
$p	Displays the current subdirectory
$v	Displays the DOS version
$n	Displays the current drive
$g	Displays a greater than sign
$l	Displays a less than sign
$b	Displays a vertical bar
$q	Displays the equal sign
$h	Displays a backspace (thus deleting the prior character)
$e	Includes an escape (Useful when ANSI.SYS is loaded)
$_	Includes a carriage return and line feed

It is important to remember that any PROMPT you develop is stored in the environmental space, along with the PATH and SET variables. A long PROMPT combined with a long PATH and a SET variable may require you to expand your environmental space, as explained later.

COMSPEC

COMSPEC is short for SET COMmand SPECification. It tells DOS where to find COMMAND.COM when a program overwrites COMMAND.COM. DOS takes up a lot of memory, which could be a problem if your computer is short of memory (either because it has less than 640K or because you have a lot of memory resident software). The lack of memory may prevent some programs from being run or could limit the size of others. DOS solves this problem by making part of itself provisionally resident (or transient) in memory. You need this part to enter DOS commands but not to run the application programs. If a program needs this space, it can overwrite the transient portion of DOS.

When you exit an application program that has overwritten the transient portion of DOS, DOS is less than complete. If you were to use this version, you wouldn't be able to enter most internal commands. DOS replenishes itself by rereading portions of COMMAND.COM into memory (coincidentally, this is why COMMAND.COM isn't a hidden file like the other two system files). Usually DOS reloads itself from the drive it booted from. Using

```
SET COMSPEC = C: \ COMMAND.COM
```

you can force DOS to reload itself from some other place. COMSPEC can also be changed using the SHELL command in the CONFIG.SYS file.

Many RAM-disk users copy COMMAND.COM to their RAM disk and then use the SET COMSPEC command to reload COMMAND.COM from the RAM-disk. This is noticeably faster than reloading from disk.

One note: while available in DOS 2.x, the SET COMSPEC command doesn't work reliably in versions of DOS prior to 3.0.

SET PATH

DOS will accept four types of commands: internal commands, .EXE program names, .COM program names, and .BAT filenames. Every time DOS receives a command, it first checks to see if that command is an internal command (like ERASE). If so, it executes that command. If the command isn't an internal command, DOS next checks the current subdirectory for an .EXE file by that name, then a .COM file, and finally a .BAT file. If DOS finds a program with the correct name, it executes that program. If DOS doesn't find a file in the current directory, it searches the PATH for a .COM, .EXE, or .BAT file. If DOS finds a program in the PATH with the correct name, it executes that program. Otherwise, DOS returns the "Bad command or filename" error message. (See Table B-3 for a PATH example.)

Table B-3   The hierarchy of DOS commands if
PATH = C; \ ; \ C: \ FIRST; \ C: \ SECOND; \ C: \ THIRD.

Internal Command	(DOS commands)
.COM	(Program in current subdirectory)
.EXE	(Program in current subdirectory)
.BAT	(Batch File in current subdirectory)
C:\FIRST\.COM	(Program)
C:\FIRST\.EXE	(Program)
C:\FIRST\.BAT	(Batch File)
C:\SECOND\.COM	(Program)
C:\SECOND\.EXE	(Program)
C:\SECOND\.BAT	(Batch File)
C:\THIRD\.COM	(Program)
C:\THIRD\.EXE	(Program)
C:\THIRD\.BAT	(Batch File)

The PATH is nothing more than a list of subdirectories for DOS to search when a program isn't in the current subdirectory. The syntax is

PATH = C: \ ;Subdirectory1;Subdirectory2;...;Last Subdirectory

If your PATH is

PATH = C: \ ; \ SYSLIB; \ DATABASE; \ WORDPROCESSOR

then DOS will only search those subdirectories on the default disk. This is normally what you want. However, if you are working on the A drive, then the PATH is really

PATH = C: \ ;A: \ SYSLIB;A: \ DATABASE;A: \ WORDPROCESSOR

because A is the default drive. Thus, you are better off to specify the full PATH, like so:

PATH = C: \ ;C: \ SYSLIB;C: \ DATABASE;C: \ WORDPROCESSOR

Unfortunately, the PATH command can only contain the same 127 characters as other DOS commands. Before DOS 3.0, there was no easy way to have a PATH longer than 127 characters. Thus, while DOS 3.0 retained the 127 character command line limit, it introduced the substitute command. The SUBST command allows you to substitute a drive letter for a subdirectory. Thus,

SUBST D: C: \ SYSLIB \ LEVEL1 \ LEVEL2

allows you to use D: anywhere you would have used C: \ SYSLIB \ LEVEL1 \ LEVEL2. Your PATH command can now be

PATH = C: \ ;D: \

instead of

PATH = C: \ ;C: \ SYSLIB \ LEVEL1 \ LEVEL2

This shortens the PATH command, making it easier to read.

Generally speaking, you won't have set the PATH before using the SUBST command. Therefore, either SUBST.EXE must be in the root directory, or you must change to the directory containing it before you issue the SUBST command. An example with SUBST.EXE in the C: \ SYSLIB directory follows:

CD \ SYSLIB
SUBST D: C: \ SYSLIB \ LEVEL1 \ LEVEL2

If you enter the PATH command with nothing after it, DOS displays the current path. If you enter PATH;, then DOS resets the PATH to nothing. This causes DOS to only search the default directory for programs and batch files. If you specify a PATH incorrectly, DOS won't find the error until it needs to search the path. If you enter an invalid directory in the PATH, DOS ignores that entry.

Using SET variables in batch files

As explained above, SET variables are variables that you have placed into the environment using the SET command or that DOS placed in the environment with a default value. A batch file can use these variables by adding a percent before and after their name (see Table B-4).

This is a very simple password system that will stop only the new users. By typing the batch file, the user can see the commands needed to run the program without the batch file. At least typing the batch file doesn't show the password.

Table B-4   PASSWORD.BAT implements a simple password system.

Batch File Line	Explanation
`ECHO OFF`	Turns command-echoing off.
`REM PASSWORD.BAT`	Remark giving the name of the batch file.
`IF (%1)==() GOTO NOPASS`	If the user did not enter a password on the command line, jumps to an error-handling routine.
`IF (%PASSWORD%)==() GOTO NOTSET`	If the environmental variable PASSWORD is blank, jumps to an error-handling routine.
`IF NOT %1==%PASSWORD% GOTO NO`	If the user's password does not match the one stored in the environmental variable, jumps to an error-handling routine.
`PROGRAM` `GOTO END`	If the user's password matches the environmental variable, runs the program and then exits the batch file.

`:NOPASS`
`ECHO You must enter a password.`
`ECHO See manual for syntax.`
`GOTO END`
	If the user did not enter a password, explains the problem and exit the batch file.

`:NOTSET`
`ECHO Password not set.`
`ECHO Call system operator.`
`GOTO END`
	If the password has not been set, explains the problem to the user and then exits the batch file.

`:NO`	Label marking the beginning of the section for handling an incorrect password.
`ECHO INCORRECT PASSWORD` `ECHO LOCKING SYSTEM`	Explains the problem.
`PAUSE>NUL`	Simulates a locked computer by pausing execution and piping the DOS message to NUL. Pressing any key will restart the batch file and allow the user to continue using the computer. The computer could be completely locked up with a CTTY NUL command followed by a PAUSE command. Using this method, the user would have to reboot the computer to use it again.
`GOTO END`	Exits the batch file if the user presses a key to restart the batch file.
`:END`	Label marking the end of the batch file.

Increasing the environment size

Most of the Microsoft compilers use one or more SET variables to point to their libraries. In fact, a couple of them use the same variables to point to different libraries! I once got a frantic call from a developer who used two Microsoft products and didn't know how to deal with this problem. I told him to construct two batch files, one to start each compiler;

he could then have each batch file custom SET the variables for that compiler. I thought the problem was solved. However, he then called me back (even more frantic) when my solution didn't work. Now I had him type in SET at the DOS prompt and read the contents back to me. It turned out that he hadn't expanded the environment; and with his long PATH and PROMPT, he just didn't have enough room to store all the information he was trying to shove into it. Thus, I walked him through the procedure to expand the environment. Finally, everything worked properly.

The default size of the environment is 160 bytes, which means that it can store 160 characters. This 160 character storage space must store the COMSPEC value, the PATH, the PROMPT, and any variables you want to enter. If this isn't enough room, you must expand the environment.

As another consideration when deciding on environment size, you must remember that each program gets a full copy of the environment. If you expand the environment to 2K and you load six memory resident programs, then each memory resident program can get a 2K copy of the environment. The result is that the 2K original environment and its six copies now occupy 14K.

However, this may not always happen. Some programs, especially memory resident programs, strip out all the free space from the environment; this retains all the variables currently in the environment but leaves no space for new ones. This is allowable because the memory resident program is the only program with access to its copy of the environment. If you load memory-resident programs that behave this way, you should wait until after loading the program before configuring your environment. Thus, the memory-resident program gets a minimal copy of the environment and uses little space storing it.

Users of DOS 3.0 and later have it easy. For them, adding one of the following lines as the first line of their CONFIG.SYS file will expand the environment:

Version 3.0   SHELL = C: \ COMMAND.COM /e:xx /p
Version 3.1   SHELL = C: \ COMMAND.COM /e:xx /p
Version 3.2   SHELL = C: \ COMMAND.COM /e:yyyyy /p
Version 3.3   SHELL = C: \ COMMAND.COM /e:yyyyy /p
Version 4.0   SHELL = C: \ COMMAND.COM /e:yyyyy /p
Version 5.0   SHELL = C: \ COMMAND.COM /e:yyyyy /p

If you are running off floppies, then change the C: \ to an A: \ . The xx is a number between 10 and 62 that represents the number of 16-byte segments to use for the environment. Thus, a 20 gives you a 320-byte environmental space. The maximum value is 992 bytes, which is an xx of 62. Beginning with v3.2, users can create a much larger environment. The yyyyy can be a number from 160 to 32,768, which allows an environmental space up to 32K! The /p is required to force COMMAND.COM to automatically run the AUTOEXEC.BAT file. Because the SHELL command is in the CONFIG.SYS file and the CONFIG.SYS file is processed prior to the AUTOEXEC.BAT file, the AUTOEXEC .BAT file will be bypassed without the /p switch.

The above SHELL statement used the /e and /p switches. These aren't SHELL but rather COMMAND.COM switches. The full set of switches are as follows:

/C   Tells COMMAND.COM to run the command listed after the /C switch. This tricks COMMAND.COM into running a subroutine batch file by giving the batch file name after the /C and having the last command in the batch file be an EXIT to unload that copy of COMMAND.COM.

/D   Causes COMMAND.COM not to run the AUTOEXEC.BAT file. It is used in conjunction with the /P switch below.

/E   Changes the environment size. It first appeared in DOS 3.0 but wasn't documented until DOS 3.1; also, it worked differently in DOS 3.0 than it did in latter versions.

/F   Causes DOS to automatically respond with a Fail anytime it displays the "Abort, retry or fail" or "Abort, ignore, retry or fail" error messages. You will still see the error message on the screen, along with DOS's Fail response. It first appeared in DOS 3.1.

/P   Tells COMMAND.COM to load in permanent mode. This causes COMMAND.COM to set a couple of switches internally. One switch causes it not to unload when you issue an EXIT command, while another switch causes it to run the AUTOEXEC.BAT file after loading.

Note that the syntax includes the .COM on the end of COMMAND.COM; this is required. These changes won't take effect until you reboot. Make sure you have a bootable system disk in case you make a mistake, as some mistakes will hang the computer. If this happens, reboot from the floppy and switch over to the hard disk to edit the problem CONFIG.SYS. As a precaution, you should make a copy of your CONFIG.SYS file before trying this change.

If you use DOS 2.x, then you must change the COMMAND.COM program in order to increase the environment. You can do this following the directions given here later. However, DOS 2.x is so old now that you really should invest in a DOS upgrade. Upgrade at least to DOS 3.3 as a minimum; and, if you have an 80386 or 80486 machine, you really should upgrade to DOS 5.0.

The example shown in Table B-5 expands the environment to 992 bytes. DOS 2.x includes a routine limiting the environment to a maximum of 992 bytes regardless of how COMMAND.COM is patched. DOS 2.x expands the environment in 16-byte increments. If you enter an odd increment, it's rounded up to the nearest 16 bytes.

Table B-5   Patching COMMAND.COM
to enlarge the environmental space for DOS 2.x.

Command	Explanation
A:<Return>	Logs onto the A drive. The modification will be made to a floppy disk (formatted as a system disk) and later transferred to the hard disk once the change is tested.
DEBUG COMMAND.COM	DOS command to start DEBUG (a DOS program editor) and edit COMMAND.COM.

Table B-5   Continued.

Command	Explanation
-	The dash is the DEBUG prompt. When you see a dash, DEBUG is waiting for a command.
-s 100 L 1000 bb 0a 00	This is the command to search for the part of COMMAND.COM that stores the size of the environment. That location will be different on different versions of DOS. NOTE: This command is case-sensitive. You must enter the command exactly as shown. Also, the 0s are zeros and not letters.
XXXX:YYYY	When DEBUG finds the correct string, it will display this information as two numbers separated by a colon. The numbers are in hexadecimal, so they might also contain letters. That is ok. You will be using the second number.
-e YYYY bb 3e 00	This is the DEBUG command to edit COMMAND.COM, so it will allocate more space for the environment. The 0a 00 two lines above was the default 160 bytes in hexadecimal. This command changes that to 992 bytes (3e 00 in hexadecimal.) NOTE: Do not use YYYY. Replace the YYYY with the second number from the line above. Do not enter YYYY.
-w	Writes the change to disk. You should see the message "Writing ZZZZ bytes" where ZZZZ will be a number.
-q	Quit DEBUG. Now reboot from the floppy disk and test it for proper operation.

To edit the COMMAND.COM program, you will use DEBUG.COM, which is a program editor coming with DOS. First, format a floppy diskette to use as a system disk. The changes will be made to this diskette, even if you have a hard disk. Once you are sure that everything works, COMMAND.COM can be copied from the modified floppy diskette to your hard disk. After formatting a system disk, copy DEBUG.COM to the floppy. Finally, change over to the A drive and perform the steps in Table B-5.

Note: I have tested this patch on IBM's PC-DOS 2.0/2.1 and Compaq's MS-DOS 2.0/2.1. While it should work on most compatibles, some vendors rewrite parts of COMMAND.COM for specific purposes and thus could prevent the patch from working. If you have trouble, you should check with the manufacturer of your computer or upgrade to a later version of DOS where you don't have this problem.

After you patch COMMAND.COM, reboot from the new floppy diskette and run the batch file TESTENVI.BAT shown in Table B-6 below. If the environment is expanded, the patch worked and you can copy COMMAND.COM to other floppy diskettes or to

Table B-6   TESTENVI.BAT determines
whether the COMMAND.COM patch shown in Table B-5 succeeded.

Batch File Line	Explanation
`ECHO OFF`	Turns command-echoing off.
`REM TESTENVI.BAT`	Remark giving the name of the batch file.

`ECHO Use this variable to test your`
`ECHO environment. The last line in`
`ECHO this batch file  will display`
`ECHO the environment. Count the`
`ECHO characters you see  before the`
`ECHO variable 1. Be sure to count`
`ECHO the variable  names and the equal`
`ECHO sign. Then add 50 for each`
`ECHO numeric variable except the last.`
`ECHO Since the last variable may have`
`ECHO been cut short, you must count`
`ECHO those characters. The resulting`
`ECHO number is the current size of the`
`ECHO environment.`
`ECHO NOTE: If you see all 19`
`ECHO variables, then your environment`
`ECHO is too large to measure using`
`ECHO this batch file.`
	Documentation remarks.

`SET 1=12345678901234567890123456789` `  0123456789012345678`	Defines an environmental variable. Including the SET 1 = this line contains 50 characters.
`SET 2=12345678901234567890123456789` `  0123456789012345678`	Defines an environmental variable.
The batch file continues in similar fashion for variables 3-18.	
`SET 19=12345678901234567890123456789` `  012345678901234567`	Defines an environmental variable.
`SET`	Displays the contents of the environment.

your hard disk. Otherwise, you must reformat the diskette and try again, contact the manufacturer for information on how to patch his version of COMMAND, or upgrade to a later version of DOS.

Summary

This appendix presents a discussion of the usefulness of the DOS environment and explains how to expand the DOS environment by patching COMMAND.COM (DOS 2.x) or by including the SHELL command in your CONFIG.SYS file. Most of the sample batch files are on the diskette.

Appendix C
Summary of batch file products

Appendix C presents an alphabetical tabular description of every batch file utility product mentioned in this book. Included in the description is the name, version, price, category, summary, author, and availability of the product.

For much more detailed information about a particular product, look under the appropriate heading in the book.

Name	Version	Price	Category	Summary	Author	Availability
Ansihere	1.0	Free	Copyrighted	A small program that tests to see if ANSI.SYS is loaded and sets ERRORLEVEL accordingly.	*PC Magazine*	Available From *PC Magazine*
Answer	1.0	Free	Public Domain	Accepts a multi-character response from the user and places it directly into the environment.	Frank Schweiger	On Disk
Ask	1.0	Free	Public Domain	Ask is an ERRORLEVEL-asker with several improvements. First, it can display a prompt. Second, it converts lower case responses to upper case. Third, it can limit responses to those listed on the command-line.	Sid Gudes	On Disk
Ask	1.0	Free	Public Domain	Ask will prompt the user for a response and only accept a y or n keystroke. It sets ERRORLEVEL accordingly. Optionally, it can display a user supplied prompt.	T. A. Davis	Available on Many Bulletin Board Systems
ASK!	Unknown	Unknown	Unknown	An ERRORLEVEL-asker that can restrict answers and timeout.	D. Robinson	Available on Many Bulletin Board Systems[1]
ASK-YN	1.0	Free	Public Domain	An ERRORLEVEL-asker that accepts only a y or n keystroke. Includes Lattice-C source code.	Skip Gilbrech	Available on Many Bulletin Board Systems
Askkey	1.0	Free	Copyrighted	A standard ERRORLEVEL-asker that can also display a prompt and convert lower case responses to upper case.	*PC Tech Journal*	Instructions to create program were published in June 1987 issue of *PC Tech Journal*
AT	1.0	Free	Copyrighted	Runs a specified program at a given time and date.	Kevyn Ford CSI Research & Development	Available on Many Bulletin Board Systems

Name	Version	Price	Category	Summary	Author	Availability
B(DISK	Unknown	Unknown	Copyrighted	A collection of a number of utilities for working with files and other aspects of running batch files.	G. Estes	Available on Many Bulletin Board Systems[2]
Bat2Exec	1.3	Free	Copyrighted	Turns batch files into stand-alone .COM programs. It does this without adding any new features to the batch language.	*PC Magazine*	Available From *PC Magazine*
BATCALL	1.0	$13.00	Shareware	Accepts input from the user, runs another batch file and passes control to that batch file.	Locksoft, Inc. 845-K Quince Orchard Blvd. Gaithersburg, MD 20878 (800) 562-5763 (301) 258-9245	Available on Many Bulletin Board Systems or From The Authors
Batcd	Unknown	Unknown	Unknown	Allows redirectable subdirectory changes.	Unknown	Available on Many Bulletin Board Systems[3]
Batch Maker	1.0	Free	Public Domain	Automates writing simple batch files.	Robert L. Miller	Available on Many Bulletin Board Systems
Batch Menu	5.4	Free[4]	Copyrighted	Automatically creates a menu on the screen. The users moves a cursor to make a select and it sets ERRORLEVEL to indicate the selection.	HFK Software 68 Wells Road Lincoln, MA 01773	Available on Many Bulletin Board Systems
Batch'in	---	$40	Commercial	Write and maintain a batch file-based menu system, including nested menus.	Leber Enterprises P.O. Box 9281 Peoria, IL 61612 (309) 693-0634	Available at Many Software Stores

---

2   While the author provides excellent documentation for the utilities, it does not indicated if they are public domain, shareware and therefore appropriate for posting on bulletin boards. The documentation does not include the author's address or phone number..

3   I was unable to determine if the program was public domain or shareware and therefore appropriate for posting on bulletin boards.

4   There is no charge for Batch Menu. The vendor sells some other shareware programs that are distributed with Batch Menu so think of Batch Menu as a "loss leader." Normally Batch Menu displays the message "Batch Menu Compliments of HFK Software" at the bottom of the menu. For a $19 fee, the vendor will change that to any 40 characters you would like to display. This is not, however, required to use Batch Menu.

Name	Version	Price	Category	Summary	Author	Availability
BATCH.EXE	Unknown	Unknown	Unknown	Converts ASCII files to batch files.	Unknown	Available on Many Bulletin Board Systems[5]
Batchman	1.0	Free	Copyrighted	A collection of 48 batch utilities into one small program.	Michael Mefford	Available From *PC Magazine*
Batcom	2.45	$59.95[6]	Commercial	A powerful batch file compiler.	Wenham Software Co. 5 Burley St. Wenham, MA 01984 (508) 774-7037	Order directly from the vendor
BatDay	1.0	Free	Copyrighted	Executes a different batch file based on the day of the week.	Tony Tortorelli	Available on Many Bulletin Board Systems
Batdel	1.0	Free	Copyrighted	A memory resident program that automatically deletes a batch file after running then removes itself from memory	Bill Wingate XenneX Enterprises 2870 East 33rd Street Tulsa, OK 74105	Available on Many Bulletin Board Systems
BATLOOP	1.0	Free	Public Domain	Implements batch file looping capabilities.	Rod L. Renner SYSOP SALEMDUG BBS Washington, D.C. (202) 646-3528	Available on Many Bulletin Board Systems Including Rod's
Batmenu	2.5[7]	$19.95	Shareware	A database program for creating, modifying and managing batch files to operate a menu system.	Masterware 2442 Tilghman Street #1 Allentown, PA 18104	Available on Many Bulletin Board Systems
Batpopup	1.0	$5.00	Shareware	Displays a moving light-bar menu and returns an ERRORLEVEL to indicate the user's selection.	J. R. McConnell Interfaces, People, & Magic P. O. Box 4496 Middletown, RI 02840	Available on Many Bulletin Board Systems

5 I was unable to determine if the program was public domain or shareware and therefore appropriate for posting on bulletin boards.
6 Includes shipping and handling.
7 The version I discuss is 2.0. Version 2.5 arrived at the last minute, too late for me to write abut but I have placed it on the disk.

Name	Version	Price	Category	Summary	Author	Availability
Batquery	1.0	Free	Public Domain	An ERRORLEVEL-asker that lets you assign ERRORLEVEL values to various keystrokes.	T. G. Browning MorganSoft 2170 Raynor Street SE Salem, Oregon 97302	Available on Many Bulletin Board Systems
BEN	March 1991	$15	Shareware	A program for controlling the screen from within a batch file using ANSI.SYS.	Hutchins Software 5323 West Townley Ave Glendale, AZ 85302	On Disk
Beyond.Bat	1.0	$99.00	Commercial	A program that completely replaces the DOS batch language with a more powerful version.	VM Personal Computing, Inc.	Available Commercially [8]
BG	Unknown	Unknown	Unknown	Generates a batch file based on the file names and text you supply.	Unknown	Available on Many Bulletin Board Systems [9]
Bigecho	1.0	Free	Postware [10]	Displays text in very large letters.	Barry Simon Richard Wilson	Available on Many Bulletin Board Systems
Bmenu	5.4	$10	Shareware	Automates displaying a menu and selecting items from that menu.	Mark Strong 6029 Eastridge Lane Cincinnati, OH 45247	Available on Many Bulletin Board Systems
BOOT.SYS	1.27	$39	Shareware	Allows the computer to boot with multiple configurations.	Hans Salvisberg Froeschmattstr. 40 CH-3018 Berne Switzerland11	Available on Many Bulletin Board Systems
Bootexec	1.0	$10	Shareware	A device driver you add to your CONFIG.SYS file. It lets you change the name of the AUTOEXEC.BAT file to any legal DOS name. In addition, you can move the AUTOEXEC.BAT file into any subdirectory.	Tom R. Donnelly Computer Software and Consulting	On Disk

8   VM Personal Computing is no longer actively marketing Beyond.Bat and they have no plans to upgrade Beyond.Bat. However, copies are still available for sale.

9   I was unable to determine if the program was public domain or shareware and therefore appropriate for posting on bulletin boards.

10 The authors ask for no money but do ask for you to send them a postcard. The address in the documentation is out of date.

11 You can also register the program with: Public software Library, P.O. Box 35705, Houston, TX 77235.

Name	Version	Price	Category	Summary	Author	Availability
BOOTLOG	1.0	Free	Copyrighted	Displays the time and date. By piping this information to a file, you can track when a program was started and ended.	Brian E. Smith 59 Main Street Piedmont, SC 29673	On Disk
BQ	2.5	$10	Shareware	An ERRORLEVEL-asker that supports a mouse. It can assign the same ERRORLEVEL value to multiple keystrokes.	T. G. Browning MorganSoft 2170 Raynor Street SE Salem, Oregon 97303	On Disk
Brkstate	1.0	Free	Public Domain	Sets ERRORLEVEL to 1 if BREAK is on, to 0 otherwise.	Unknown	On Disk
BUBA	1.0	Free	Public Domain	Five utilities to measure file and disk space, input information and select files.	Bill Reamy 9426 Dubarry Ave. Seabrook, MD 20706	Available on Many Bulletin Board Systems
Builder	1.5	$149.95	Commercial	A very powerful batch file compiler.	Hyperkinetix, Inc.	Available Commercially
Call	Unknown	Unknown	Unknown	Allows batch files running under DOS 3.21 and earlier to run another batch file where control will return to the original batch file.	George Palecek	Available on Many Bulletin Board Systems[12]
Check	11-18-87	Free	Copyrighted	A program that can determine a great deal of information about the computer hardware and pass that information back to the batch file. It can also prompt the user for a single character response to a question. All information is passed using the ERRORLEVEL.	PC Magazine	Available From PC Magazine
Checkerr	1.0	Free	Public Domain	A program you run once to create a long batch file that checks every possible ERRORLEVEL value by stepping through them one-at-a-time.	Marek Majewski	Available on Many Bulletin Board Systems
CHENV	1.0	Free	Public Domain	Copies the specified files to replace the AUTOEXEC.BAT and CONFIG.SYS configuration files and reboots.	Pedro P. Polakoff III	Available on Many Bulletin Board Systems
CHKVOLID	1.0	Free	Public Domain	Check the volume label on a disk, return status or display the volume label. Will also return disk type or status.	Wayne Mingee	Available on Many Bulletin Board Systems

---

[12] I was unable to determine if the program was public domain or shareware and therefore appropriate for posting on bulletin boards.

Name	Version	Price	Category	Summary	Author	Availability
Choices	Unknown	Unknown	Unknown	Accepts a number 0-250 and sets ERRORLEVEL t o that number.	Ted W. Allen	Available on Many Bulletin Board Systems[13]
CLUTIL	1.3	$18.00	Shareware	A collection of 12 utility programs. All require ANSI.SYS. Most are command-line utilities but a few are useful in batch files.	William S. Mezian 105 1/2 20th Avenue Apartment 2 St. Petersburg Beach, Florida 33706	Available on Many Bulletin Board Systems
COMMENT.SYS	Unknown	Free	Copyrighted	A device driver for displaying comments and entering ANSI.SYS escape sequences in the CONFIG.SYS file.	Skip Gilbrech	Available on Many Bulletin Board Systems
CONFIG.CTL	1.0	Free	Copyrighted	A device driver you add to your CONFIG.SYS file. It lets you edit portions of your CONFIG.-SYS file during booting so you can boot with a custom configuration.	PC Magazine	Available From PC Magazine
CTRL-P	1.0	Free	Copyrighted	Simulates pressing Ctrl-PrintScreen.	Keith P. Graham	Available on Many Bulletin Board Systems
DATETIME	4.4	Free	Copyrighted	A quick way to set the date and time on machines without a built-in clock.	Paul S. Burney 10800 Alpharetta Hwy Suite 200-N8 Roswell, GA 30076	Available on Many Bulletin Board Systems
DDDBATCH	1.0	$10 Single $30 Site	Shareware	A collection of 12 batch file utilities.	J. Barrett	On Disk
DELAYOP	1.03	Free	Copyrighted	Delays the batch file until a given time is reached.	Don Gloistein	Available on Many Bulletin Board Systems
DO-ONCE	2.20	Free	Copyrighted	Runs programs once a day/week/month.	Glenn Snow 1 Carmel Parkway Mundelein, IL 60060	Available on Many Bulletin Board Systems
Dissolve	Unknown	Unknown	Unknown	Slowly clears the screen.	Unknown	Available on Many Bulletin Board Systems

---

13   I was unable to determine if the program was public domain or shareware and therefore appropriate for posting on bulletin boards.

Name	Version	Price	Category	Summary	Author	Availability
Drvdir	2.0	Free	Public Domain	Places the current drive and subdirectory into environmental variables.	Richard N. Wisan	On Disk
Drvrdy	1.0	Free	Copyrighted	Checks a drive and returns an ERRORLEVEL to indicate if the drive is ready. The nice thing about the program is it does not cause a DOS "Abort, Retry, Fail" error-message if the drive is not ready.	*PC Magazine*	Available From *PC Magazine*
Dskchk	1.0	Free	Public Domain	Tests to see if the specified drive can be read and written to and sets ERRORLEVEL accordingly.	Richard N. Wisan	On Disk
DynaBoot	1.1	$15	Shareware	Boots the computer in one of up to one hundred different configurations.	Matthew J. Palcic MJP Enterprises 1030 Dayton-Yellow Spg Rd Xenia, OH 45385	Available on Many Bulletin Board Systems
EC	1.00	Free	Public Domain	Pauses a batch file until the specified time is reached then runs EXEC-CLK.BAT.	Lonnie J. Rolland	Available on Many Bulletin Board Systems
ECHO-N	Unknown	Free	Copyrighted	Displays text on the screen like the ECHO command except it does not move the cursor to the next line after writing the text and it does not strip off leading spaces.	Paul Johnson	Available on Many Bulletin Board Systems
ECHOF	1.02	$15	Shareware	A replacement for the ECHO command that allows you to include control characters in messages.	Steven M. Georgiades	Available on Many Bulletin Board Systems
Ecoh	1.0	Free	Public Domain	Functions just like the DOS ECHO command except it displays text in inverse video.	Glen Hammond	On Disk[14]
EMSCHK	1.0	Free	Public Domain	Checks to see if EMS memory is present and if so, what type. Sets ERRORLEVEL to indicate what it finds.	Christopher J. Dunford The Cove Software Group	Available on Many Bulletin Board Systems
ENV	1.00b	$5.00	Shareware	An environmental editor that lets you modify environmental variables in both batch and interactive mode and to expand your PATH beyond the DOS limit of 127 characters.	Thuan-Tit Ewe P. O. Box 1016 Capitola, CA 95010	On Disk
Envcount	1.0	Free	Copyrighted	Displays the amount of information stored in the environment.	Richard Hale	Available From *PC Magazine*

14   This is one of several programs stored in a file called HAMMOND.ZIP.

Name	Version	Price	Category	Summary	Author	Availability
Errlevel	1.0	Free	Copyrighted	Tests for one of the following in a batch file and sets ERRORLEVEL accordingly: date, Julian date, weekday, hour, month or year. It can also force the ERRORLEVEL to a specific value.	Paul M. Sittler	Available on Many Bulletin Board Systems
EX	1.0	Free	Copyrighted	Allows one batch file to call another where control will return to the original batch file.	Doctor Debug Steel City Software	Available on Many Bulletin Board Systems
Extended Batch Language Plus	4.02	$79.00	Shareware	A complete replacement for the DOS batch language that greatly extends the power of batch files.	Frank Cannova	Available On Many Bulletin Board Systems
EZ-EXEC	1.0	$10	Shareware	Allows you to modify your AUTOEXEC.BAT file while the computer is booting.	T.H.E. SoftWareHouse PO Box 34246 Omaha, NE 68134	Available on Many Bulletin Board Systems
F1toF10	1.0	Free	Public Domain	An ERRORLEVEL-asker that only accepts function keys.	Glen Hammond	On Disk[15]
FD	Unknown	Unknown	Unknown	Checks to see if a file or subdirectory exists and sets the ERRORLEVEL accordingly.	Martin Telfer	Available On Many Bulletin Board Systems
Findenv	1.0	Free	Copyrighted	Displays the starting address of the environment, its total space, the amount of spaced used and the free space.	PC Magazine	Available From PC Magazine
Flip	Unknown	Unknown	Unknown	Changes the settings for several togglable operatons.	Unknown	Available on Many Bulletin Board Systems[16]
Fly	1.0	A Few Dollars[17]	Shareware	Creates a temporary batch file, runs that batch file then deletes it.	Bob Halsall	Available on Many Bulletin Board Systems
FT	1.0	Free	Copyrighted	Displays the status of floppy drives.	Jeffrey S. Morley	Available on Many Bulletin Board Systems

15   This is one of several programs stored in a file called HAMMOND.ZIP.
16   I was unable to determine if the program was public domain or shareware and therefore appropriate for posting on bulletin boards.
17   The author asks that if you like the program, you donate a few dollars to the American Cancer Society.

Summary of batch file products   **347**

Name	Version	Price	Category	Summary	Author	Availability
GENEL	1.0	Free	Copyrighted	Sets the ERRORLEVEL to the specified value.	Brian E. Smith 59 Main Street Piedmont, SC 29673	On Disk
Getecho	2.0	Free	Public Domain	Displays a prompt then waits for the user to press any key. That key is converted to uppercase and its ASCII value is stored in ERRORLEVEL.	Richard N. Wisan	On Disk
Getkey	1.0	Free	Public Domain	Accepts a keystroke in a batch file and sets the ERRORLEVEL accordingly.	Glen Hammond	On Disk[18]
Getkey	1.0	Free	Public Domain	An ERRORLEVEL-asker that allows you to control the acceptable keystrokes and displays a message.	Ken Hipple	Available on Many Bulletin Board Systems
Getyes	1.1	Free	Public Domain	Displays a prompt then waits for the user to press Y or N in either case. For any other keystroke, it beeps. It sets ERRORLEVEL to zero for a Y and to one for a N.	Richard N. Wisan	On Disk
Getyorn	1.0	Free	Public Domain	An ERRORLEVEL-asker that accepts only a capital Y or N and sets ERRORLEVEL accordingly.	Glen Hammone	On Disk[19]
GOODDAY	1.0	Free	Copyrighted	Reads the time from the clock and responds with different greeting, like Good Evening, depending on the time.	Brian E. Smith 59 Main Street Piedmont SC 29673	On Disk
Gpause	Unknown	Unknown	Unknown	A replacement for the DOS PAUSE command that requires you to type "GO" before continuing.	Unknown	Available On Many Bulletin Board Systems[20]
HITAKEY.SYS	3.0	Free	Copyrighted	A device driver that pauses the CONFIG.SYS until the user presses a key.	Raymond P. Tackett	Available on Many Bulletin Board Systems

18   This is one of several programs stored in a file called HAMMOND.ZIP.

19   This is one of several programs stored in a file called HAMMOND.ZIP.

20   I was unable to determine if the program was public domain or shareware and therefore appropriate for posting on bulletin boards.

Name	Version	Price	Category	Summary	Author	Availability
InKey	1.0	Free	Copyrighted[21]	InKey asks the user a question and waits for a response. That response is placed in ERRORLEVEL. InKey converts all lower case responses to upper case to reduce the amount of testing that is required.	Steven Moore	On Disk
INPUT	1.0	Free	Copyrighted	Accepts a multi-character response from the user and places it directly into the environment.	William C. Parke for Capitol Health Users' Group P. O. Box 16406 Arlington, VA 22215	Available on Many Bulletin Board Systems
INPUT	1.0	$10.00	Shareware	Accepts a multi-character response from the user and places it in the environment under the name of your choice.	Mike Palmer 12316 Langshaw Drive Thonotosassa, FL 33592	Available on Many Bulletin Board Systems
Insist Insist2	1.0	Free	Public Domain	Insist beeps constantly until the user presses a key. Once a key is pressed, it converts it to uppercase then returns its ASCII value in the ERRORLEVEL. Insist2 works the same way except it only beeps 600-times.	Richard N. Wisan	On Disk
Isdev	1.0	Free	Copyrighted	A small program that can check to see if a device driver is loaded into memory.	Chris DeVoney	Instruction to Create In Feb 1991 *PC/Computing*
IsDir	1.0	Free	Public Domain	Checks to see if a subdirectory exists and sets the ERRORLEVEL accordingly.	Richard N. Wisan	On Disk
Isit	1.0	Free	Copyrighted	Checks to see if the day matches the day entered on the command line and sets ERRORLEVEL accordingly.	Brian E. Smith 59 Main Street Piedmont SC 29673	On Disk
Key-Fake	1.0	Free	Copyrighted	A small memory-resident program that feeds keystrokes into a program once a batch file loads it.	Charles Petzold	Available From *PC Magazine*

21   You may use InKey on all of the machines you own, no matter how many, but you may not give copies of the program to anyone else.

Name	Version	Price	Category	Summary	Author	Availability
Keypress	1.0	Free	Copyrighted	Asks the user a question and returns their response as an ERRORLEVEL. You enter a list of acceptable responses on the command line. It returns the first one with an ERRORLEVEL value on 1, the second with a 2, and so on. If the user presses an unacceptable key, it returns an ERRORLEVEL of zero.	Louis J. Cutrona Jr.	Available From *PC Magazine*
Keypress	1.0	Free	Public Domain	Keypress is an ERRORLEVEL-asker. You include the acceptable keystrokes after the command. It sets ERRORLEVEL to one for the first, two for the second, and so on. The ERRORLEVEL assignments are case-insensitive. If the user presses an unacceptable keystroke, the program exits and sets ERRORLEVEL to zero.	Glen Hammond	On Disk[22]
Lastdir	2.0	Free	Public Domain	Stores the current drive and subdirectory in an environmental variable. **Does not work under DOS 4.0 or DOS 5.0.**	Key Hipple	Available on Many Bulletin Board Systems
Locate	1.0	Free	Public Domain	Positions the cursor on the screen.	Glen Hammone	On Disk[23]
Lookfor	1.0	Free	Public Domain	Checks to see if a file exists and sets ERROR-LEVEL accordingly.	Wayne King	Available on Many Bulletin Board Systems
Lptchk	1.0	Free	Public Domain	Checks the status of the printer and sets ERROR-LEVEL accordingly.	R. Vander Kinter	Available on Many Bulletin Board Systems
MicroMacro-Bat	3.0	$35	Shareware	An extremely powerful tool for creating advanced screens within batch files.	Sitting Duck Software Post Office Box 130 Veneta, OR 97487	On Disk[24]
MSG	1.0	Free	Copyrighted	Improves the ability to display messages from within a batch file.	Ralph Dratman	Available on Many Bulletin Board Systems

22   This is one of several programs stored in a file called HAMMOND.ZIP.

23   This is one of several programs stored in a file called HAMMOND.ZIP.

24   The version on the disk is the standard shareware version. You obtain additional features and enhancements for registering.

Name	Version	Price	Category	Summary	Author	Availability
MultiBoot	1.0	Free	Copyrighted	A small program that allows you to boot from one of four different environments. These four environments can consist of four different AUTOEXEC.BAT and CONFIG.SYS files or even different operating systems.	Douglas Boiling	Available From *PC Magazine*
MWBAT2	1.0	$10^{25}	Shareware	A collection of twelve utilities for counting in a batch file and measuring time.	J. R. McConnell Interfaces, People, & Magic P. O. Box 4496 Middletown, RI 02840	Available on Many Bulletin Board Systems
MYMENU	1.0	Free	Copyrighted	A small ERRORLEVEL-asker that reads a file from disk and creates a moving lightbar menu based on that file.	Brian E. Smith 59 Main Street Piedmont, SC 29673	On Disk
Noboot	1.0	Free	Copyrighted	A small memory-resident program that disables Control-Alt-Delete. This is useful if you are running a batch file you want to make sure is not interrupted.	Ethan Winer	Available From *PC Magazine*
Nobrk	1.0	Free	Copyrighted	A small device driver that prevents Ctrl-Break from stopping a batch file.	John Pulliam Walter Cox Benjamin Diss	Available on Many Bulletin Board Systems
Norton Batch Enhancer	5.0	$150	Commercial	A small portion of the Norton Utilities that offers a number of batch file enhancements.	Peter Norton Computing	Available Commercially
ONBOOT	1.01	Free	Copyrighted	Can perform specified tasks daily on boot up, or everytime a warm or cold boot occurs.	Christopher J. Dunford Cove Software Group P. O. Box 1072 Columbia, MD 21044	Available on Some Bulletin Board Systems[26]
Option	1.0	Free	Copyrighted	Asks the user a question and waits for a response. That response is placed in ERRORLEVEL. Option allows you customize the ERRORLEVEL values associated with a specific keystroke; however, the process is more difficult than it should be.	Edward Morris	Available From *PC Magazine*

---

[25] The author adds a strange extension to shareware called menuware. Under this, the author allows you to register only those programs you want to use. The individual registration fee is one dollar. However, many of the utilities, especially the system variable ones, work together so it seems to me you would be better off just registering all twelve of them.

[26] The documentation strictly prohibits any commercial company, including commercial bulletin board systems or shareware distribution companies from distributing ONBOOT. As a result, you may have difficulty finding it.

Name	Version	Price	Category	Summary	Author	Availability
PALRUN	1.0	$20.00	Shareware	Allows you to run batch files and programs stored inside a common archive file.	PAL Software NY, Inc 51 Cedar Lane Ossining, NY 105662	Available on Many Bulletin Board Systems of From Authors
PAUSE3	1.0	Free	Public Domain	A replacement for the PAUSE command that also displays a message.	Scott Pakin 6007 N. Sheridan Rd. Chicago, IL 60660	Available on Many Bulletin Board Systems
PAWS	1.51	$2.00	Shareware[27]	Pauses the batch file with a nice moving message.	Michael L. Wilson 134 Oak Lane Scotts Valley, CA 95066	Available From Your Local User's Group[28]
PED	Unknown	Unknown	Unknown	An excellent program for modifying your PATH interactively. Can write the results back to the AUTOEXEC.BAT file.	Unknown	Available on Many Bulletin Board Systems[29]
PPD	3.01	Free	Public Domain	Can store the current drive and subdirectory to a file and later change back to that drive and subdirectory using the information in that file.	Richard N. Wisan	On Disk
PPPD	3.01	Free	Public Domain	Can store the current drive, subdirectory and path to a file and later change back to that drive and subdirectory and restore the path using the information in that file.	Richard N. Wisan	On Disk
Prnstate	1.0	Free	Public Domain	Tests the status of the printer and sets ERROR-LEVEL accordingly.	Mike Gribble	Available on Many Bulletin Board Systems
ProBat	1.0	$35 USA $45 Canada	Shareware	A batch file development environment including a word processor, screen processor and simple menu program.	Mark Tigges 2925 Altamont Cir. West Vancouver BC Canada V7V 3B9	Available on Many Bulletin Board Systems

27   The author labels the program as "freeware" but requests a $2.00 fee for the program, making it shareware.

28   The author specifically prohibits shareware vendors from distributing PAWS so it may be hard for you to find.

29   I was unable to determine if the program was public domain or shareware and therefore appropriate for posting on bulletin boards.

Name	Version	Price	Category	Summary	Author	Availability
QUERY.COM	1.0	Free	Copyrighted	Accepts a multi-character response from the user and creates a batch file to store that response in the environment.	Brett Glass	Program Instructions appear in *PC/Computing* on March '91
Query2	1.0	Free	Public Domain	An ERRORLEVEL-asker that can display a prompt and restrict choices to those specified on the command-line.	Torsten Hoff	Available on Many Bulletin Board Systems
Rebeep	1.0	Free	Copyrighted	Beeps at a user defined interval until the user presses a key.	Community Educations Services Foundation P.O. Box 636 Arlington, VA 22216	Available on Many Bulletin Board Systems
Reboot	1.0	Free	Public Domain	Performs a warm reboot.	Glen Hammond	On Disk[30]
Reboot1	1.0	Free	Copyrighted	Performs a cold reboot.	*PC Magazine*	Available From *PC Magazine*
Reboot2	1.0	Free	Copyrighted	Performs a warm reboot. (Would not work properly on several computers I used to test it.)	*PC Magazine*	Available From *PC Magazine*
Reset	1.2	Free	Public Domain	Manages multiple AUTOEXEC.BAT and CONFIG.SYS configuration files.	Bruce Travers	Available on Many Bulletin Board Systems
Rite	1.0	Free	Public Domain	A program for displaying text on the screen while controlling its location and color.	Laurence Shusta 523 Green Hill Road Madison, CT 06443	Available on Many Bulletin Board Systems[31]
Ronset	2.1	$20.00	Shareware	A very powerful tool for manipulating environmental variables. Version 21 will not work with DOS 3.3 or later.	Ron Bemis 9601 Forest Lane Apartment 222 Dallas, TX 75243	Available on Many Bulletin Board Systems
Run	1.0	Free	Copyrighted	Allows you to run a program or batch file that is not in the PATH. It is most useful to user of DOS 2.x as DOS 3.0 and beyond allows you to specify the path to the file on the command line.	Michael J. Mefford	Available From PC Magazine

30   This is one of several programs stored in a file called HAMMOND.ZIP.
31   Generally distributed as a set containing both Rite and Well under a file named BATIN-IT, named after the example batch file.

Name	Version	Price	Category	Summary	Author	Availability
SCR	1.0	$30.00	Shareware	An alternative to the batch language with very strong looping and screen control features.	T. G. Browning MorganSoft 2170 Raynor Street SE Salem, Oregon 97302	On Disk
Scroll	3a	Free	Copyrighted	Pauses the batch file while displaying a scrolling large message on the screen.	Bill Stewart	Available on Many Bulletin Board Systems
Sebfu	2.2	$9.95 + (varies)	Shareware	A collection of over 100 small .COM files. Each program provides a single batch file enhancement.	Paul Scanlon	On Disk
Select	Unknown	Unknown	Unknown	An ERRORLEVEL-asker that converts the user's response to uppercase.	Steve Olensky	Available on Many Bulletin Board Systems[32]
Send	1.6	Free	Public Domain	An advanced screen display program for controlling text by sending commands to ANSI.SYS.	Howard Rumsey	Available on Many Bulletin Board Systems
SetError	1.0	Free	Copyrighted[33]	Sets the ERRORLEVEL to the value specified on the command line.	Ronny Richardson	On Disk
Show	Unknown	Free	Copyrighted	Displays text in various combinations of bright, underline, inverse and blinking from within a batch file.	HBP Systems	Available on Many Bulletin Board Systems
Showerr	1.0	Free	Public Domain	A small memory resident program that displays the ERRORLEVEL value every time it changes.	Ken Hipple	Available on Many Bulletin Board Systems
Signalx	Unknown	Unknown	Unknown	A replacement for the DOS PAUSE command that constantly beeps until a key is pressed.	Unknown	Available On Many Bulletin Board Systems
SkipLine	1.0	Free	Copyrighted[34]	Inserts a blank line on the screen.	Ronny Richardson	On Disk

---

32   I was unable to determine if the program was public domain or shareware and therefore appropriate for posting on bulletin boards.

33   You may use SetError on all of the machines you own, no matter how many, but you may not give copies of the program to anyone else.

34   You may use SkipLine on all of the machines you own, no matter how many, but you may not give copies of the program to anyone else.

Name	Version	Price	Category	Summary	Author	Availability
Sleep	1.1	Unknown	Unknown	Pauses the batch file for a specified period of time or until a given time is reached.	John Parnell & Associates	Available on Many Bulletin Board Systems[35]
Son of a Batch	1.01	$69.95	Commercial	A simple batch file compiler.	Hyperkinetix, Inc.	Available Commercially[36]
Spy	1.1	Free	Public Domain	Logs the time and date a batch file is run.	Danny Walters	Available on Many Bulletin Board Systems
State	Unknown	Free	Copyrighted	Checks to see if a file exists and sets ERROR-LEVEL accordingly. Differs from "IF EXIST" because it ignores 0-length files.	Keith P. Graham	Available on Many Bulletin Board Systems
SYSCFG	3.0[37]	$19.95	Shareware	Maintains a database of CONFIG.SYS and AUTOEXEC.BAT configuration files so you can boot from multiple configurations.	Masterware 2442 Tilghman Street #1 Allentown, PA 18194	On Disk
T_Minus	1.2	Free	Copyrighted	Pauses the batch file for the specified number of seconds.	Harry M. Carver	Available on Many Bulletin Board Systems
tBU	3.0	Free	Copyrighted	A powerful set of tools for storing information about the system in environmental variables.	Todd R. Hill Claude W. Warren Jr.	Available on Many Bulletin Board Systems
THRASHER	1.0	Free	Public Domain	Tests your computer and reports on the appropriate value for the BUFFERS= statement in your CONFIG.SYS configuration file.	Monte Ferguson 833 W. Highland Ravenna, OH 44266	Available on Many Bulletin Board Systems
Time Runner	1.0	$25.00	Shareware	Time Runner is a utility that will run up to five programs at preselected times. These programs can be .COM, .EXE or .BAT programs.	Brian Albright Allsoft Computer Products 2404 Sugar Maple Court Monmouth Jnct, NJ 08852	Available on Many Bulletin Board Systems

35 I was unable to determine if the program was public domain or shareware and therefore appropriate for posting on bulletin boards.

36 Hyperkinetix, Inc. is not promoting Son of a Batch and has no plans to upgrade the program, although they do have copies for sale. Hyperkinetix has replaced Son of a Batch with a much more powerful compiler called Builder.

37 The version I discuss is 2.5. Version 3.0 arrived at the last minute, too late for me to write about but I have placed it on the disk.

Name	Version	Price	Category	Summary	Author	Availability
Time_In	1.0	Free	Copyrighted	Allows the user to run a program based on a configured time limit.	John W. Wulff Wulff Enterpriese, Inc. 260 Terranova Drive Wattenton, VA 22186	Available on Many Bulletin Board Systems
Timedget	1.0	Free	Public Domain	Pauses briefly for the user to enter a keystroke. Sets the ERRORLEVEL to 255 if the user presses the spacebar and to zero for any other keystroke or if the program times out.	C. David Moran	Available on Many Bulletin Board Systems
TIMEJOB	Unknown	Unknown	Unknown	A pausing program that restarts the batch file at a specified time.	Unknown[38]	Available on Many Bulletin Board Systems
Title	1.0	Free	Public Domain	Displays a message of up to 32 characters in very large letters.	D. W. Martin	Available on Many Bulletin Board Systems
Typo	1.0	$5.00	Shareware	Replaces the ECHO command with a program that can center text and easily display blank lines.	Sapphire Software 4141 Ball Road Suite 166 Cypress, CA 90630	Available on Many Bulletin Board Systems
Ultimate Screen Manager	1.20	$39.00[39]	Shareware	Creates, maintains and modifies advanced batch file screens and menus.	MDFlynn Associates P. O. Box 5034 Redwood City, CA 94063 (415) 487-6482	On Disk
Until	1.0	Free	Copyrighted	Pauses the batch file until the specified time is reached.	Jerry A. Shank 2596 Old Philadelphia Bird-in-Hand, PA 17505	Available on Many Bulletin Board Systems
Wait	1.0	Free	Public Domain	Pauses a batch file for up to 59 seconds in one second increments.	Glen Hammond	On Disk[40]
Wait	Unknown	Unknown	Unknown	Pauses a batch file until a specified time is reached.	Software Research	Available on Many Bulletin Board Systems[41]

38   I was unable to determine if the program was public domain or shareware and therefore appropriate for posting on bulletin boards.
39   When you register, in addition to a printed manual you receive additional screen editing functions and several additional utilities.
40   This is one of several programs stored in a file called HAMMOND.ZIP.
41   I was unable to determine if the program was public domain or shareware and therefore appropriate for posting on bulletin boards.

Name	Version	Price	Category	Summary	Author	Availability
Wait10	1.0	Unknown	Unknown	Causes the batch file to pause for 10 seconds.	Unknown	Available on Many Bulletin Board Systems[42]
Waitil	1.0	Free	Copyrighted	Pauses the batch file until the specified time is reached.	George A. Stanislav	Available on Many Bulletin Board Systems[43]
Warmboot	1.0	Free	Copyrighted	Reboots the computer.	*PC Magazine*	Available From *PC Magazine*
Well	1.0	Free	Public Domain	An ERRORLEVEL-asker that allows you to control the ERRORLEVEL assigned to different characters.	Laurence Shusta 523 Green Hill Road Madison, CT 06443	Available on Many Bulletin Board Systems[44]
What	1.47	Free	Public Domain	A program that can determine a great deal of information about the computer and pass that information back to the batch file. It can also prompt the user for a single character response to a question. Information is passed using a combination of ERRORLEVEL and an environmental variable called what.	Tom Peters	Available on Many Bulletin Board Systems
Write	1.1	Free	Public Domain	Replaces the echo command and includes advanced formatting switches.	Markus Fischer University of Geneva Department of Anthropology 12, rue Gustave Revilliod 1227 Carouge (Geneve) Switerland	On Disk
Zerobat	Unknown	Free	Copyrighted	A batch file to create 0-length files, a program to accept a y or n keystroke and a replacement for the PAUSE command.	John C. Van Lund	Available on Many Bulletin Board Systems

42   I was unable to determine if the program was public domain or shareware and therefore appropriate for posting on bulletin boards.

43   The author has restricted distribution of this program to non-profit organizations so it may be hard to find.

44   Generally distributed as a set containing both Rite and Well under a file named BATIN-IT, named after the example batch file.

Appendix D
Inkey ERRORLEVEL values

Extended keycodes and upshifted
ERRORLEVEL values for 83/84-key PC keyboard.

Extended Key Code	ERROR-LEVEL	Key	Extended Key Code	ERROR-LEVEL	Key
15	138	Shift-Tab	90	213	Shift-F7
16	139	Alt-Q	91	214	Shift-F8
17	140	Alt-W	92	215	Shift-F9
18	141	Alt-E	93	216	Shift-F10
19	142	Alt-R	94	217	Ctrl-F1
20	143	Alt-T	95	218	Ctrl-F2
21	144	Alt-Y	96	219	Ctrl-F3
22	145	Alt-U	97	220	Ctrl-F4
23	146	Alt-I	98	221	Ctrl-F5
24	147	Alt-O	99	222	Ctrl-F6
25	148	Alt-P	100	223	Ctrl-F7
30	153	Alt-A	101	224	Ctrl-F8
31	154	Alt-S	102	225	Ctrl-F9
32	155	Alt-D	103	226	Ctrl-F10
33	156	Alt-F	104	227	Alt-F1
34	157	Alt-G	105	228	Alt-F2
35	158	Alt-H	106	229	Alt-F3
36	159	Alt-J	107	230	Alt-F4
37	160	Alt-K	108	231	Alt-F5
38	161	Alt-L	109	232	Alt-F6
44	167	Alt-Z	110	233	Alt-F7
45	168	Alt-X	111	234	Alt-F8
46	169	Alt-C	112	235	Alt-F9
47	170	Alt-V	113	236	Alt-F10
48	171	Alt-B	114	237	Ctrl-PrtSc
49	172	Alt-N	115	238	Ctrl-Lt-Arrow
50	173	Alt-M	116	239	Ctrl-Rt-Arrow
59	182	F1	117	240	Ctrl-End
60	183	F2	118	241	Ctrl-PgDn
61	184	F3	119	242	Ctrl-Home
62	185	F4	120	243	Alt-1
63	186	F5	121	244	Alt-2
64	187	F6	122	245	Alt-3
65	188	F7	123	246	Alt-4
66	189	F8	124	247	Alt-5
67	190	F9	125	248	Alt-6
68	191	F10	126	249	Alt-7
84	207	Shift-F1	127	250	Alt-8
85	208	Shift-F2	128	251	Alt-9
86	209	Shift-F3	129	252	Alt-0
87	210	Shift-F4	130	253	Alt-Hyphen
88	211	Shift-F5	131	254	Alt-=
89	212	Shift-F6	132	255	Ctrl-PgUp

Extended keycodes and upshifted
ERRORLEVEL values for IBM Enhanced keyboard.

Extended Key Code	ERROR-LEVEL	Key	Extended Key Code	ERROR-LEVEL	Key
44	133	Alt-Z	115	204	Ctrl-Lt-Arrow
45	134	Alt-X	116	205	Ctrl-Rt-Arrow
46	135	Alt-C	117	206	Ctrl-End
47	136	Alt-V	118	207	Ctrl-PgDn
48	137	Alt-B	119	208	Ctrl-Home
49	138	Alt-N	120	209	Alt-1
50	139	Alt-M	121	210	Alt-2
59	148	F1	122	211	Alt-3
60	149	F2	123	212	Alt-4
61	150	F3	124	213	Alt-5
62	151	F4	125	214	Alt-6
63	152	F5	126	215	Alt-7
64	153	F6	127	216	Alt-8
65	154	F7	128	217	Alt-9
66	155	F8	129	218	Alt-0
67	156	F9	130	219	Alt-Hyphen
68	157	F10	131	220	Alt-=
84	173	Shift-F1	132	221	Ctrl-PgUp
85	174	Shift-F2	133	222	F11
86	175	Shift-F3	134	223	F12
87	176	Shift-F4	135	224	Shift-F11
88	177	Shift-F5	136	225	Shift-F12
89	178	Shift-F6	137	226	Ctrl-F11
90	179	Shift-F7	138	227	Ctrl-F12
91	180	Shift-F8	139	228	Alt-F11
92	181	Shift-F9	140	229	Alt-F12
93	182	Shift-F10	141	230	Ctrl-Up-Arrow
94	183	Ctrl-F1	142	231	Ctrl-Pad-(-)
95	184	Ctrl-F2	143	232	Ctrl-Pad-5
96	185	Ctrl-F3	144	233	Ctrl-Pad-(+)
97	186	Ctrl-F4	145	234	Ctrl-Dn-Arrow
98	187	Ctrl-F5	146	235	Ctrl-Ins
99	188	Ctrl-F6	147	236	Ctrl-Del
100	189	Ctrl-F7	148	237	Ctrl-Tab
101	190	Ctrl-F8	149	238	Ctrl-/
102	191	Ctrl-F9	150	239	Ctrl-*
103	192	Ctrl-F10	151	240	Alt-Home
104	193	Alt-F1	152	241	Alt-Up-Arrow
105	194	Alt-F2	153	242	Alt-PgUp
106	195	Alt-F3	155	243	Alt-Lt-Arrow
107	196	Alt-F4	157	244	Alt-Rt-Arrow
108	197	Alt-F5	159	248	Alt-End

Continued.

Extended Key Code	ERROR-LEVEL	Key	Extended Key Code	ERROR-LEVEL	Key
109	198	Alt-F6	160	249	Alt-Dn-Arrow
110	199	Alt-F7	161	250	Alt-PgDn
111	200	Alt-F8	162	251	Alt-Ins
112	201	Alt-F9	163	252	Alt-Del
113	202	Alt-F10	164	253	Alt-/
114	203	Ctrl-PrtSc	165	254	Alt-Tab
166	255	Alt-Enter			

Extended keycodes and upshifted ERRORLEVEL values for Tandy keyboard.

Extended Key Code	ERROR-LEVEL	Key	Extended Key Code	ERROR-LEVEL	Key
44	---	Alt-Z	112	184	Alt-F9
45	---	Alt-X	113	185	Alt-F10
46	---	Alt-C	114	186	Ctrl-PrtSc
47	---	Alt-V	115	187	Ctrl-Lt-Arrow
48	---	Alt-B	116	188	Ctrl-Rt-Arrow
49	---	Alt-N	117	189	Ctrl-End
50	---	Alt-M	118	190	Ctrl-PgDn
59	131	F1	119	191	Ctrl-Home
60	132	F2	120	192	Alt-1
61	133	F3	121	193	Alt-2
62	134	F4	122	194	Alt-3
63	135	F5	123	195	Alt-4
64	136	F6	124	196	Alt-5
65	137	F7	125	197	Alt-6
66	138	F8	126	198	Alt-7
67	139	F9	127	199	Alt-8
68	140	F10	128	200	Alt-9
70	142	Alt-PrtSc	129	201	Alt-0
71	143	Home	130	202	Alt-Hyphen
72	144	Up-Arrow	131	203	Alt-=
73	145	Shift-PgUp	132	204	Ctrl-PgUp
74	146	Shift-Home	133	205	Shift-Up-Arrow
75	147	Lt-Arrow	134	206	Shift-Dn-Arrow
77	149	Rt-Arrow	135	207	Shift-Lt-Arrow
79	151	Shift-End	136	208	Shift-Rt-Arrow
80	152	Dn-Arrow	140	212	Alt-Backspace
81	153	Shift-PgDn	141	213	Ctrl-Tab
83	155	Shift-Del	142	214	Alt-Tab
84	156	Shift-F1	143	215	Alt-Enter
85	157	Shift-F2	144	216	Ctrl-Up-Arrow

Extended Key Code	ERROR-LEVEL	Key	Extended Key Code	ERROR-LEVEL	Key
86	158	Shift-F3	145	217	Alt-Up-Arrow
87	159	Shift-F4	146	218	Alt-Lt-Arrow
88	160	Shift-F5	147	219	Ctrl-7
89	161	Shift-F6	148	220	Ctrl-8
90	162	Shift-F7	149	221	Ctrl-4
91	163	Shift-F8	150	222	Ctrl-Dn-Arrow
92	164	Shift-F9	151	223	Alt-Dn-Arrow
93	165	Shift-F10	152	224	F11
94	166	Ctrl-F1	153	225	F12
95	167	Ctrl-F2	154	226	Ctrl-2 (pad)
96	168	Ctrl-F3	155	227	Shift-0 (pad)
97	169	Ctrl-F4	156	228	Ctrl-0 (pad)
98	170	Ctrl-F5	157	229	Ctrl-Del
99	171	Ctrl-F6	158	230	Alt-Del
100	172	Ctrl-F7	159	231	Ctrl-Ins
101	173	Ctrl-F8	160	232	Alt-Ins
102	174	Ctrl-F9	161	233	Shift-. (pad)
103	175	Ctrl-F10	162	234	Shift-F11
104	176	Alt-F1	163	235	Shift-F12
105	177	Alt-F2	164	236	Ctrl-. (pad)
106	178	Alt-F3	165	237	Alt-. (pad)
107	179	Alt-F4	166	238	Alt-Home
108	180	Alt-F5	172	244	Ctrl-F11
109	181	Alt-F6	173	245	Ctrl-F12
110	182	Alt-F7	182	254	Alt-F11
111	183	Alt-F8	183	255	Alt-F12

Index

BUILDER

from *hyperkinetix, inc.*

Dear Computer Enthusiast,

We can help you to:

* Quickly code intelligent installations and utilities
* Create slick DropDown, PopUp & LightBar menus
* User-proof your batch files

Stop suffering under the limitations of batch. Quit making compromises forced by batch *interpreters*. Get a true *compiler* that can do it all for you, including allowing you to distribute .COM or .EXE files royalty free.

One of BUILDER's users compiled a 2000 line batch file and it now runs in a fraction of the time it used to! Compiling converts the interpreted code into machine language, increasing speed. *A major U.S. airline is using BUILDER as a security front end on its networked PC's.* The PASSWORD command, machine language conversion, and optional data ENCRYPTION give you batch file security never before possible. Instead of using C and spending days on the project, *one software developer wrote a complex installation script in BUILDER in less than half a day!* We've built in the commands to check memory, disk label, change AUTOEXEC.BAT and CONFIG.SYS, etc.; it's quick and easy.

If you need a fast, efficient way to write DOS systems level programs, then BUILDER is your answer. It's only $149.95! **Use the coupon on the back side of this page and you get 25% off!** We give you free telephone tech support, great user documentation, and 30 days of free upgrades. BUILDER is shipped on both 3.5" and 5.25" diskettes.

Call or send your order today and begin mastering DOS tomorrow!

Sincerely,

Douglas J. Amaral
Douglas J. Amaral
BUILDER Developer

hyperkinetix, inc. 615 North Poplar, Orange, CA 92667 714-935-0823

Eliminate 99% of
your batch file problems
for 25% off!

Big savings on BUILDER
Only $112.46 with this coupon

hyperkinetix, inc.
Builder Mail Order Form

Name: _____

Company: _____

Address: _____

City: _____ State: _____ Zip: _____

Country: _____ Phone: (   )_____

Visa/Mastercard Card #:_____Exp Date:_____

Name on card:_____Check Enclosed _____COD _____

	Builder	$112.46
	Sales Tax (CA only)	_____
	Shipping (US only)	$5.00
	C.O.D. Charge ($4.00)	_____
	Total	_____

Signature:_____
(Required for Credit Card and C.O.D. orders)

Mail to: 615 North Poplar   Fax to: 714-935-0831
                Orange, CA 92667

MS-DOS Batch File Utilities

Now that your appetite's been whetted by reading *MS-DOS Batch File Utilities* (TAB Book No. 3915), you probably want to try out your new disk packed full of nifty shareware utilities. You should have no problems, at least when using the great majority of modern computers. Still, the disk included with this book is double-density and formatted at 1.2M. Older machines might not be able to read it properly, instead claiming that a disk failure has occurred and probably frustrating you to no end.

Don't lose hope! If you face this problem, TAB is willing to exchange your unreadable disk for a set of 5.25″ 360K floppies containing almost all of the same utilities. Merely send us your old disk with the coupon below, and your troubles will be over. Please include $2.50 ($5.00 if outside the U.S.) for shipping and handling costs.

YES, I'm interested. With this coupon, I've included my 1.2M disk containing the batch file utilities. In return, please send me my free replacement disks formatted at 360K.

Shipping & Handling: $2.50 per disk in U.S.
($5.00 per disk outside U.S.) $ _____

☐ Check or money order enclosed made payable to TAB Books

Charge my ☐ VISA ☐ MasterCard ☐ American Express

Acct No. _____ Exp. Date _____

Signature _____

Name _____

Address _____

City _____ State _____ Zip _____

TOLL-FREE ORDERING: 1-800-822-8158
(in PA, AK, and Canada call 1-717-794-2191)

or write to TAB Books, Blue Ridge Summit, PA 17294-0214

Prices subject to change. Orders outside the U.S. must be paid in international money order in U.S. dollars.

TAB-3915